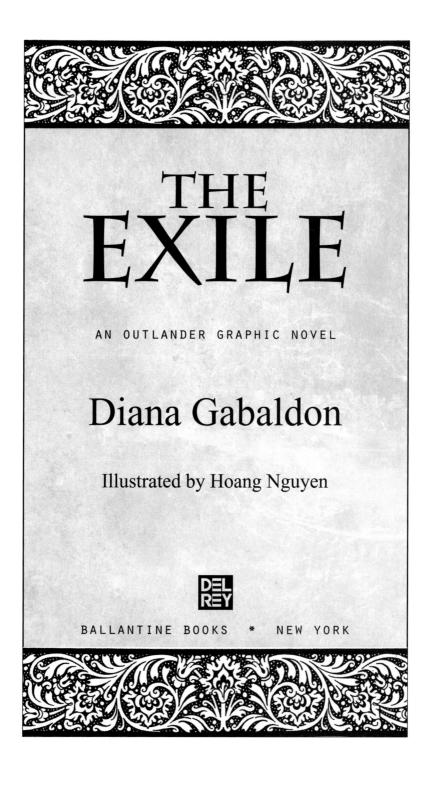

# THE EXILE

AN OUTLANDER GRAPHIC NOVEL

## Diana Gabaldon

Illustrated by Hoang Nguyen

DEL REY

BALLANTINE BOOKS ✳ NEW YORK

# TO DEL CONNELL,
# A TRUE GENT WITH A
# SENSE OF HUMOR.

Published in the United States by Del Rey, an imprint of The Random House Publishing Group, a division of Random House, Inc., New York.

Del Rey is a registered trademark and the Del Rey colophon is a trademark of Random House, Inc.

ISBN 978-0-345-50538-5

Illustrations by Hoang Nguyen

Lettering by Bill Tortolini

Printed in the United States of America on acid-free paper

www.delreybooks.com

2 4 6 8 9 7 5 3 1

First Edition

# HOW THIS BOOK CAME TO BE

My mother taught me to read at the age of three—in part by reading me Walt Disney Comics. I never stopped (and was consequently appalled when I ran into Dick and Jane in kindergarten. Flipped through *See Spot Run* and put it back, wondering—aloud—why anybody would want to read *that*? I was not a diplomatic child).

Twenty-odd years later, I read a rather sub-par Disney story, though, and spurred by the reckless notion that surely I could write better than *that*, I sent a medium-rude letter to the editor of said comic line, essentially saying, "Dear Sir—I've been reading your Walt Disney Comics for twenty-five years now, and they've been getting worse and worse. I don't *know* that I could do better myself, but I'd like to try."

Evidently age had taught me nothing about diplomacy, but I did have the luck to have written to Del Connell, a true gent with a sense of humor, who wrote back to me and said, "OK. Try."

So I did. Del didn't buy my first story, but he did something much more valuable: He told me what was wrong with it. He did buy my second story (my first fiction sale ever; I literally bounced off the walls when I got his letter with the contract), and I wrote scripts for Disney for several years: Uncle Scrooge, the Beagle Boys, Daisy and Donald, Big Bad Wolf and Three Little Pigs, even the occasional Mickey Mouse story (I always preferred the ducks; Mickey was too much the straight arrow to be a really interesting character).

Eventually, the comics program stopped buying new scripts (someone at headquarters, having suddenly realized that they had forty years of Carl Barks scripts in the files, thought to ask why they were paying for new stories instead of simply reprinting those?), Disney sold their comics license, and I moved on to other things. But once a lover of comic books...

And so, when (years later) I had a literary agent and novels to my name, I told said agent that IF the opportunity to write a graphic novel should ever come along, I would seize it with both hands. And thus when a production company contracted for a movie option of my novels, I insisted that we must include an exemption in the option contract, since comic books would normally be covered under the "merchandising" clause—so that IF someone happened to come along and offer me the chance to write a graphic novel...

Well, one month later, someone did. That was Betsy Mitchell, the wonderful editor of the book you're holding. "I don't want a straight adaptation of *Outlander*," she said to me. "I want a new Jamie and Claire story, set within the parameters of *Outlander*."

"Well, *that's* a cool challenge," I said, scratching my head. "What if...?" So the story you're holding here begins slightly before *Outlander,* and is essentially the story as told from the point of view of Jamie's godfather, Murtagh. If you've read *Outlander,* you'll recognize some of the major events, but you'll also see a completely new storyline woven through them—all the things Claire *didn't* see or know about—as well as getting Murtagh's unexpurgated opinions of the whole affair.

Through Betsy's auspices, I found Hoang Nguyen, the magnificent artist who drew the story from my script, and the wonderful team of production people who've made this book a visual marvel.

So you and I have a lot of people to thank for this: Betsy and Hoang, Catherine MacGregor and Catherine-Ann MacPhee (who supplied the Gaelic), Russell Galen (my literary agent), Del Connell—and my mother. I hope you enjoy reading it as much as I enjoyed writing it!

Yours truly,

*Diana Gabaldon*

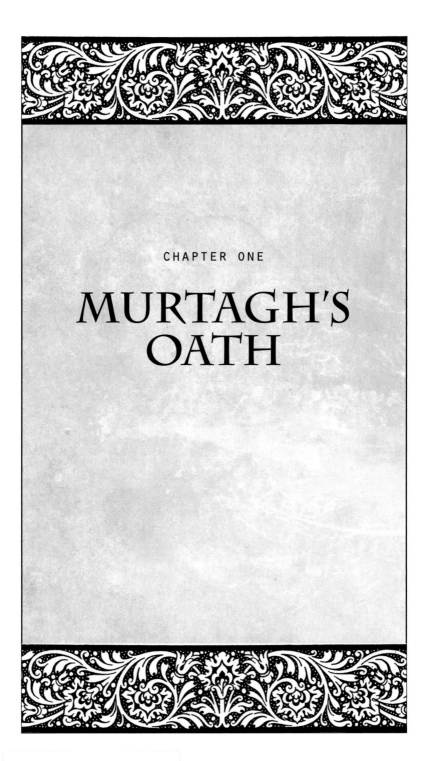

CHAPTER ONE

# MURTAGH'S OATH

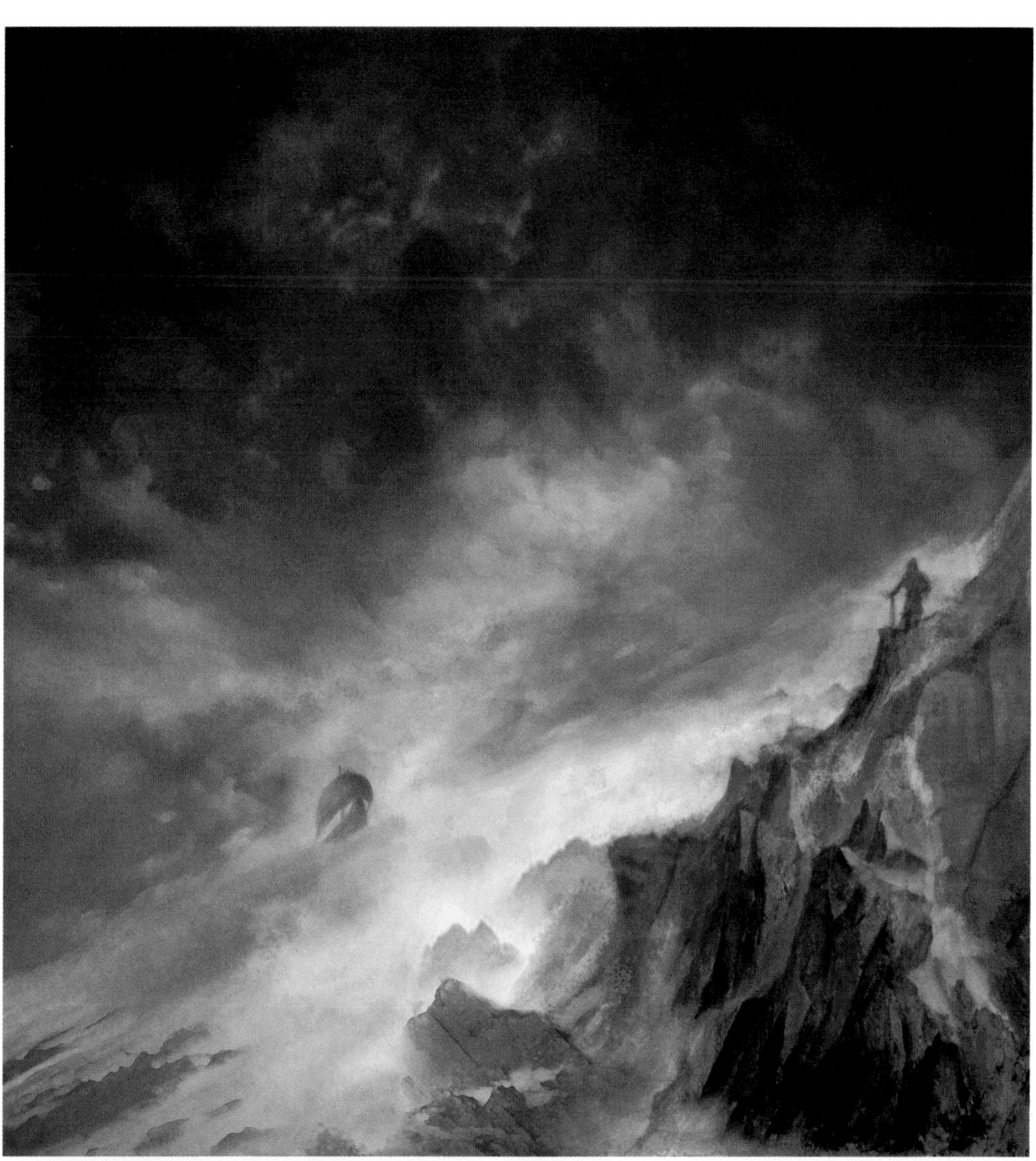

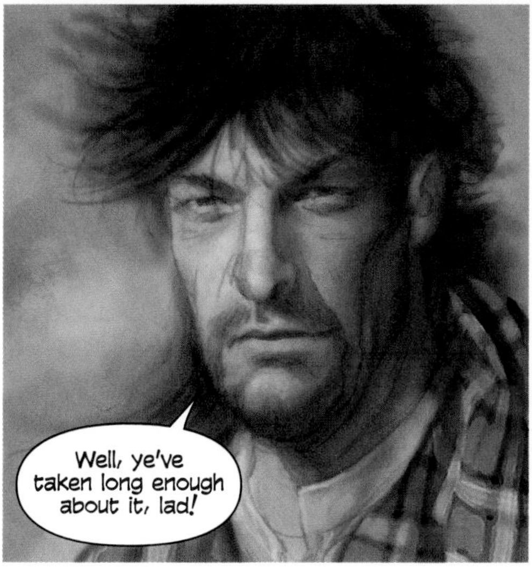
Well, ye've
taken long enough
about it, lad!

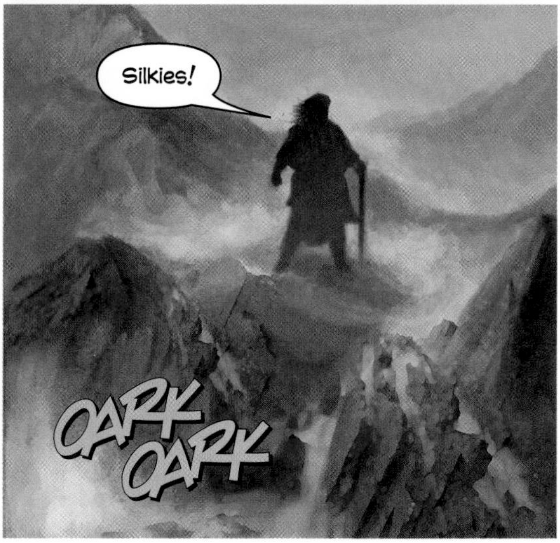
Silkies!
OARK
OARK

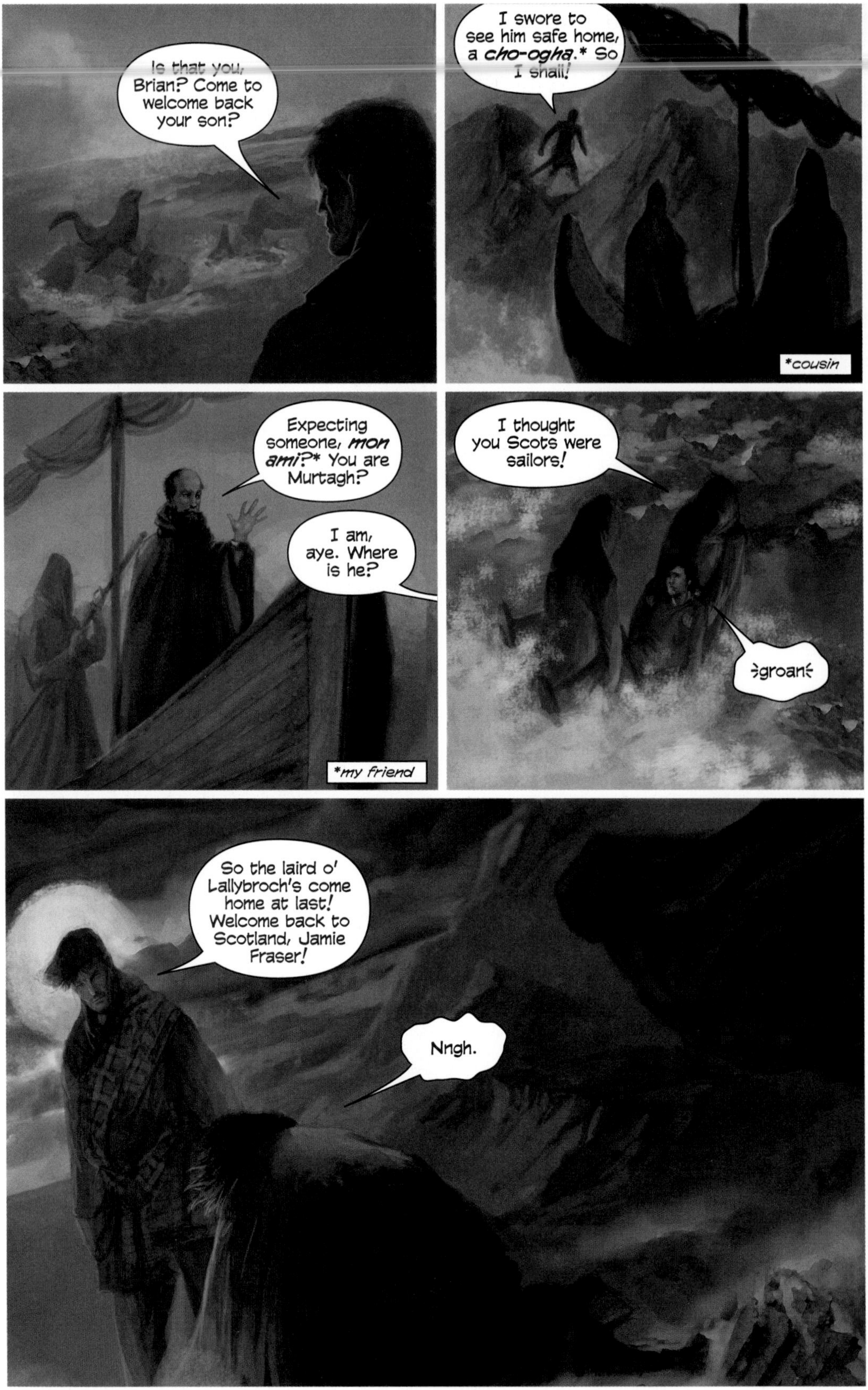
Is that you, Brian? Come to welcome back your son?
I swore to see him safe home, a cho-ogha.* So I shall!
*cousin
Expecting someone, mon ami?* You are Murtagh?
I am, aye. Where is he?
*my friend
I thought you Scots were sailors!
groan
So the laird o' Lallybroch's come home at last! Welcome back to Scotland, Jamie Fraser!
Nngh.

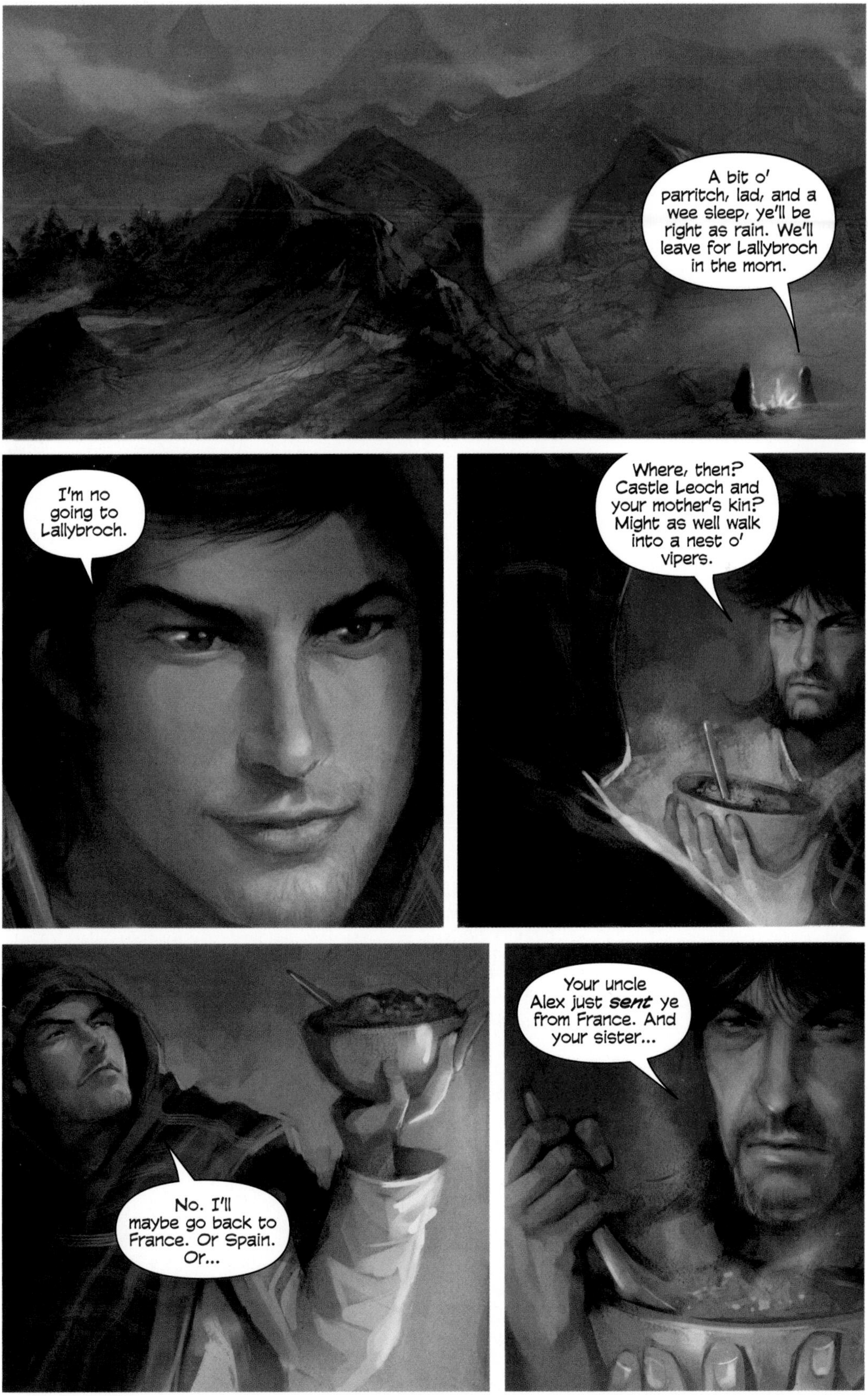
A bit o' parritch, lad, and a wee sleep, ye'll be right as rain. We'll leave for Lallybroch in the morn.
I'm no going to Lallybroch.
Where, then? Castle Leoch and your mother's kin? Might as well walk into a nest o' vipers.
No. I'll maybe go back to France. Or Spain. Or...
Your uncle Alex just *sent* ye from France. And your sister...

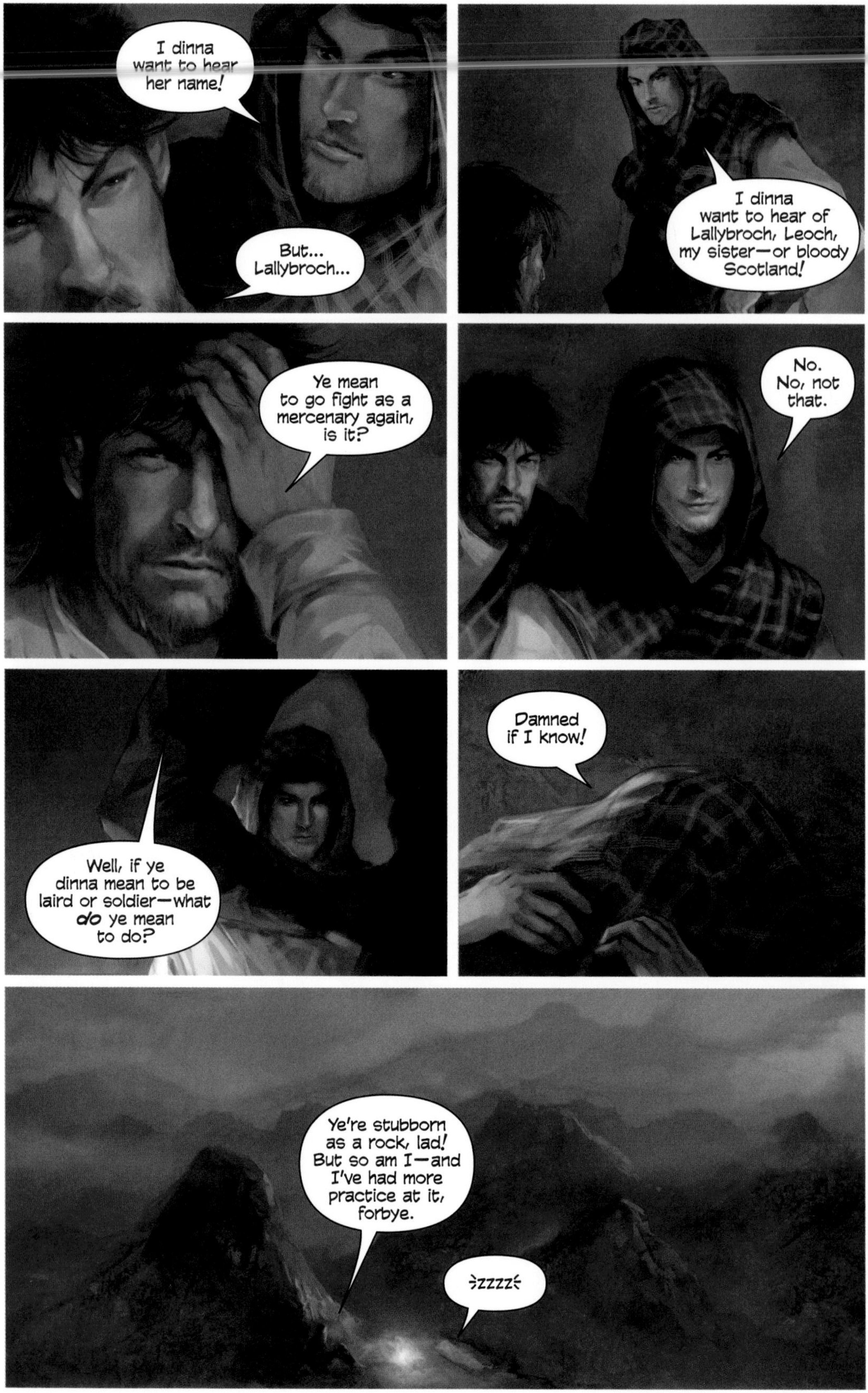
I dinna want to hear her name!
But... Lallybroch...
I dinna want to hear of Lallybroch, Leoch, my sister—or bloody Scotland!
Ye mean to go fight as a mercenary again, is it?
No. No, not that.
Well, if ye dinna mean to be laird or soldier—what *do* ye mean to do?
Damned if I know!
Ye're stubborn as a rock, lad! But so am I—and I've had more practice at it, forbye.
ZZZZ

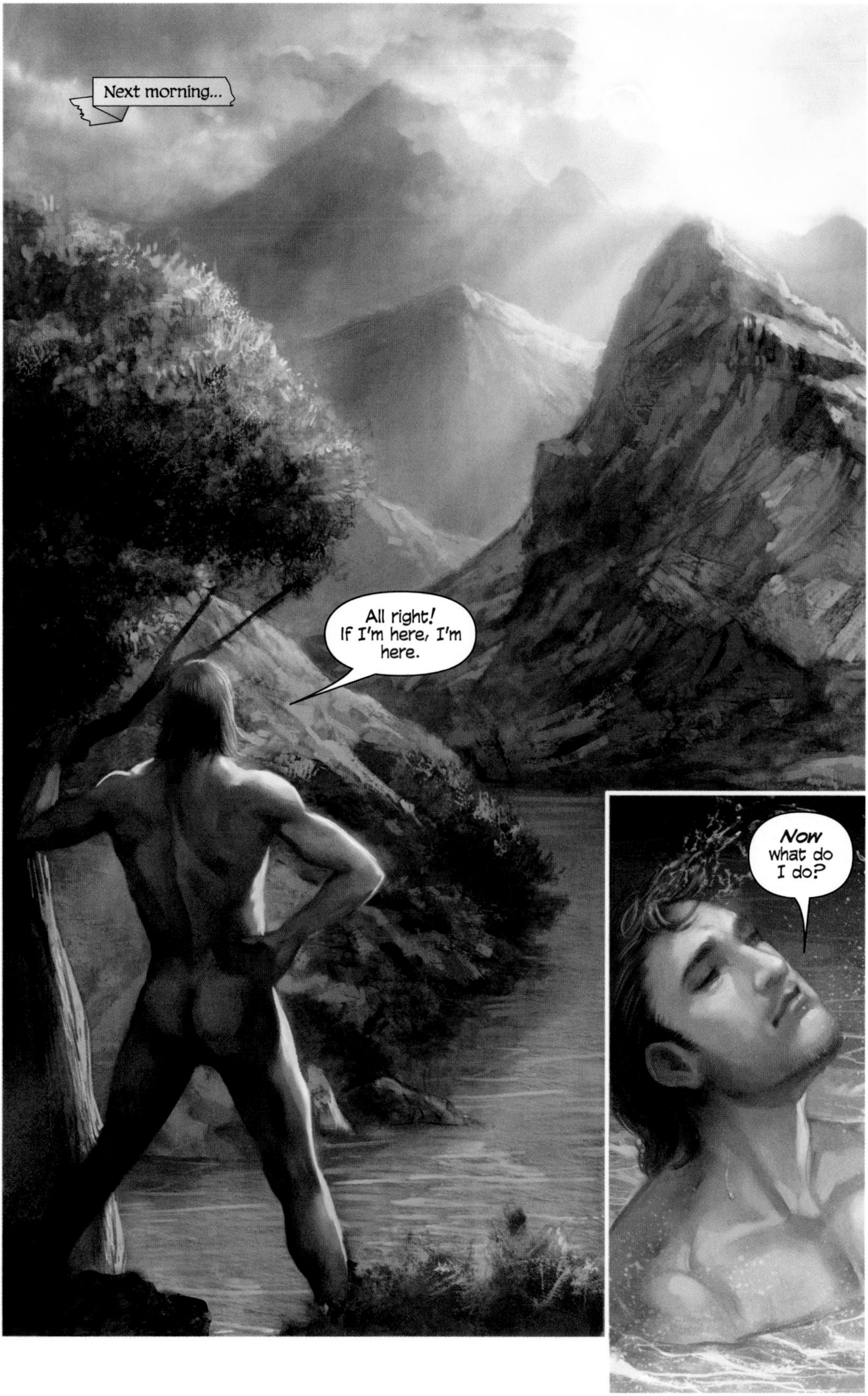
Next morning...
All right! If I'm here, I'm here.
Now what do I do?

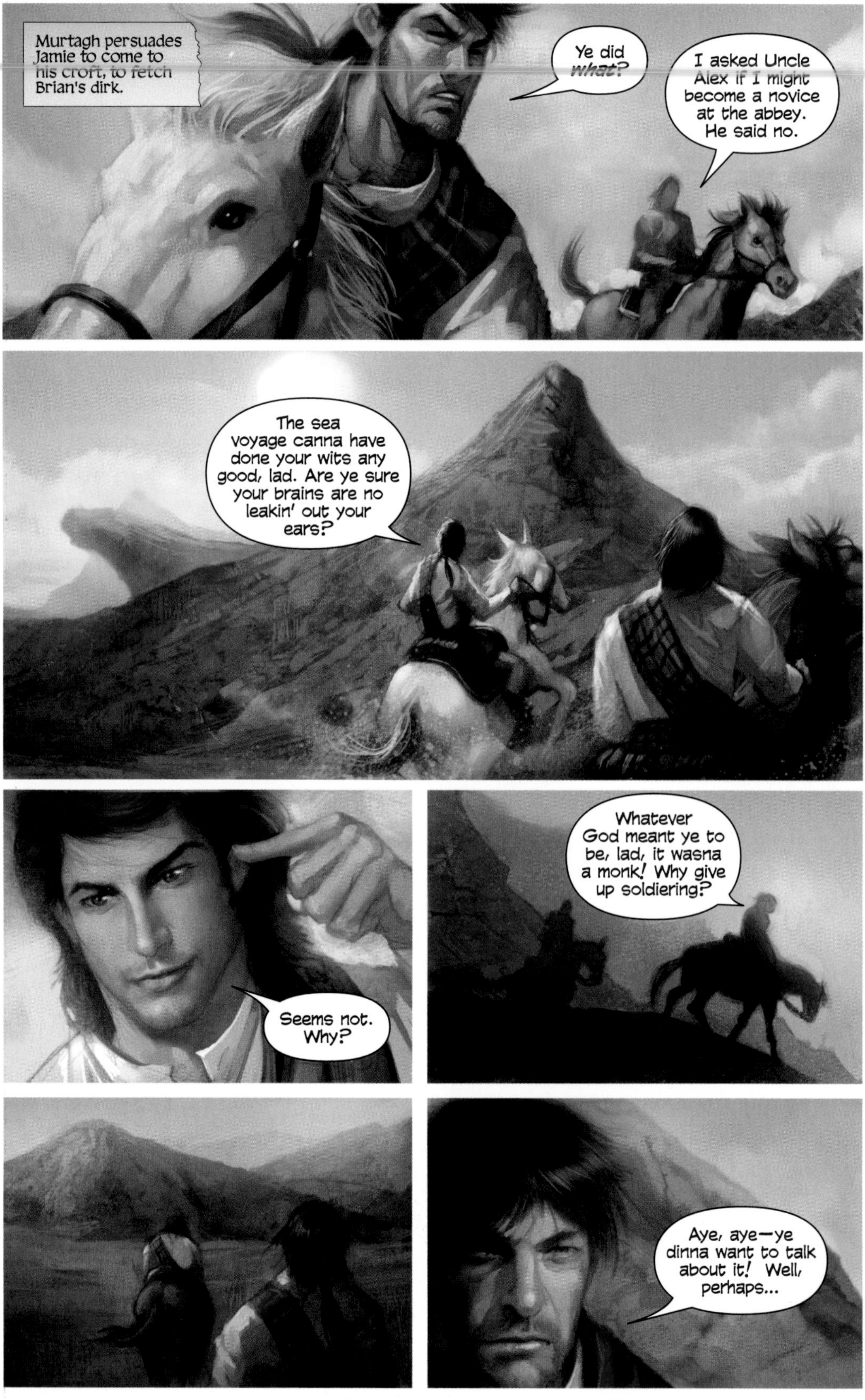
Murtagh persuades Jamie to come to his croft, to fetch Brian's dirk.
Ye did *what?*
I asked Uncle Alex if I might become a novice at the abbey. He said no.
The sea voyage canna have done your wits any good, lad. Are ye sure your brains are no leakin' out your ears?
Seems not. Why?
Whatever God meant ye to be, lad, it wasna a monk! Why give up soldiering?
Aye, aye—ye dinna want to talk about it! Well, perhaps...

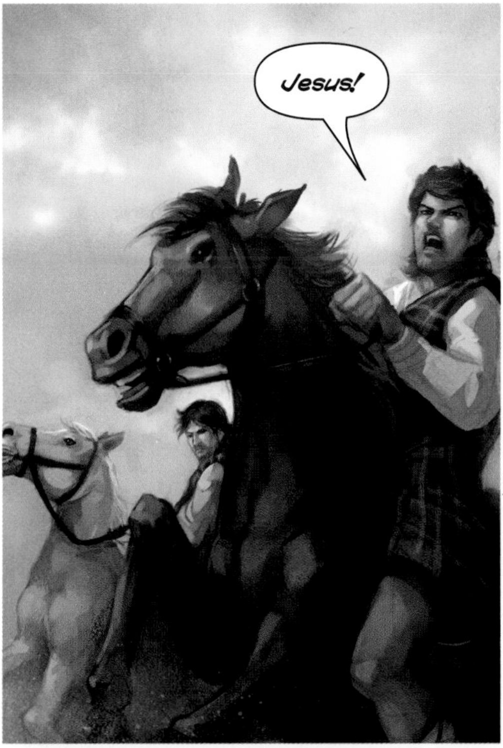
Jesus!

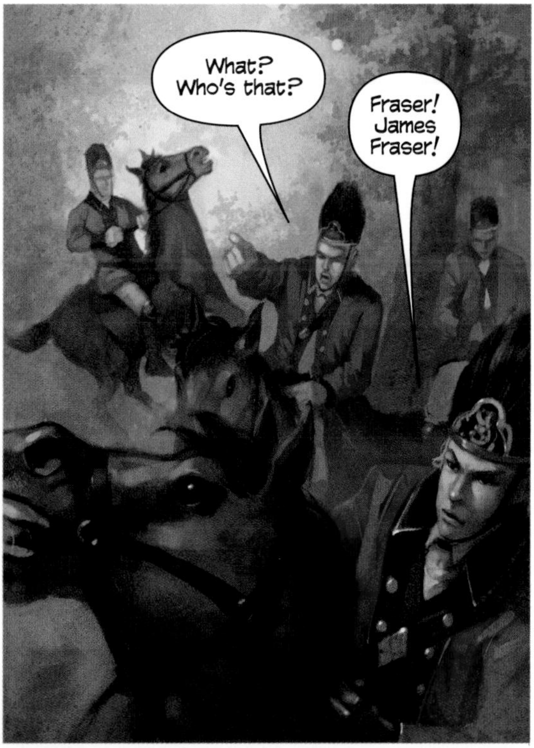
What? Who's that?
Fraser! James Fraser!

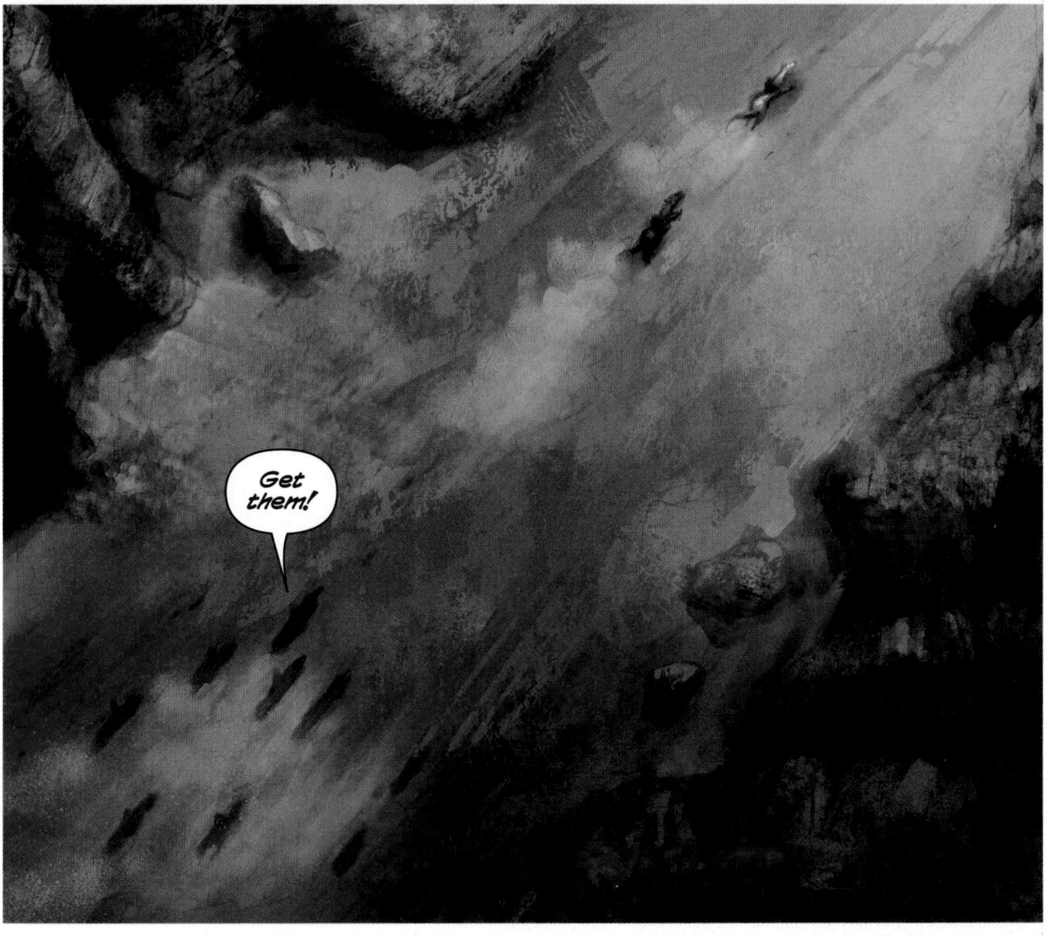
Get them!

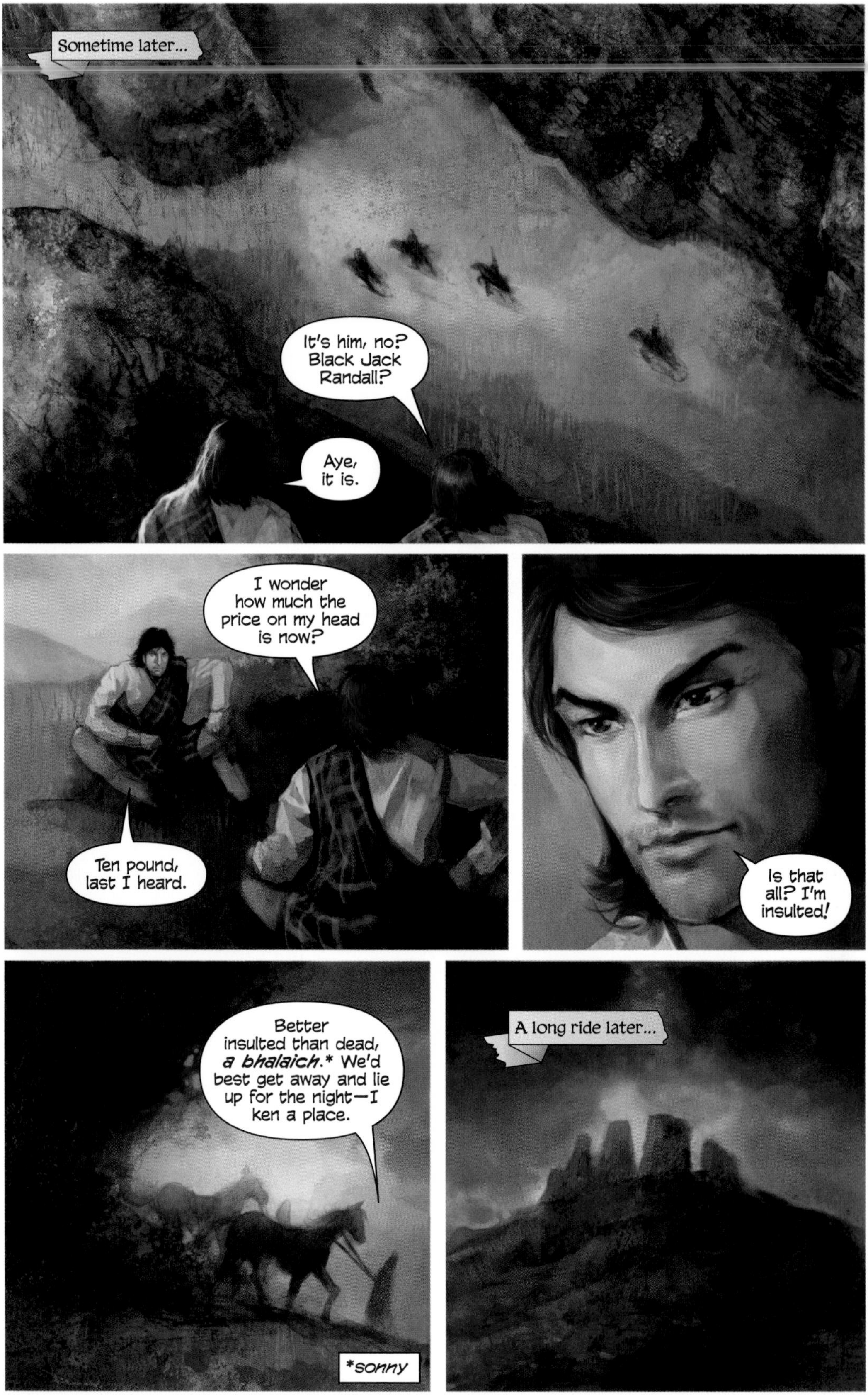
Sometime later...
It's him, no? Black Jack Randall?
Aye, it is.
I wonder how much the price on my head is now?
Ten pound, last I heard.
Is that all? I'm insulted!
Better insulted than dead, *a bhalaich*.* We'd best get away and lie up for the night—I ken a place.
*sonny
A long ride later...

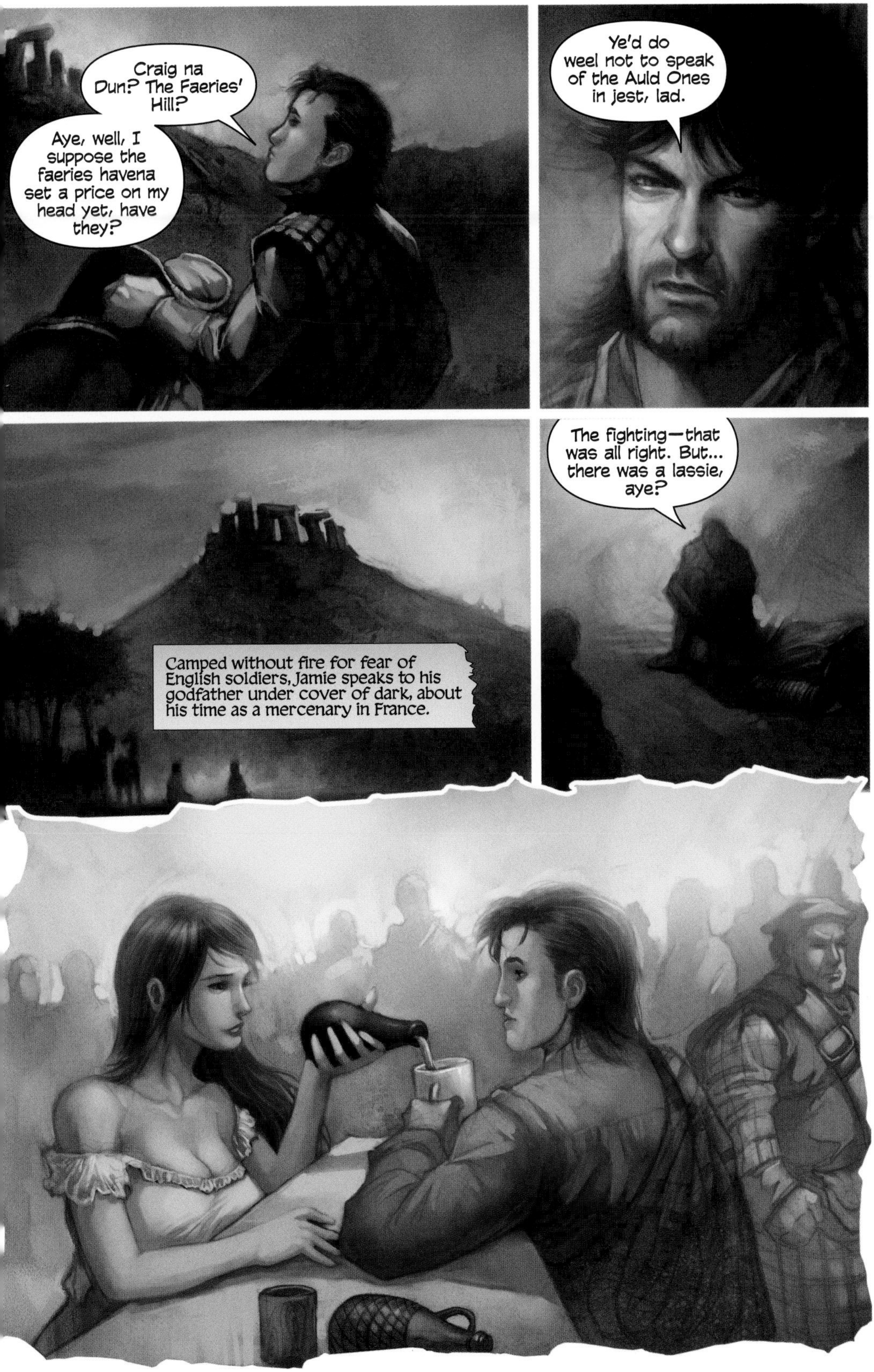
Craig na Dun? The Faeries' Hill?
Aye, well, I suppose the faeries havena set a price on my head yet, have they?
Ye'd do weel not to speak of the Auld Ones in jest, lad.
Camped without fire for fear of English soldiers, Jamie speaks to his godfather under cover of dark, about his time as a mercenary in France.
The fighting—that was all right. But... there was a lassie, aye?

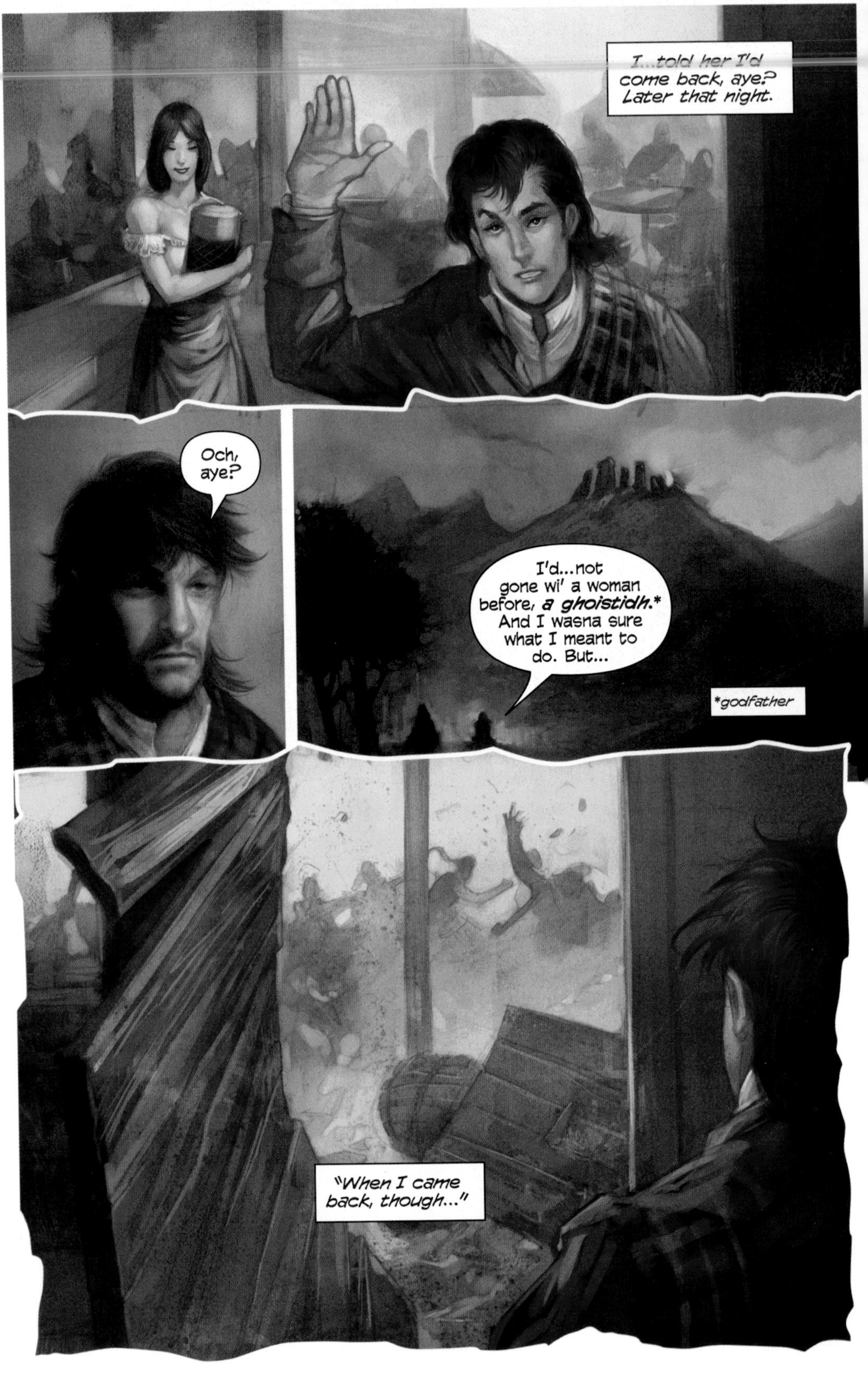
I...told her I'd come back, aye? Later that night.
Och, aye?
I'd...not gone wi' a woman before, a ghoistidh.* And I wasna sure what I meant to do. But...
*godfather
"When I came back, though..."

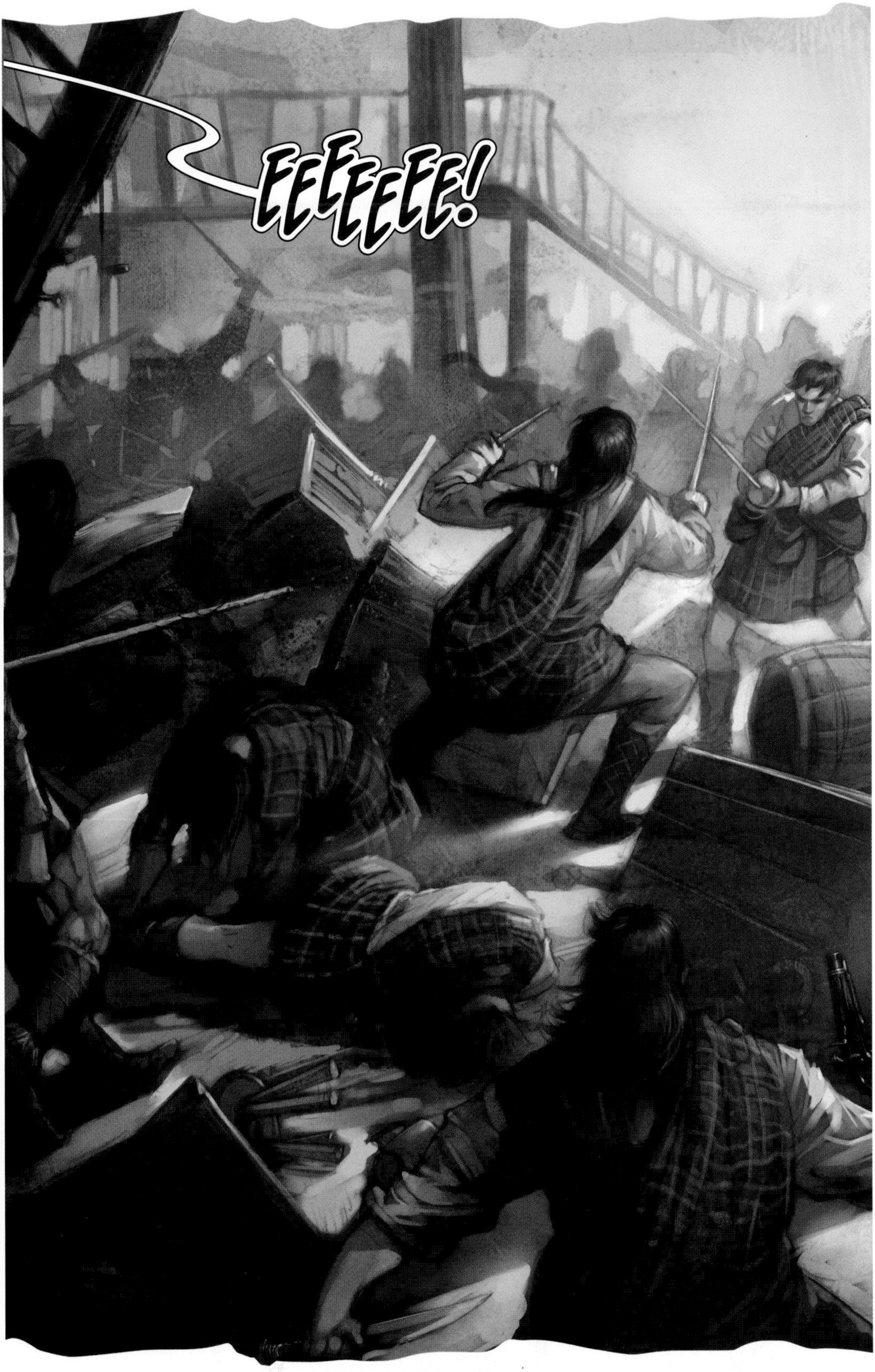
EEEEEEEE!

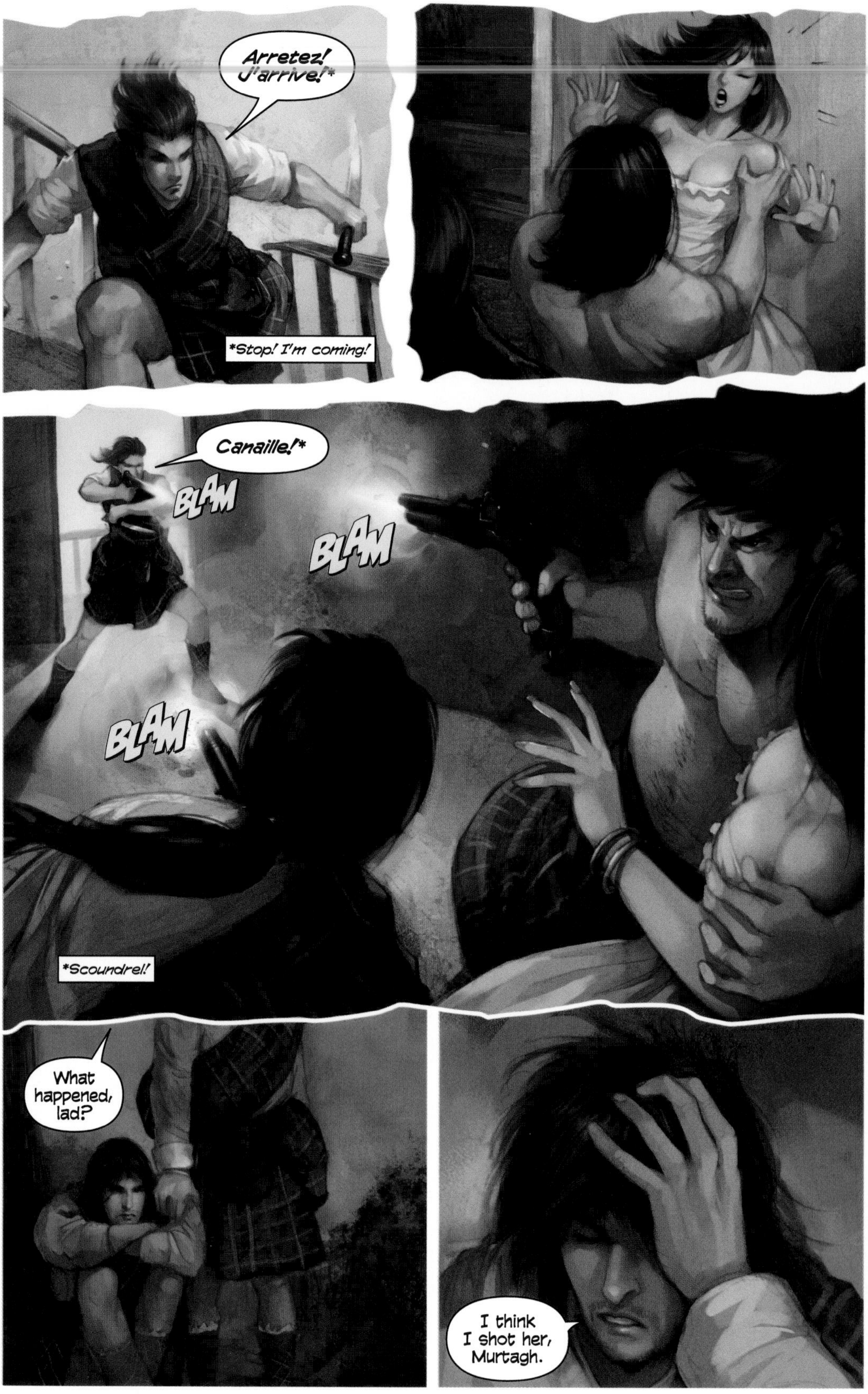
Arretez! J'arrive!*
*Stop! I'm coming!
Canaille!*
BLAM
BLAM
BLAM
*Scoundrel!
What happened, lad?
I think I shot her, Murtagh.

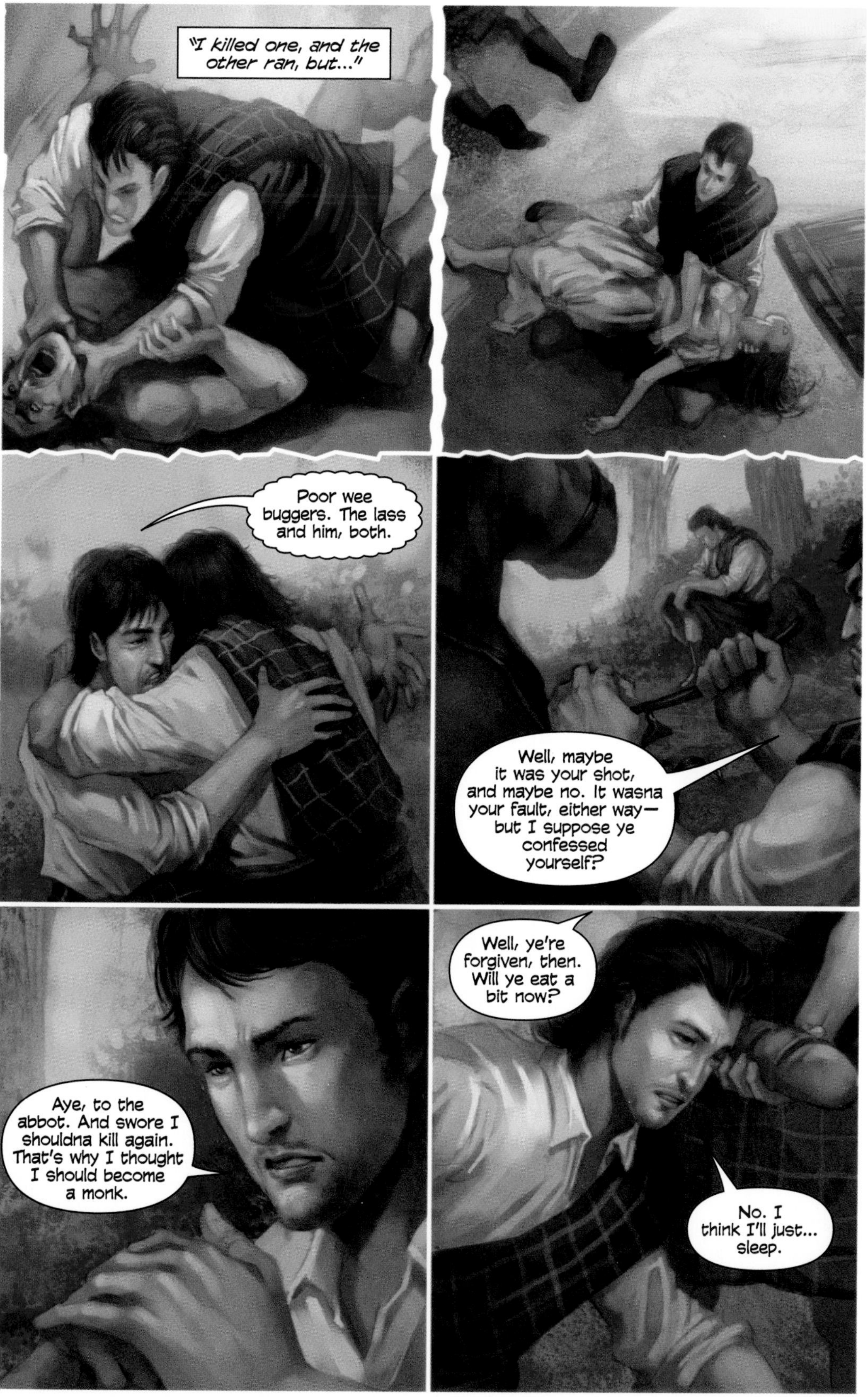
"I killed one, and the other ran, but..."
Poor wee buggers. The lass and him, both.
Well, maybe it was your shot, and maybe no. It wasna your fault, either way— but I suppose ye confessed yourself?
Aye, to the abbot. And swore I shouldna kill again. That's why I thought I should become a monk.
Well, ye're forgiven, then. Will ye eat a bit now?
No. I think I'll just... sleep.

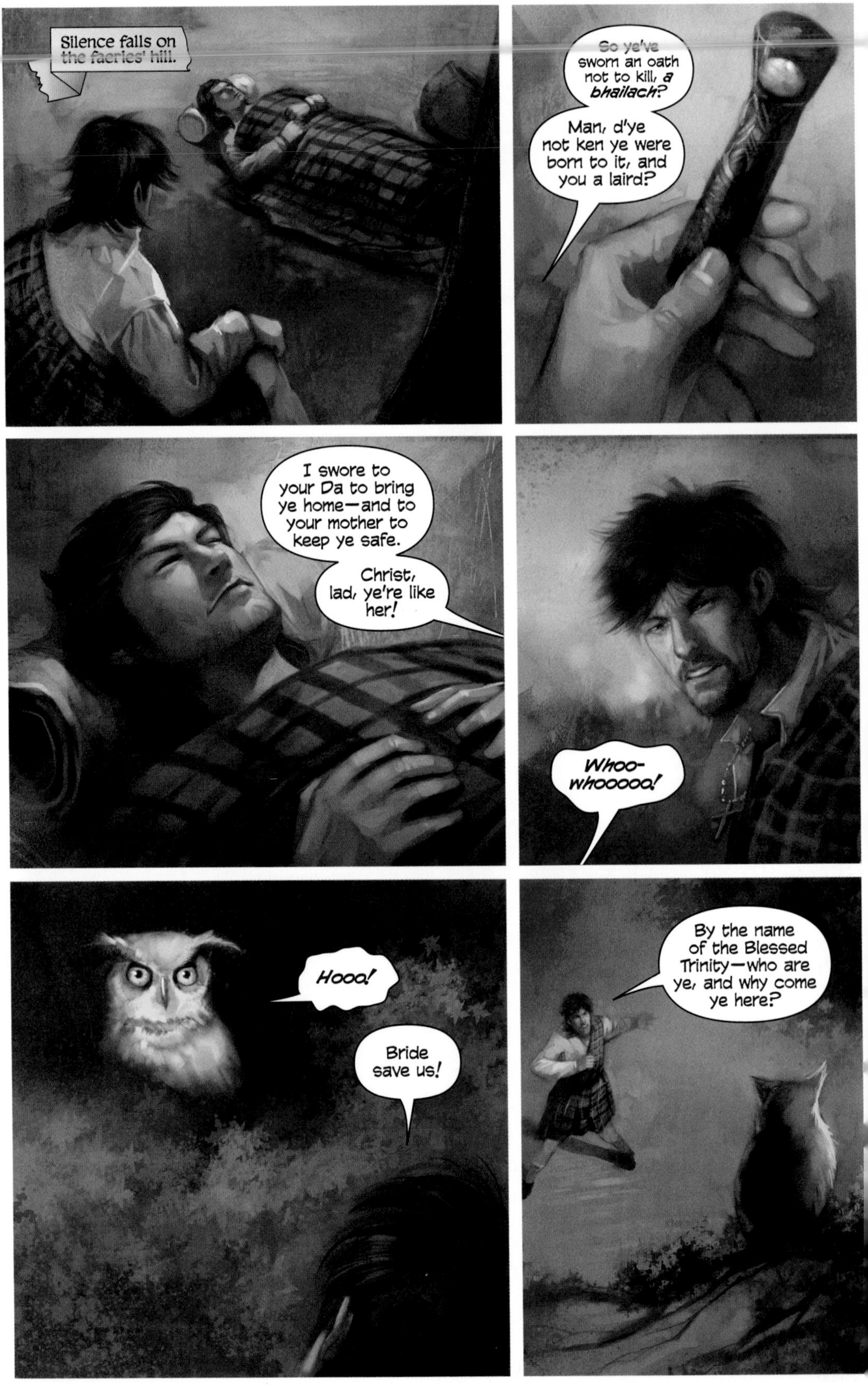

Silence falls on the faeries' hill.
So ye've sworn an oath not to kill, *a bhailach*?
Man, d'ye not ken ye were born to it, and you a laird?
I swore to your Da to bring ye home—and to your mother to keep ye safe.
Christ, lad, ye're like her!
*Whoo-whoooooo!*
*Hooo!*
Bride save us!
By the name of the Blessed Trinity—who are ye, and why come ye here?

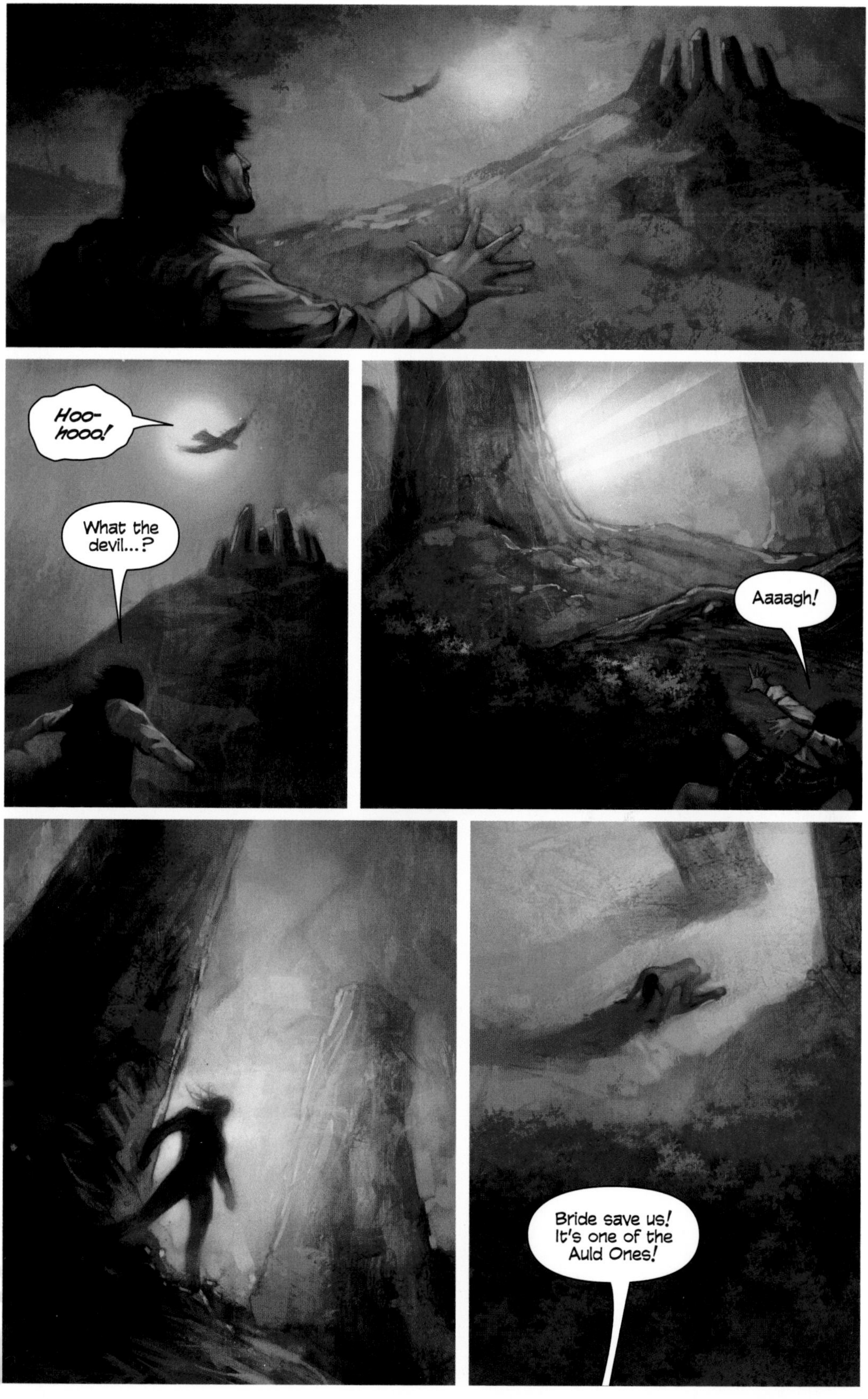
Hoo-hooo!
What the devil...?
Aaaagh!
Bride save us! It's one of the Auld Ones!

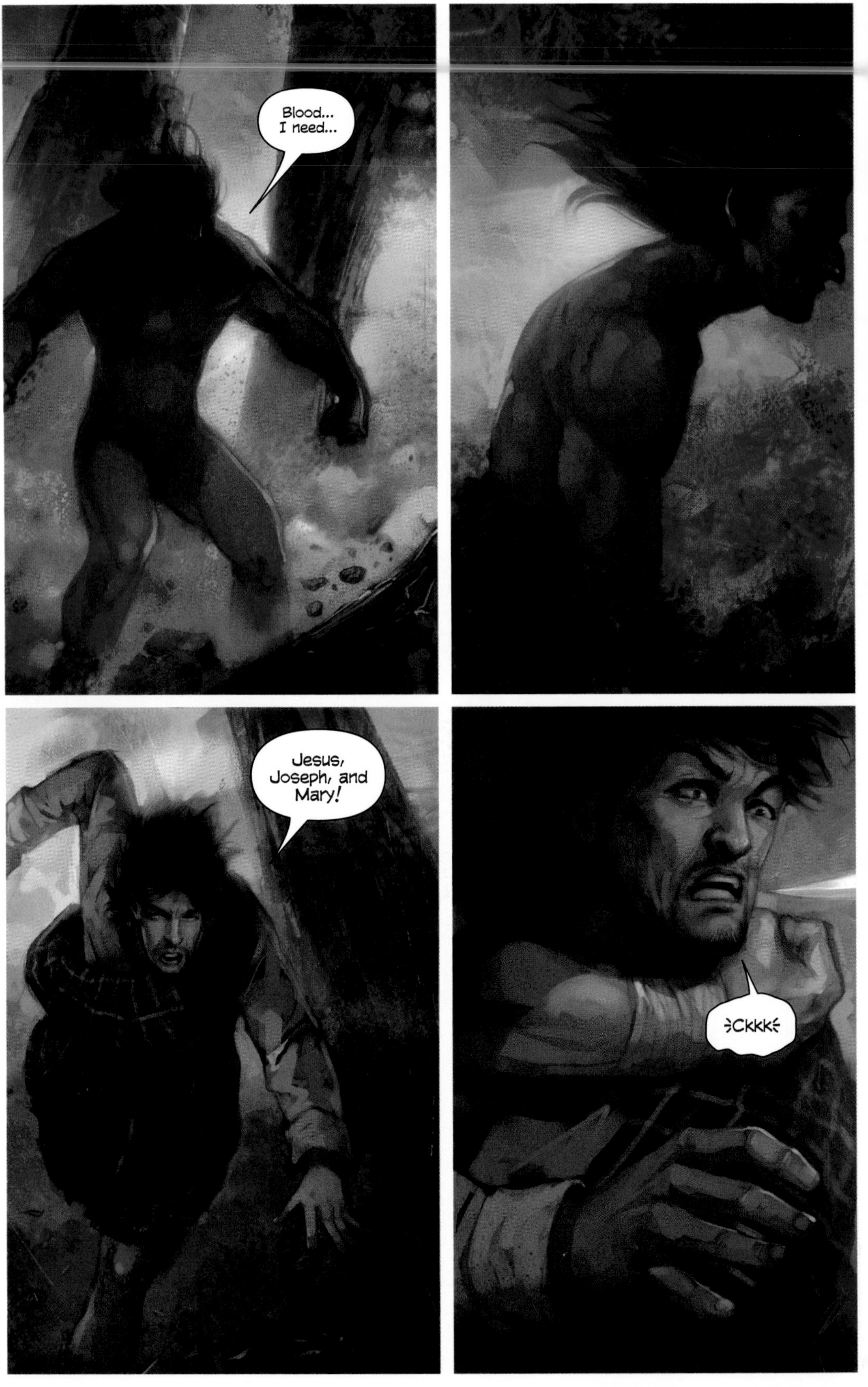
Blood... I need...
Jesus, Joseph, and Mary!
Ckkk

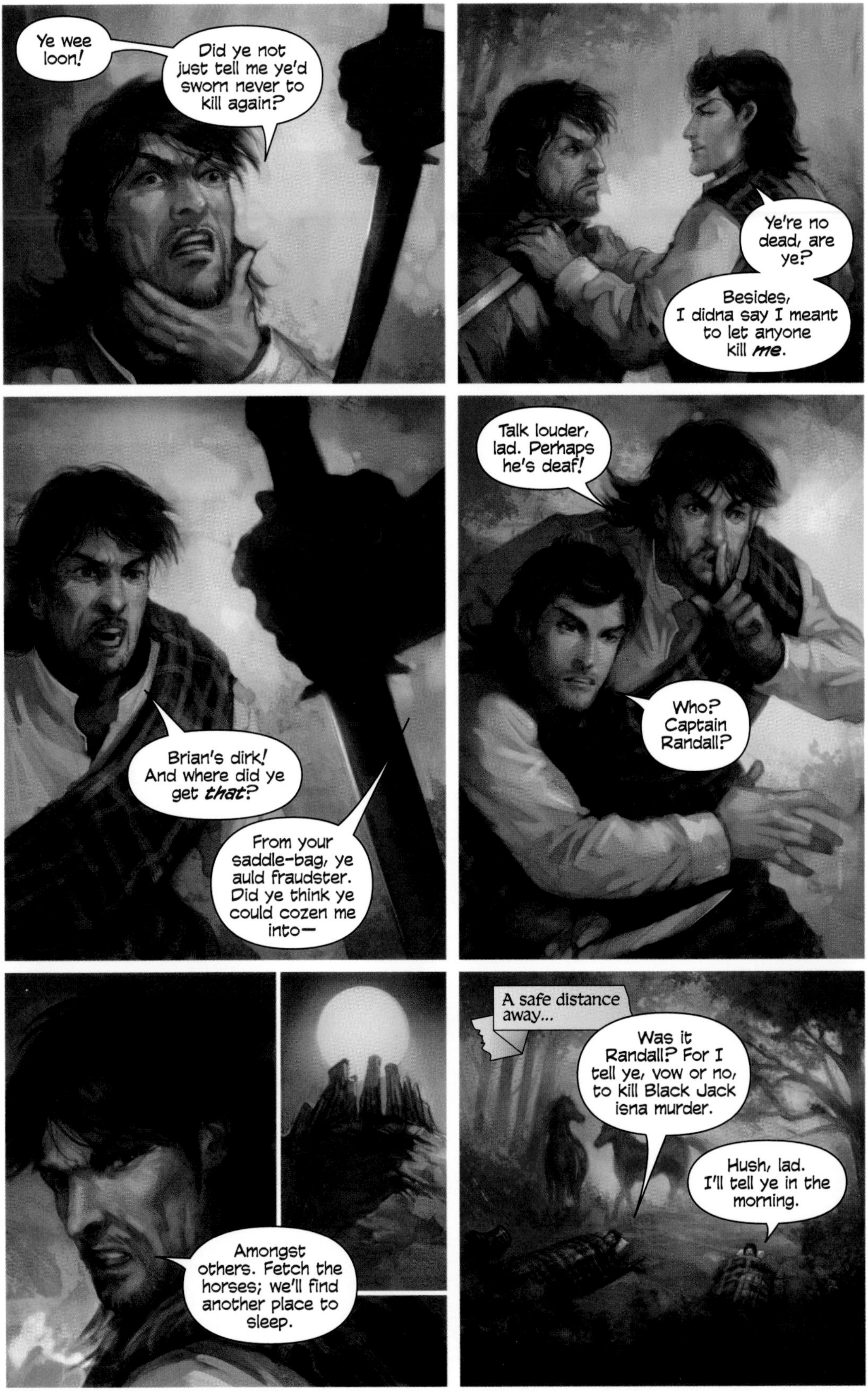
Ye wee loon!
Did ye not just tell me ye'd sworn never to kill again?
Ye're no dead, are ye?
Besides, I didna say I meant to let anyone kill *me*.
Brian's dirk! And where did ye get *that*?
From your saddle-bag, ye auld fraudster. Did ye think ye could cozen me into—
Talk louder, lad. Perhaps he's deaf!
Who? Captain Randall?
Amongst others. Fetch the horses; we'll find another place to sleep.
A safe distance away...
Was it Randall? For I tell ye, vow or no, to kill Black Jack isna murder.
Hush, lad. I'll tell ye in the morning.

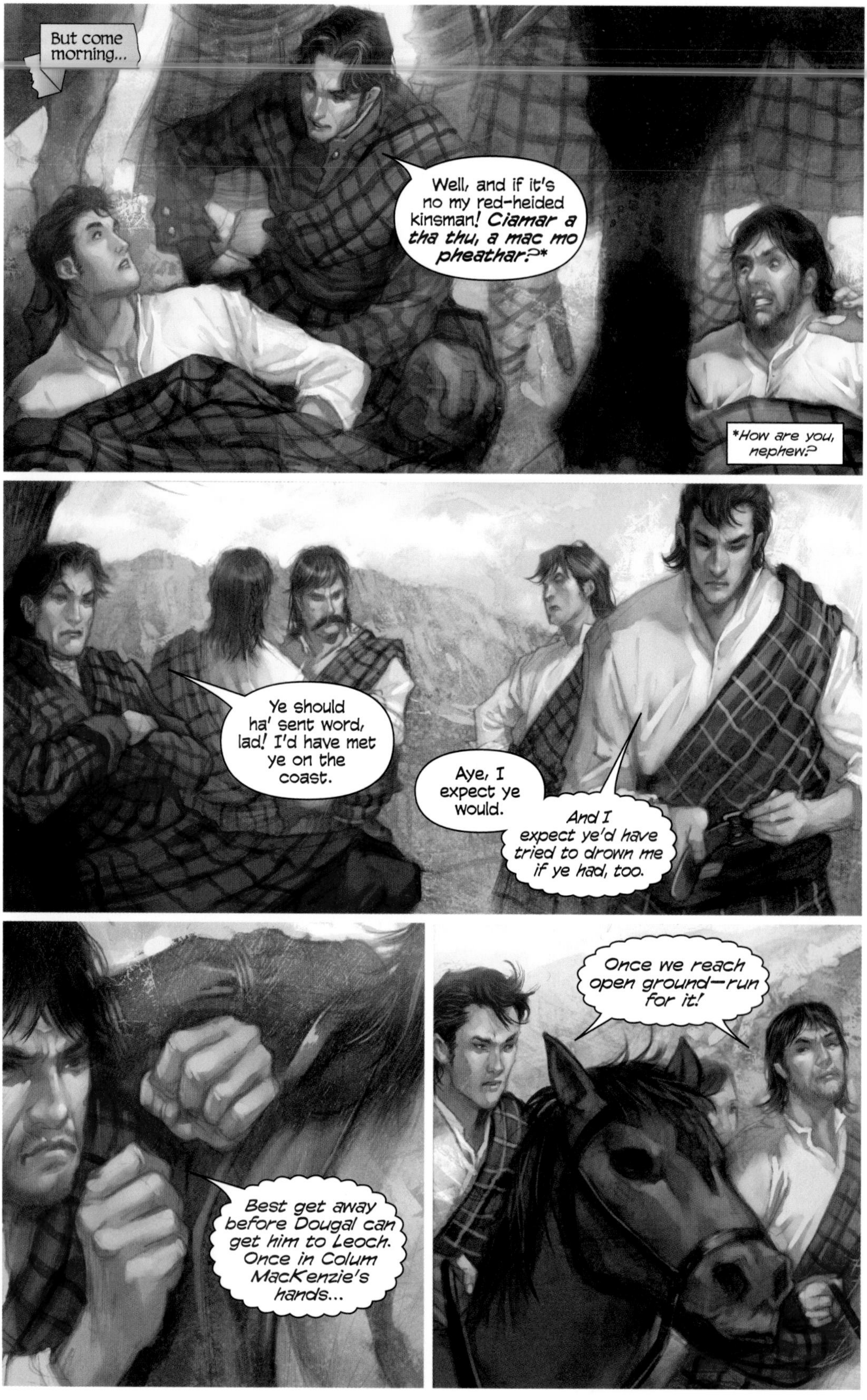

But come morning...
Well, and if it's no my red-heided kinsman! *Ciamar a tha thu, a mac mo pheathar?**
*How are you, nephew?
Ye should ha' sent word, lad! I'd have met ye on the coast.
Aye, I expect ye would.
And I expect ye'd have tried to drown me if ye had, too.
Best get away before Dougal can get him to Leoch. Once in Colum MacKenzie's hands...
Once we reach open ground—run for it!

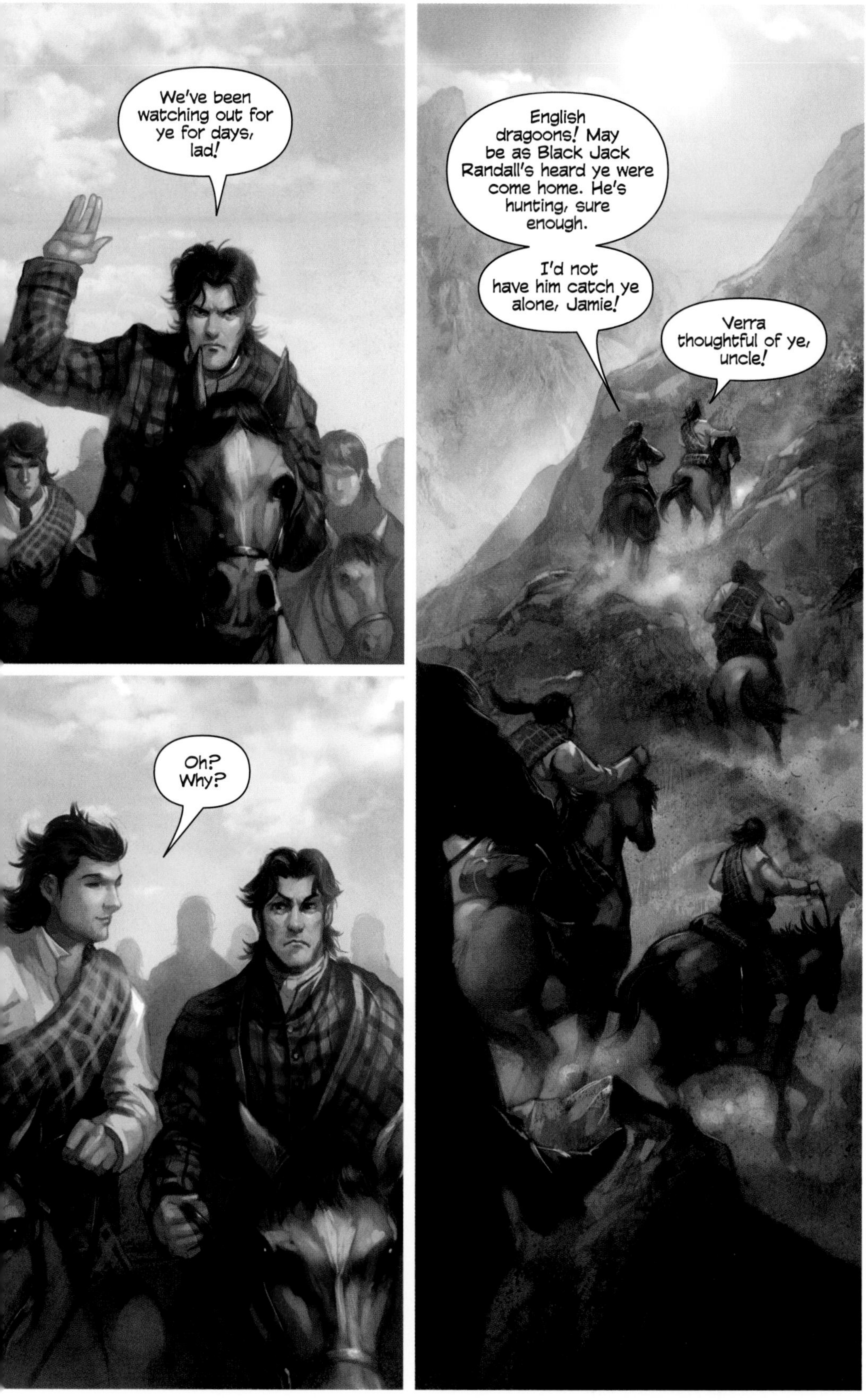
We've been watching out for ye for days, lad!
Oh? Why?
English dragoons! May be as Black Jack Randall's heard ye were come home. He's hunting, sure enough.
I'd not have him catch ye alone, Jamie!
Verra thoughtful of ye, uncle!

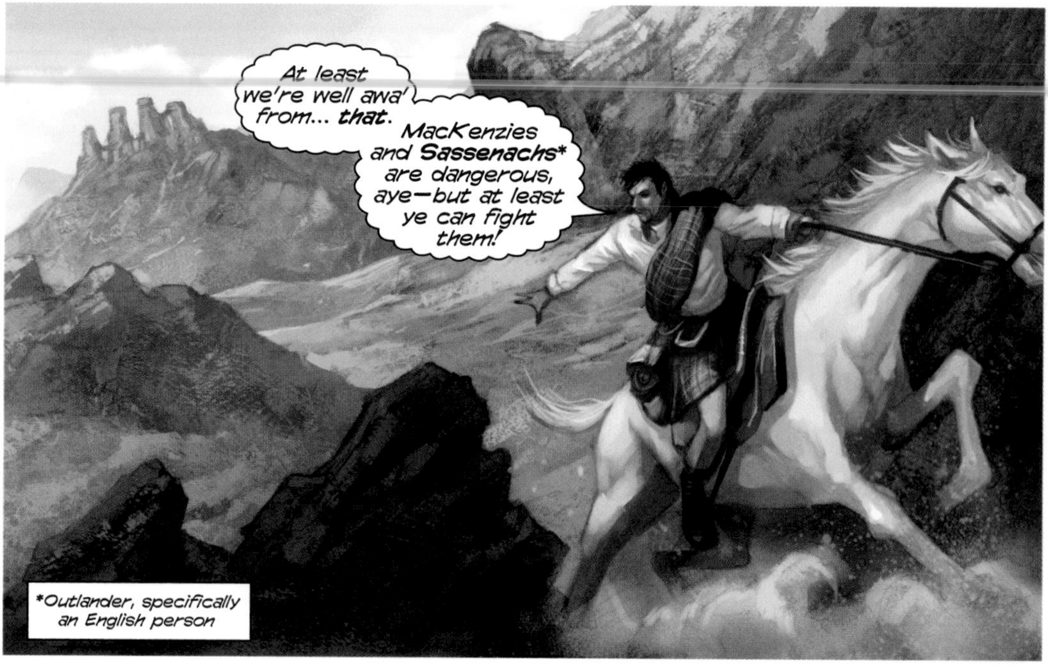
At least we're well awa' from... **that**.
MacKenzies and **Sassenachs*** are dangerous, aye—but at least ye can fight them!
*Outlander, specifically an English person

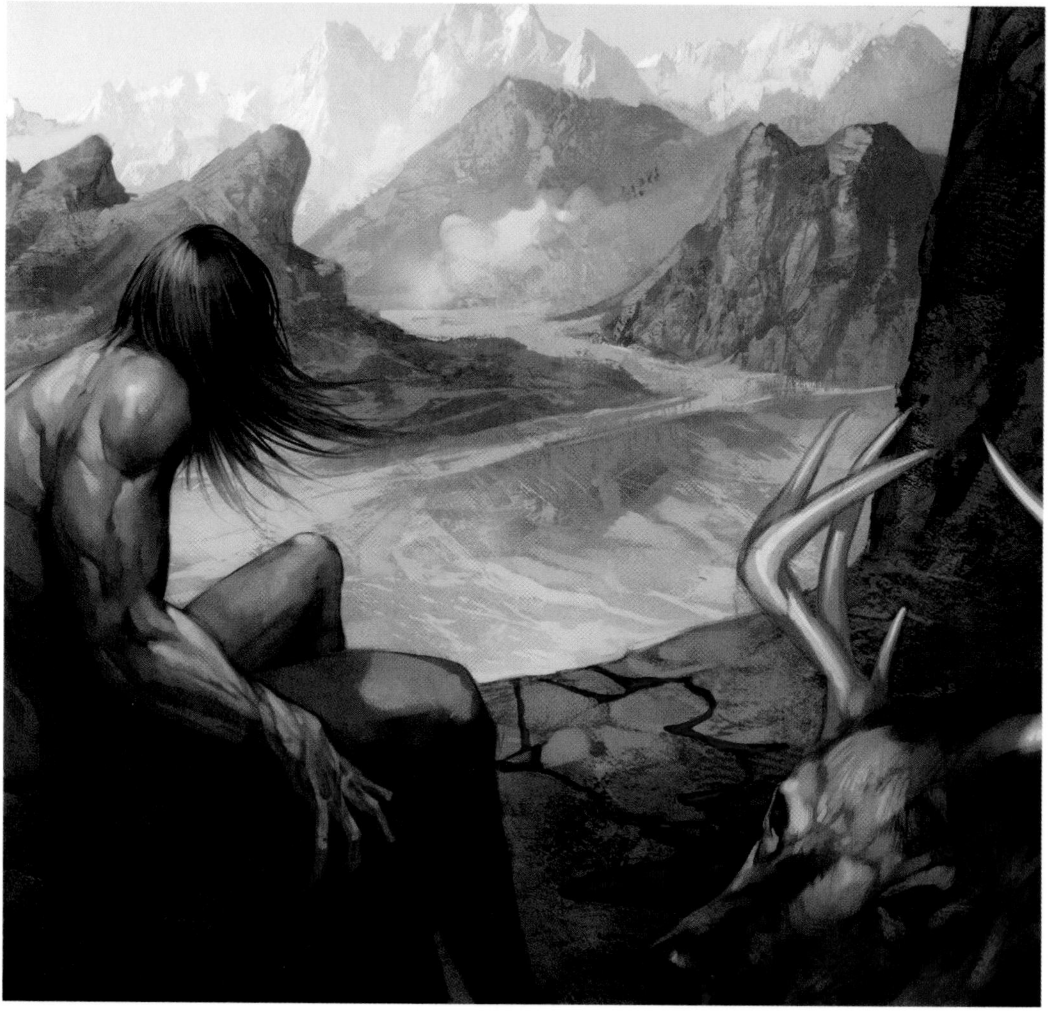

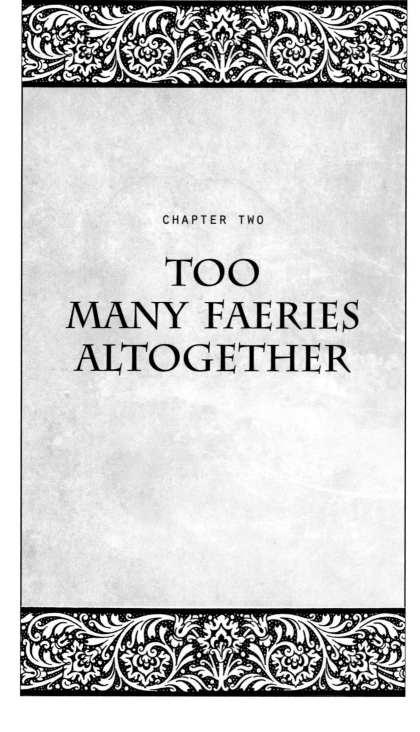

CHAPTER TWO

# TOO
# MANY FAERIES
# ALTOGETHER

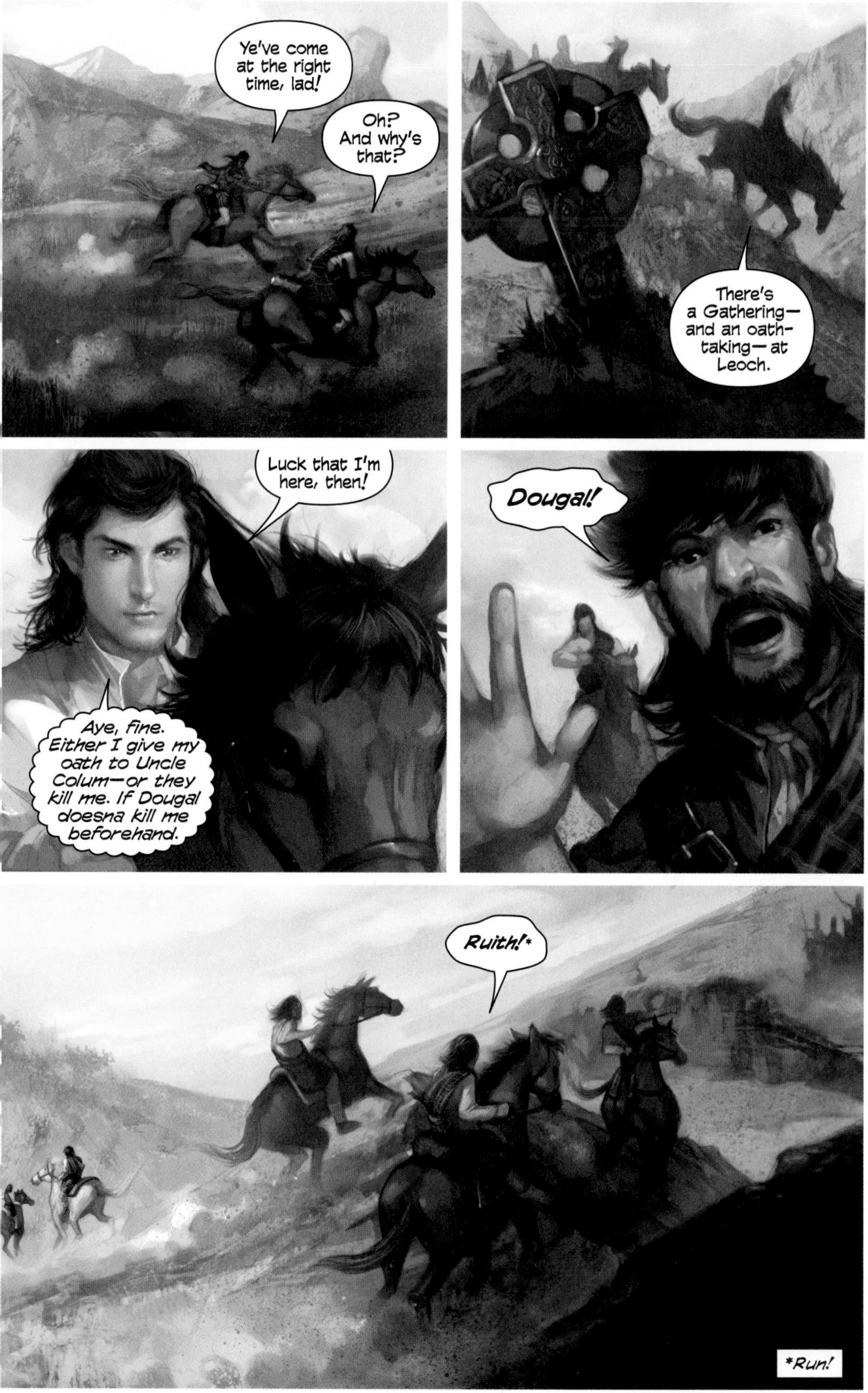
Ye've come at the right time, lad!
Oh? And why's that?
There's a Gathering—and an oath-taking—at Leoch.
Luck that I'm here, then!
Aye, fine. Either I give my oath to Uncle Colum—or they kill me. If Dougal doesna kill me beforehand.
Dougal!
Ruith!*
*Run!

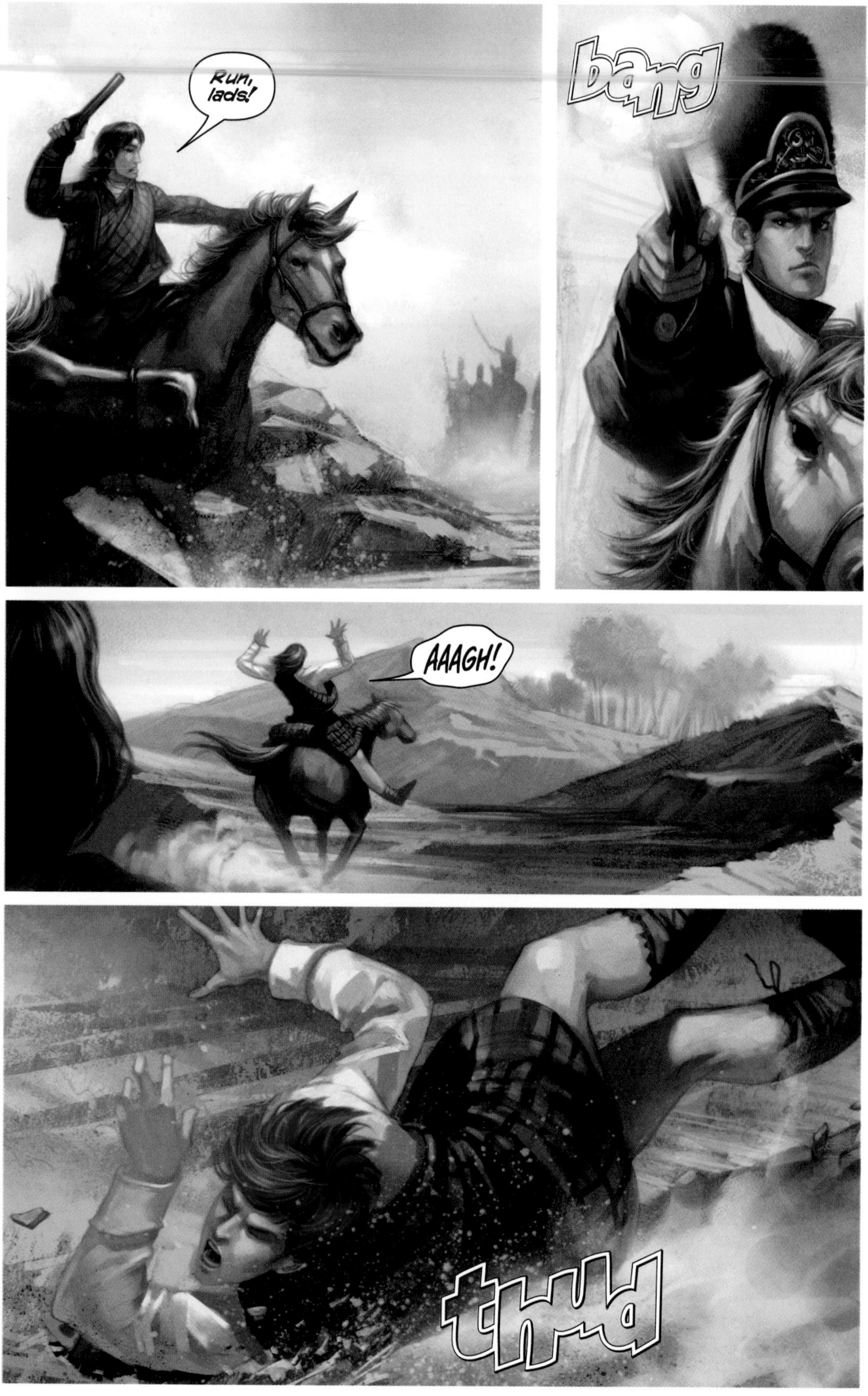
Run, lads!
bang
AAAGH!
thud

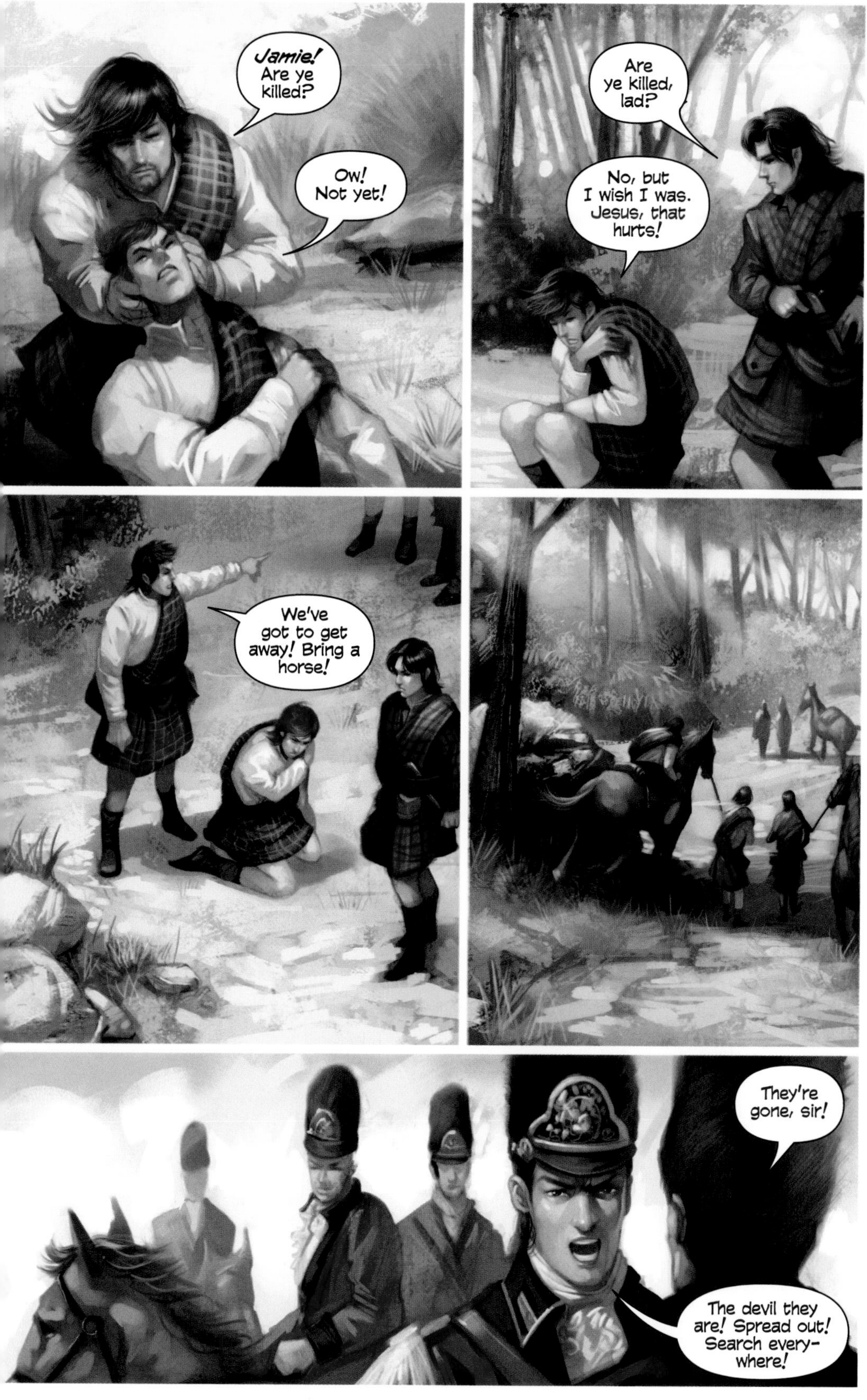
Jamie! Are ye killed?
Ow! Not yet!
Are ye killed, lad?
No, but I wish I was. Jesus, that hurts!
We've got to get away! Bring a horse!
They're gone, sir!
The devil they are! Spread out! Search every-where!

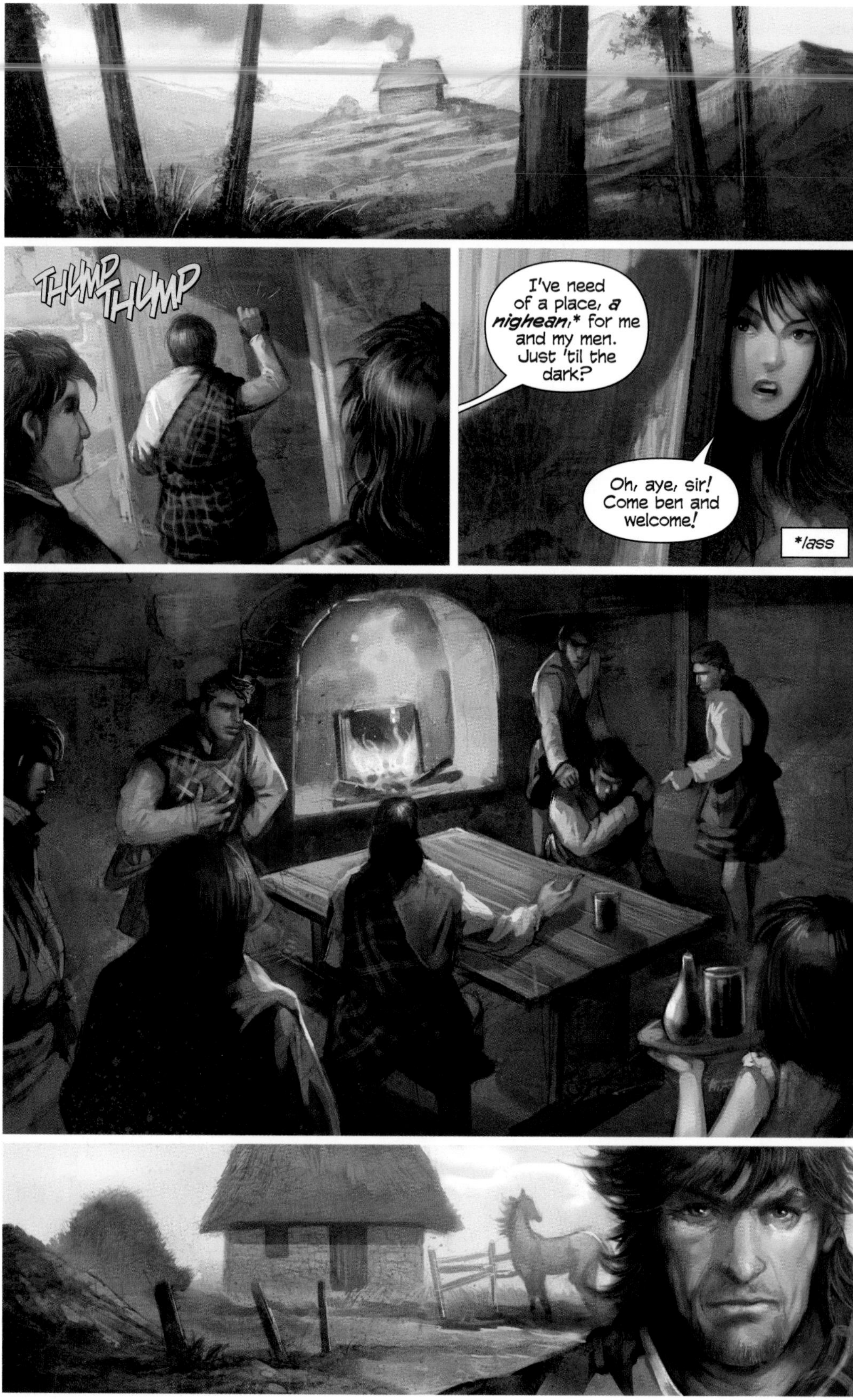
THUMP THUMP
I've need of a place, a nighean,* for me and my men. Just 'til the dark?
Oh, aye, sir! Come ben and welcome!
*lass

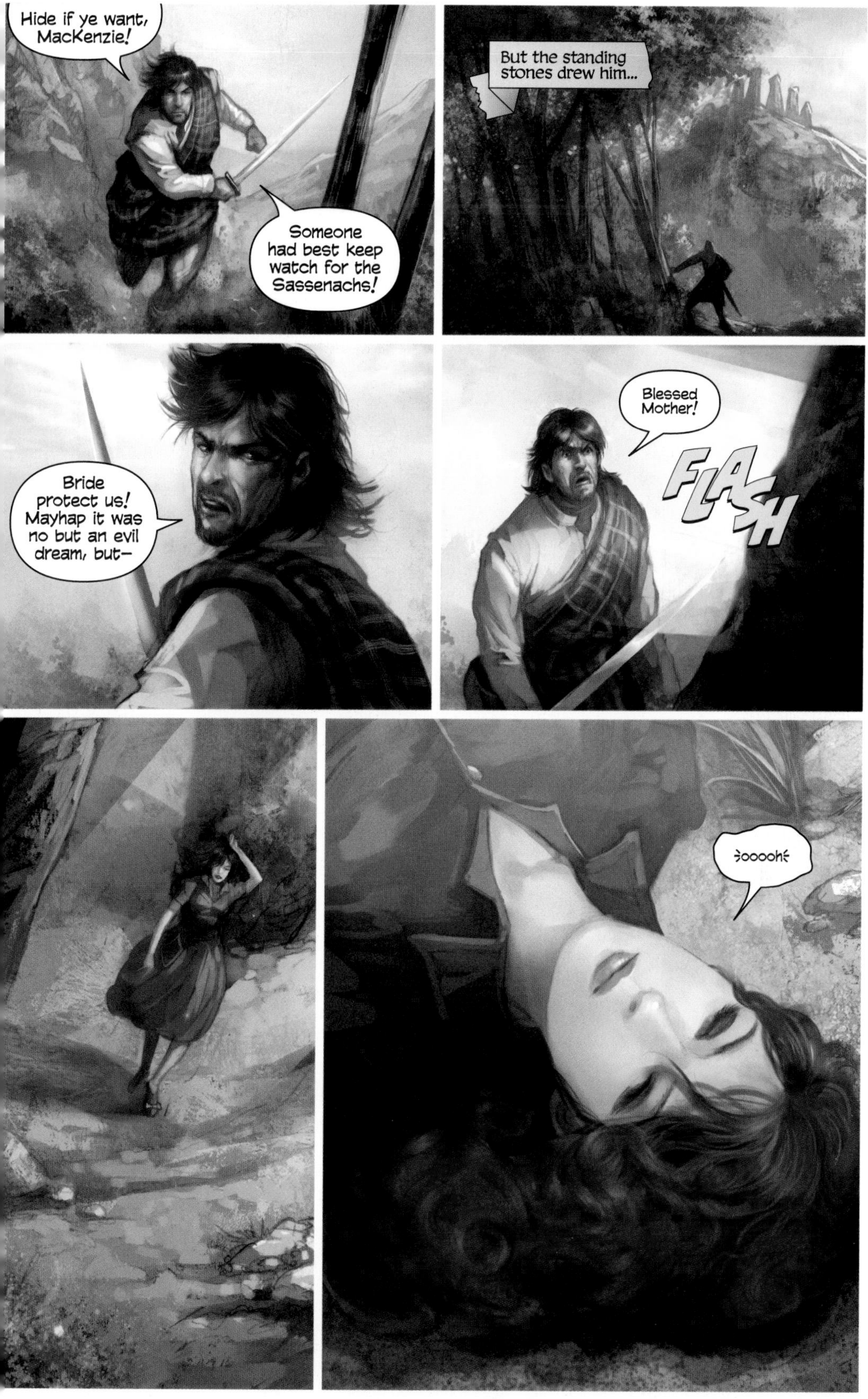
Hide if ye want, MacKenzie!
Someone had best keep watch for the Sassenachs!
But the standing stones drew him...
Bride protect us! Mayhap it was no but an evil dream, but—
Blessed Mother!
FLASH
ooooh

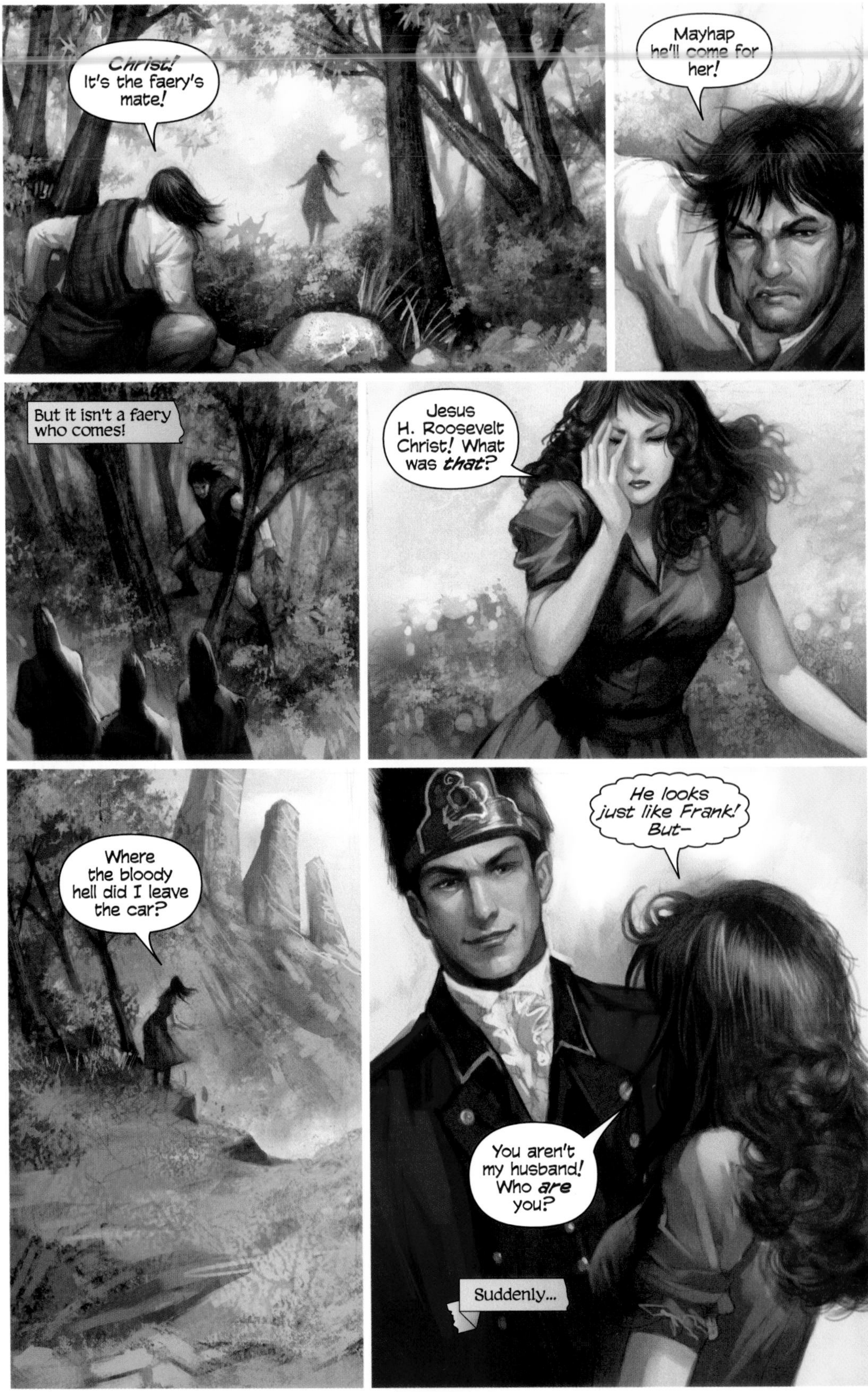
Christ! It's the faery's mate!
Mayhap he'll come for her!
But it isn't a faery who comes!
Jesus H. Roosevelt Christ! What was that?
Where the bloody hell did I leave the car?
He looks just like Frank! But-
You aren't my husband! Who are you?
Suddenly...

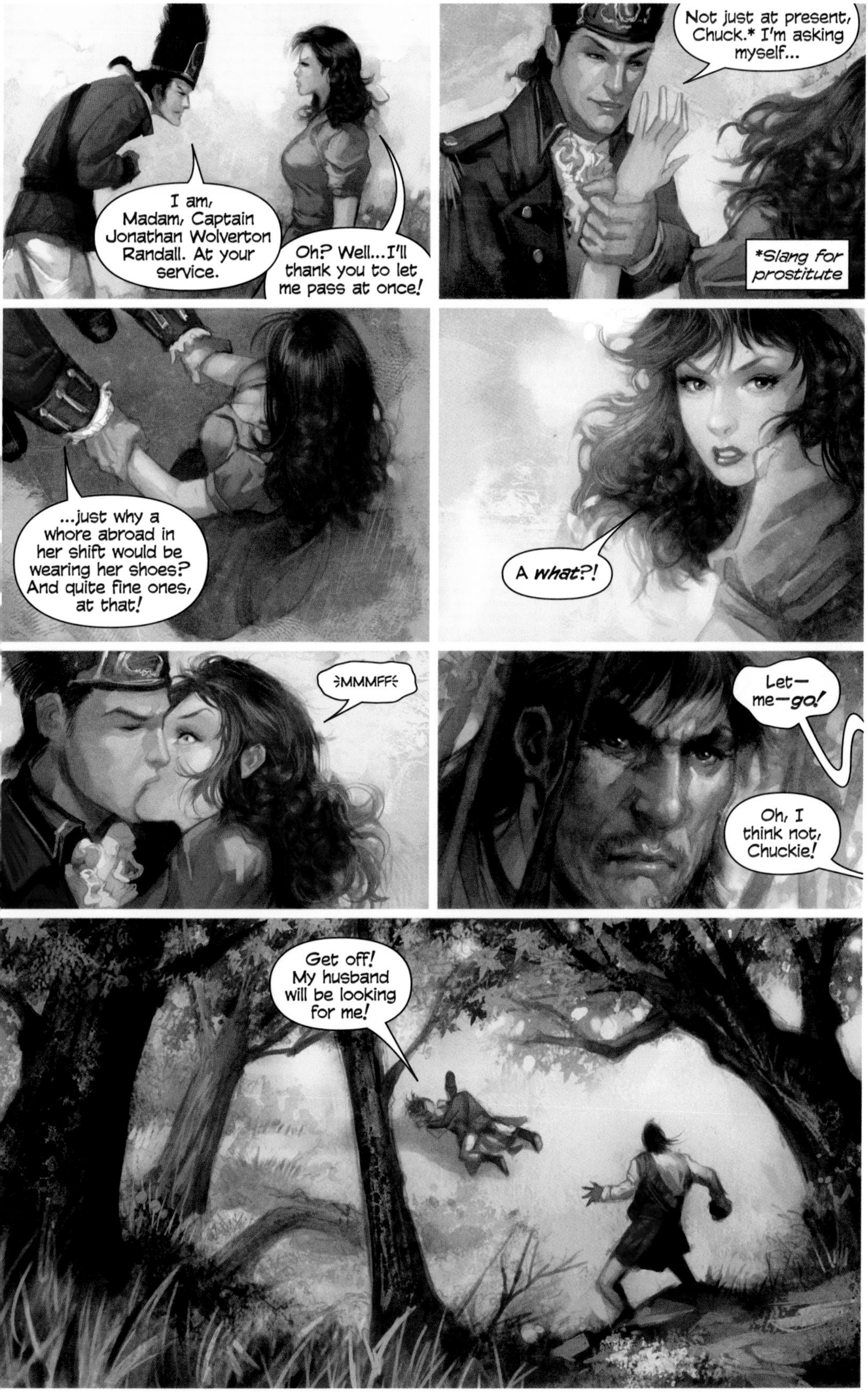
I am, Madam, Captain Jonathan Wolverton Randall. At your service.
Oh? Well...I'll thank you to let me pass at once!
Not just at present, Chuck.* I'm asking myself...
*Slang for prostitute
...just why a whore abroad in her shift would be wearing her shoes? And quite fine ones, at that!
A what?!
MMMFF
Let—me—go!
Oh, I think not, Chuckie!
Get off! My husband will be looking for me!

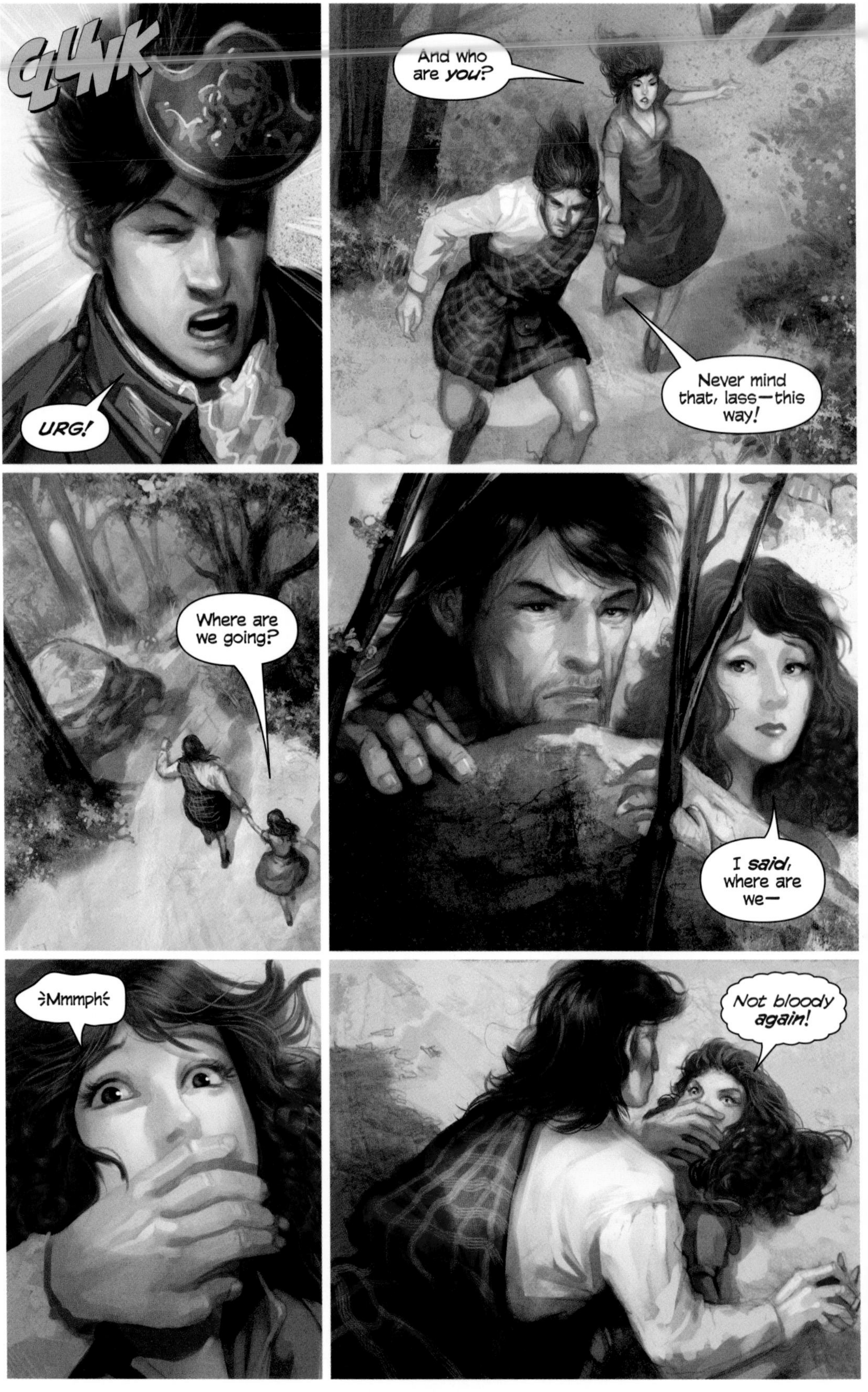
CLUNK
URG!
And who are *you*?
Never mind that, lass—this way!
Where are we going?
I *said*, where are we—
Mmmph
Not bloody *again*!

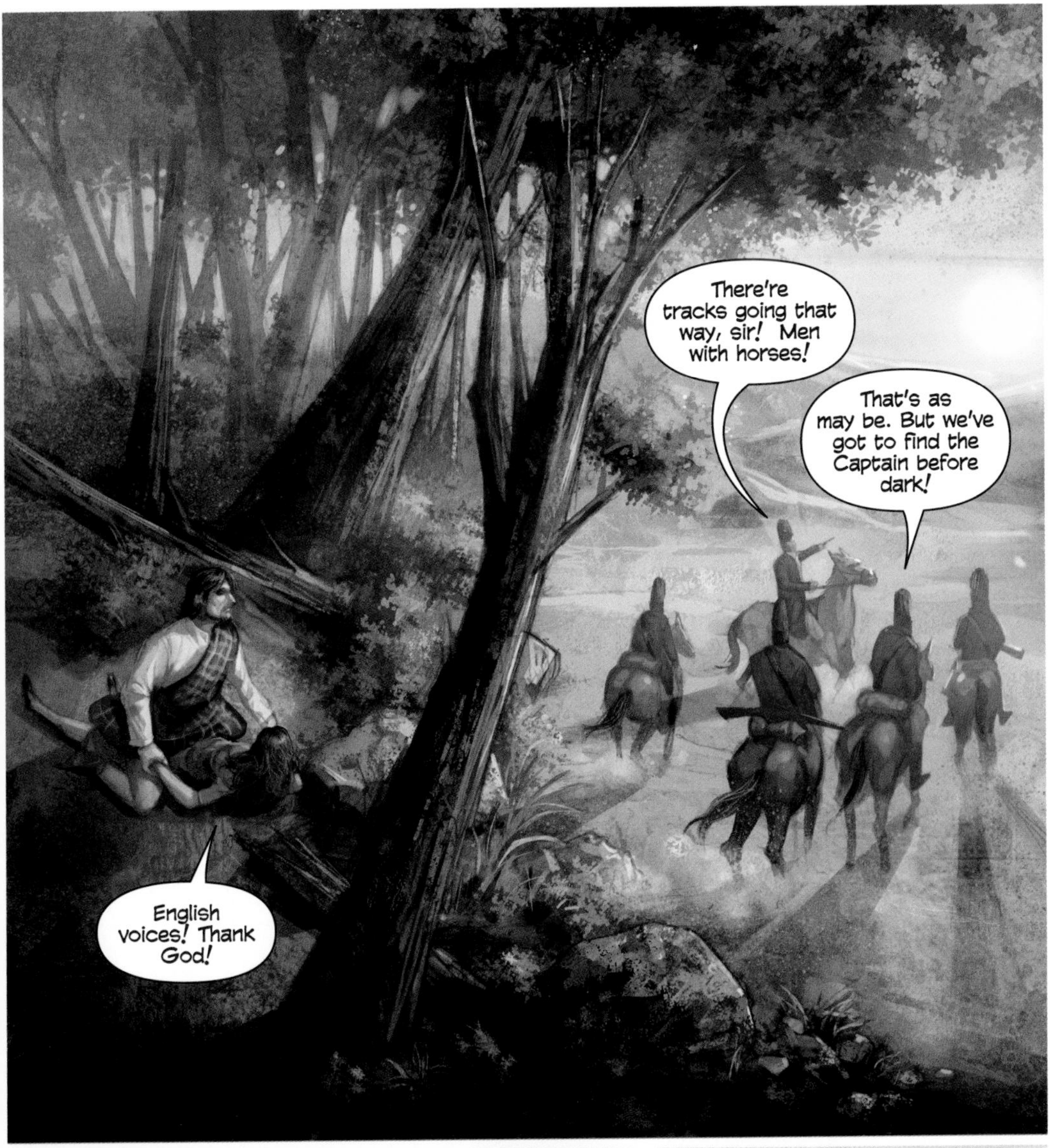
There're tracks going that way, sir! Men with horses!
That's as may be. But we've got to find the Captain before dark!
English voices! Thank God!

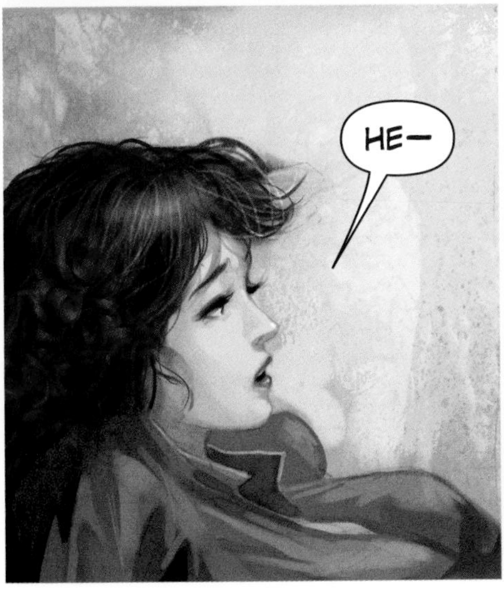
HE—

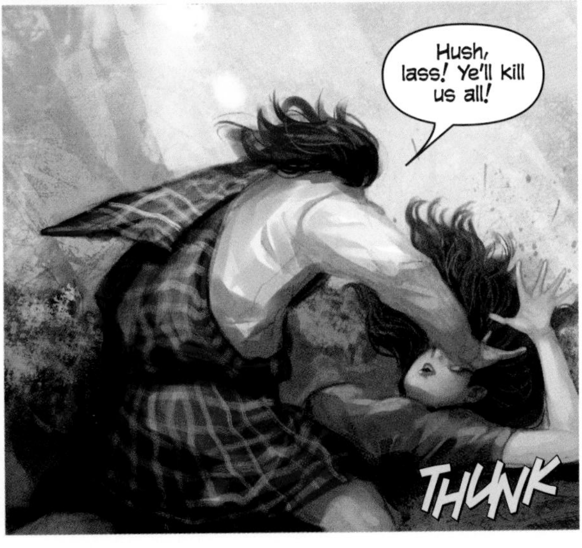
Hush, lass! Ye'll kill us all!
THUNK

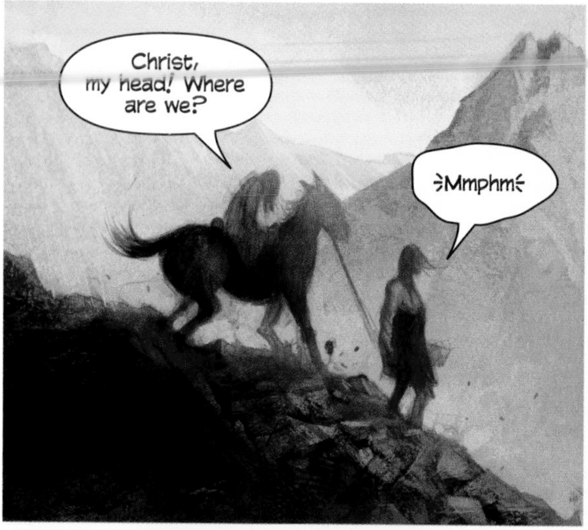
Christ, my head! Where are we?
Mmphm

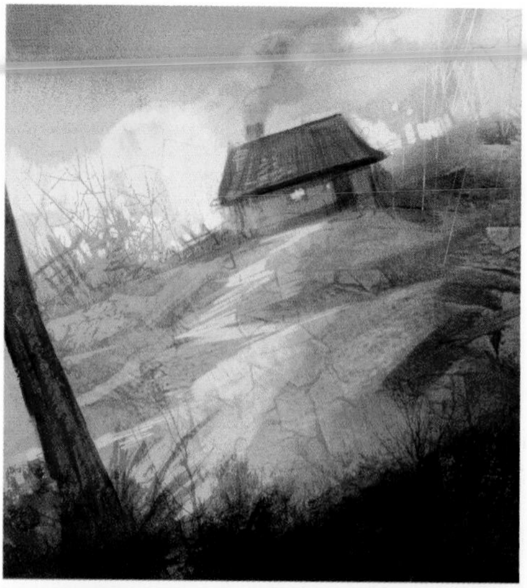

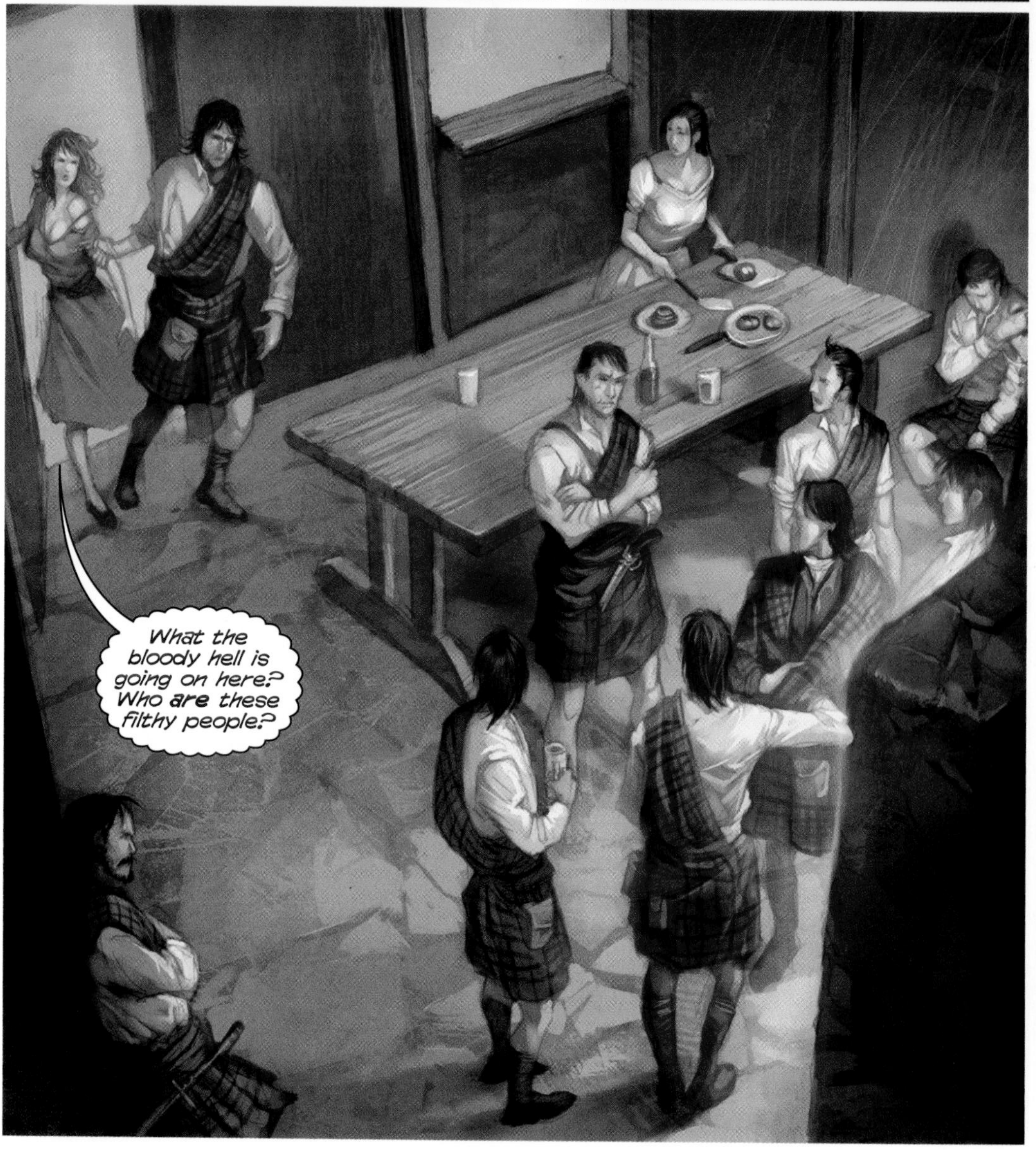
What the bloody hell is going on here? Who **are** these filthy people?

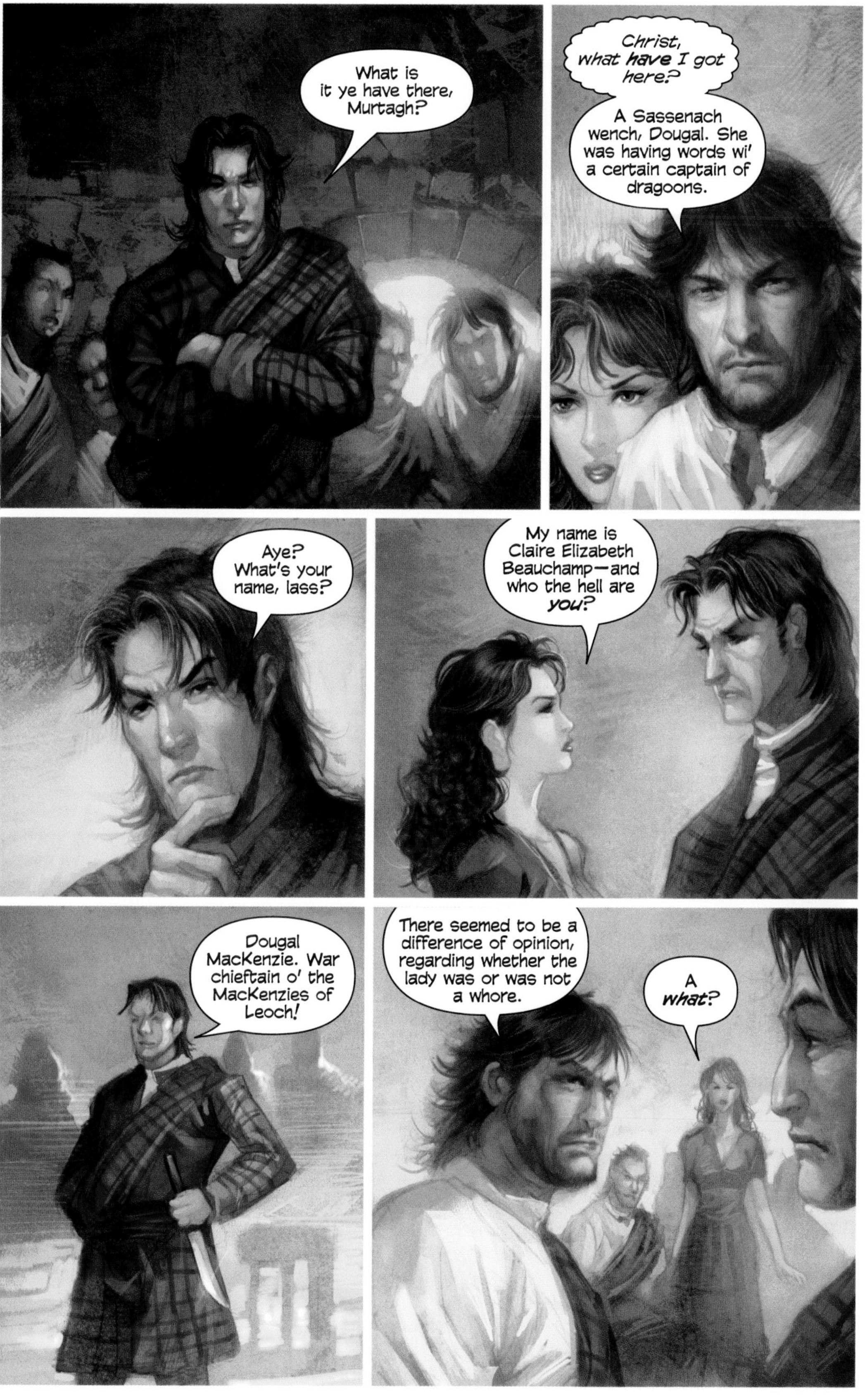
What is it ye have there, Murtagh?
Christ, what have I got here?
A Sassenach wench, Dougal. She was having words wi' a certain captain of dragoons.
Aye? What's your name, lass?
My name is Claire Elizabeth Beauchamp—and who the hell are you?
Dougal MacKenzie. War chieftain o' the MacKenzies of Leoch!
There seemed to be a difference of opinion, regarding whether the lady was or was not a whore.
A what?

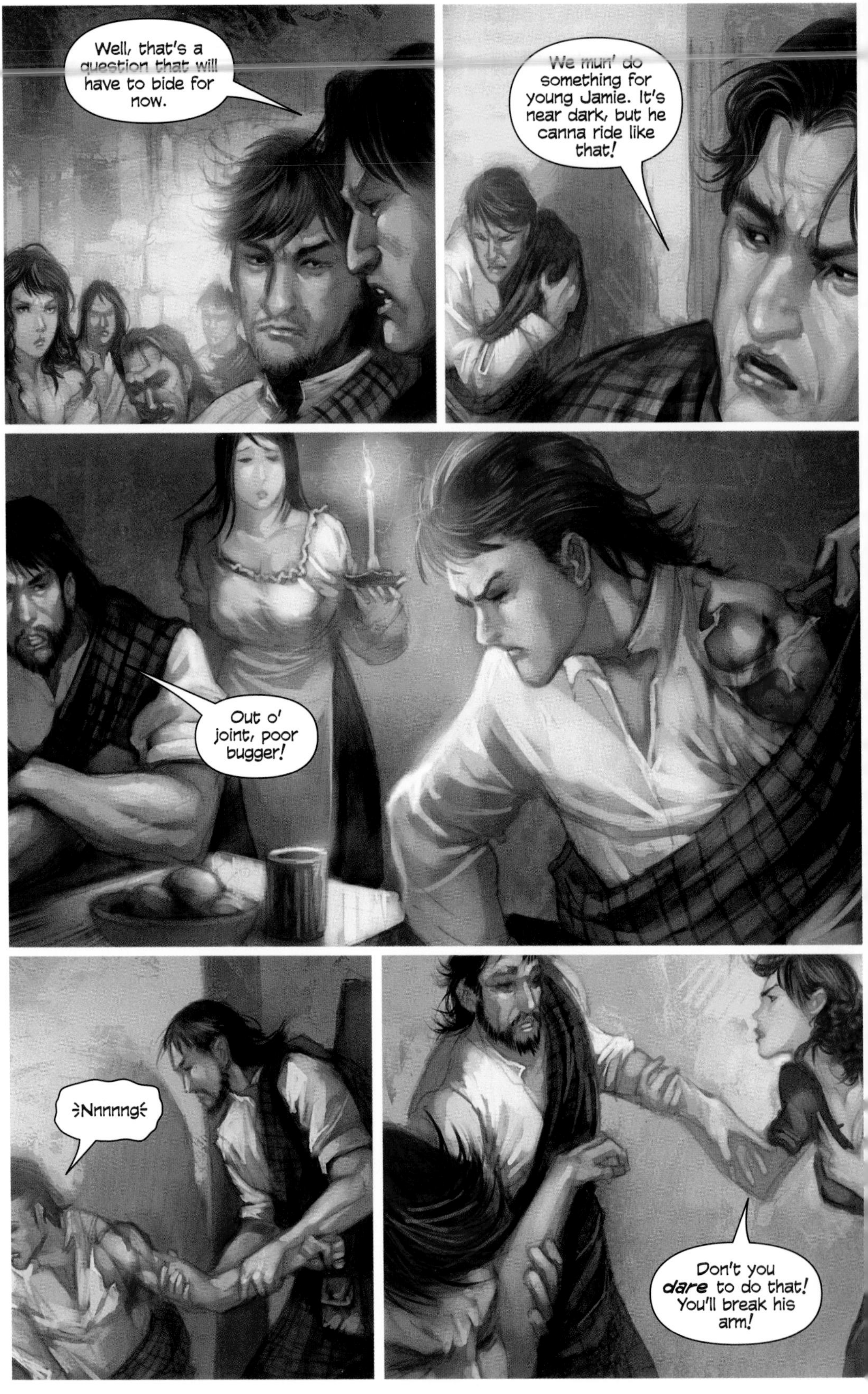
Well, that's a question that will have to bide for now.
We mun' do something for young Jamie. It's near dark, but he canna ride like that!
Out o' joint, poor bugger!
Nnnnng
Don't you *dare* to do that! You'll break his arm!

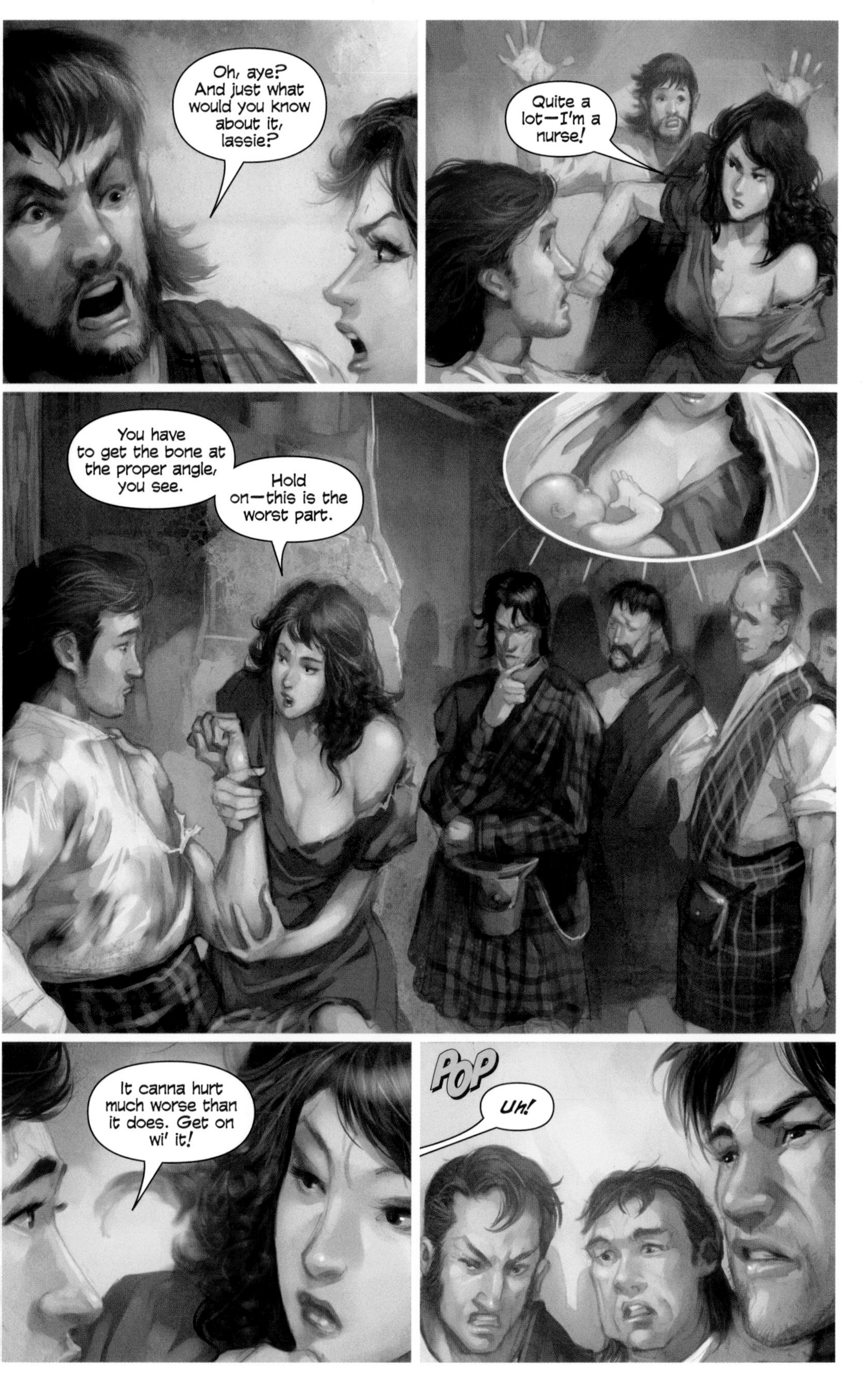
Oh, aye? And just what would you know about it, lassie?
Quite a lot—I'm a nurse!
You have to get the bone at the proper angle, you see.
Hold on—this is the worst part.
It canna hurt much worse than it does. Get on wi' it!
POP
Uh!

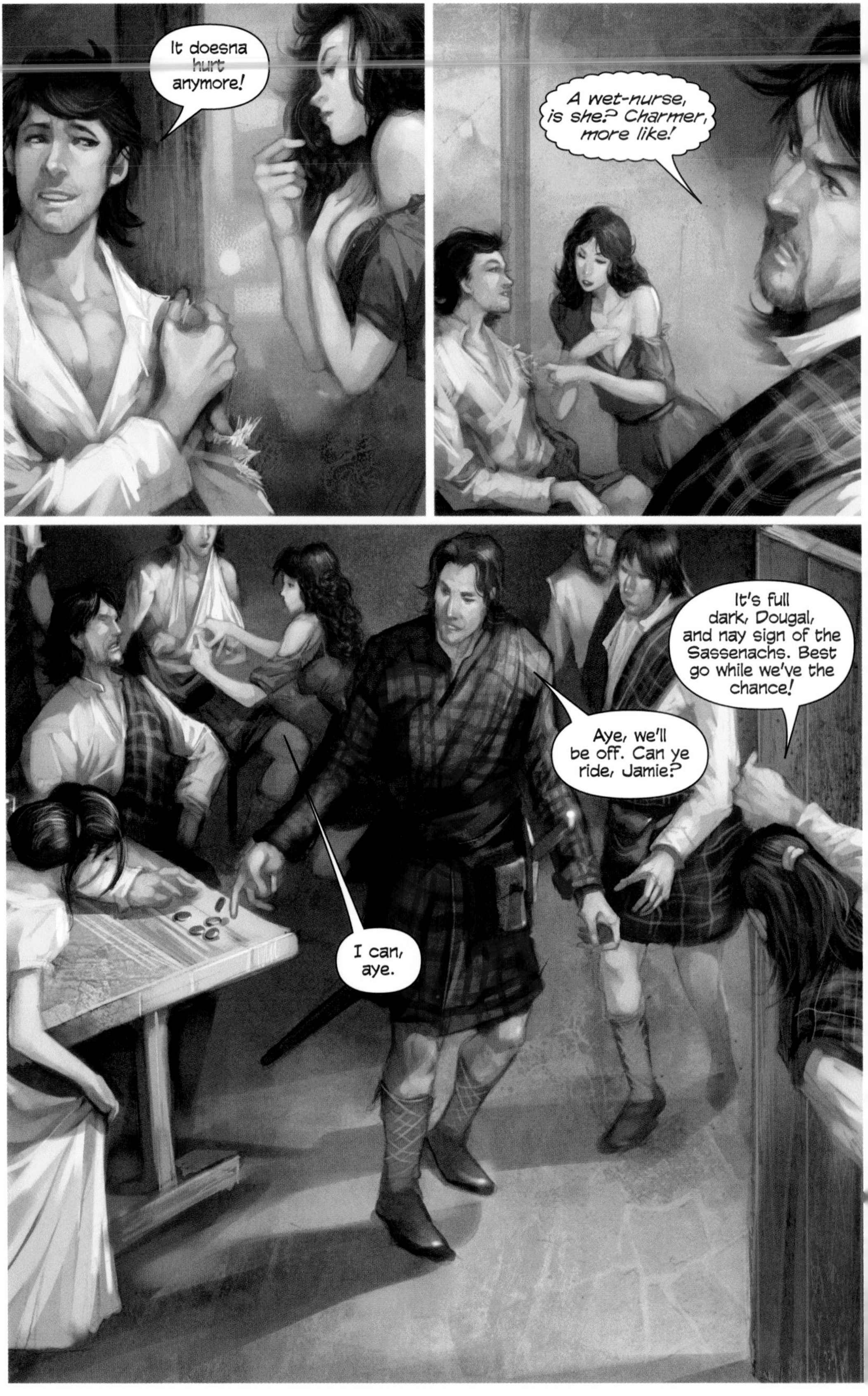

It doesna hurt anymore!
A wet-nurse, is she? Charmer, more like!
It's full dark, Dougal, and nay sign of the Sassenachs. Best go while we've the chance!
Aye, we'll be off. Can ye ride, Jamie?
I can, aye.

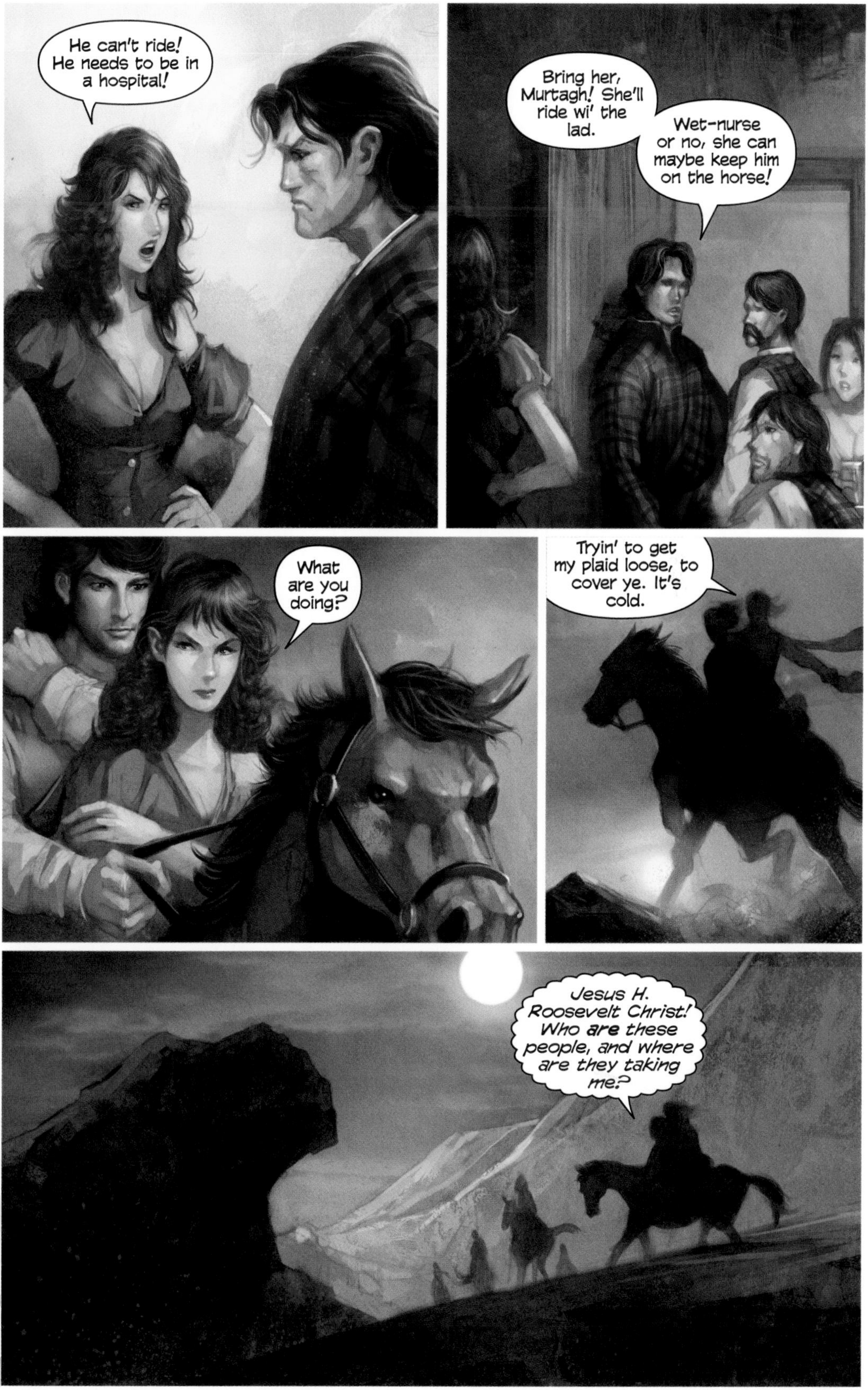
He can't ride! He needs to be in a hospital!
Bring her, Murtagh! She'll ride wi' the lad.
Wet-nurse or no, she can maybe keep him on the horse!
What are you doing?
Tryin' to get my plaid loose, to cover ye. It's cold.
*Jesus H. Roosevelt Christ! Who **are** these people, and where are they taking me?*

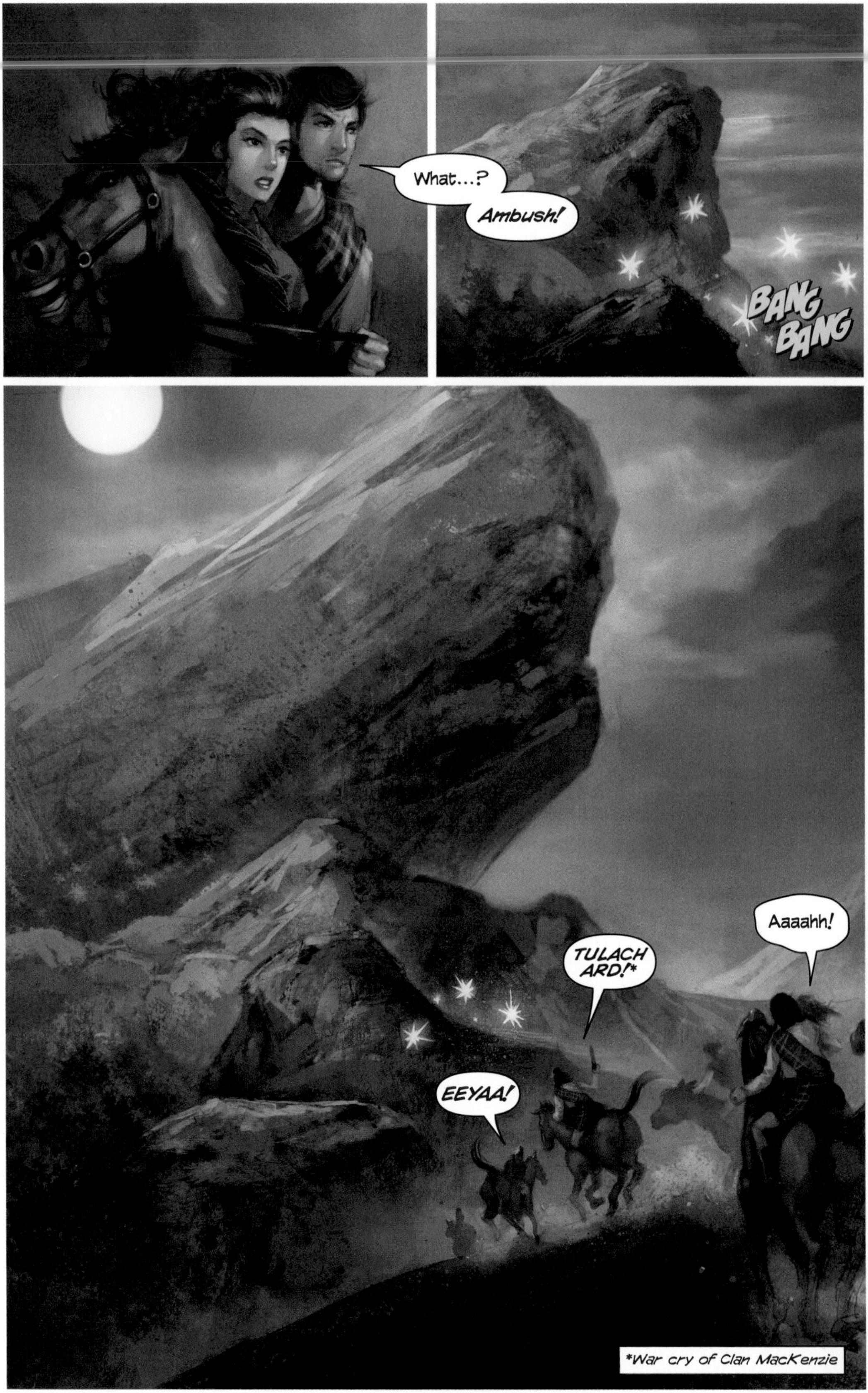
What...?
Ambush!
BANG
BANG
Aaaahh!
TULACH ARD!*
EEYAA!
*War cry of Clan MacKenzie

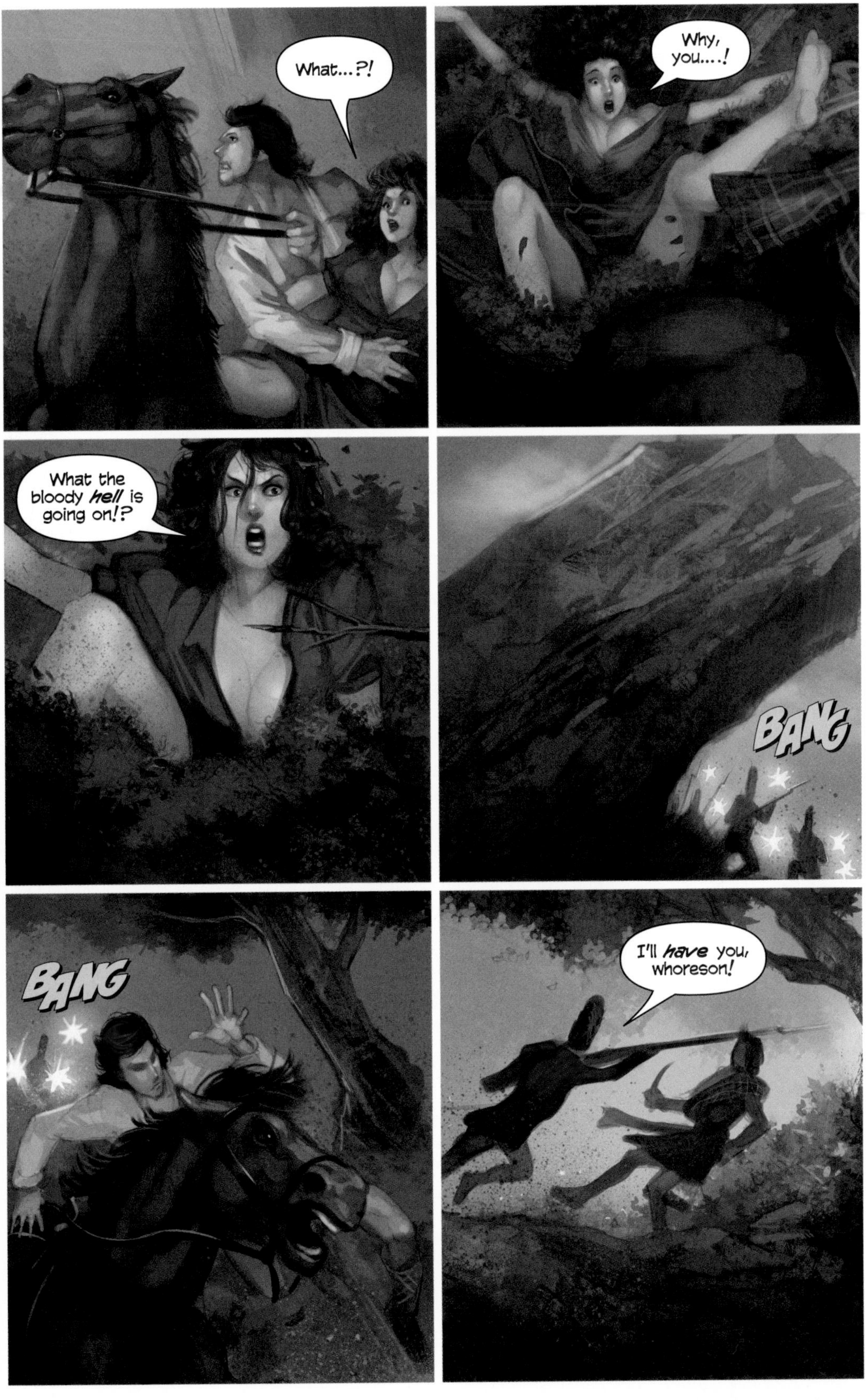
What...?!
Why, you....!
What the bloody *hell* is going on!?
BANG
BANG
I'll *have* you, whoreson!

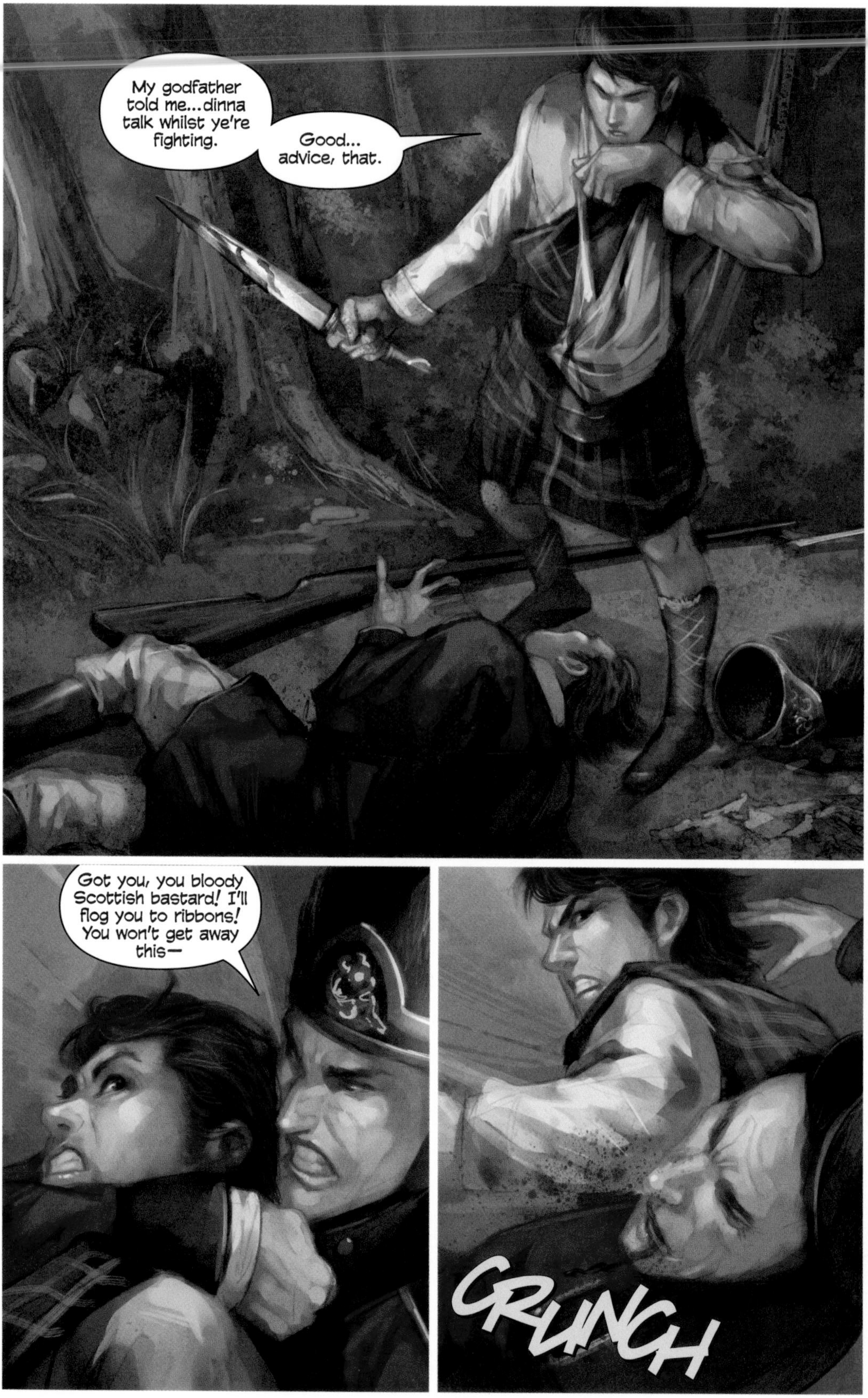
My godfather told me...dinna talk whilst ye're fighting.
Good... advice, that.
Got you, you bloody Scottish bastard! I'll flog you to ribbons! You won't get away this—
CRUNCH

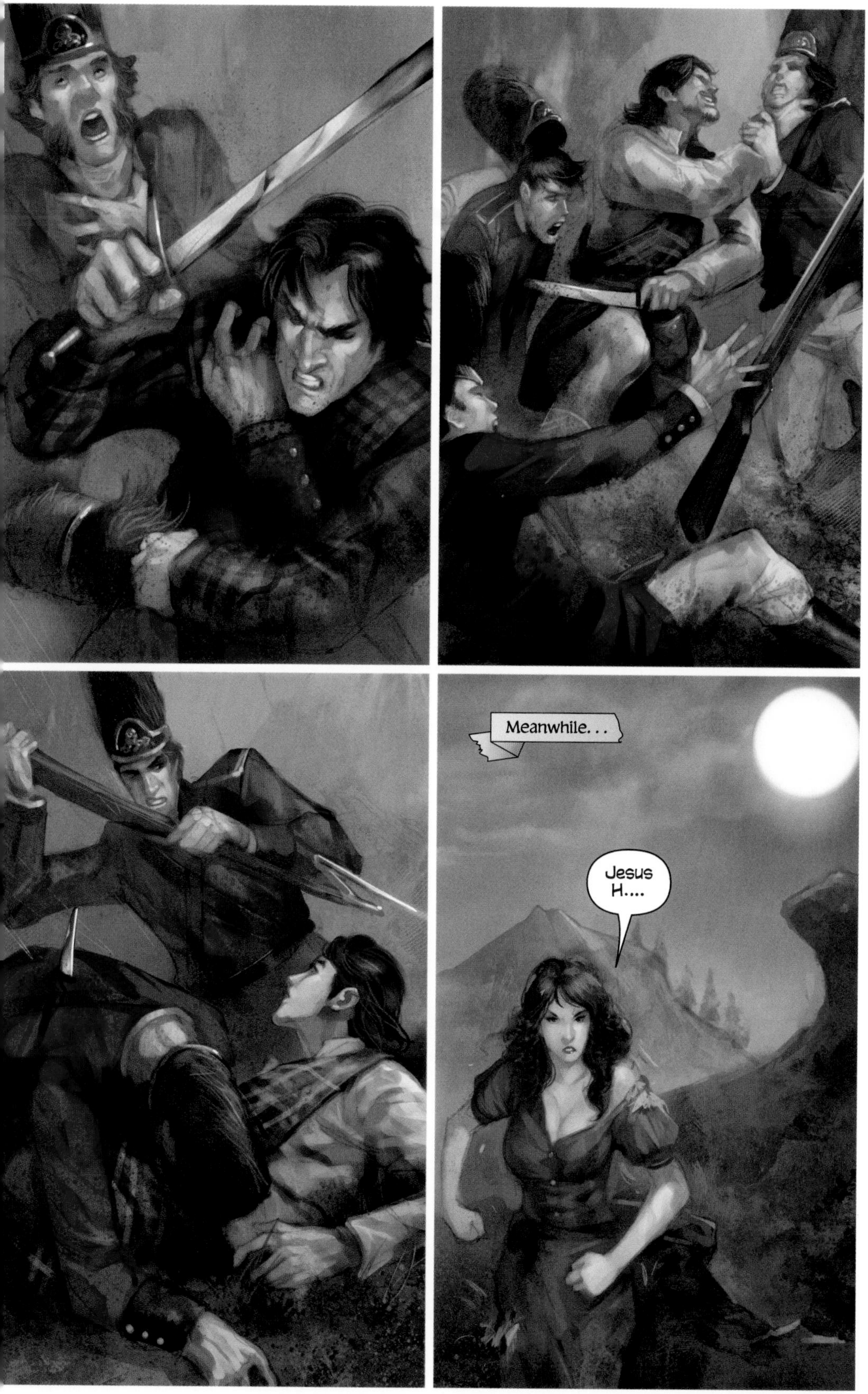
Meanwhile...
Jesus H....

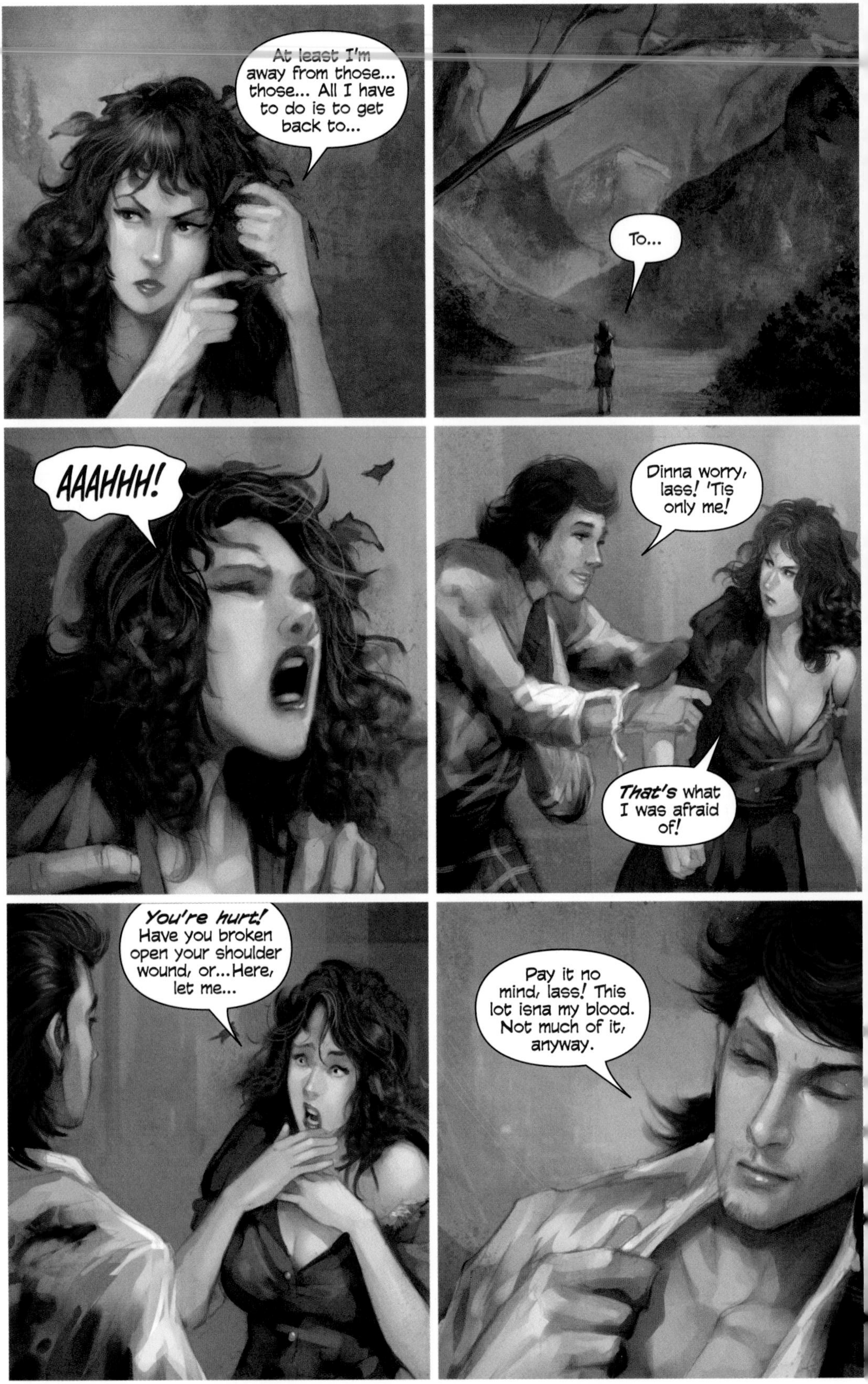
At least I'm away from those... those... All I have to do is to get back to...
To...
AAAHHH!
Dinna worry, lass! 'Tis only me!
*That's* what I was afraid of!
*You're hurt!* Have you broken open your shoulder wound, or...Here, let me...
Pay it no mind, lass! This lot isna my blood. Not much of it, anyway.

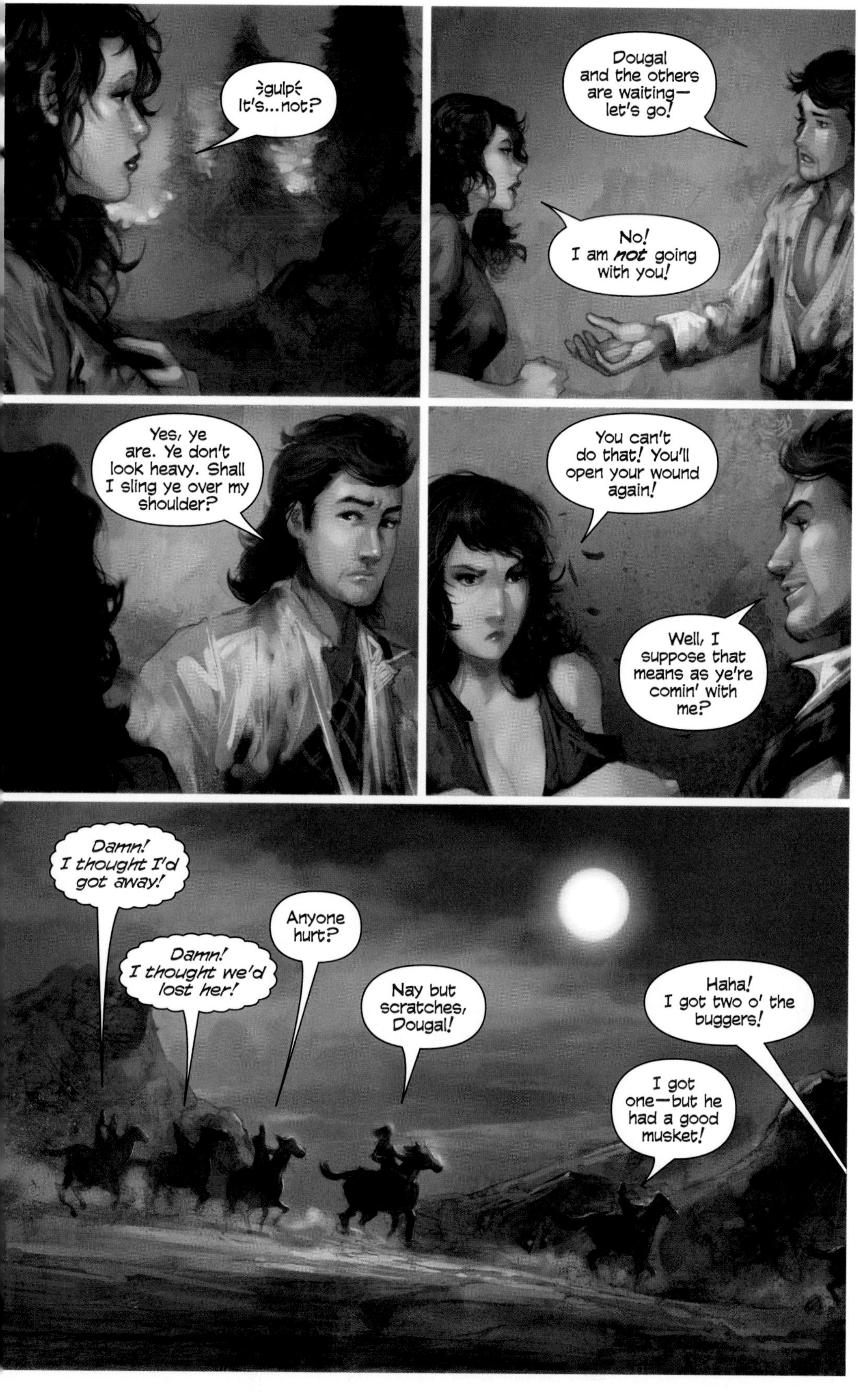

≥gulp≤ It's...not?
Dougal and the others are waiting—let's go!
No! I am *not* going with you!
Yes, ye are. Ye don't look heavy. Shall I sling ye over my shoulder?
You can't do that! You'll open your wound again!
Well, I suppose that means as ye're comin' with me?
*Damn! I thought I'd got away!*
*Damn! I thought we'd lost her!*
Anyone hurt?
Nay but scratches, Dougal!
Haha! I got two o' the buggers!
I got one—but he had a good musket!

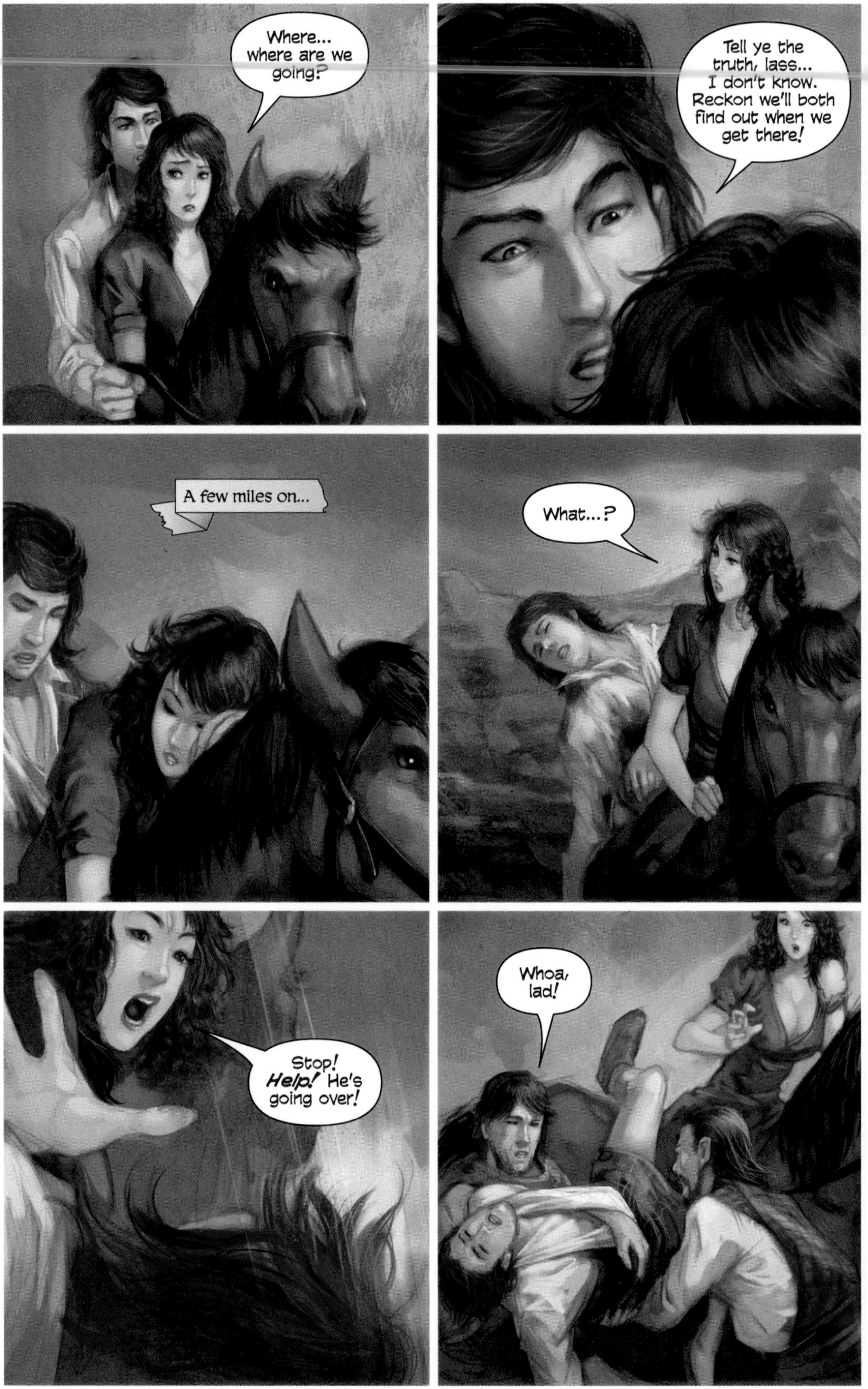

Where... where are we going?
Tell ye the truth, lass... I don't know. Reckon we'll both find out when we get there!
A few miles on...
What...?
Stop! *Help!* He's going over!
Whoa, lad!

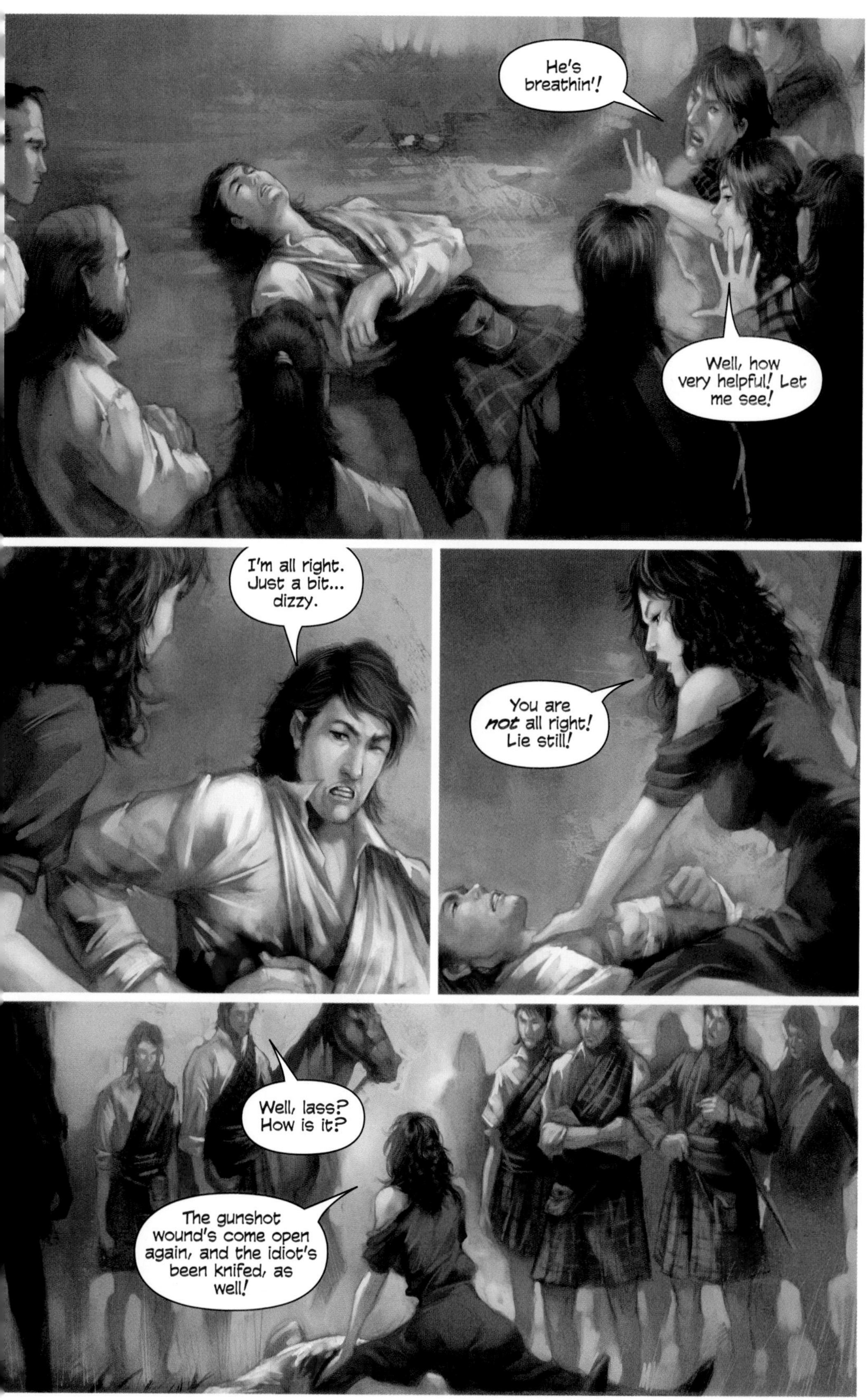
He's breathin'!
Well, how very helpful! Let me see!
I'm all right. Just a bit... dizzy.
You are *not* all right! Lie still!
Well, lass? How is it?
The gunshot wound's come open again, and the idiot's been knifed, as well!

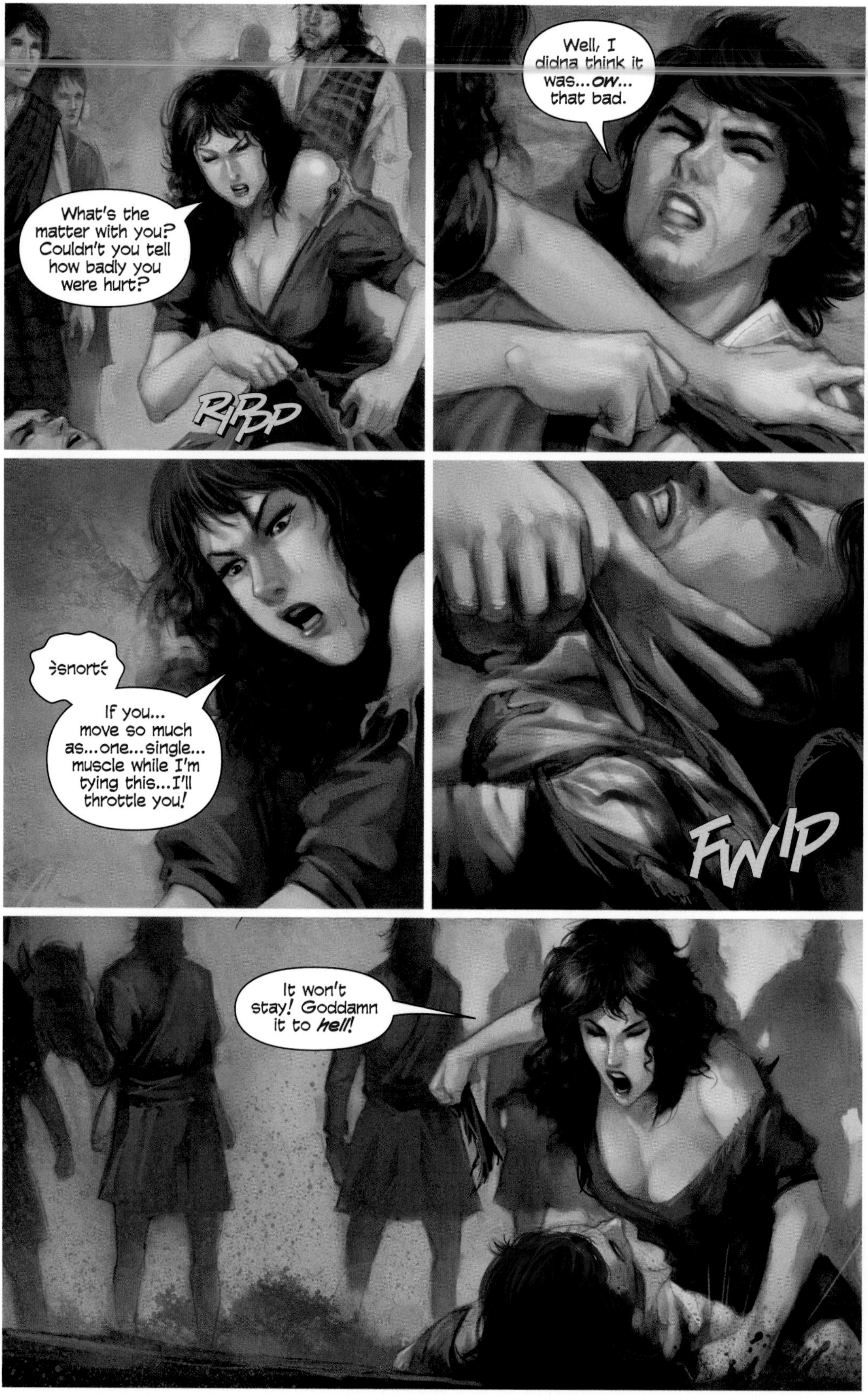
What's the matter with you? Couldn't you tell how badly you were hurt?
RIPP
Well, I didna think it was...*ow*... that bad.
≯snort≮
If you... move so much as...one...single... muscle while I'm tying this...I'll throttle you!
FWIP
It won't stay! Goddamn it to *hell*!

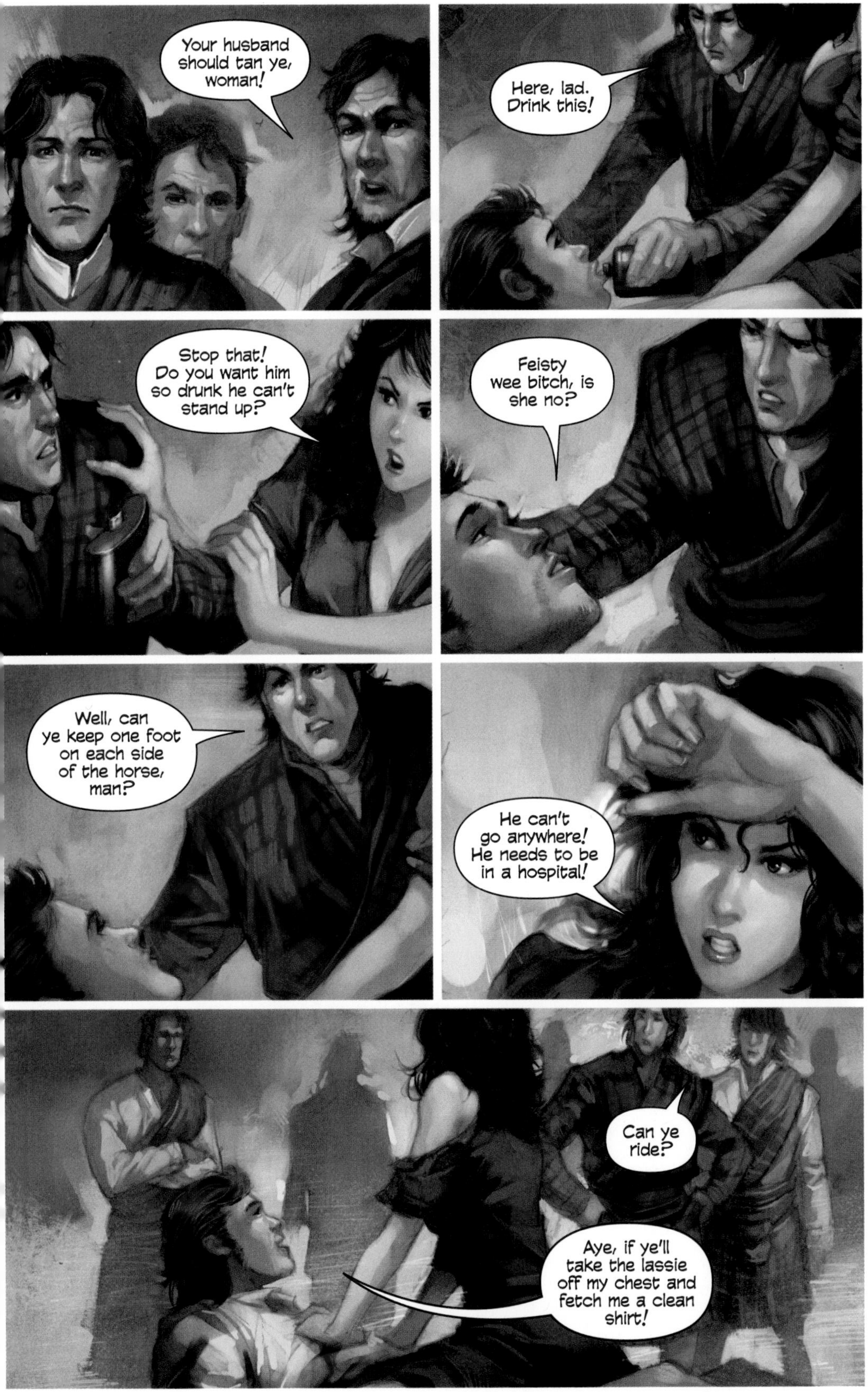
Your husband should tan ye, woman!
Here, lad. Drink this!
Stop that! Do you want him so drunk he can't stand up?
Feisty wee bitch, is she no?
Well, can ye keep one foot on each side of the horse, man?
He can't go anywhere! He needs to be in a hospital!
Can ye ride?
Aye, if ye'll take the lassie off my chest and fetch me a clean shirt!

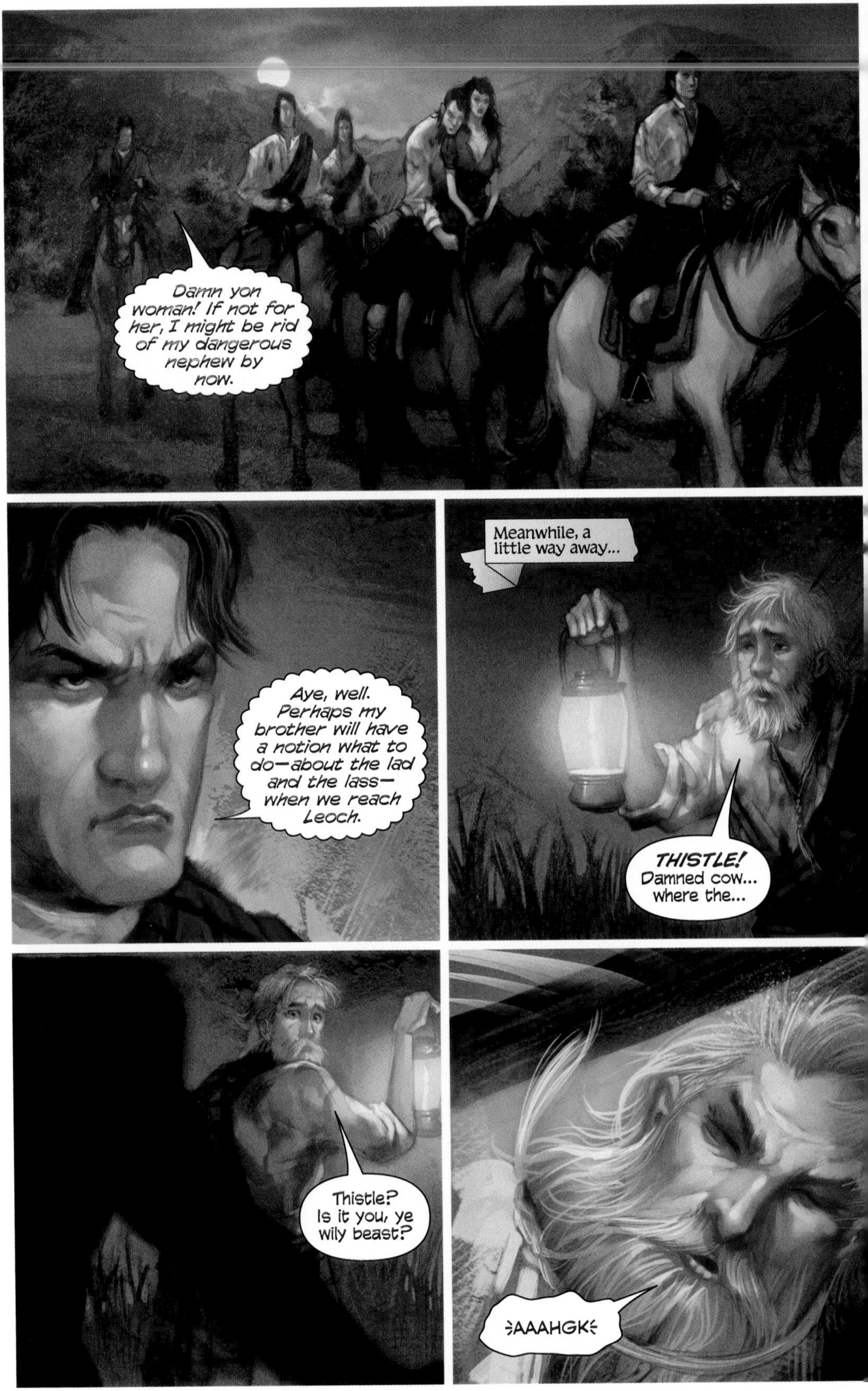
Damn yon woman! If not for her, I might be rid of my dangerous nephew by now.
Aye, well. Perhaps my brother will have a notion what to do—about the lad and the lass—when we reach Leoch.
Meanwhile, a little way away...
THISTLE! Damned cow... where the...
Thistle? Is it you, ye wily beast?
AAAHGK

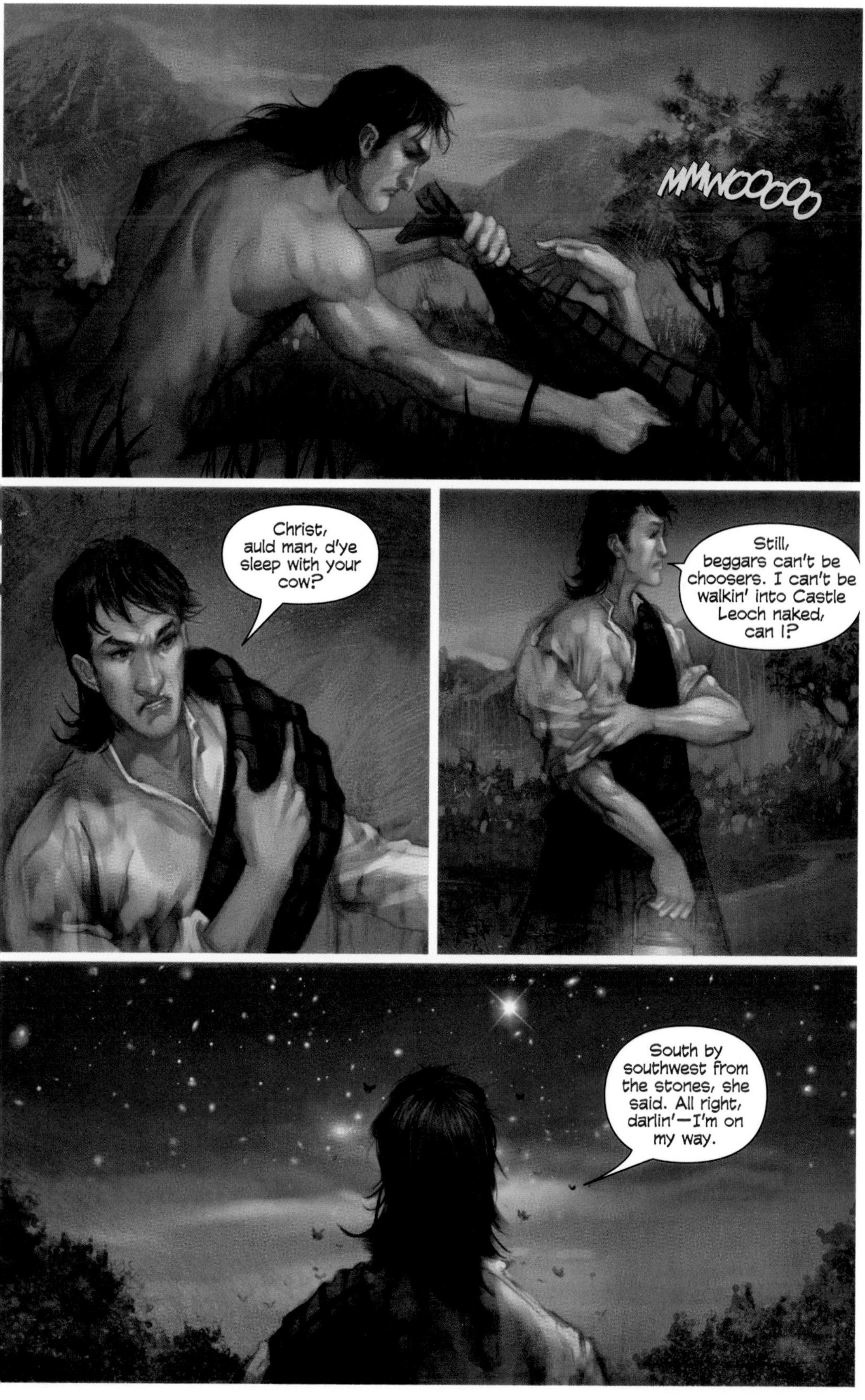
MMWOOOOO
Christ, auld man, d'ye sleep with your cow?
Still, beggars can't be choosers. I can't be walkin' into Castle Leoch naked, can I?
South by southwest from the stones, she said. All right, darlin'—I'm on my way.

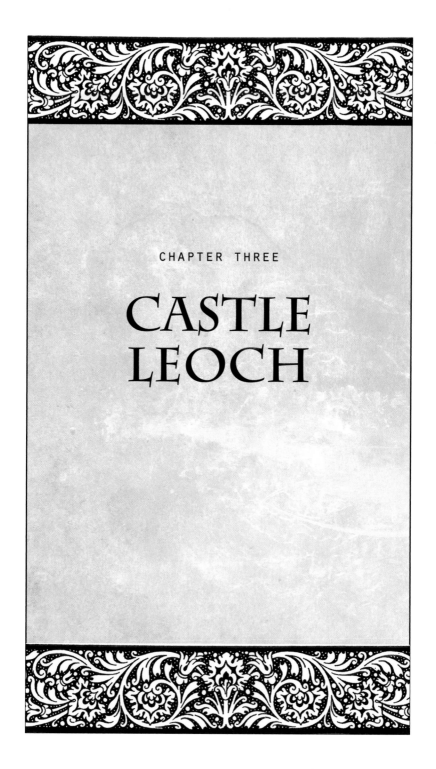

CHAPTER THREE

# CASTLE
# LEOCH

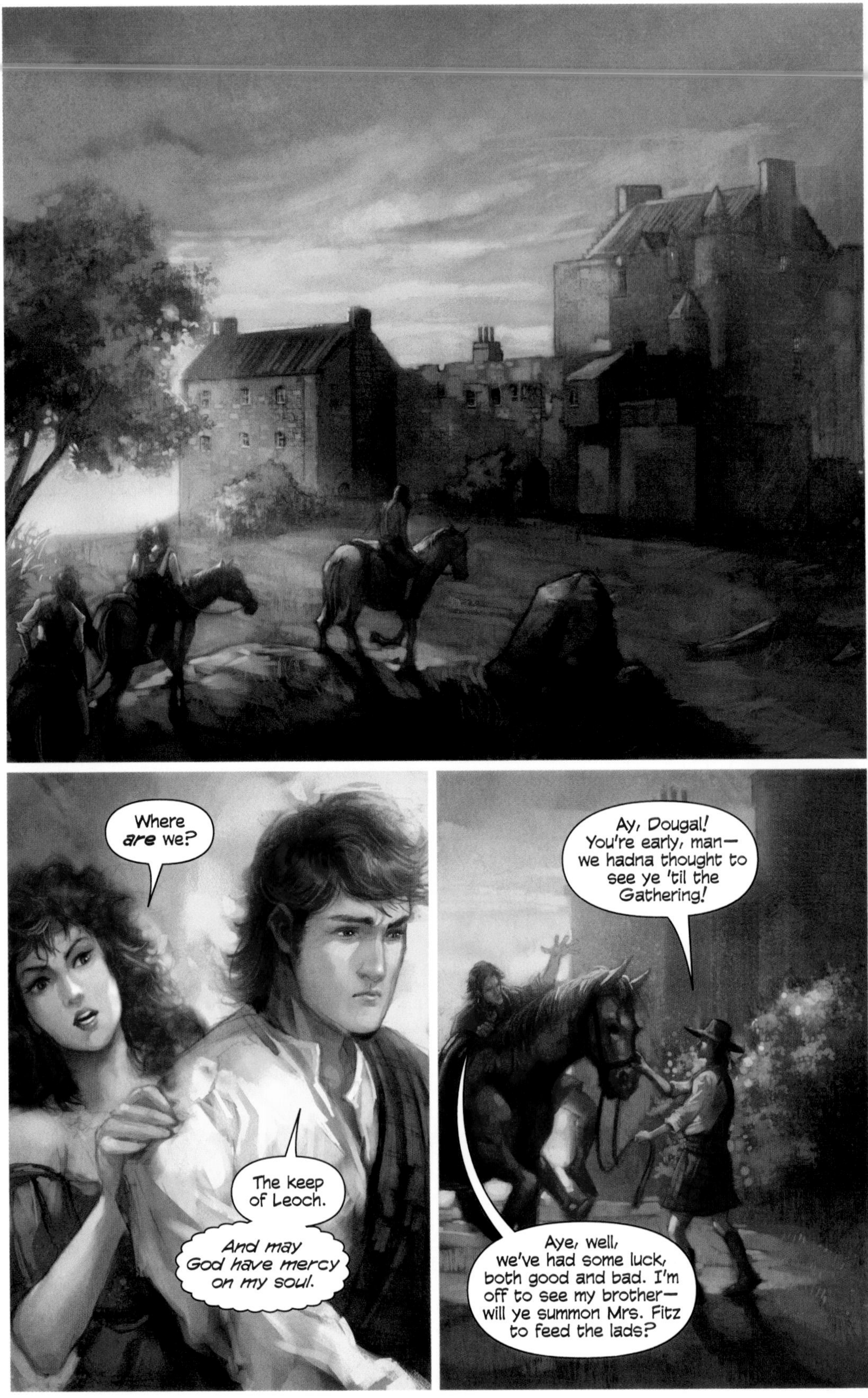
Where *are* we?
The keep of Leoch.
*And may God have mercy on my soul.*
Ay, Dougal! You're early, man— we hadna thought to see ye 'til the Gathering!
Aye, well, we've had some luck, both good and bad. I'm off to see my brother— will ye summon Mrs. Fitz to feed the lads?

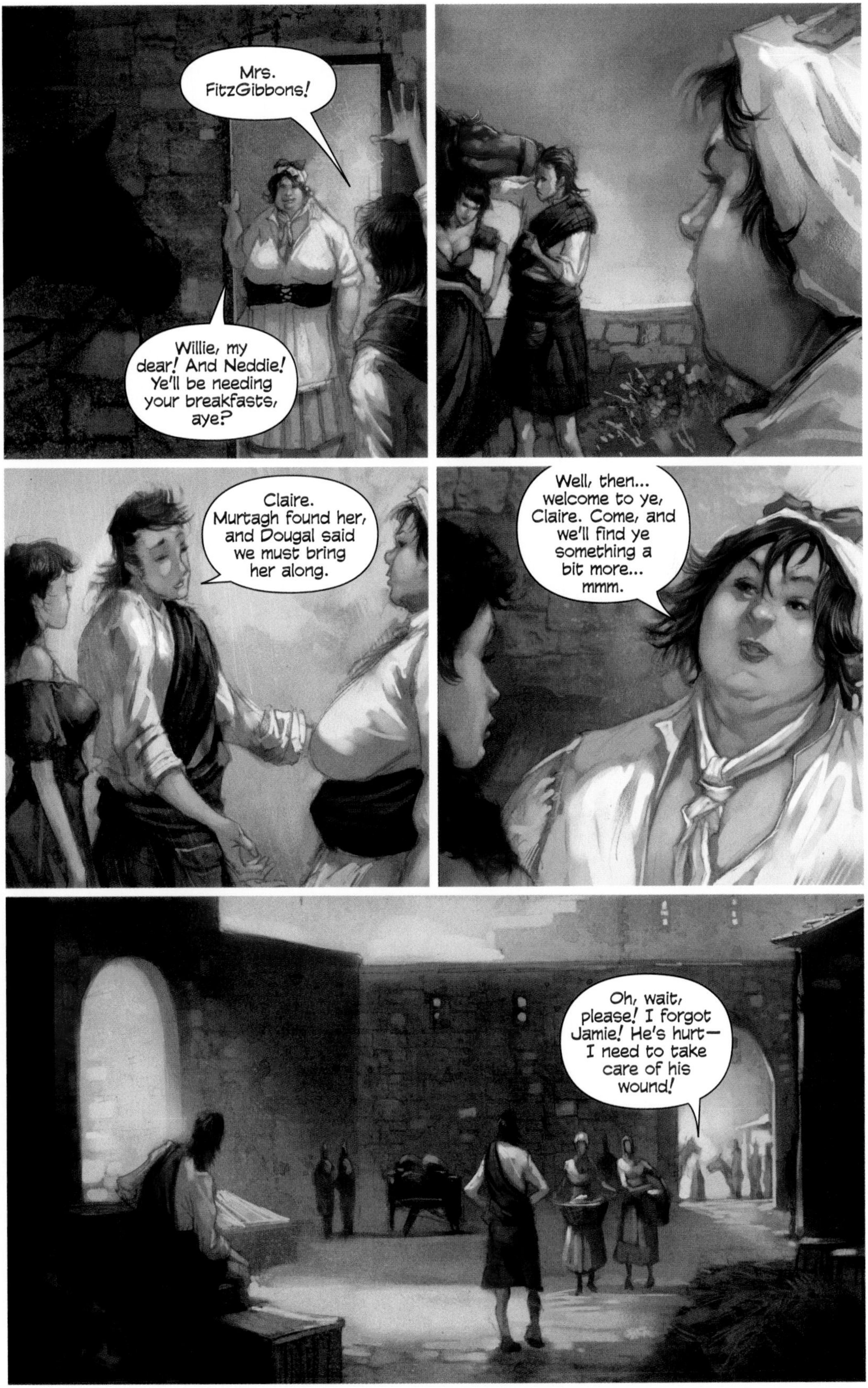
Mrs. FitzGibbons!
Willie, my dear! And Neddie! Ye'll be needing your breakfasts, aye?
Claire. Murtagh found her, and Dougal said we must bring her along.
Well, then... welcome to ye, Claire. Come, and we'll find ye something a bit more... mmm.
Oh, wait, please! I forgot Jamie! He's hurt— I need to take care of his wound!

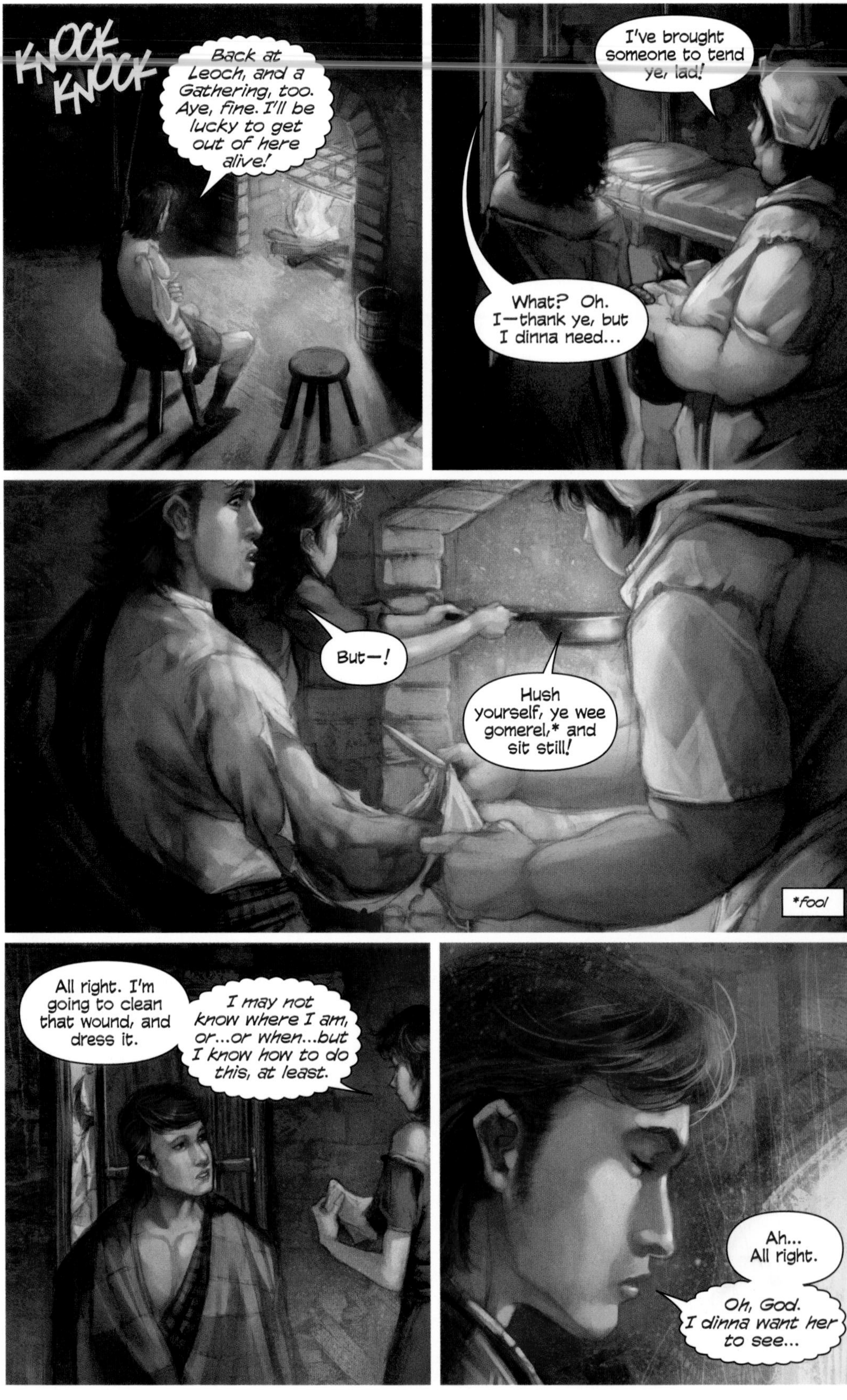
KNOCK KNOCK
Back at Leoch, and a Gathering, too. Aye, fine. I'll be lucky to get out of here alive!
I've brought someone to tend ye, lad!
What? Oh. I—thank ye, but I dinna need...
But—!
Hush yourself, ye wee gomerel,* and sit still!
*fool
All right. I'm going to clean that wound, and dress it.
I may not know where I am, or...or when...but I know how to do this, at least.
Ah... All right.
Oh, God. I dinna want her to see...

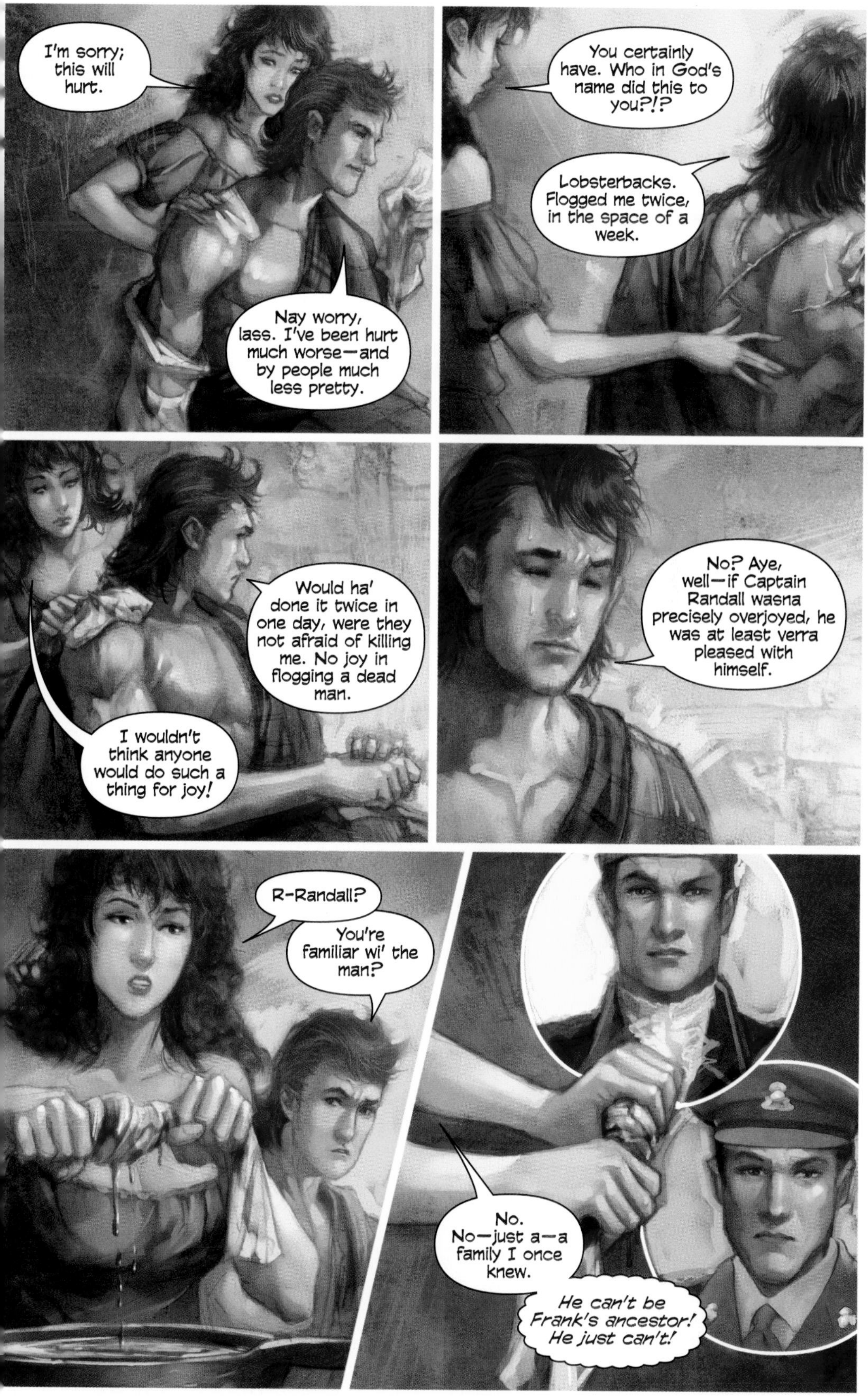
I'm sorry; this will hurt.
Nay worry, lass. I've been hurt much worse—and by people much less pretty.
You certainly have. Who in God's name did this to you?!?
Lobsterbacks. Flogged me twice, in the space of a week.
Would ha' done it twice in one day, were they not afraid of killing me. No joy in flogging a dead man.
I wouldn't think anyone would do such a thing for joy!
No? Aye, well—if Captain Randall wasna precisely overjoyed, he was at least verra pleased with himself.
R-Randall?
You're familiar wi' the man?
No. No—just a—a family I once knew.
*He can't be Frank's ancestor! He just can't!*

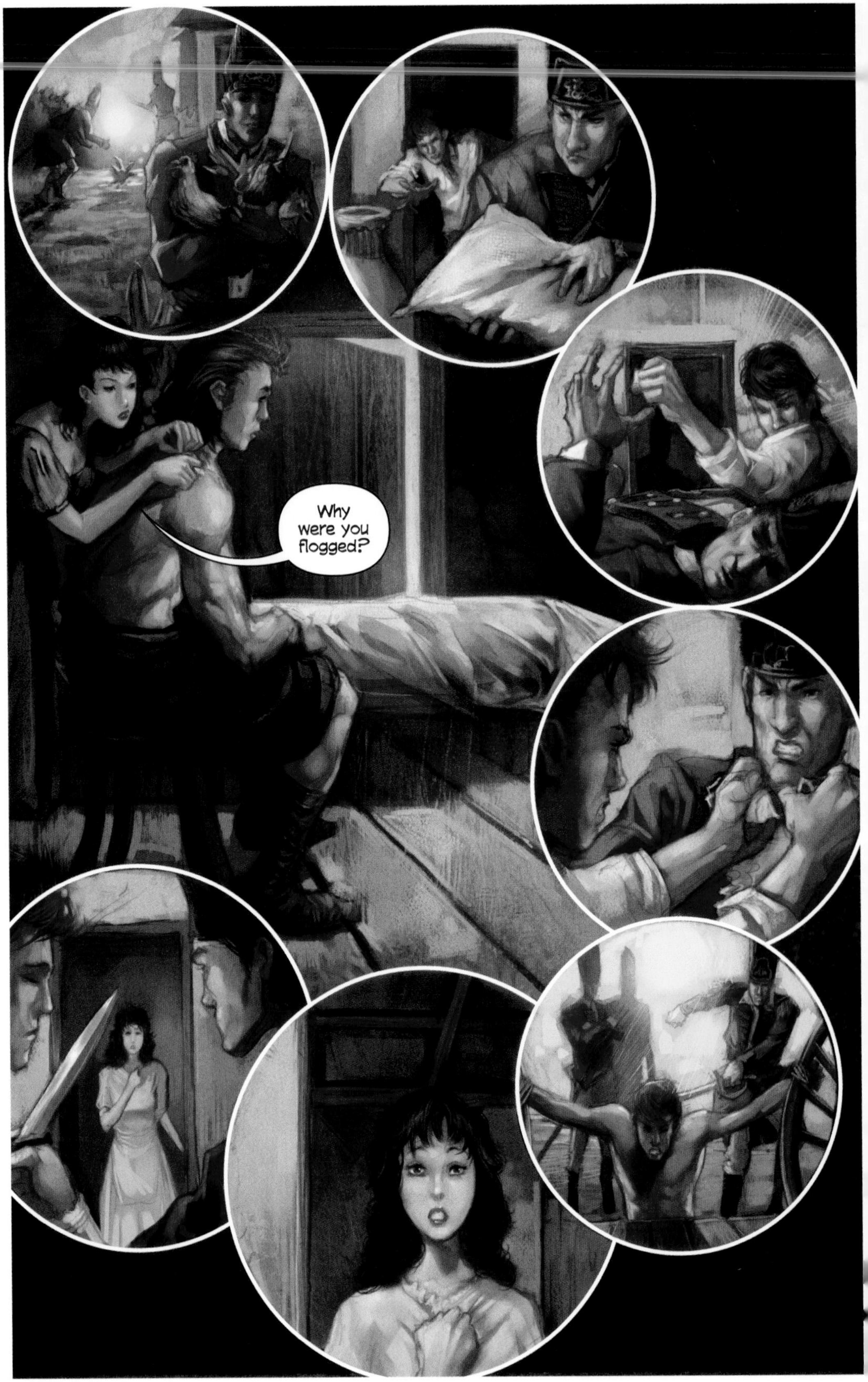
Why were you flogged?

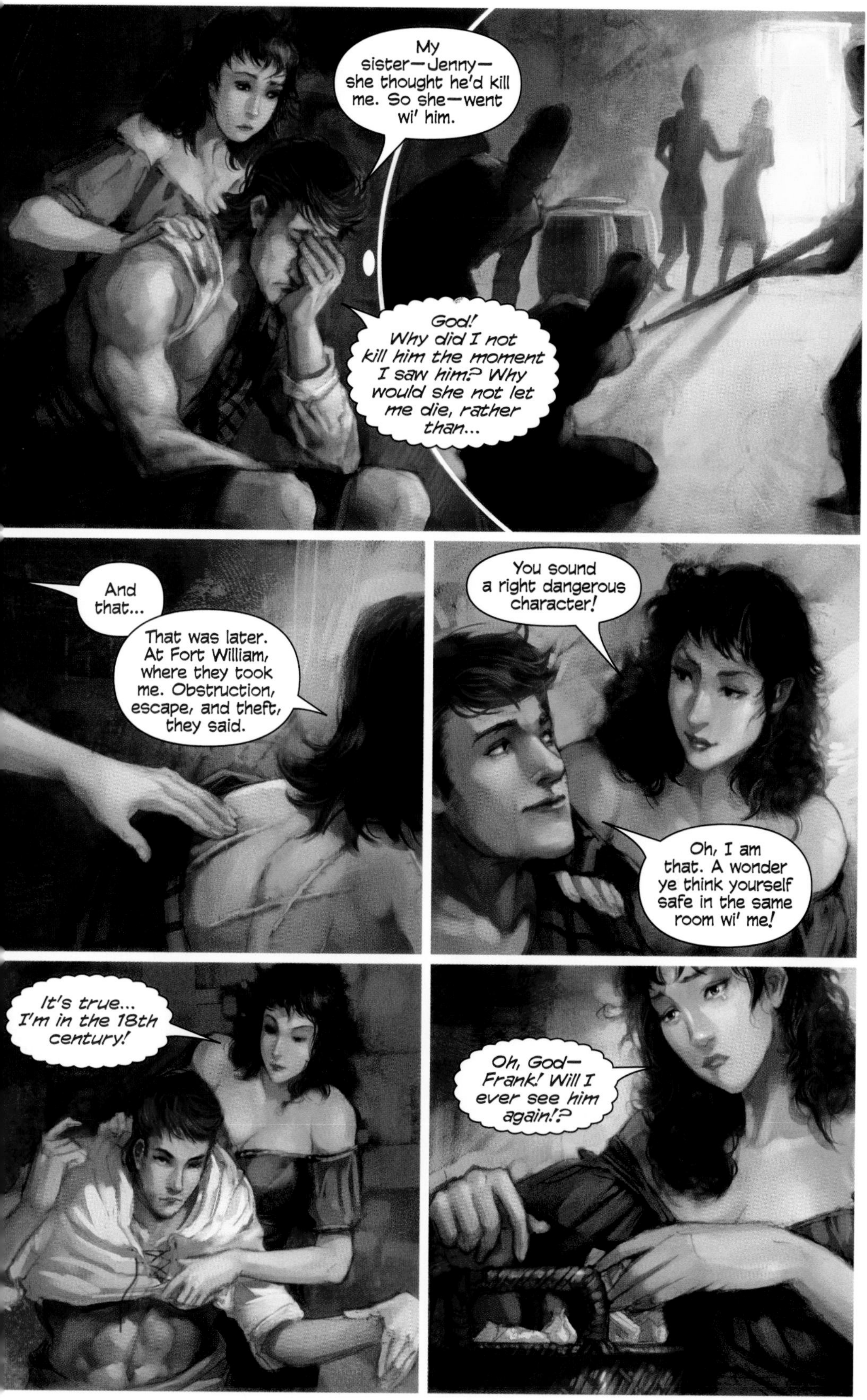
My sister—Jenny—she thought he'd kill me. So she—went wi' him.
God! Why did I not kill him the moment I saw him? Why would she not let me die, rather than...
And that...
That was later. At Fort William, where they took me. Obstruction, escape, and theft, they said.
You sound a right dangerous character!
Oh, I am that. A wonder ye think yourself safe in the same room wi' me!
It's true... I'm in the 18th century!
Oh, God—Frank! Will I ever see him again!?

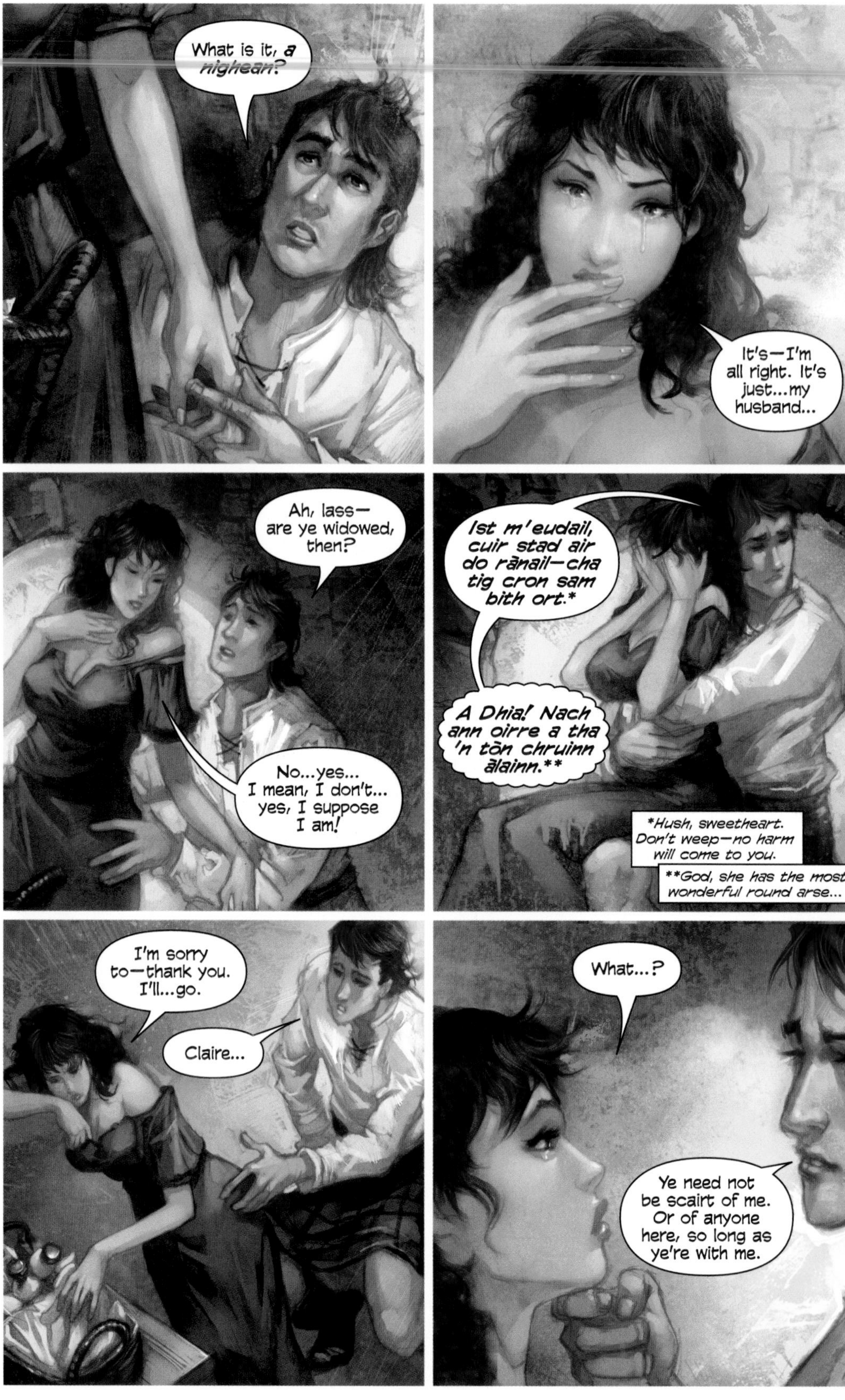
What is it, *a nighean?*
It's—I'm all right. It's just...my husband...
Ah, lass—are ye widowed, then?
No...yes... I mean, I don't... yes, I suppose I am!
*Ist m'eudail, cuir stad air do rànail—cha tig cron sam bith ort.**
*A Dhia! Nach ann oirre a tha 'n tòn chruinn àlainn.***
**Hush, sweetheart. Don't weep—no harm will come to you.*
***God, she has the most wonderful round arse...*
I'm sorry to—thank you. I'll...go.
Claire...
What...?
Ye need not be scairt of me. Or of anyone here, so long as ye're with me.

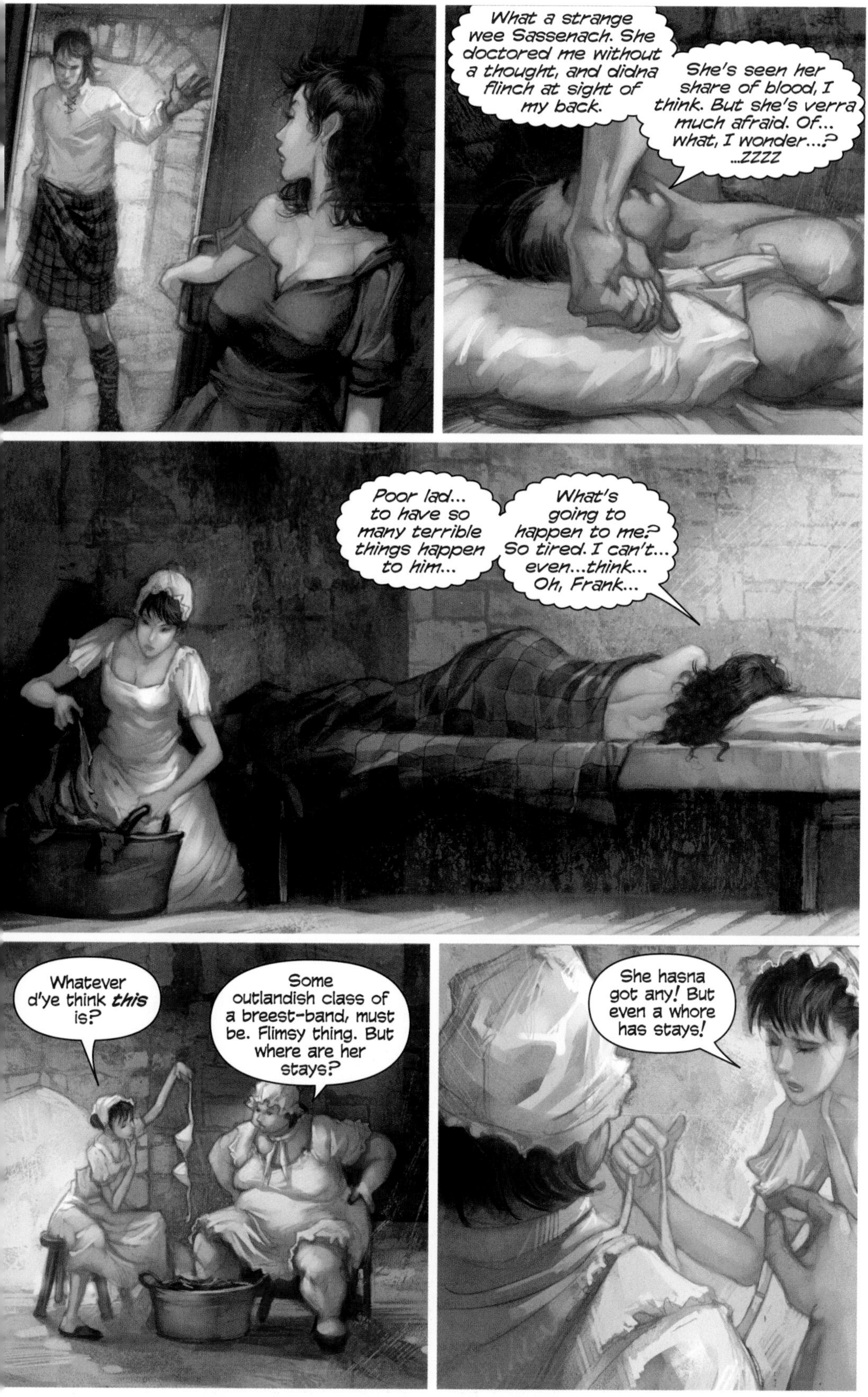
What a strange wee Sassenach. She doctored me without a thought, and didna flinch at sight of my back.
She's seen her share of blood, I think. But she's verra much afraid. Of... what, I wonder...? ...ZZZZ
Poor lad... to have so many terrible things happen to him...
What's going to happen to me? So tired. I can't... even...think... Oh, Frank...
Whatever d'ye think *this* is?
Some outlandish class of a breest-band, must be. Flimsy thing. But where are her stays?
She hasna got any! But even a whore has stays!

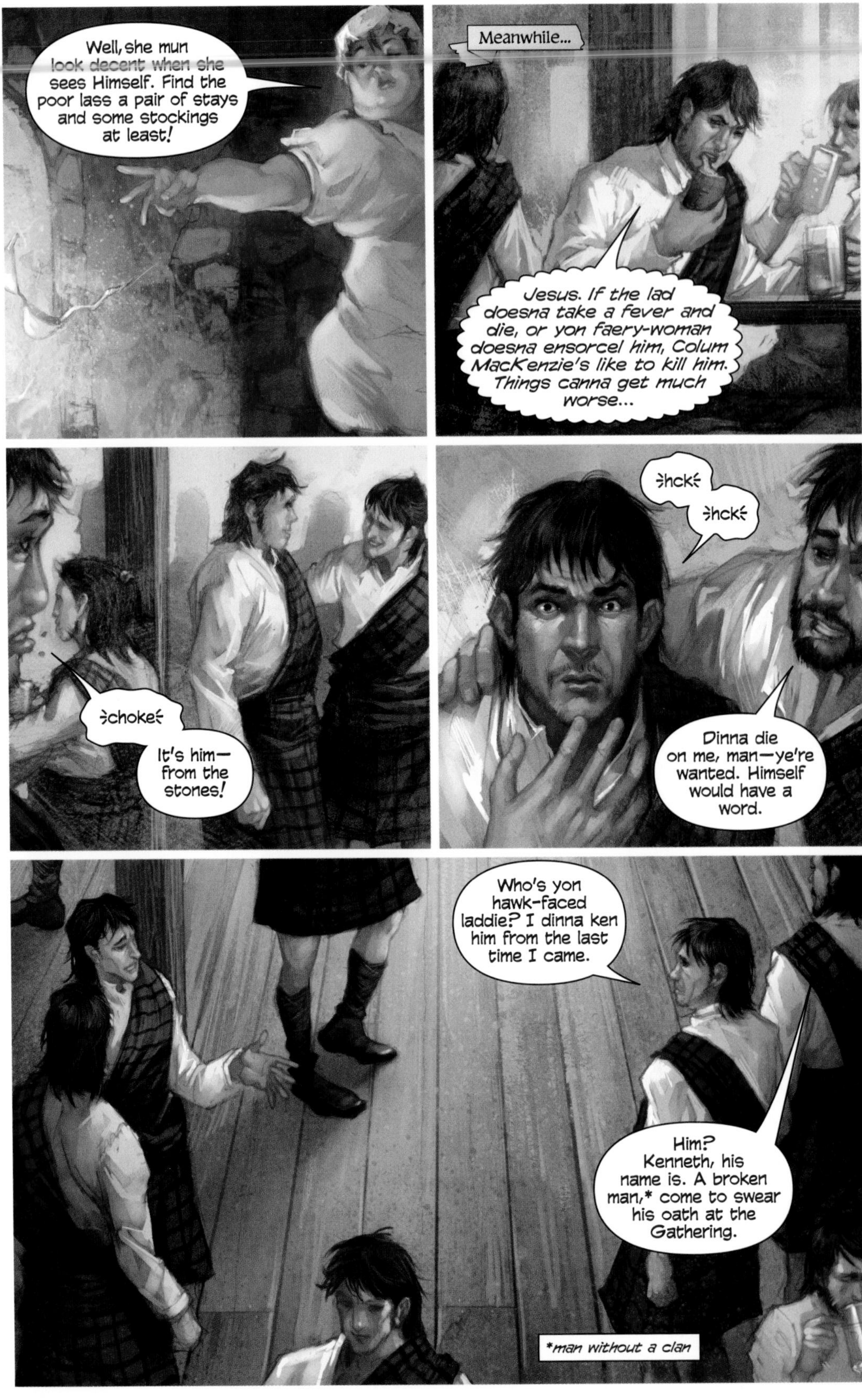
Well, she mun look decent when she sees Himself. Find the poor lass a pair of stays and some stockings at least!
Meanwhile...
Jesus. If the lad doesna take a fever and die, or yon faery-woman doesna ensorcel him, Colum MacKenzie's like to kill him. Things canna get much worse...
choke
It's him—from the stones!
hck
hck
Dinna die on me, man—ye're wanted. Himself would have a word.
Who's yon hawk-faced laddie? I dinna ken him from the last time I came.
Him? Kenneth, his name is. A broken man,* come to swear his oath at the Gathering.
*man without a clan

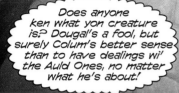

Does anyone ken what yon creature is? Dougal's a fool, but surely Colum's better sense than to have dealings wi' the Auld Ones, no matter what he's about!

Murtagh FitzGibbons Fraser. I hadna expected to see you at Leoch again.

Aye, that'll be the two of us, then.

We'd ha' been about our own business, the lad and I, had your brother not had other notions.

Why, I couldna let a kinsman pass and not offer hospitality, now, could I?

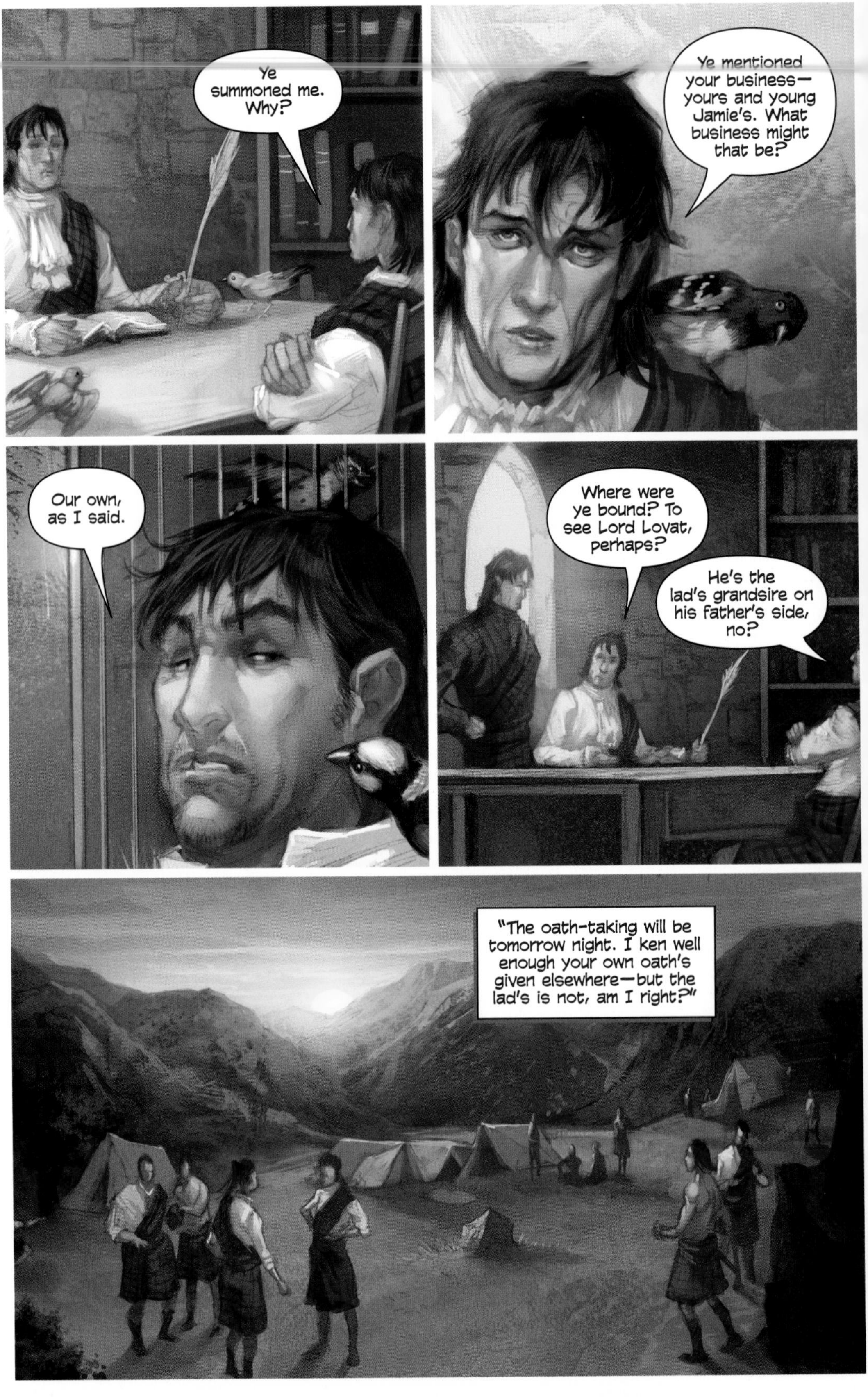
Ye summoned me. Why?
Ye mentioned your business—yours and young Jamie's. What business might that be?
Our own, as I said.
Where were ye bound? To see Lord Lovat, perhaps?
He's the lad's grandsire on his father's side, no?
"The oath-taking will be tomorrow night. I ken well enough your own oath's given elsewhere—but the lad's is not, am I right?"

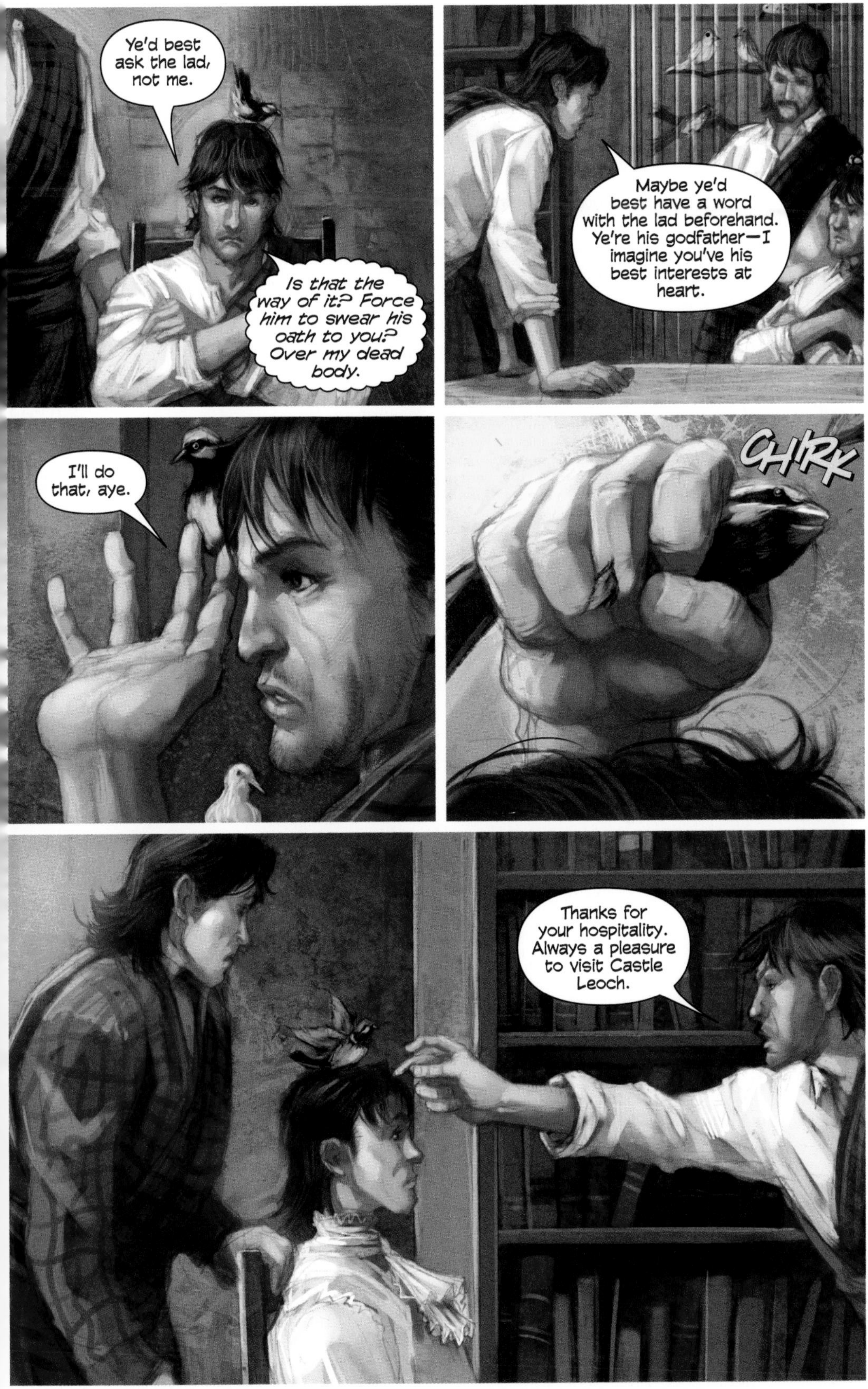
Ye'd best ask the lad, not me.
Is that the way of it? Force him to swear his oath to you? Over my dead body.
Maybe ye'd best have a word with the lad beforehand. Ye're his godfather—I imagine you've his best interests at heart.
I'll do that, aye.
CHIRK
Thanks for your hospitality. Always a pleasure to visit Castle Leoch.

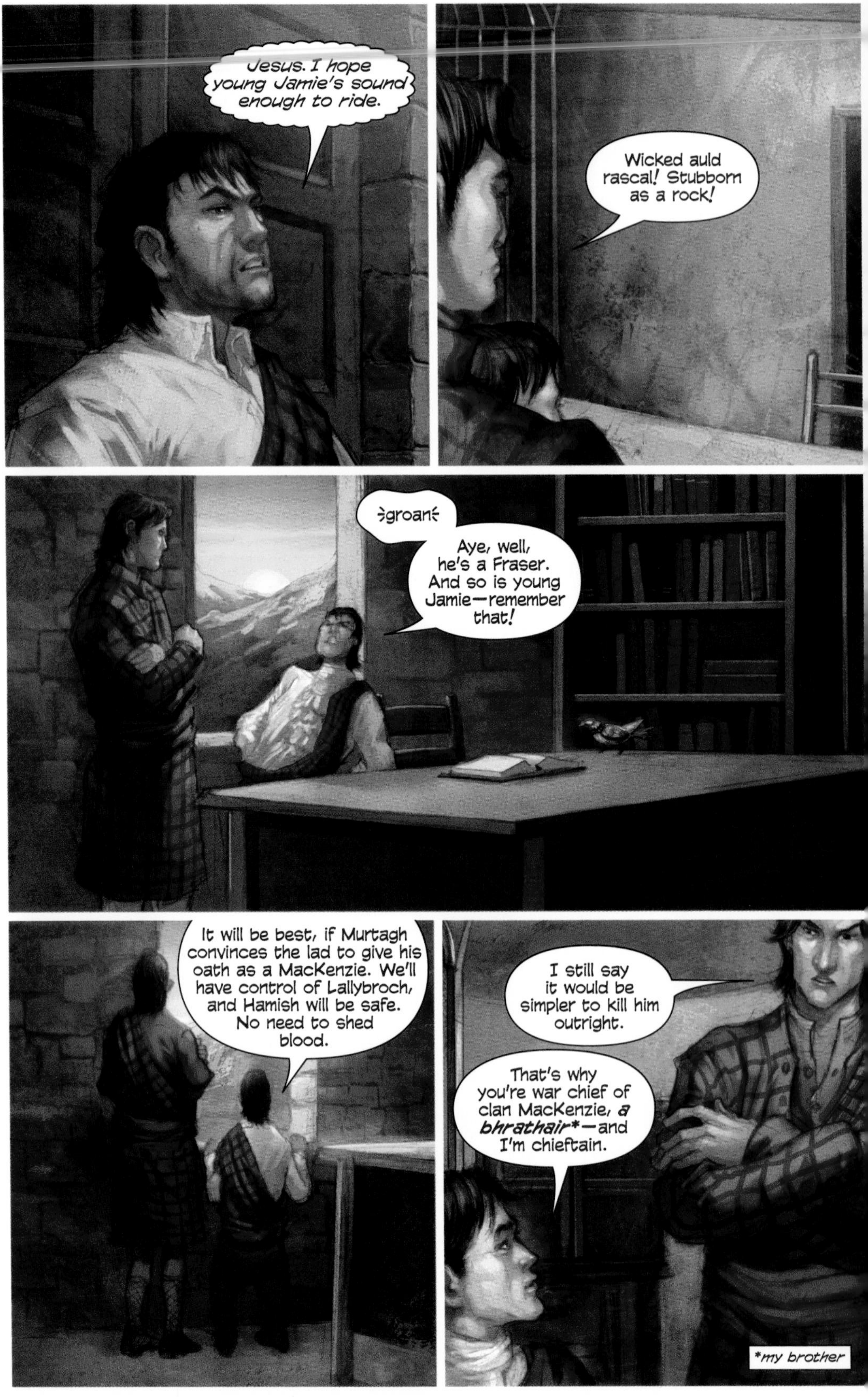
Jesus. I hope young Jamie's sound enough to ride.
Wicked auld rascal! Stubborn as a rock!
groan
Aye, well, he's a Fraser. And so is young Jamie—remember that!
It will be best, if Murtagh convinces the lad to give his oath as a MacKenzie. We'll have control of Lallybroch, and Hamish will be safe. No need to shed blood.
I still say it would be simpler to kill him outright.
That's why you're war chief of clan MacKenzie, *a bhrathair**—and I'm chieftain.
*my brother

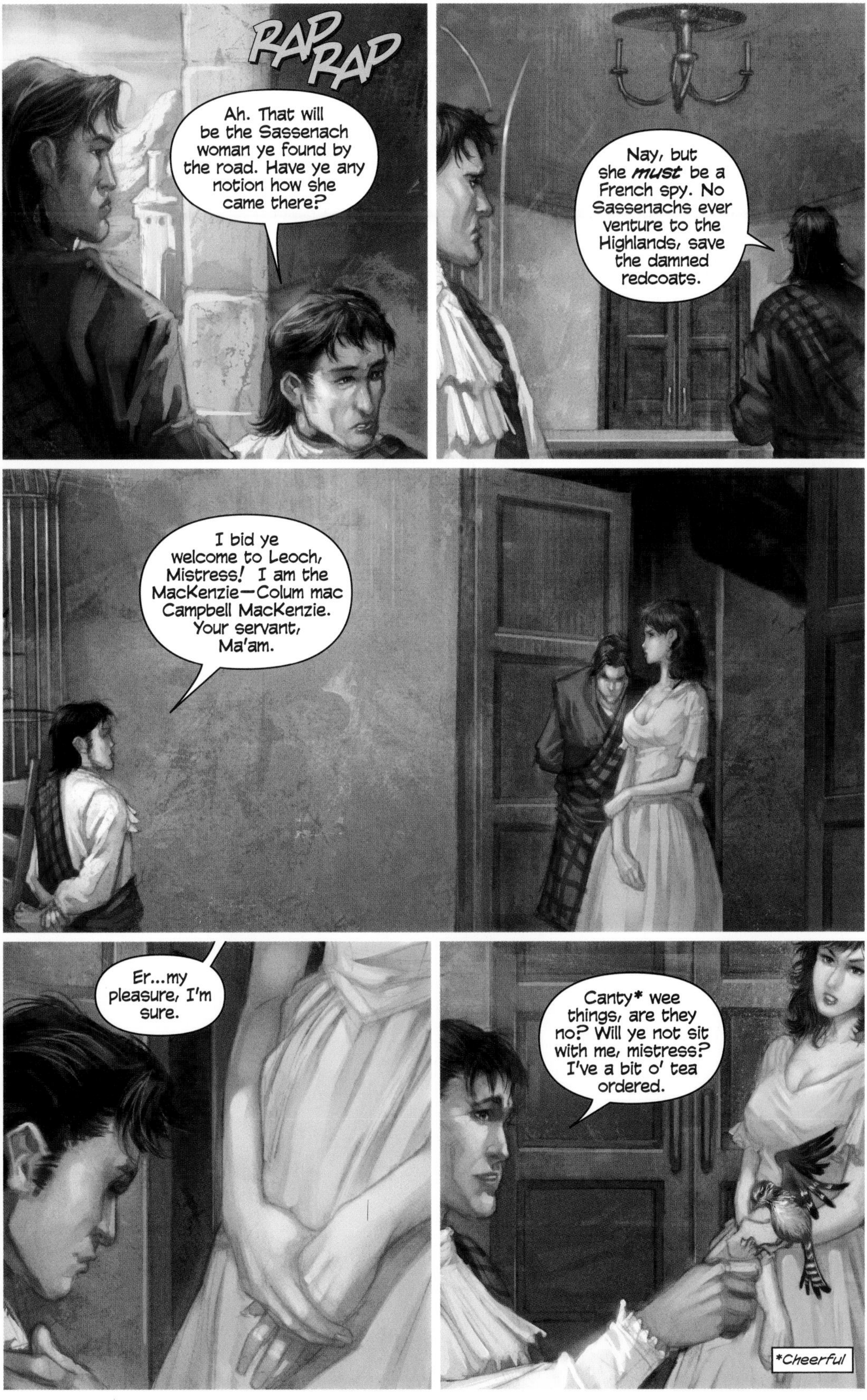
RAP RAP
Ah. That will be the Sassenach woman ye found by the road. Have ye any notion how she came there?
Nay, but she *must* be a French spy. No Sassenachs ever venture to the Highlands, save the damned redcoats.
I bid ye welcome to Leoch, Mistress! I am the MacKenzie—Colum mac Campbell MacKenzie. Your servant, Ma'am.
Er...my pleasure, I'm sure.
Canty* wee things, are they no? Will ye not sit with me, mistress? I've a bit o' tea ordered.
*Cheerful

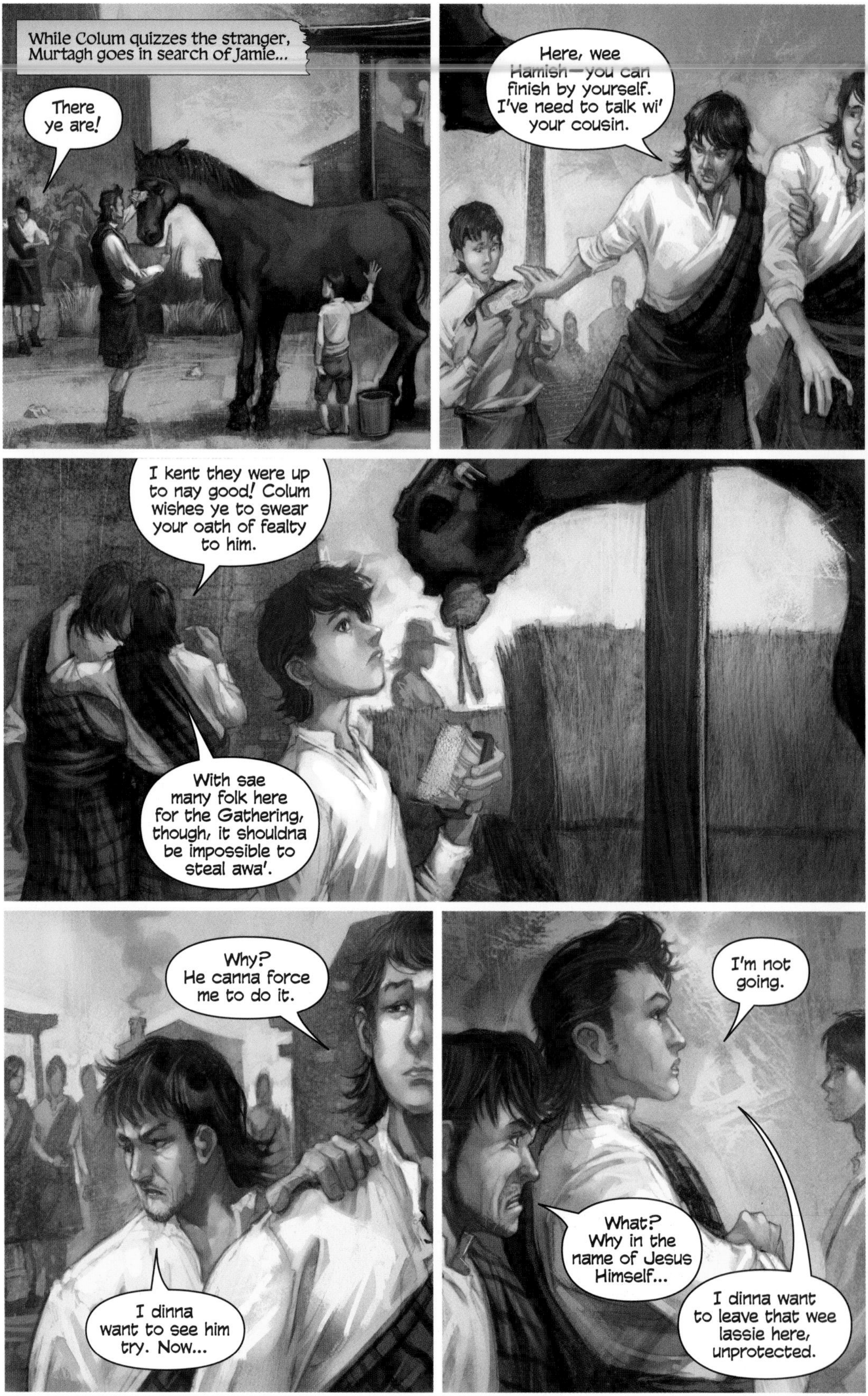
While Colum quizzes the stranger, Murtagh goes in search of Jamie...
There ye are!
Here, wee Hamish—you can finish by yourself. I've need to talk wi' your cousin.
I kent they were up to nay good! Colum wishes ye to swear your oath of fealty to him.
With sae many folk here for the Gathering, though, it shouldna be impossible to steal awa'.
Why? He canna force me to do it.
I dinna want to see him try. Now...
I'm not going.
What? Why in the name of Jesus Himself...
I dinna want to leave that wee lassie here, unprotected.

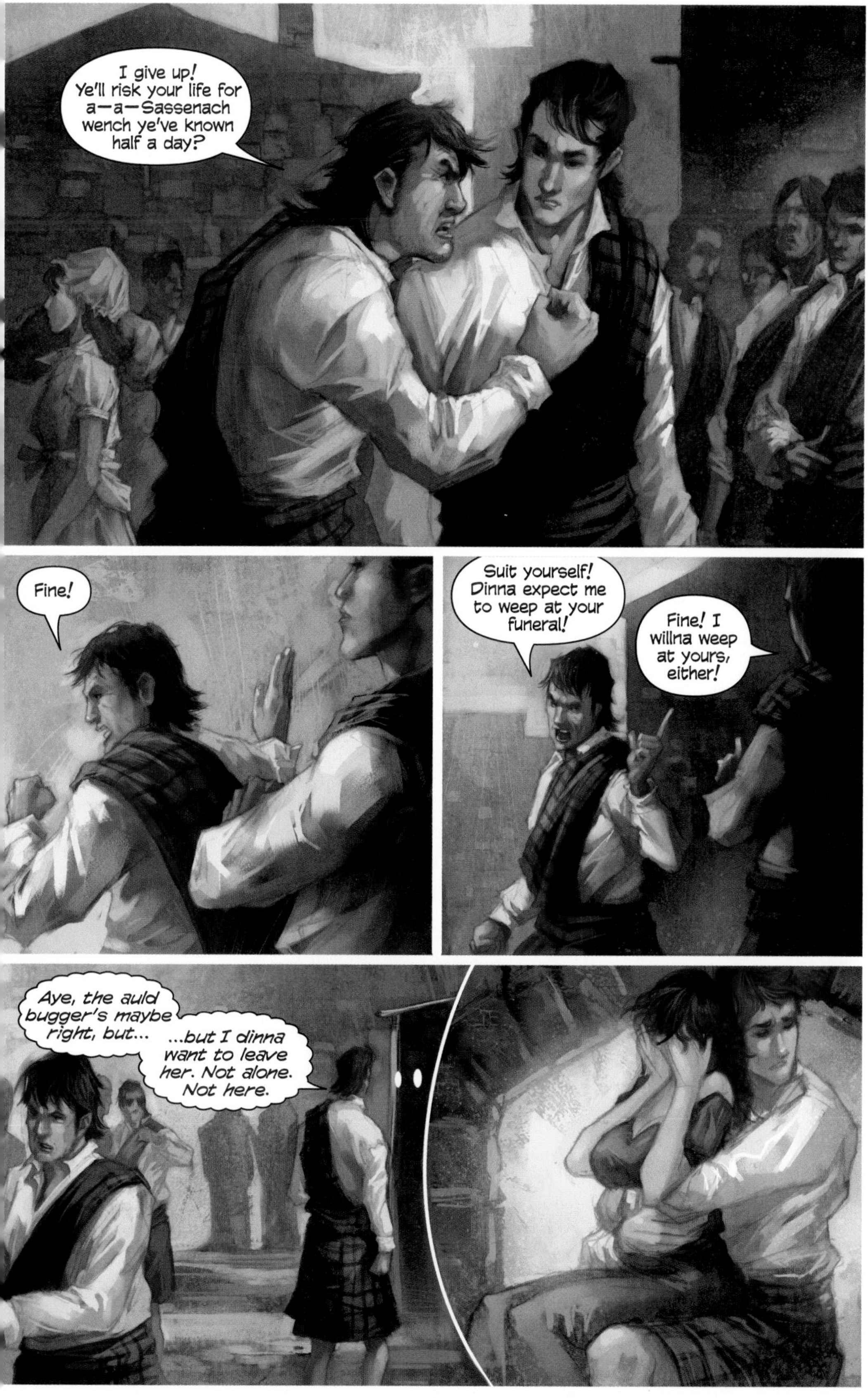
I give up! Ye'll risk your life for a—a—Sassenach wench ye've known half a day?
Fine!
Suit yourself! Dinna expect me to weep at your funeral!
Fine! I willna weep at yours, either!
Aye, the auld bugger's maybe right, but...
...but I dinna want to leave her. Not alone. Not here.

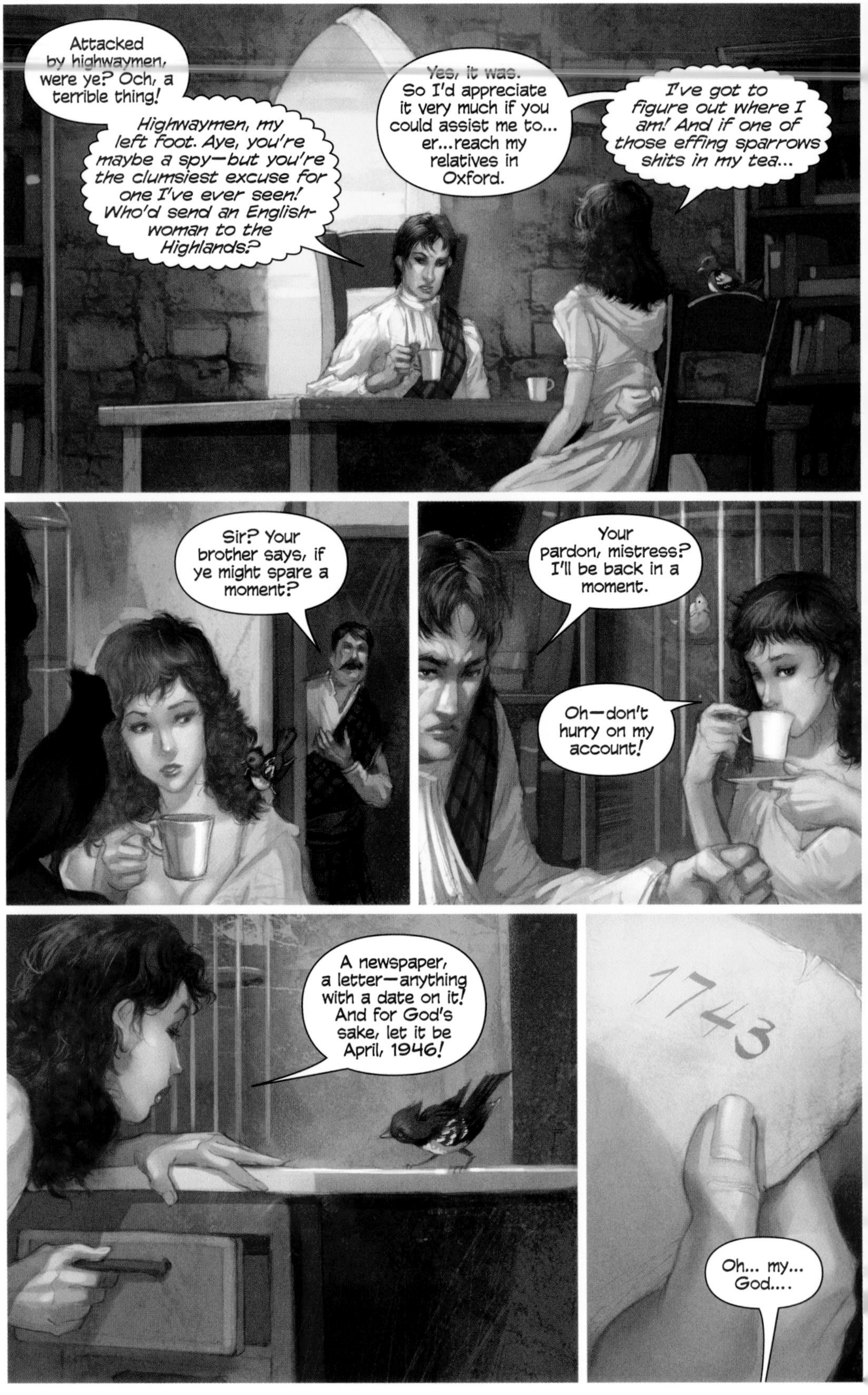
Attacked by highwaymen, were ye? Och, a terrible thing!
Highwaymen, my left foot. Aye, you're maybe a spy—but you're the clumsiest excuse for one I've ever seen! Who'd send an English-woman to the Highlands?
Yes, it was. So I'd appreciate it very much if you could assist me to... er...reach my relatives in Oxford.
I've got to figure out where I am! And if one of those effing sparrows shits in my tea...
Sir? Your brother says, if ye might spare a moment?
Your pardon, mistress? I'll be back in a moment.
Oh—don't hurry on my account!
A newspaper, a letter—anything with a date on it! And for God's sake, let it be April, 1946!
1743
Oh... my... God....

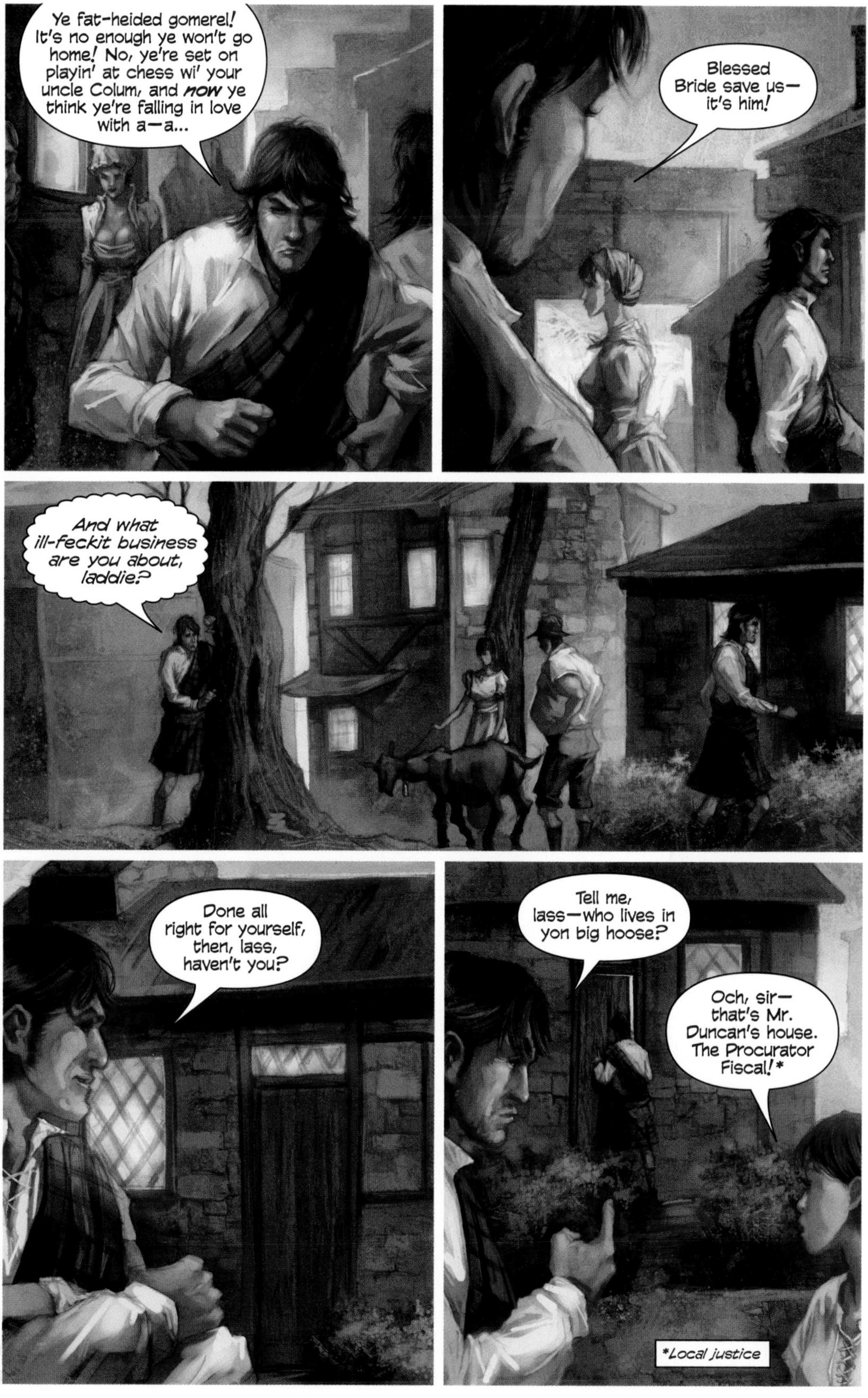
Ye fat-heided gomerel! It's no enough ye won't go home! No, ye're set on playin' at chess wi' your uncle Colum, and *now* ye think ye're falling in love with a—a...
Blessed Bride save us—it's him!
*And what ill-feckit business are you about, laddie?*
Done all right for yourself, then, lass, haven't you?
Tell me, lass—who lives in yon big hoose?
Och, sir—that's Mr. Duncan's house. The Procurator Fiscal!*
*Local justice

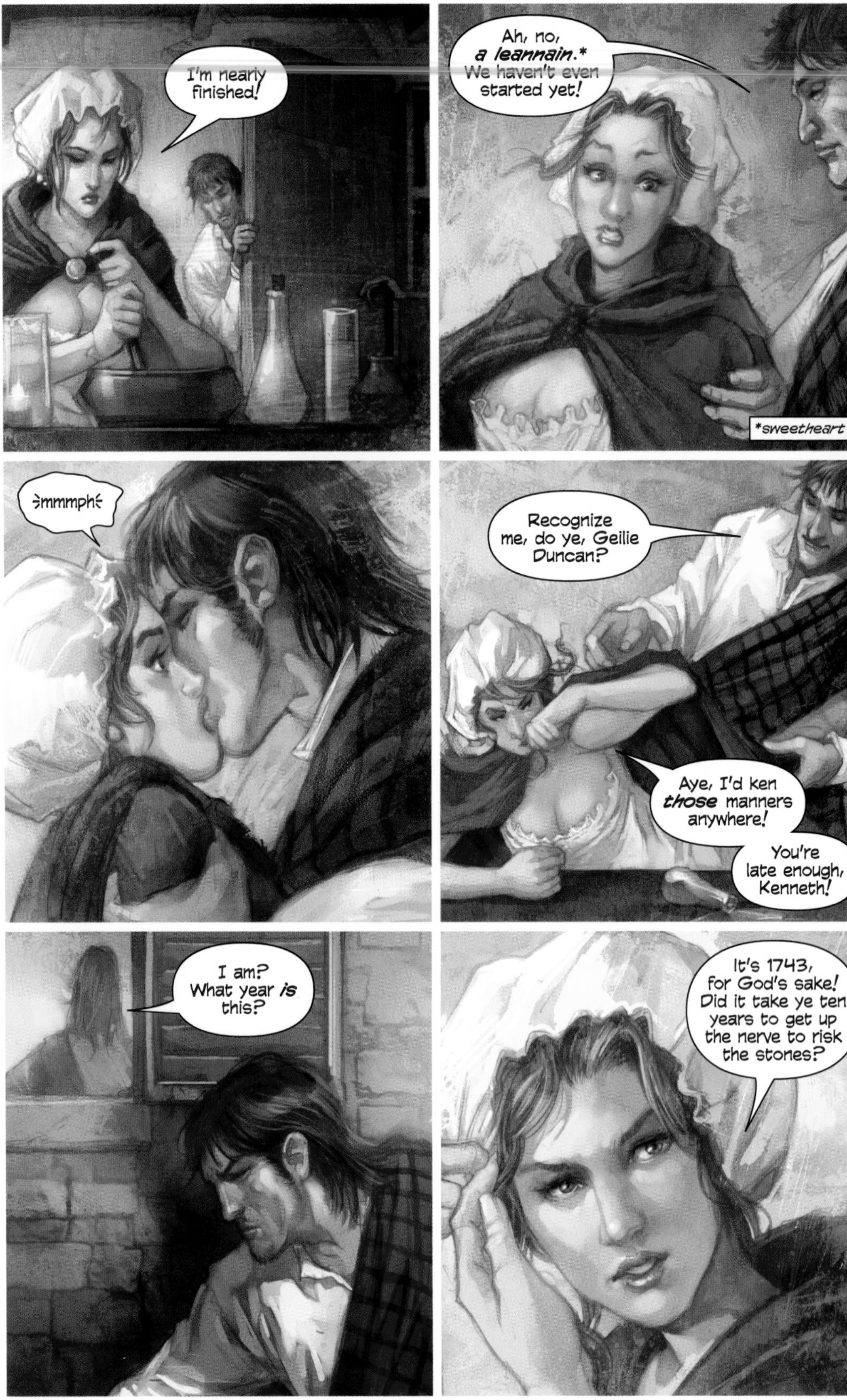
I'm nearly finished!
Ah, no, a leannain.* We haven't even started yet!
*sweetheart
≥mmmph≤
Recognize me, do ye, Geilie Duncan?
Aye, I'd ken those manners anywhere!
You're late enough, Kenneth!
I am? What year is this?
It's 1743, for God's sake! Did it take ye ten years to get up the nerve to risk the stones?

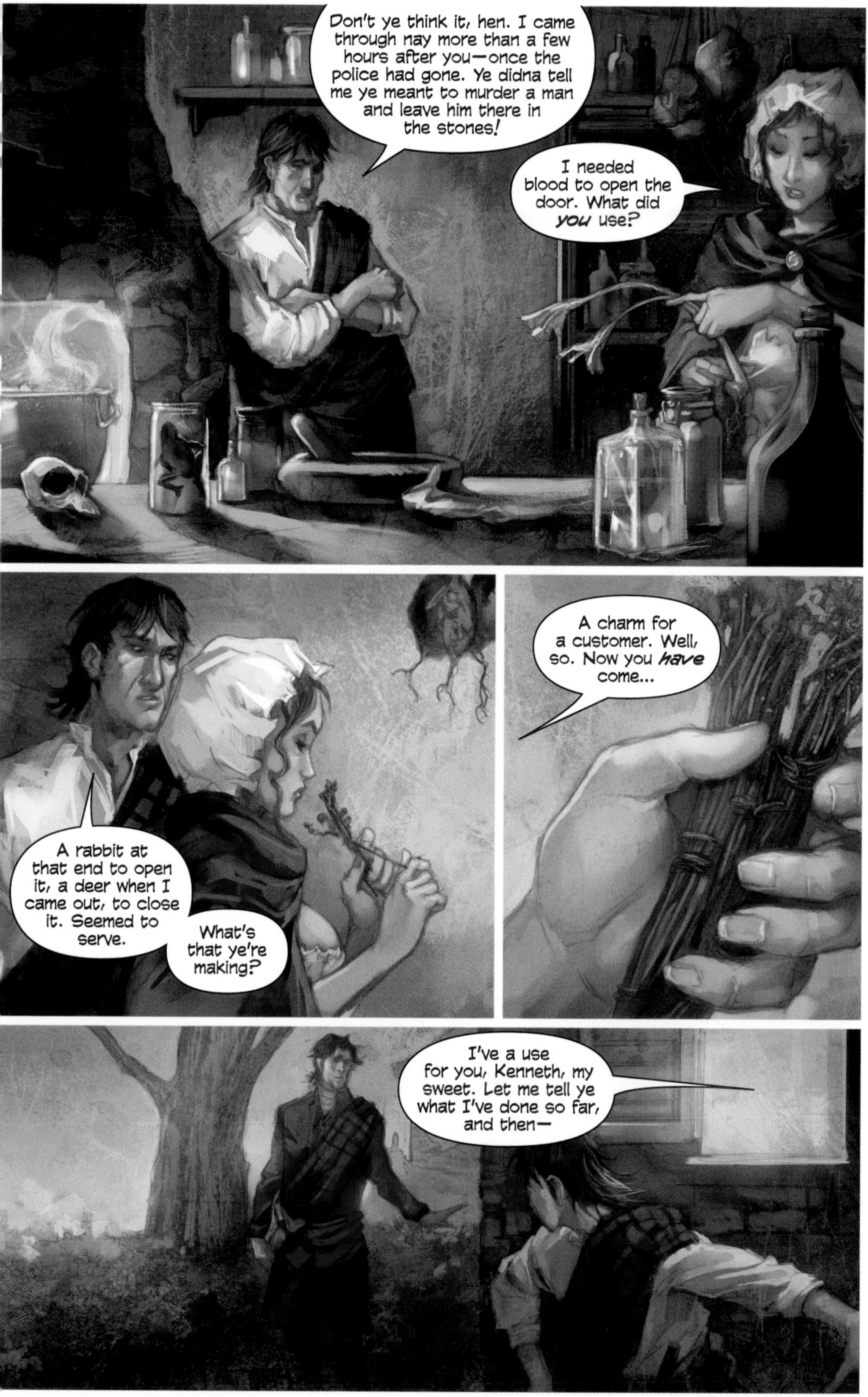
Don't ye think it, hen. I came through nay more than a few hours after you—once the police had gone. Ye didna tell me ye meant to murder a man and leave him there in the stones!
I needed blood to open the door. What did *you* use?
A rabbit at that end to open it, a deer when I came out, to close it. Seemed to serve.
What's that ye're making?
A charm for a customer. Well, so. Now you *have* come...
I've a use for you, Kenneth, my sweet. Let me tell ye what I've done so far, and then—

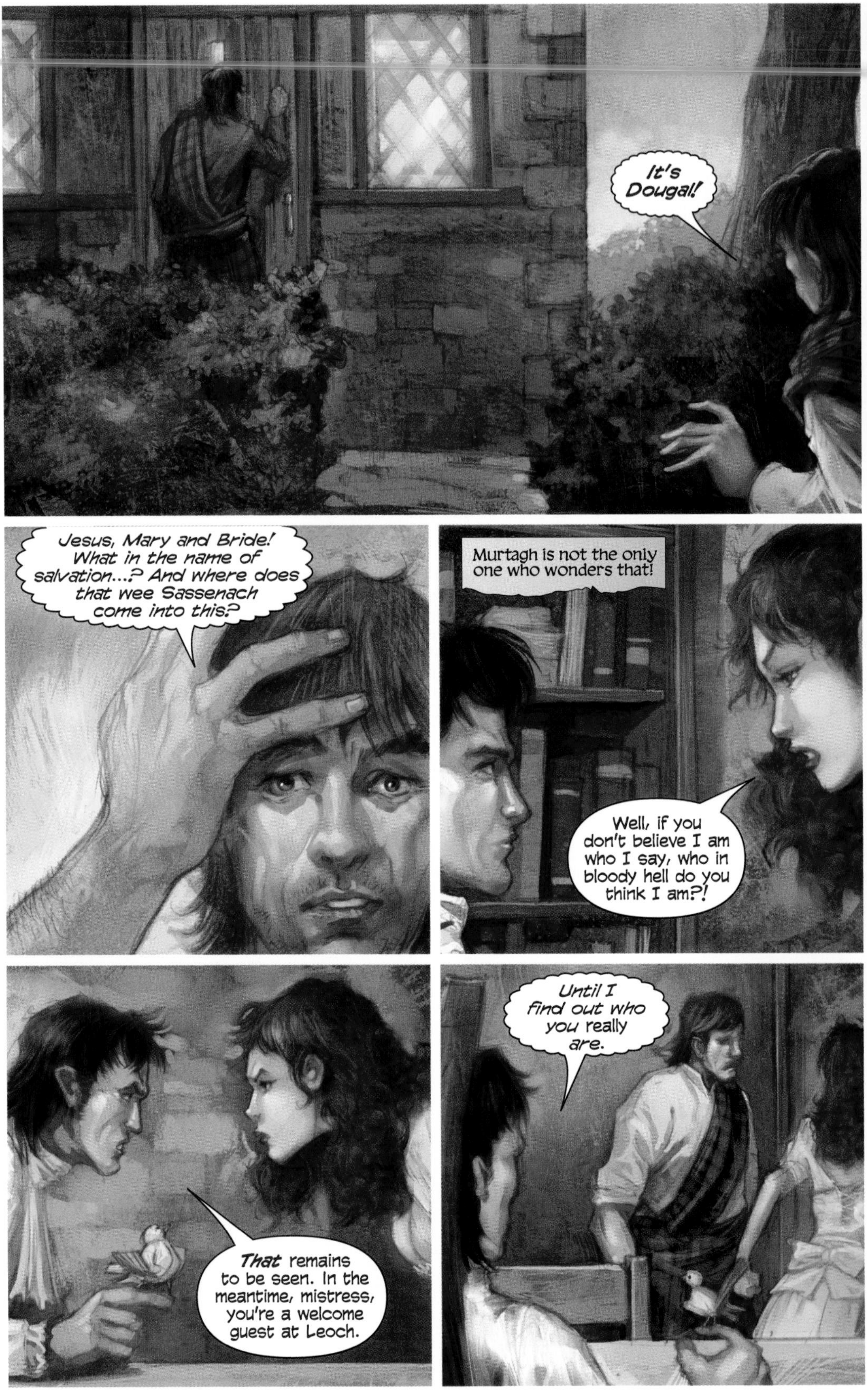
It's Dougal!
Jesus, Mary and Bride! What in the name of salvation...? And where does that wee Sassenach come into this?
Murtagh is not the only one who wonders that!
Well, if you don't believe I am who I say, who in bloody hell do you think I am?!
That remains to be seen. In the meantime, mistress, you're a welcome guest at Leoch.
Until I find out who you really are.

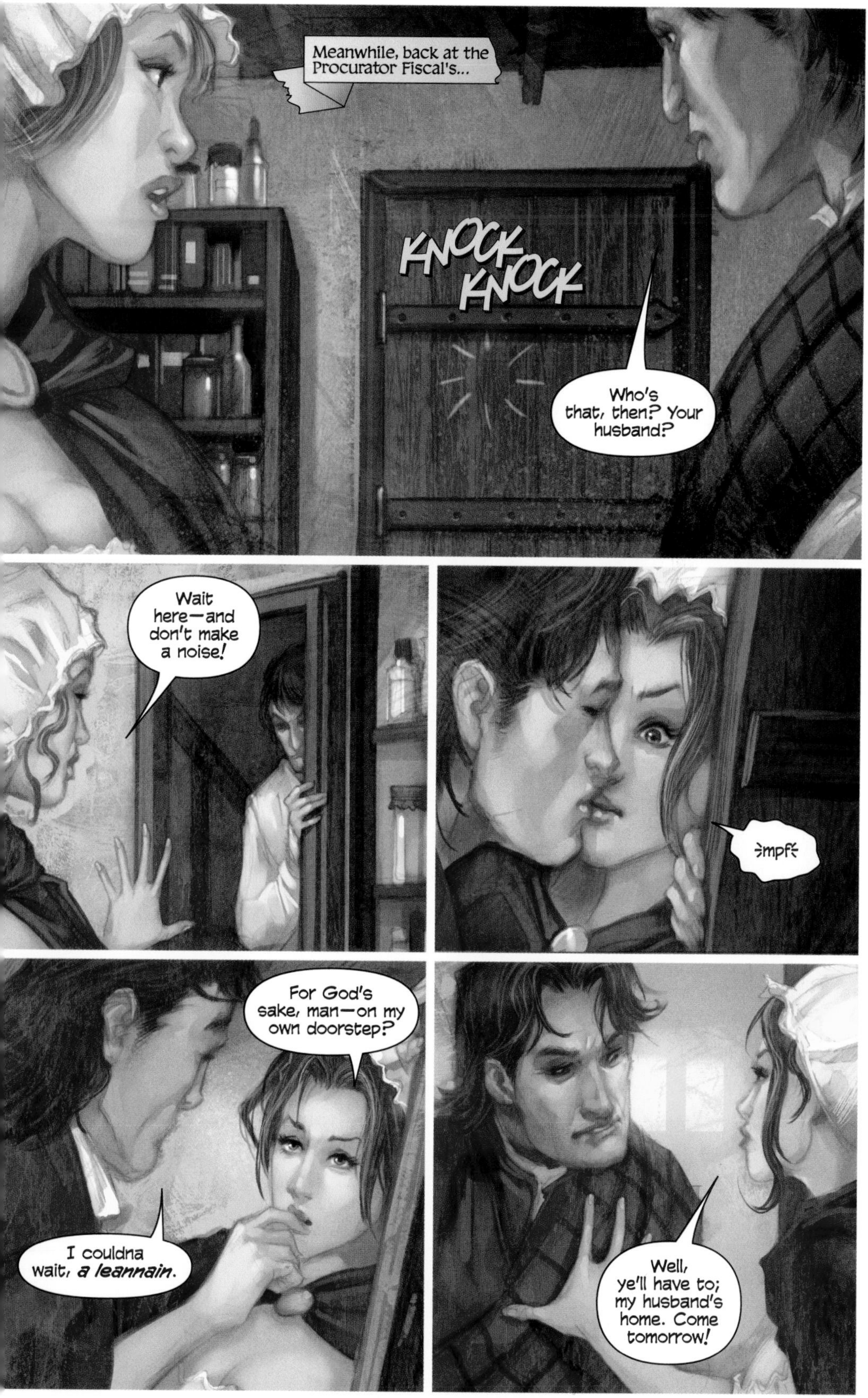
Meanwhile, back at the Procurator Fiscal's...
KNOCK KNOCK
Who's that, then? Your husband?
Wait here—and don't make a noise!
mpf
For God's sake, man—on my own doorstep?
I couldna wait, *a leannain*.
Well, ye'll have to; my husband's home. Come tomorrow!

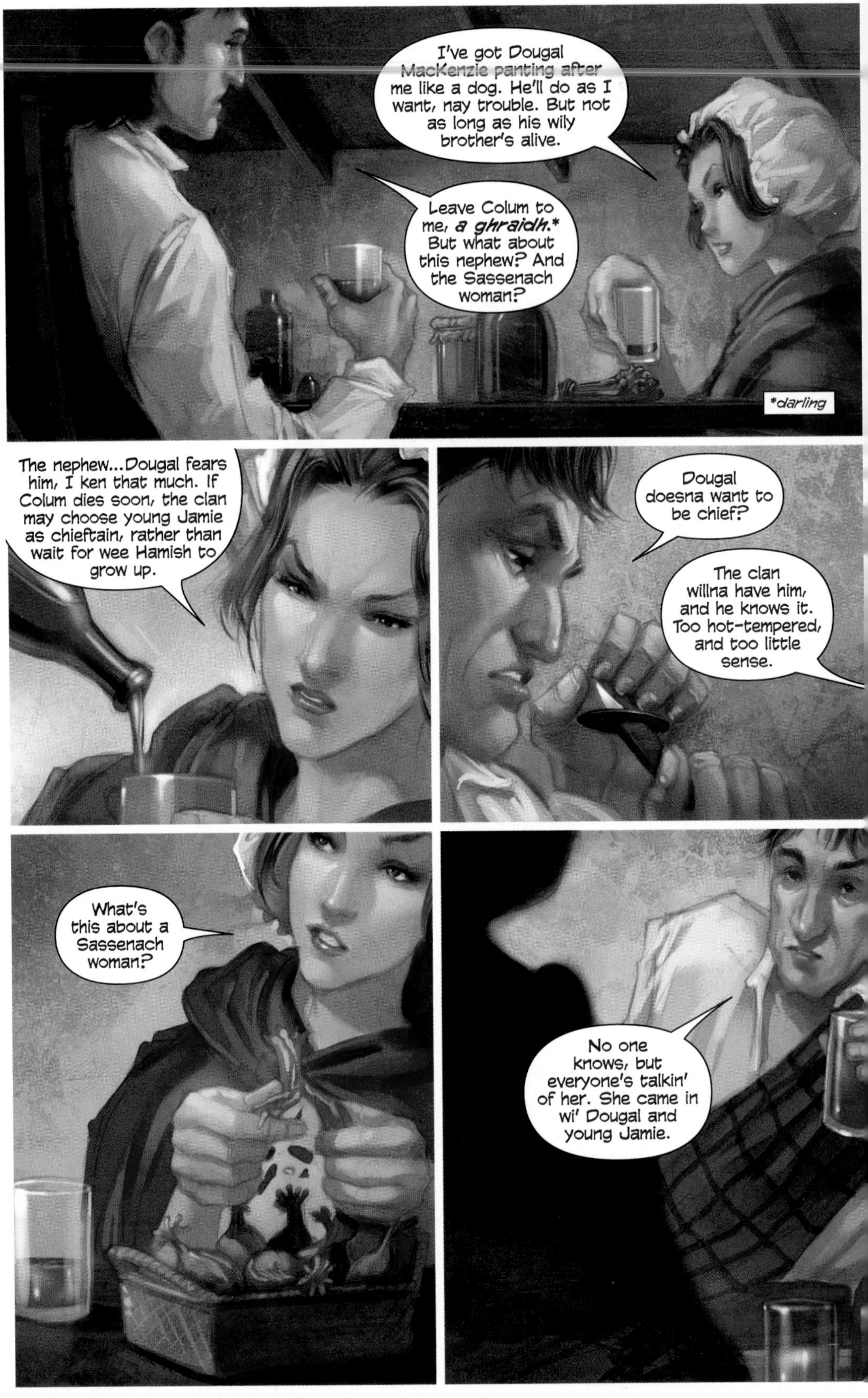
I've got Dougal MacKenzie panting after me like a dog. He'll do as I want, nay trouble. But not as long as his wily brother's alive.
Leave Colum to me, *a ghraidh.** But what about this nephew? And the Sassenach woman?
*darling
The nephew...Dougal fears him, I ken that much. If Colum dies soon, the clan may choose young Jamie as chieftain, rather than wait for wee Hamish to grow up.
Dougal doesna want to be chief?
The clan willna have him, and he knows it. Too hot-tempered, and too little sense.
What's this about a Sassenach woman?
No one knows, but everyone's talkin' of her. She came in wi' Dougal and young Jamie.

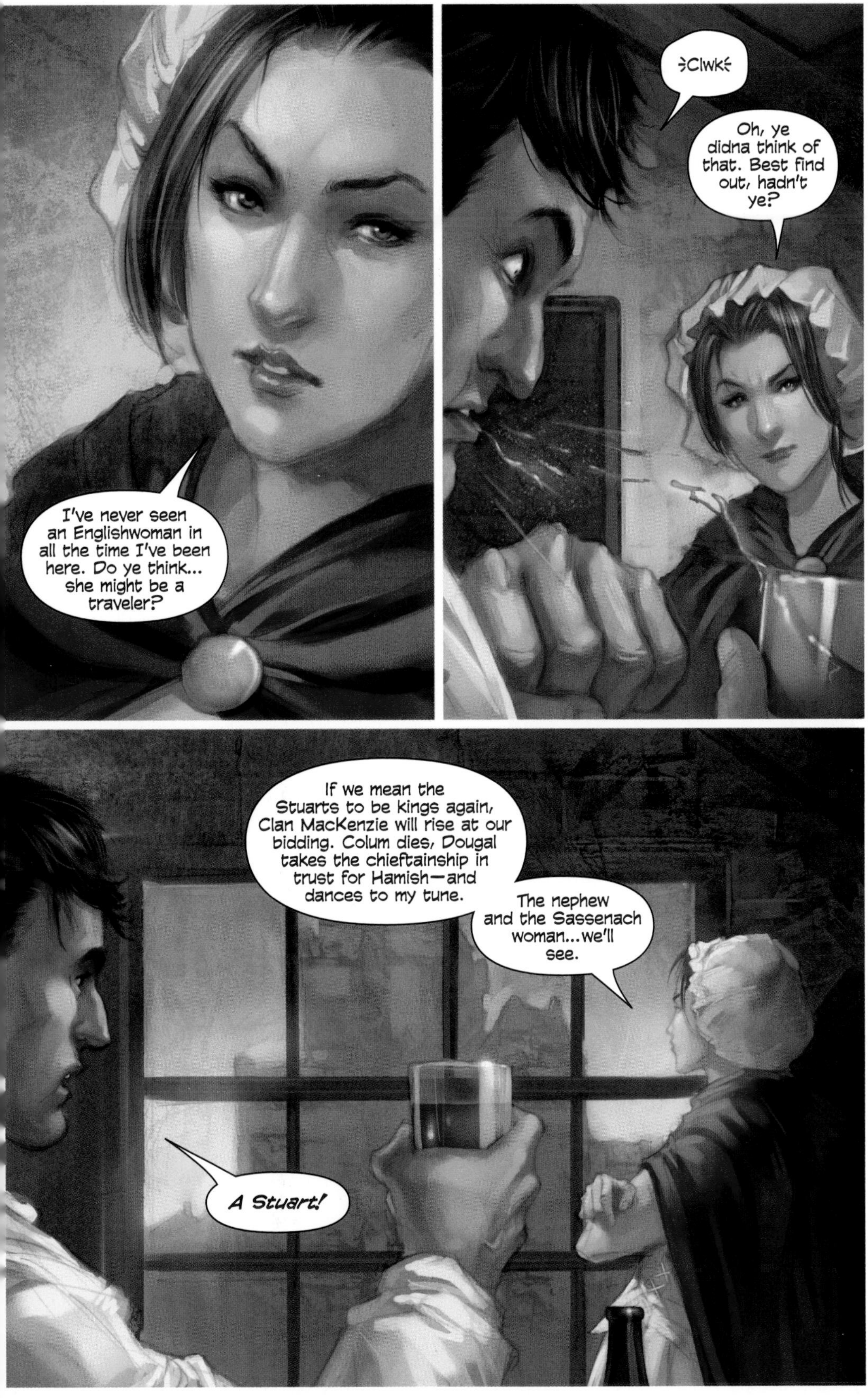
I've never seen an Englishwoman in all the time I've been here. Do ye think... she might be a traveler?
⩥Clwk⩤
Oh, ye didna think of that. Best find out, hadn't ye?
If we mean the Stuarts to be kings again, Clan MacKenzie will rise at our bidding. Colum dies, Dougal takes the chieftainship in trust for Hamish—and dances to my tune.
The nephew and the Sassenach woman...we'll see.
A Stuart!

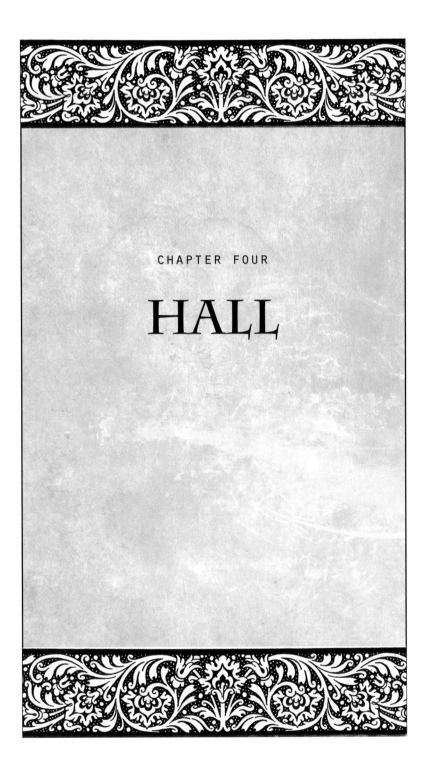

CHAPTER FOUR

# HALL

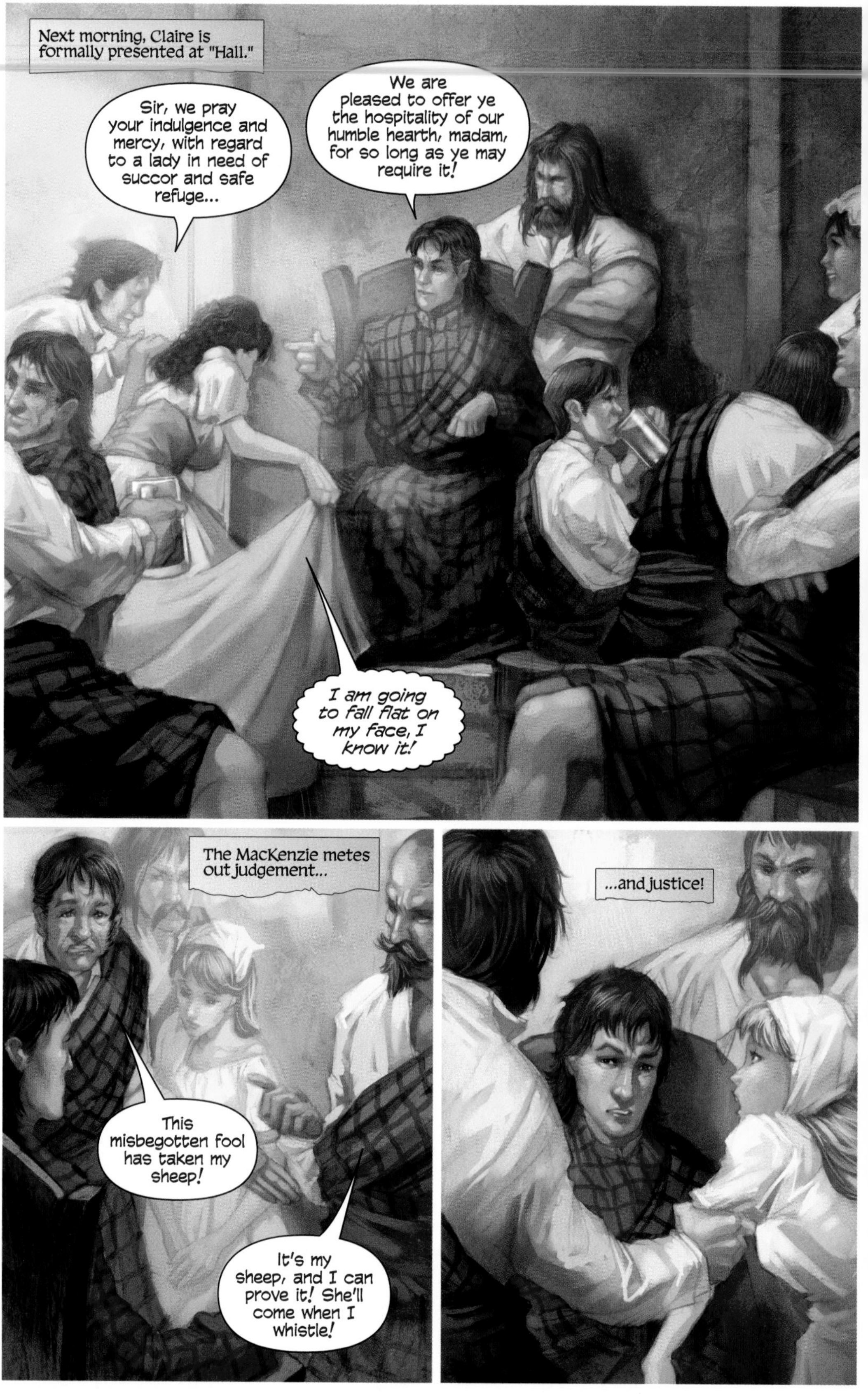
Next morning, Claire is formally presented at "Hall."
Sir, we pray your indulgence and mercy, with regard to a lady in need of succor and safe refuge...
We are pleased to offer ye the hospitality of our humble hearth, madam, for so long as ye may require it!
I am going to fall flat on my face, I know it!
The MacKenzie metes out judgement...
This misbegotten fool has taken my sheep!
It's my sheep, and I can prove it! She'll come when I whistle!
...and justice!

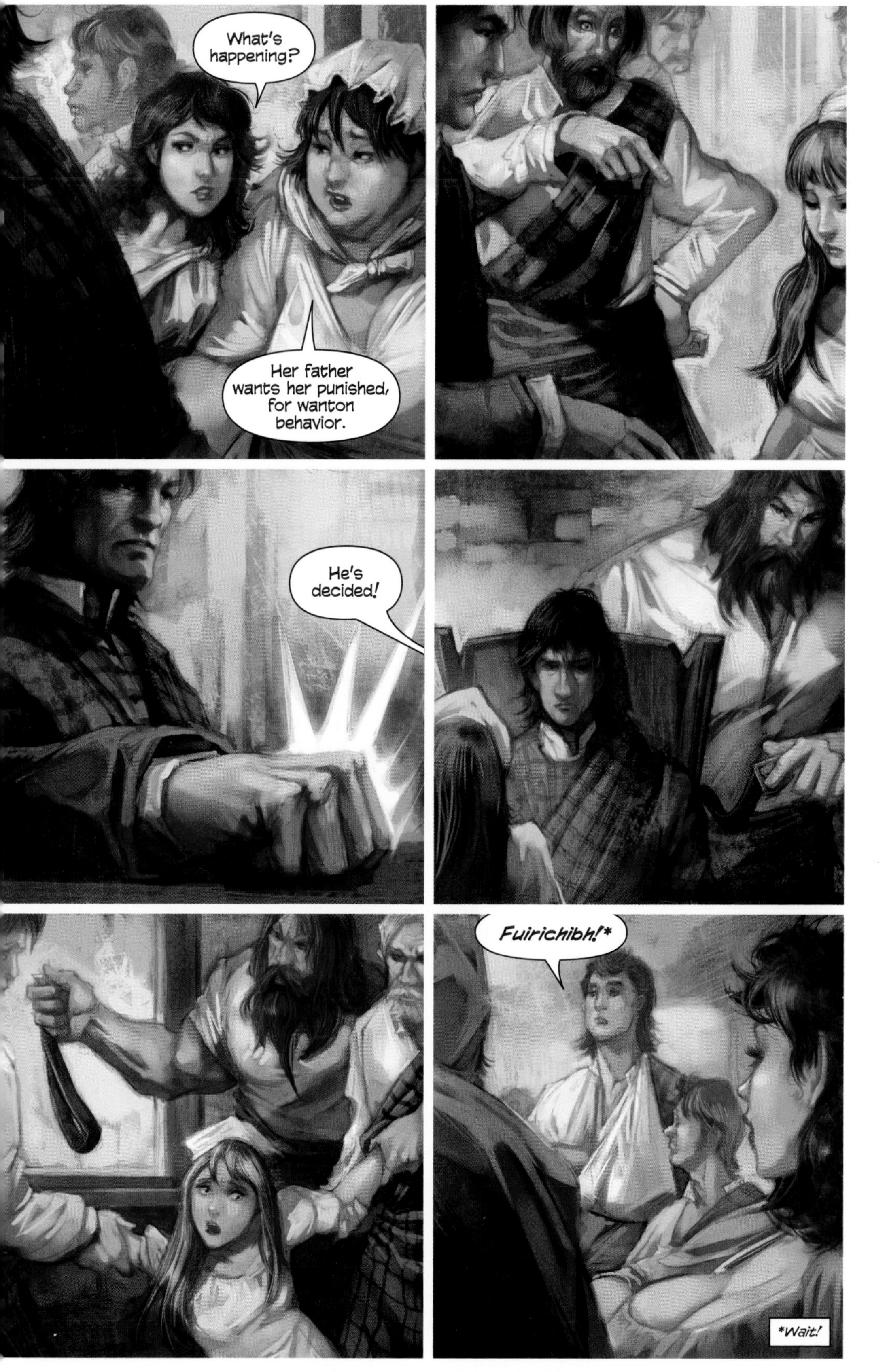
What's happening?
Her father wants her punished, for wanton behavior.
He's decided!
Fuirichibh!*
*Wait!

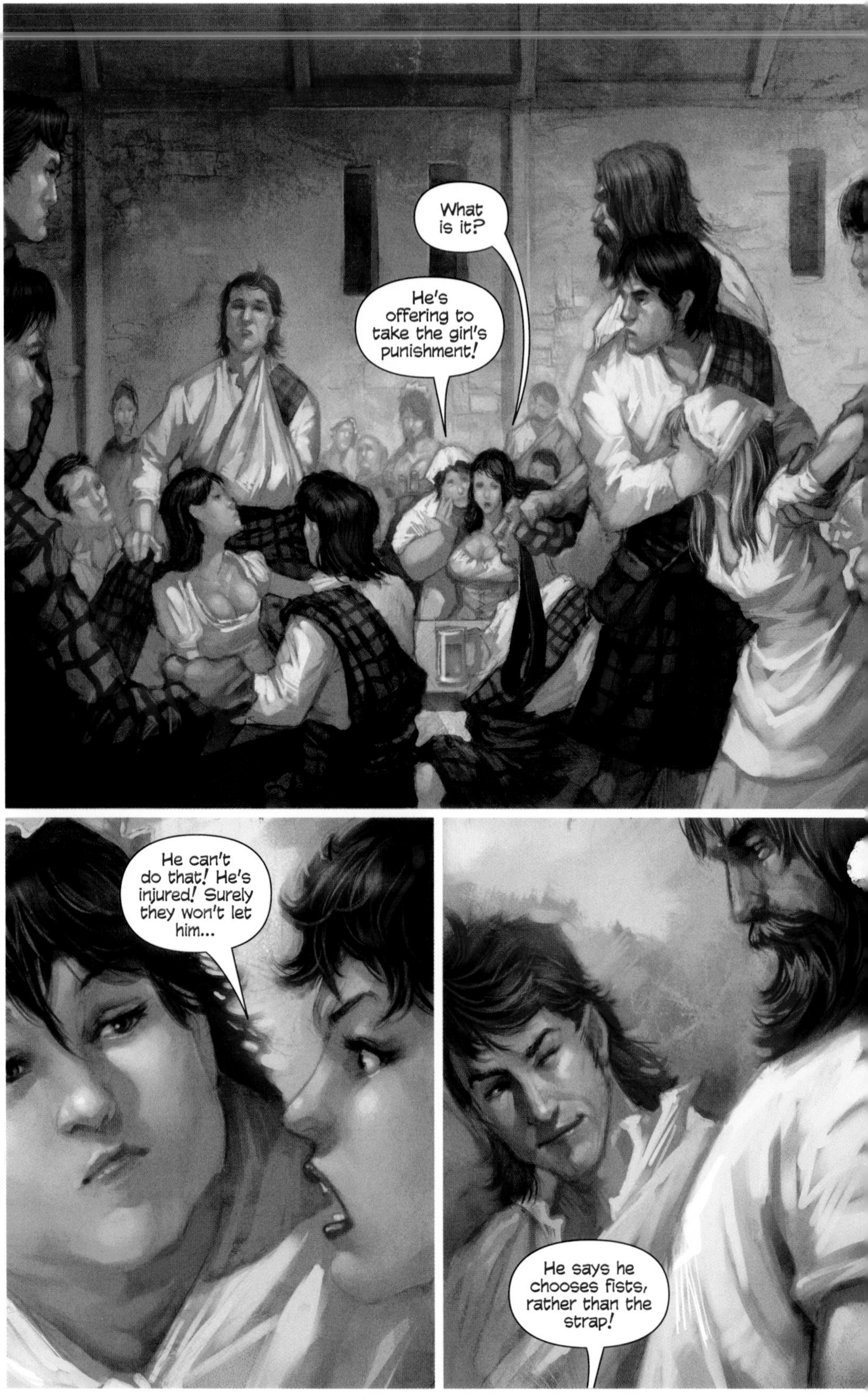
What is it?
He's offering to take the girl's punishment!
He can't do that! He's injured! Surely they won't let him...
He says he chooses fists, rather than the strap!

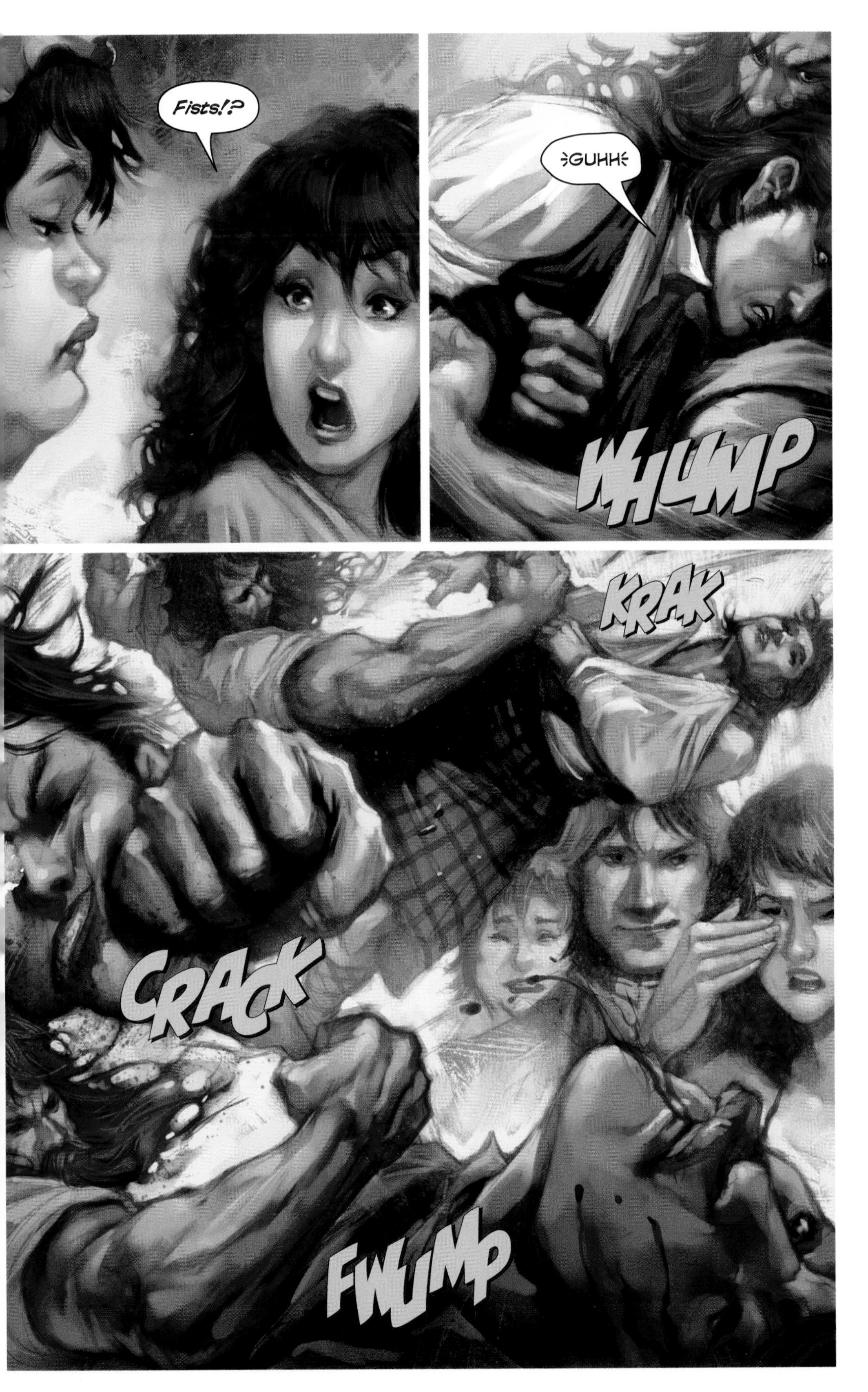
Fists!?
GUHH
WHUMP
KRAK
CRACK
FWUMP

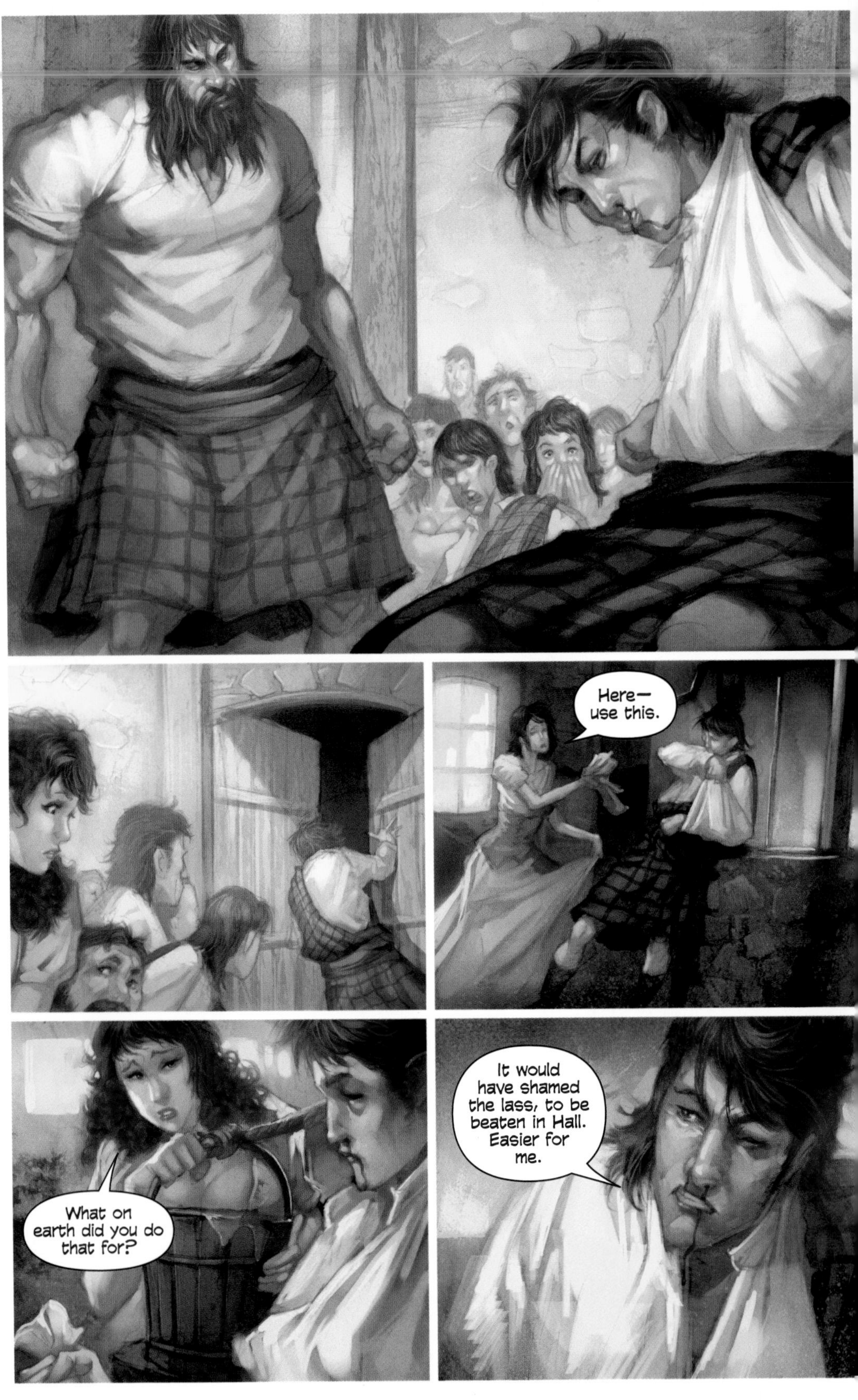
Here—use this.
What on earth did you do that for?
It would have shamed the lass, to be beaten in Hall. Easier for me.

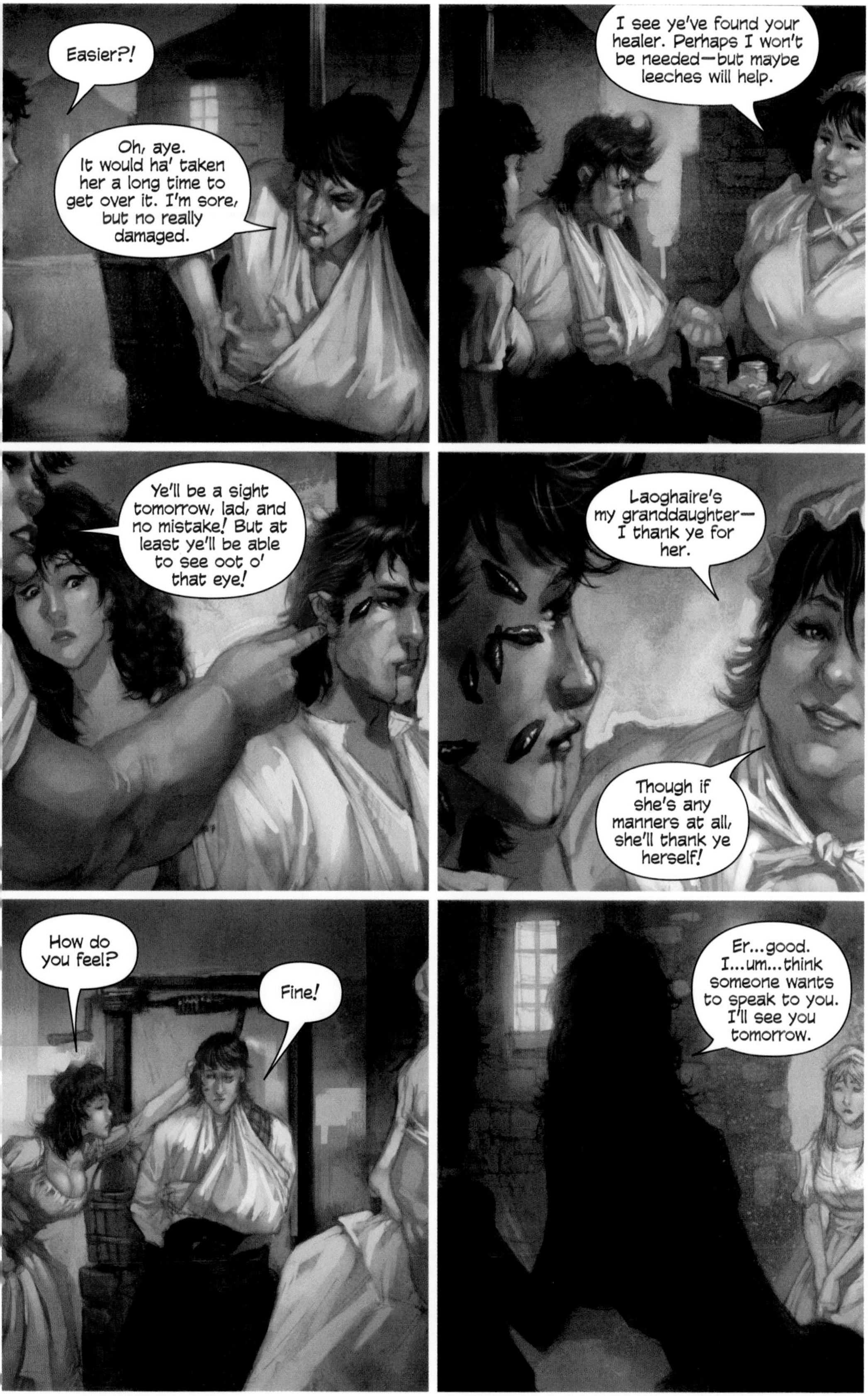
Easier?!
Oh, aye. It would ha' taken her a long time to get over it. I'm sore, but no really damaged.
I see ye've found your healer. Perhaps I won't be needed—but maybe leeches will help.
Ye'll be a sight tomorrow, lad, and no mistake! But at least ye'll be able to see oot o' that eye!
Laoghaire's my granddaughter—I thank ye for her.
Though if she's any manners at all, she'll thank ye herself!
How do you feel?
Fine!
Er...good. I...um...think someone wants to speak to you. I'll see you tomorrow.

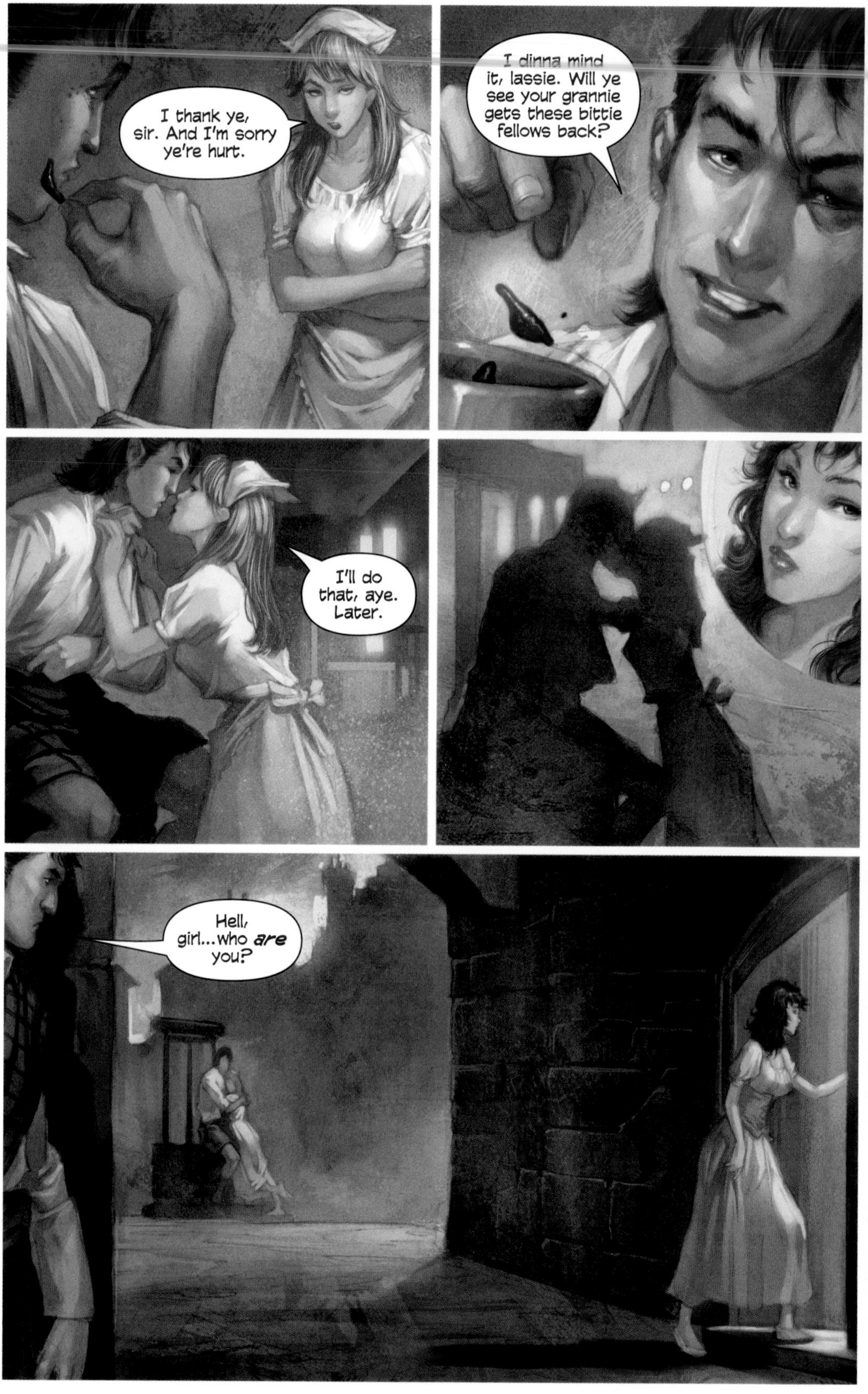
I thank ye, sir. And I'm sorry ye're hurt.
I dinna mind it, lassie. Will ye see your grannie gets these bittie fellows back?
I'll do that, aye. Later.
Hell, girl...who *are* you?

CHAPTER FIVE

# THE GATHERING

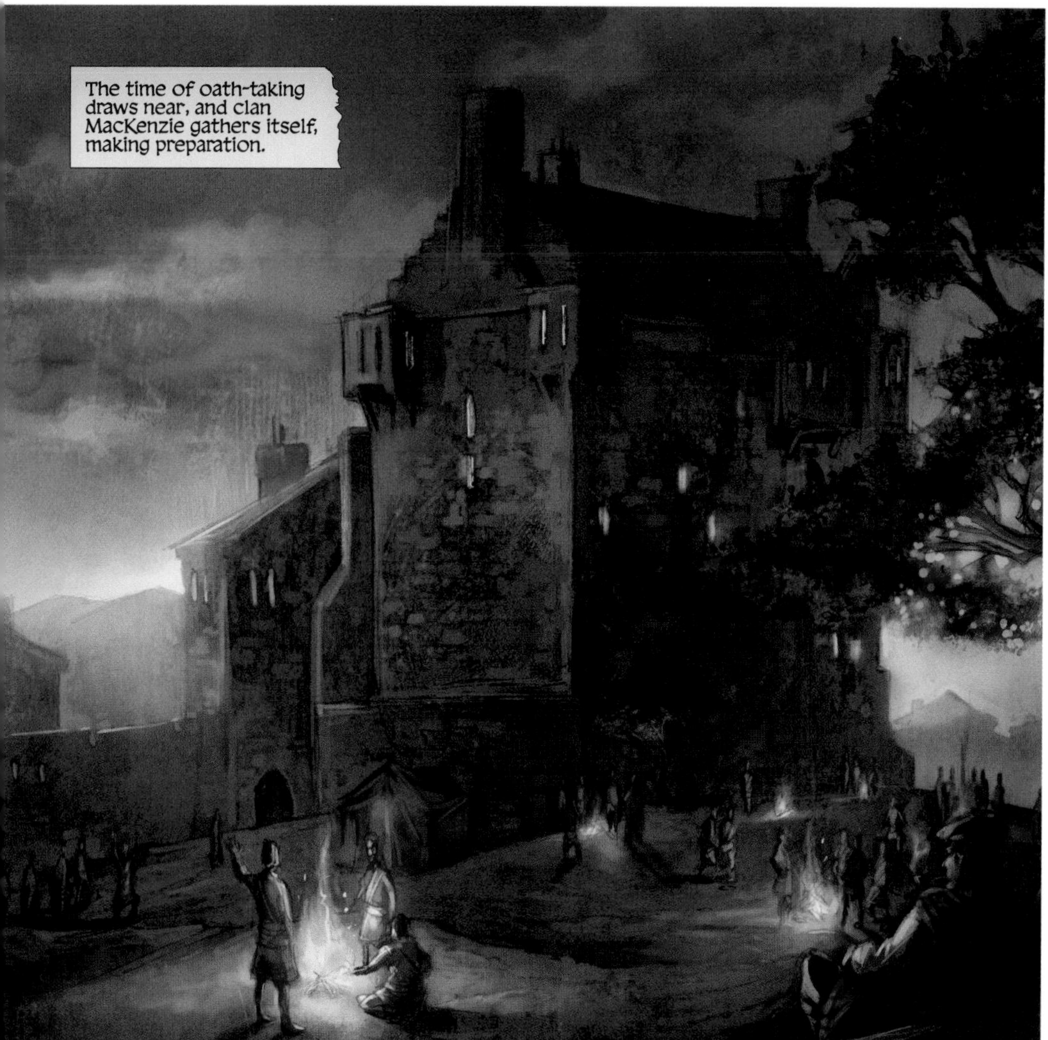
The time of oath-taking draws near, and clan MacKenzie gathers itself, making preparation.

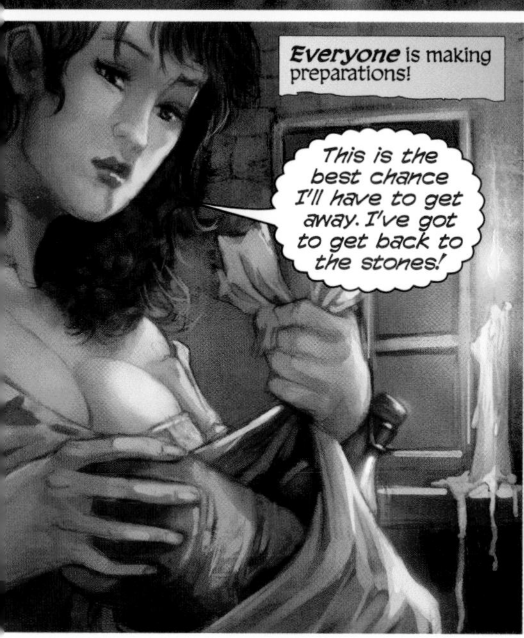
Everyone is making preparations!
This is the best chance I'll have to get away. I've got to get back to the stones!

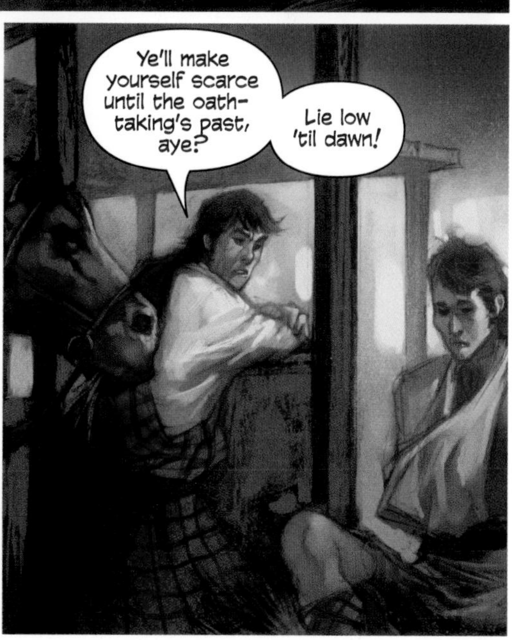
Ye'll make yourself scarce until the oath-taking's past, aye?
Lie low 'til dawn!

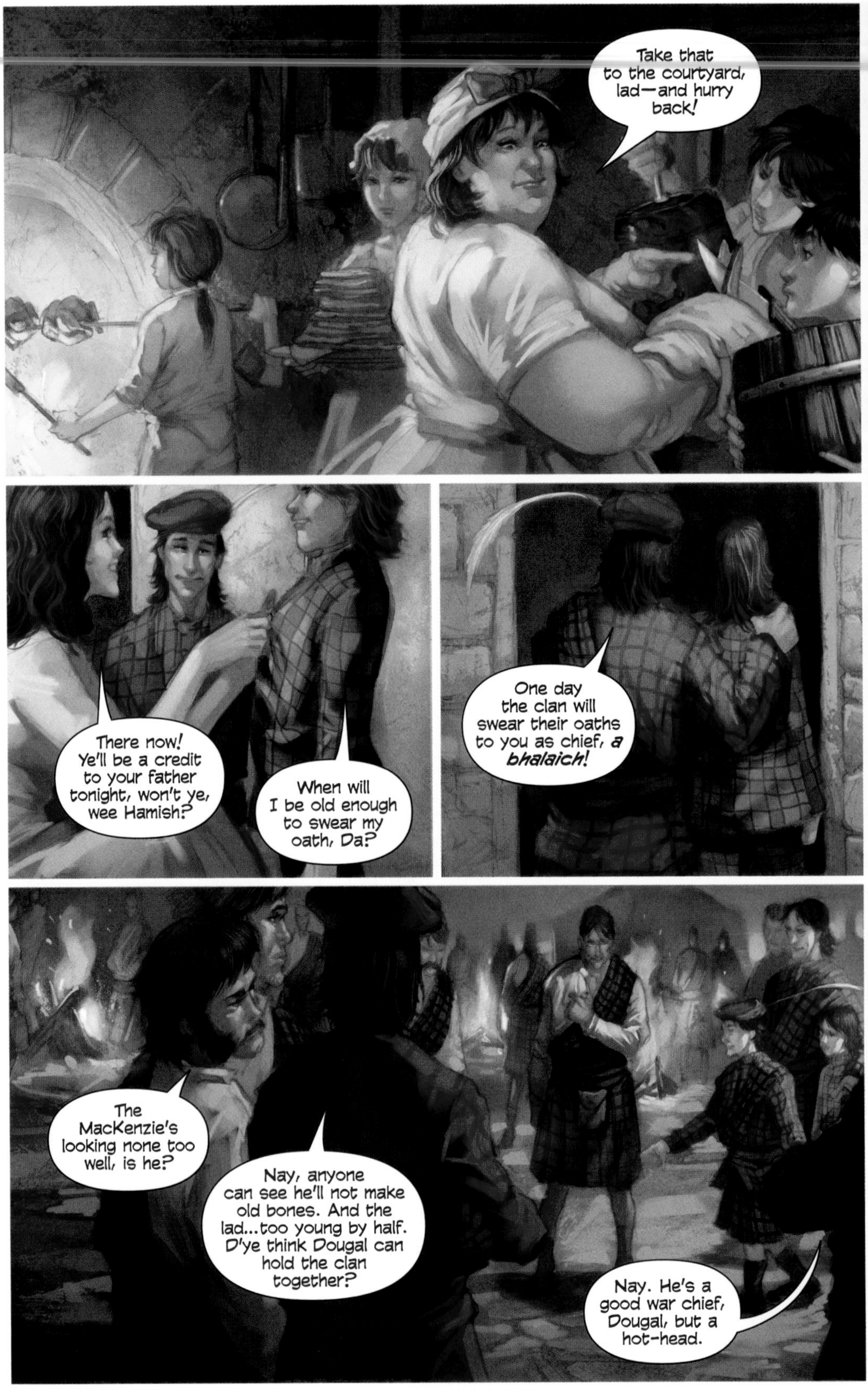
Take that to the courtyard, lad—and hurry back!
There now! Ye'll be a credit to your father tonight, won't ye, wee Hamish?
When will I be old enough to swear my oath, Da?
One day the clan will swear their oaths to you as chief, *a bhalaich!*
The MacKenzie's looking none too well, is he?
Nay, anyone can see he'll not make old bones. And the lad...too young by half. D'ye think Dougal can hold the clan together?
Nay. He's a good war chief, Dougal, but a hot-head.

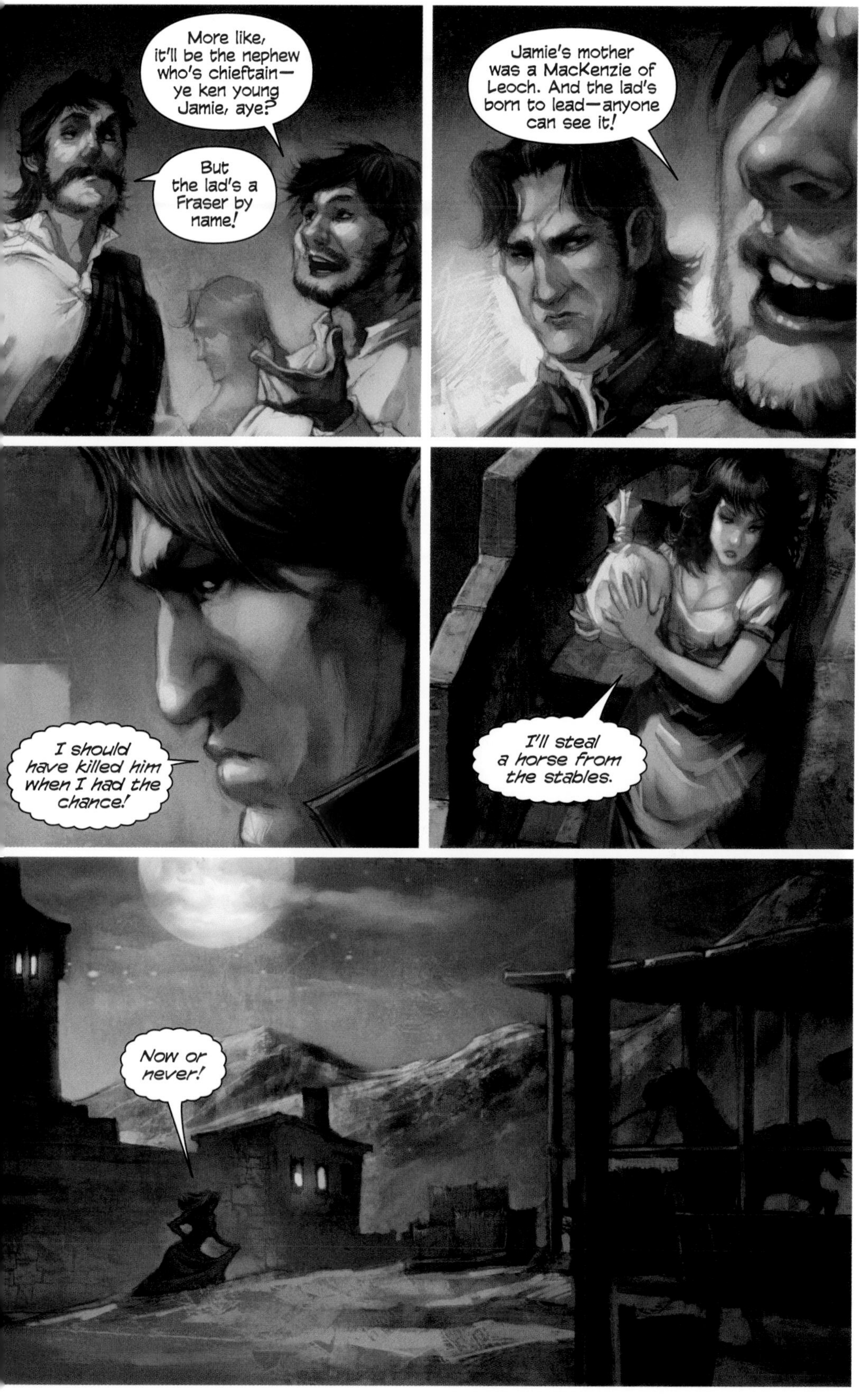
More like, it'll be the nephew who's chieftain—ye ken young Jamie, aye?
But the lad's a Fraser by name!
Jamie's mother was a MacKenzie of Leoch. And the lad's born to lead—anyone can see it!
I should have killed him when I had the chance!
I'll steal a horse from the stables.
Now or never!

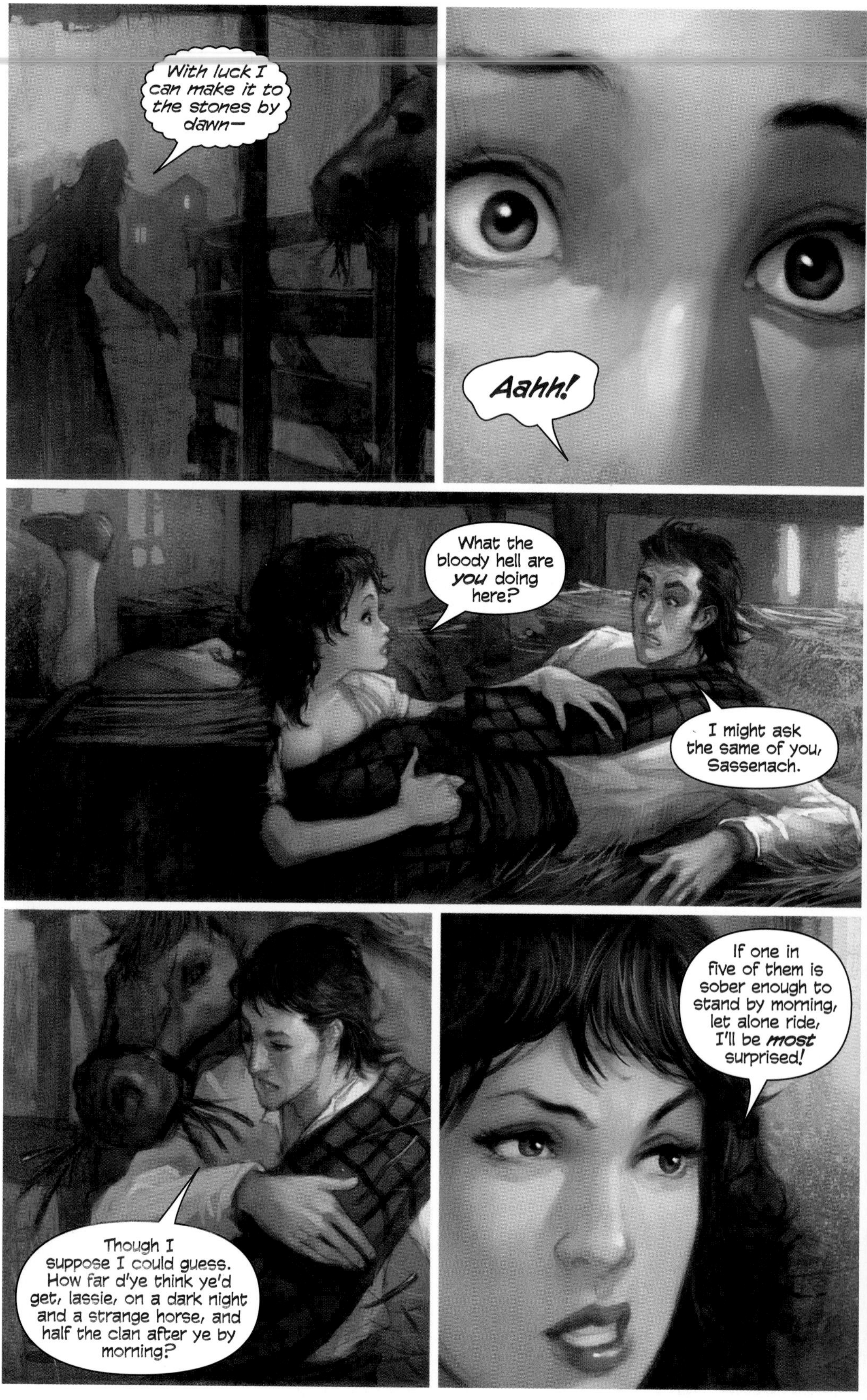

With luck I can make it to the stones by dawn—
Aahh!
What the bloody hell are *you* doing here?
I might ask the same of you, Sassenach.
Though I suppose I could guess. How far d'ye think ye'd get, lassie, on a dark night and a strange horse, and half the clan after ye by morning?
If one in five of them is sober enough to stand by morning, let alone ride, I'll be *most* surprised!

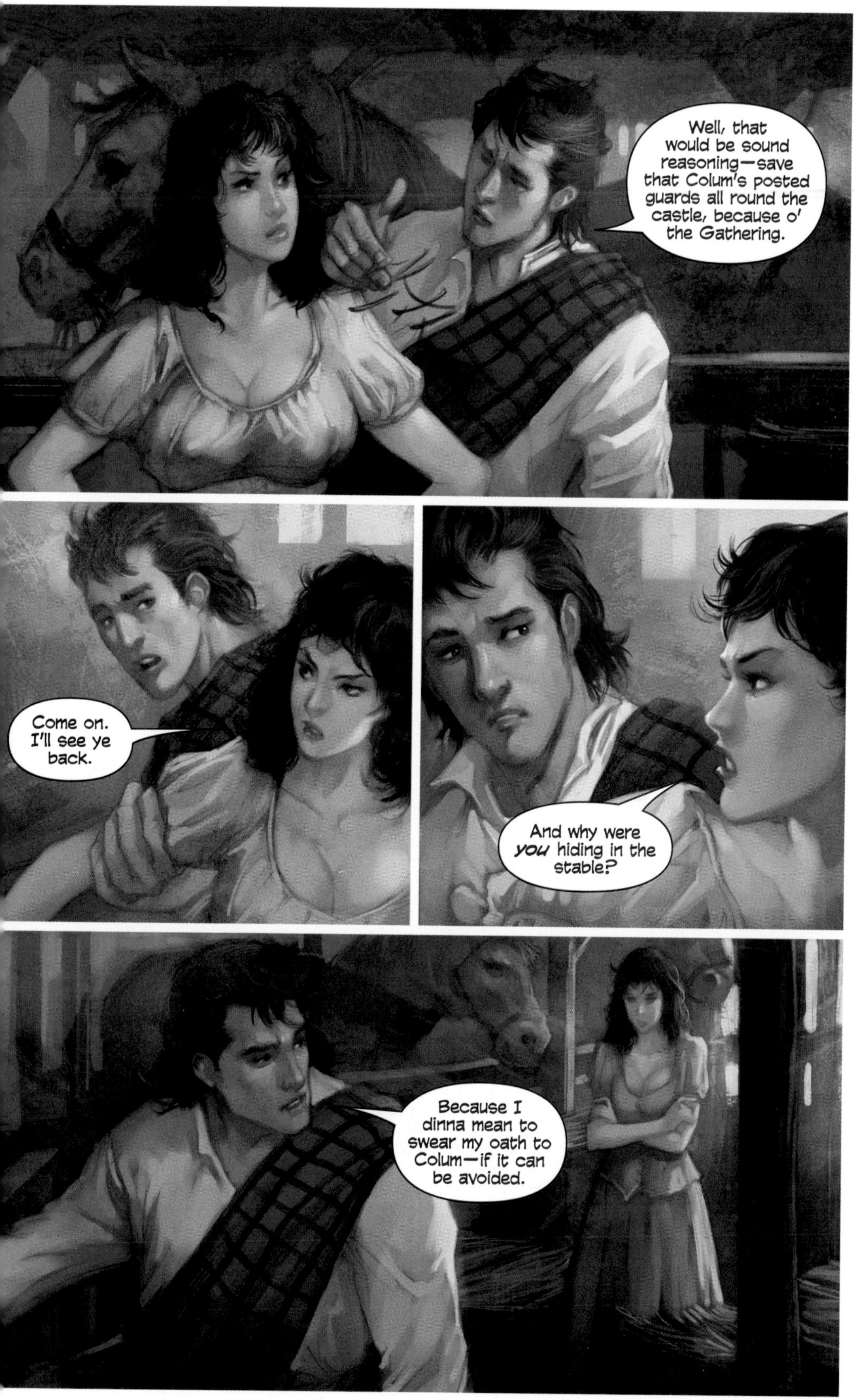
Well, that would be sound reasoning—save that Colum's posted guards all round the castle, because o' the Gathering.
Come on. I'll see ye back.
And why were *you* hiding in the stable?
Because I dinna mean to swear my oath to Colum—if it can be avoided.

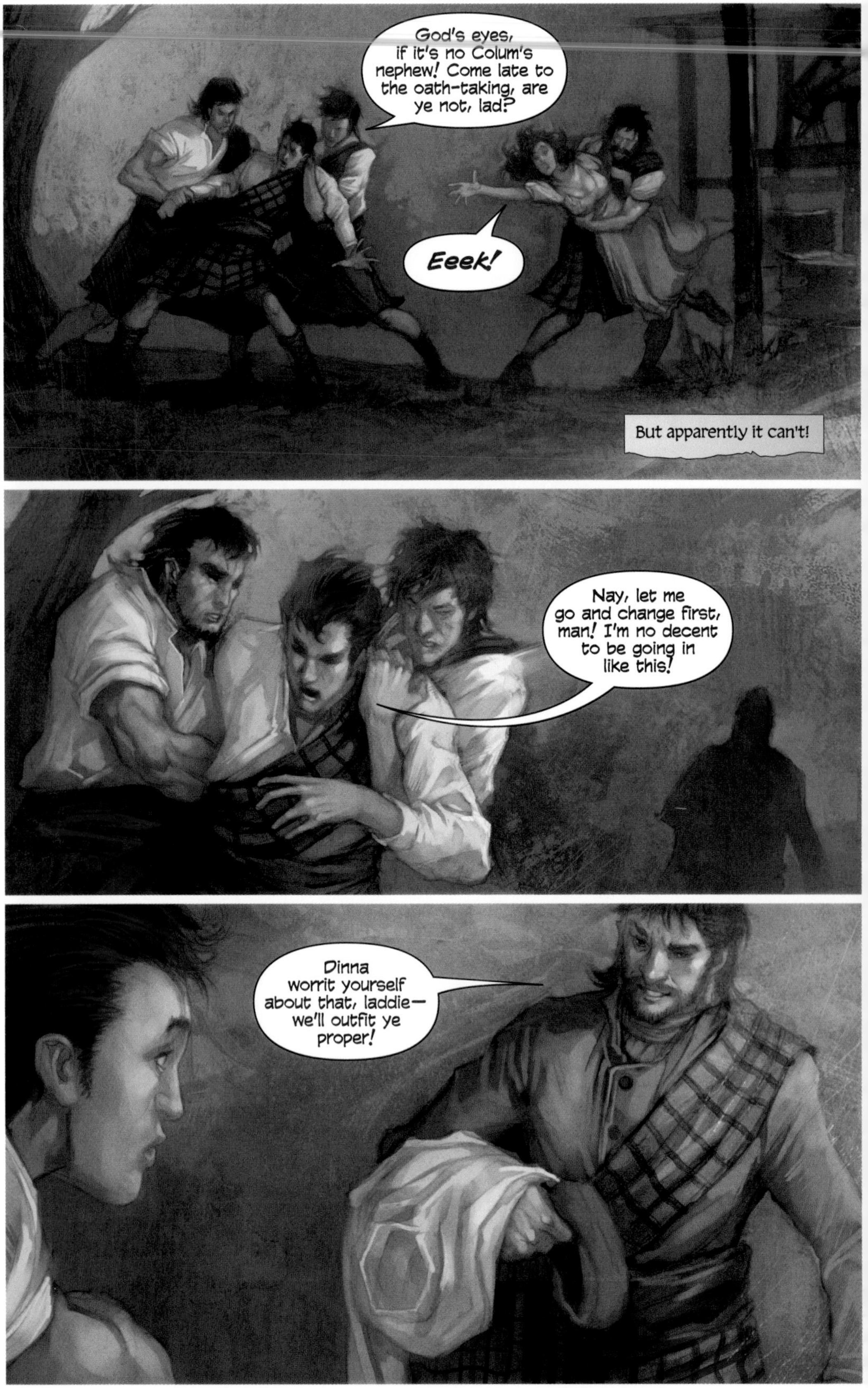
God's eyes, if it's no Colum's nephew! Come late to the oath-taking, are ye not, lad?
Eeek!
But apparently it can't!
Nay, let me go and change first, man! I'm no decent to be going in like this!
Dinna worrit yourself about that, laddie—we'll outfit ye proper!

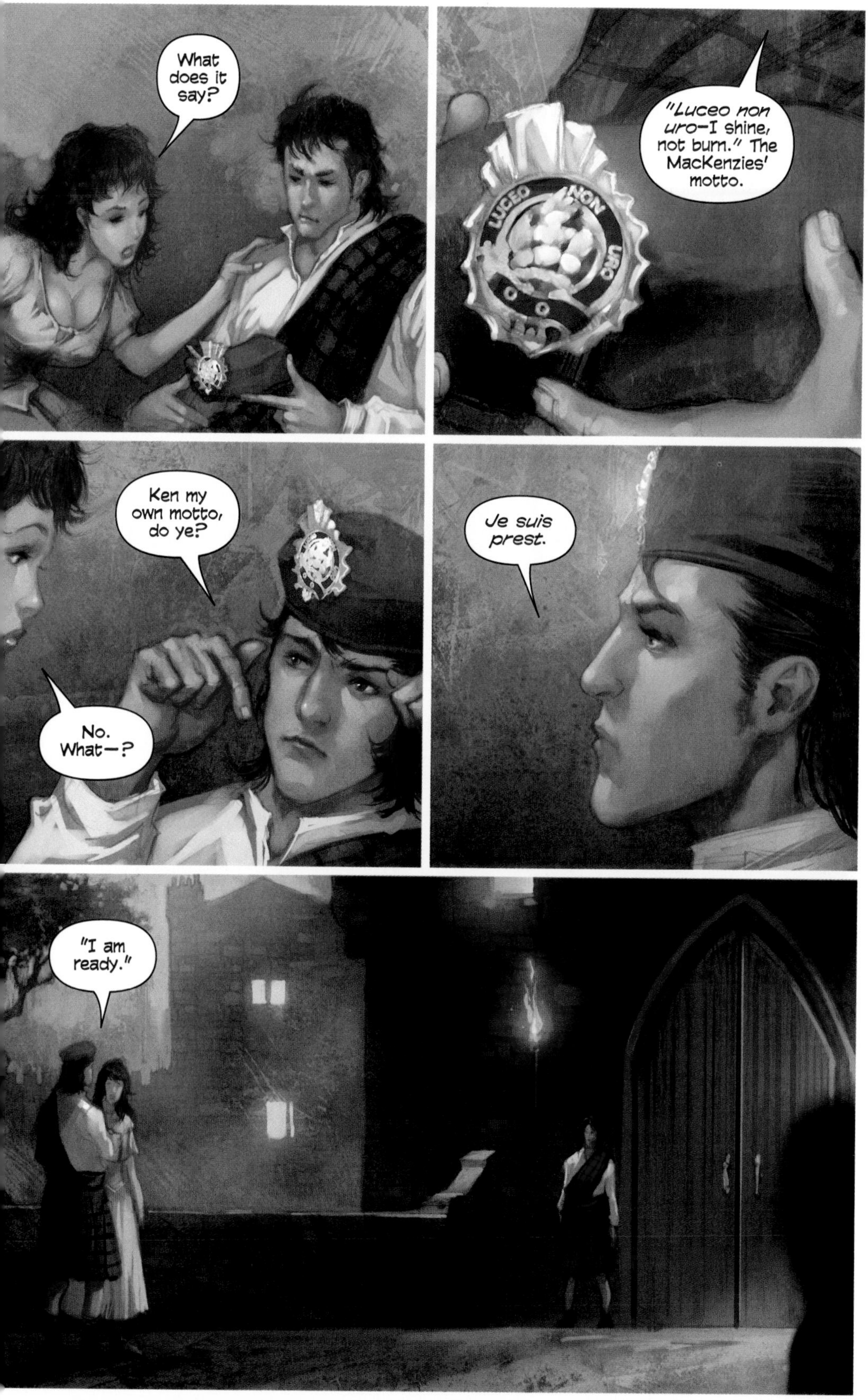
What does it say?
"Luceo non uro—I shine, not burn." The MacKenzies' motto.
Ken my own motto, do ye?
No. What—?
Je suis prest.
"I am ready."

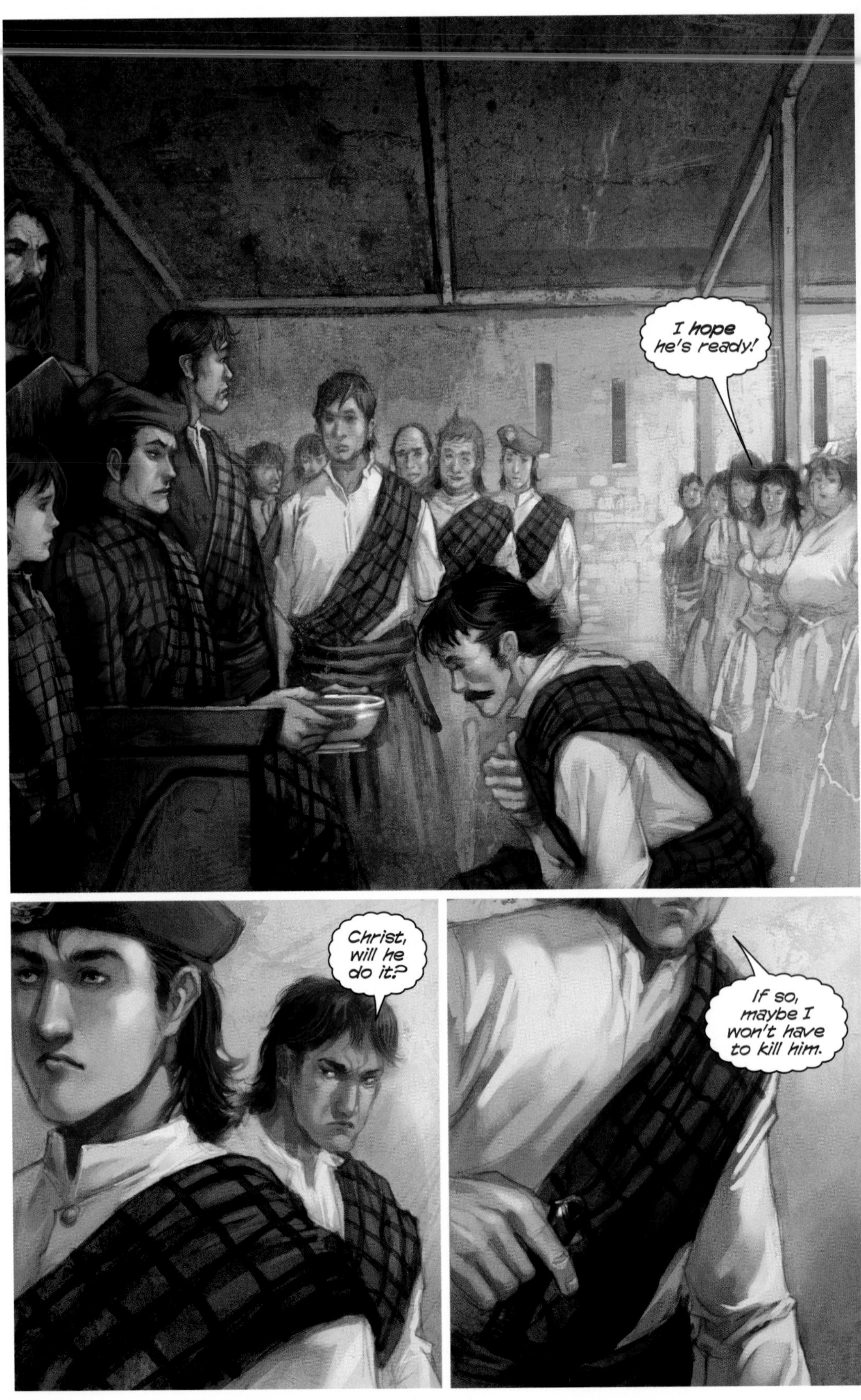
I hope he's ready!
Christ, will he do it?
If so, maybe I won't have to kill him.

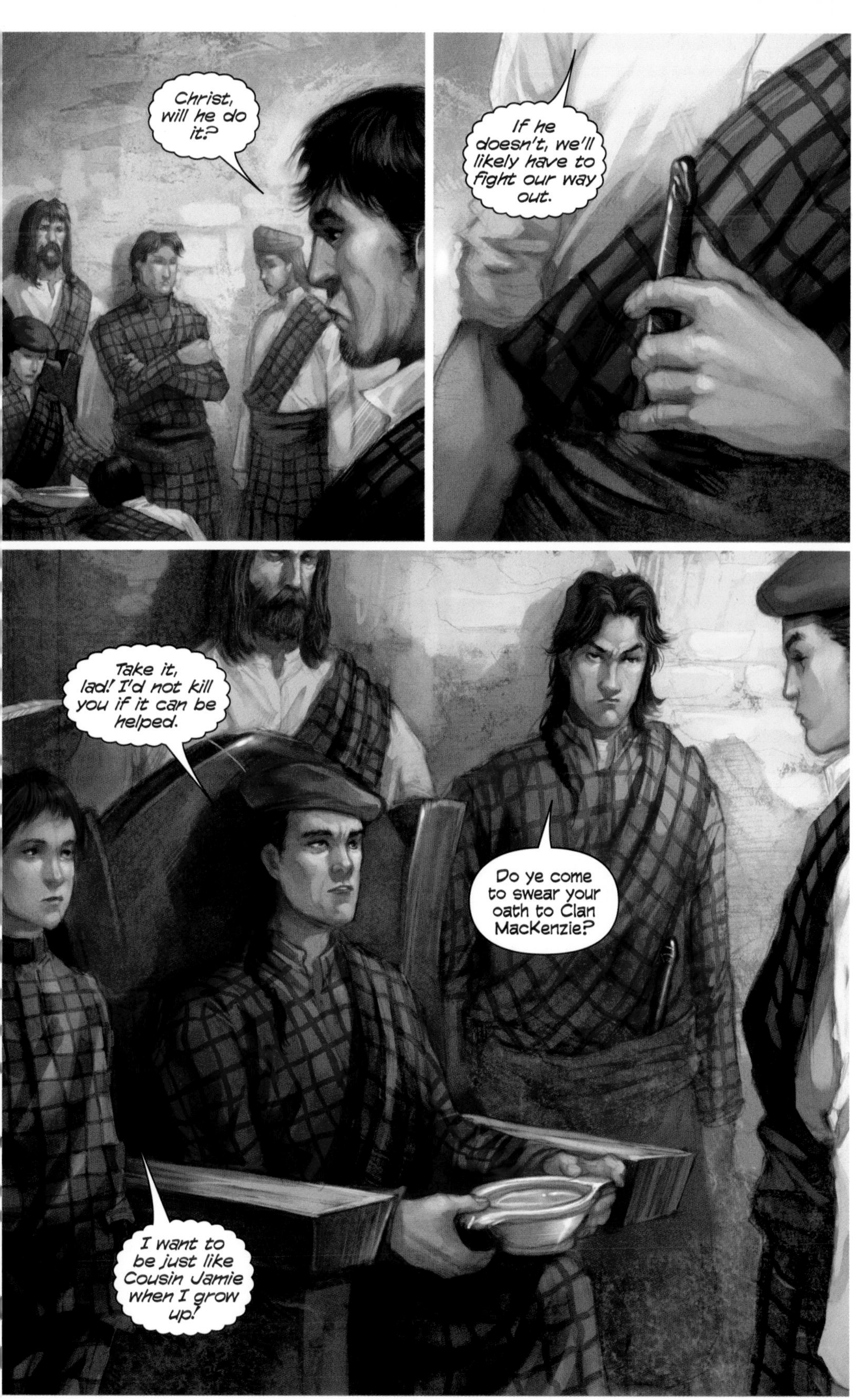
Christ, will he do it?
If he doesn't, we'll likely have to fight our way out.
Take it, lad! I'd not kill you if it can be helped.
Do ye come to swear your oath to Clan MacKenzie?
I want to be just like Cousin Jamie when I grow up!

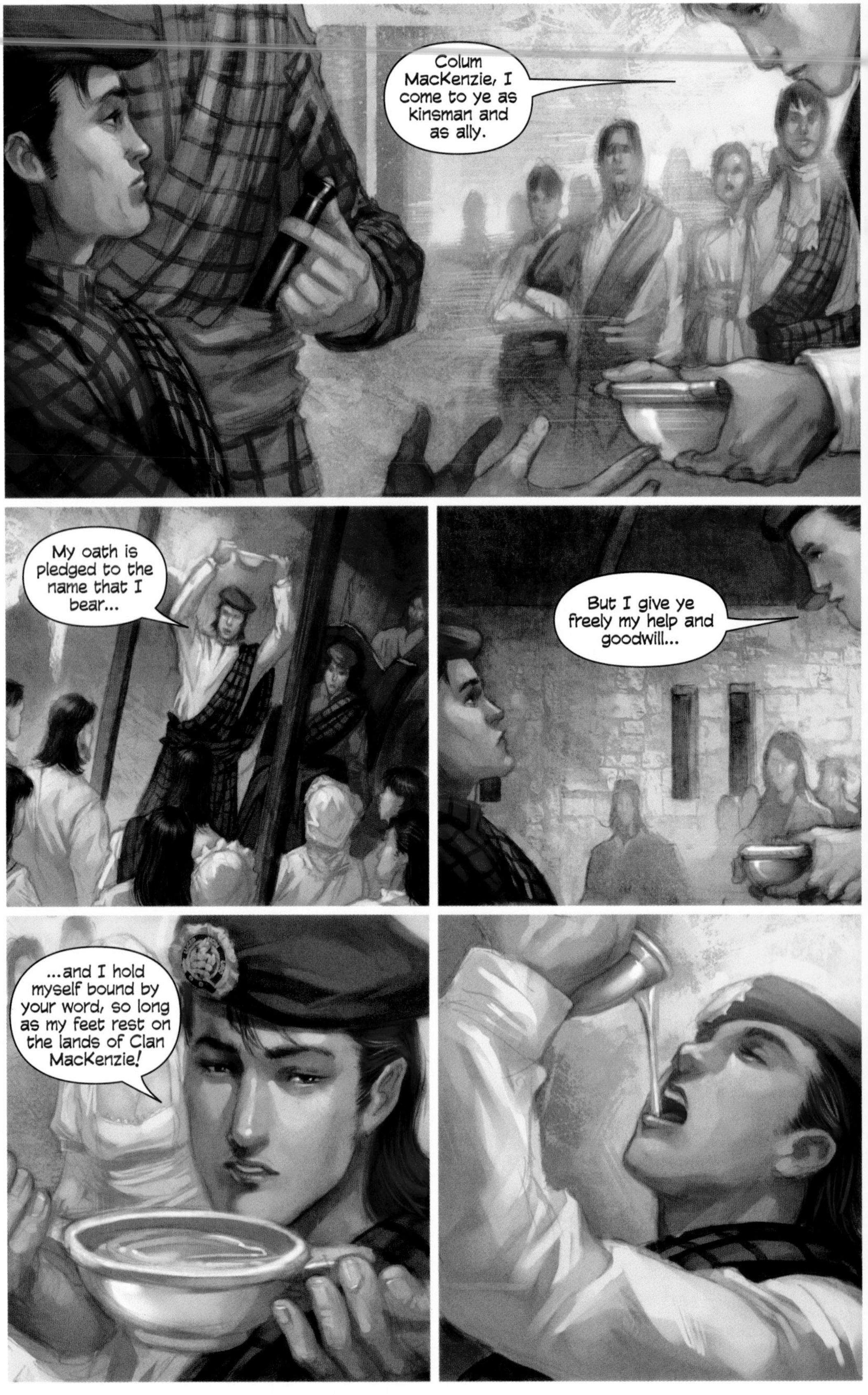
Colum MacKenzie, I come to ye as kinsman and as ally.
My oath is pledged to the name that I bear...
But I give ye freely my help and goodwill...
...and I hold myself bound by your word, so long as my feet rest on the lands of Clan MacKenzie!

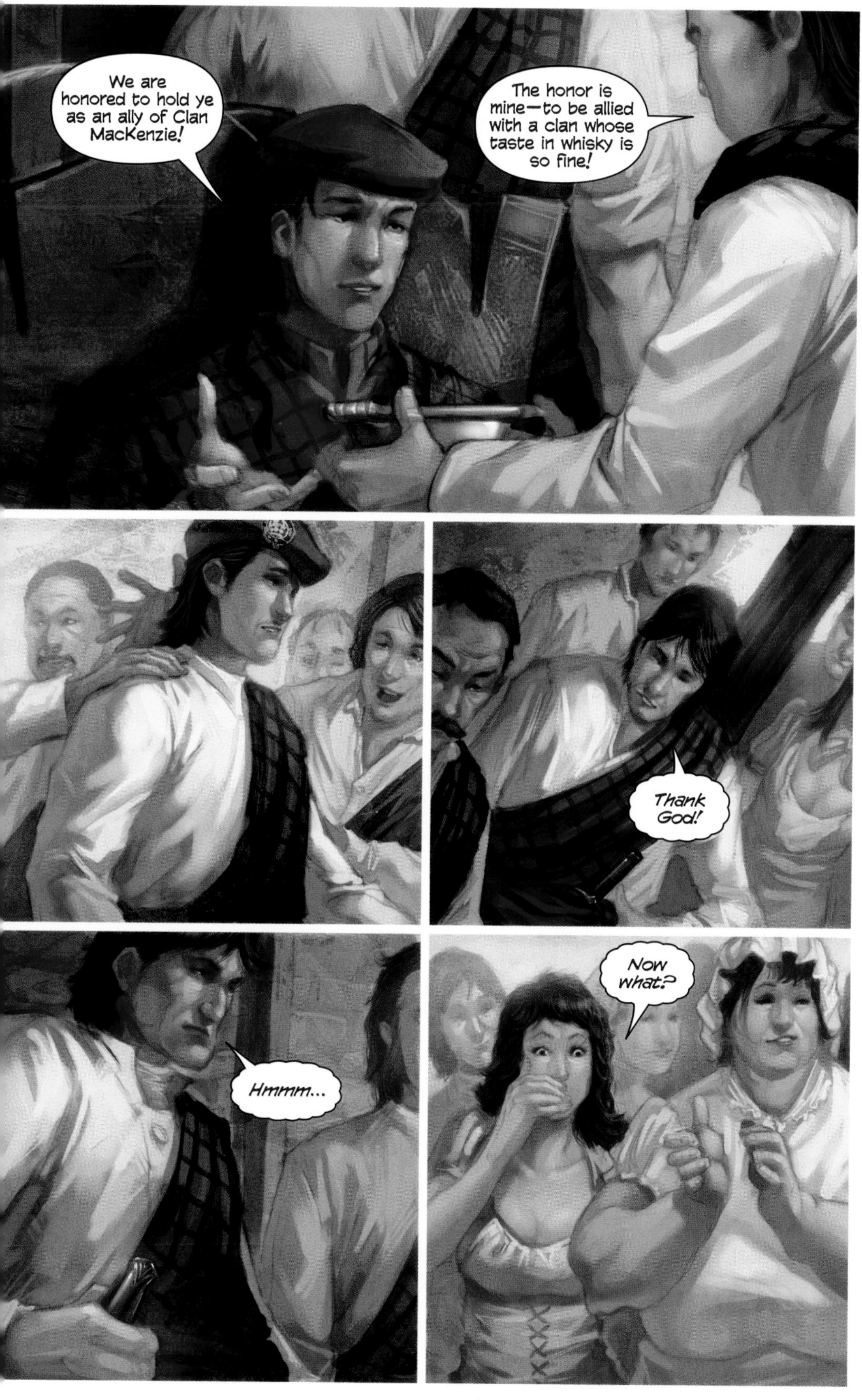
We are honored to hold ye as an ally of Clan MacKenzie!
The honor is mine—to be allied with a clan whose taste in whisky is so fine!
Thank God!
Hmmm...
Now what?

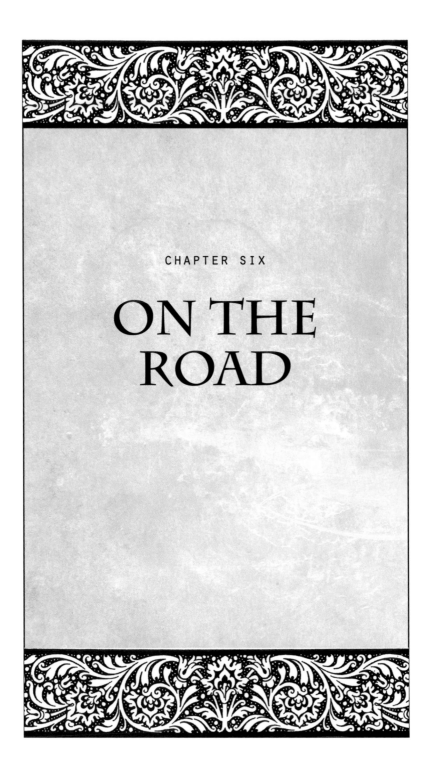

CHAPTER SIX

# ON THE ROAD

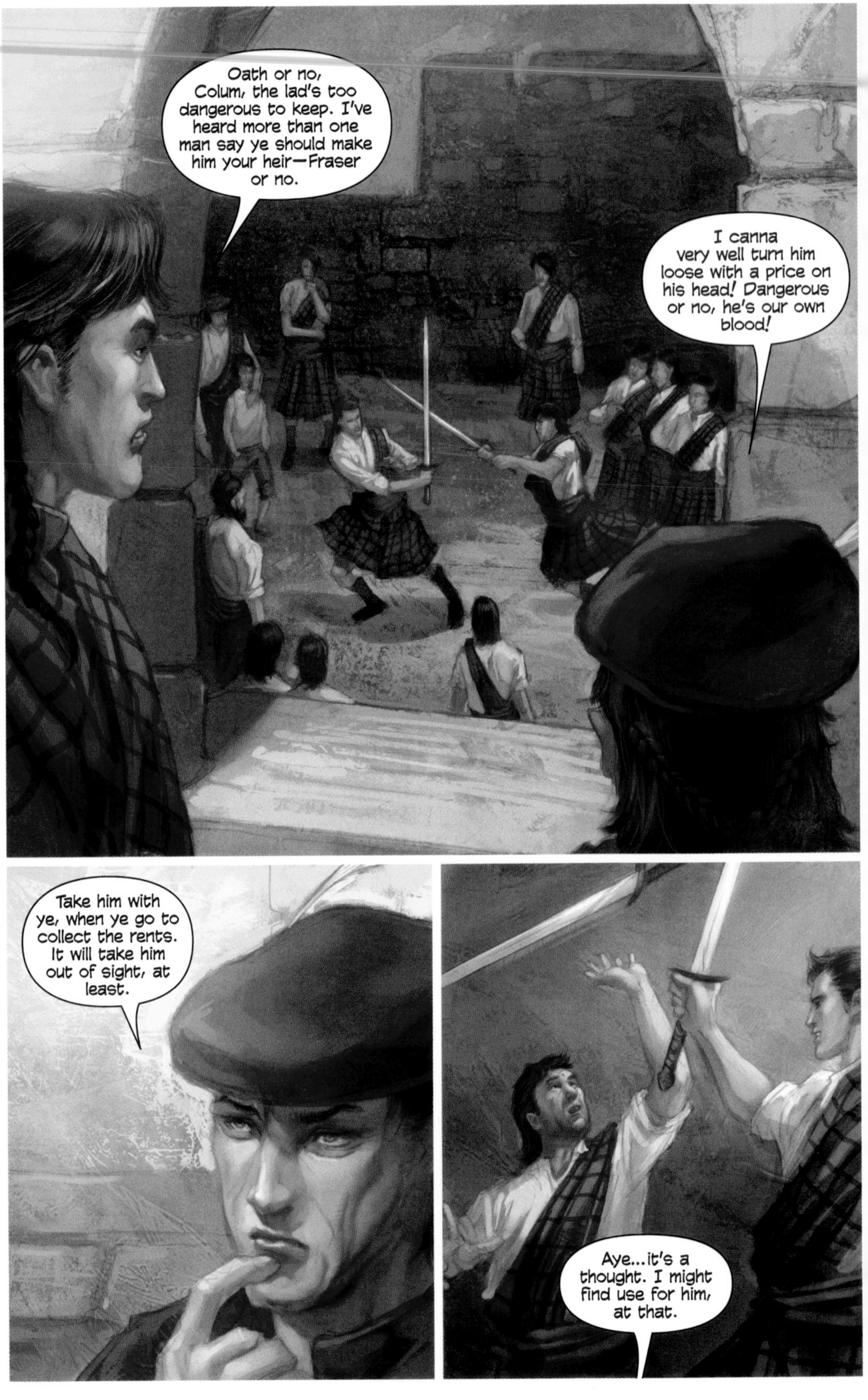
Oath or no, Colum, the lad's too dangerous to keep. I've heard more than one man say ye should make him your heir—Fraser or no.
I canna very well turn him loose with a price on his head! Dangerous or no, he's our own blood!
Take him with ye, when ye go to collect the rents. It will take him out of sight, at least.
Aye...it's a thought. I might find use for him, at that.

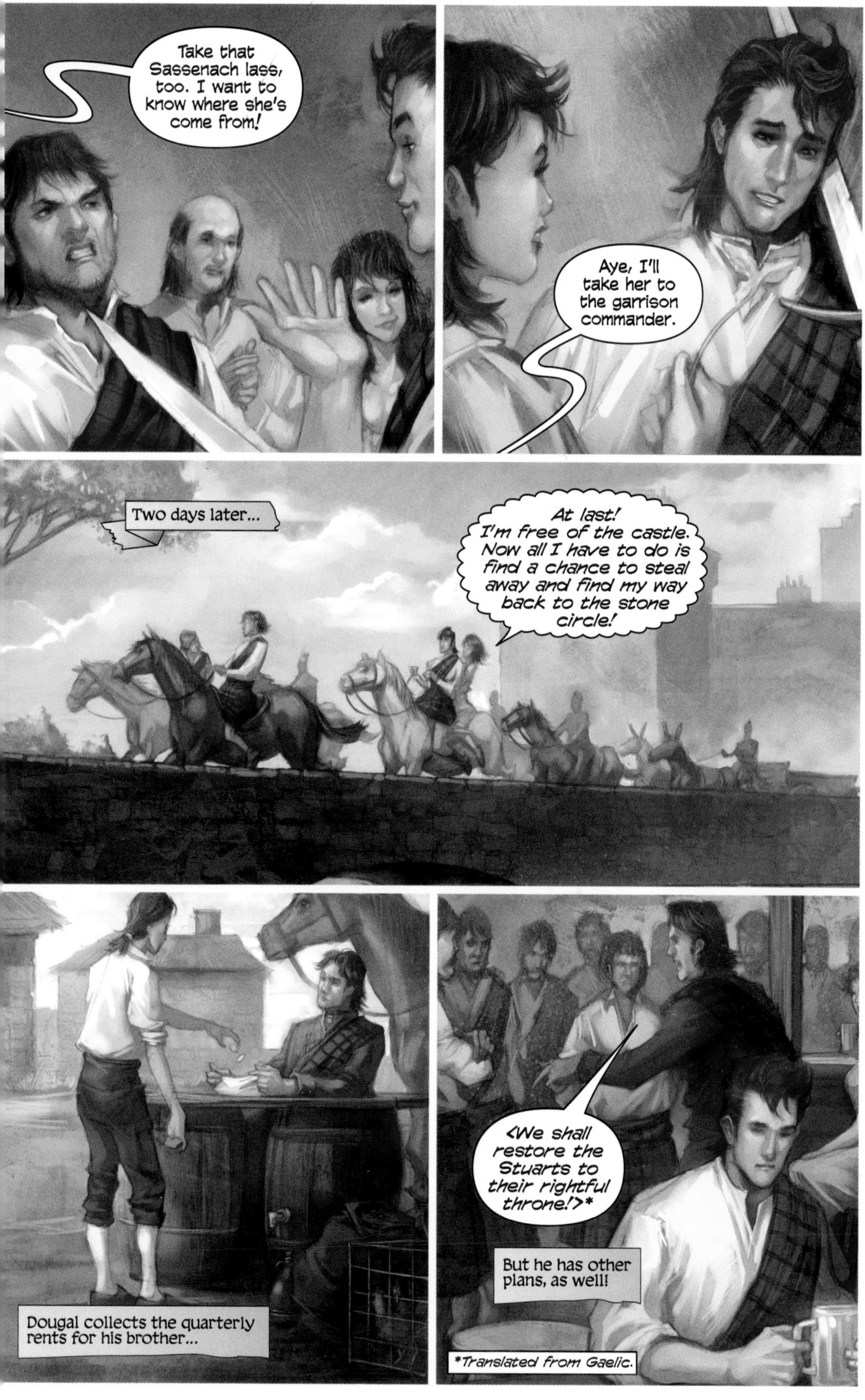
Take that Sassenach lass, too. I want to know where she's come from!
Aye, I'll take her to the garrison commander.
Two days later...
At last! I'm free of the castle. Now all I have to do is find a chance to steal away and find my way back to the stone circle!
Dougal collects the quarterly rents for his brother...
<We shall restore the Stuarts to their rightful throne!>*
But he has other plans, as well!
*Translated from Gaelic.

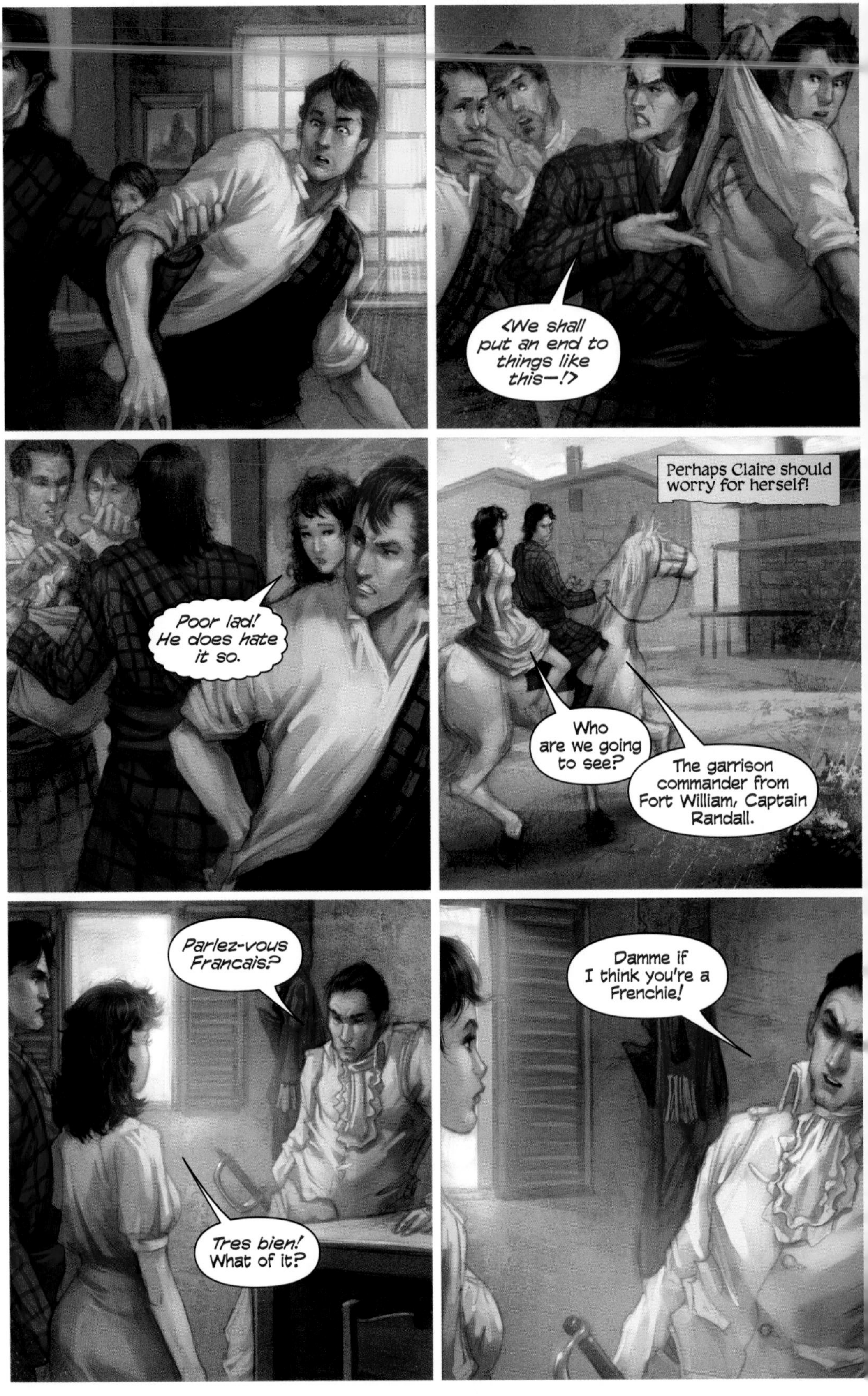
<We shall put an end to things like this—!>
Poor lad! He does hate it so.
Perhaps Claire should worry for herself!
Who are we going to see?
The garrison commander from Fort William, Captain Randall.
Parlez-vous Francais?
Tres bien! What of it?
Damme if I think you're a Frenchie!

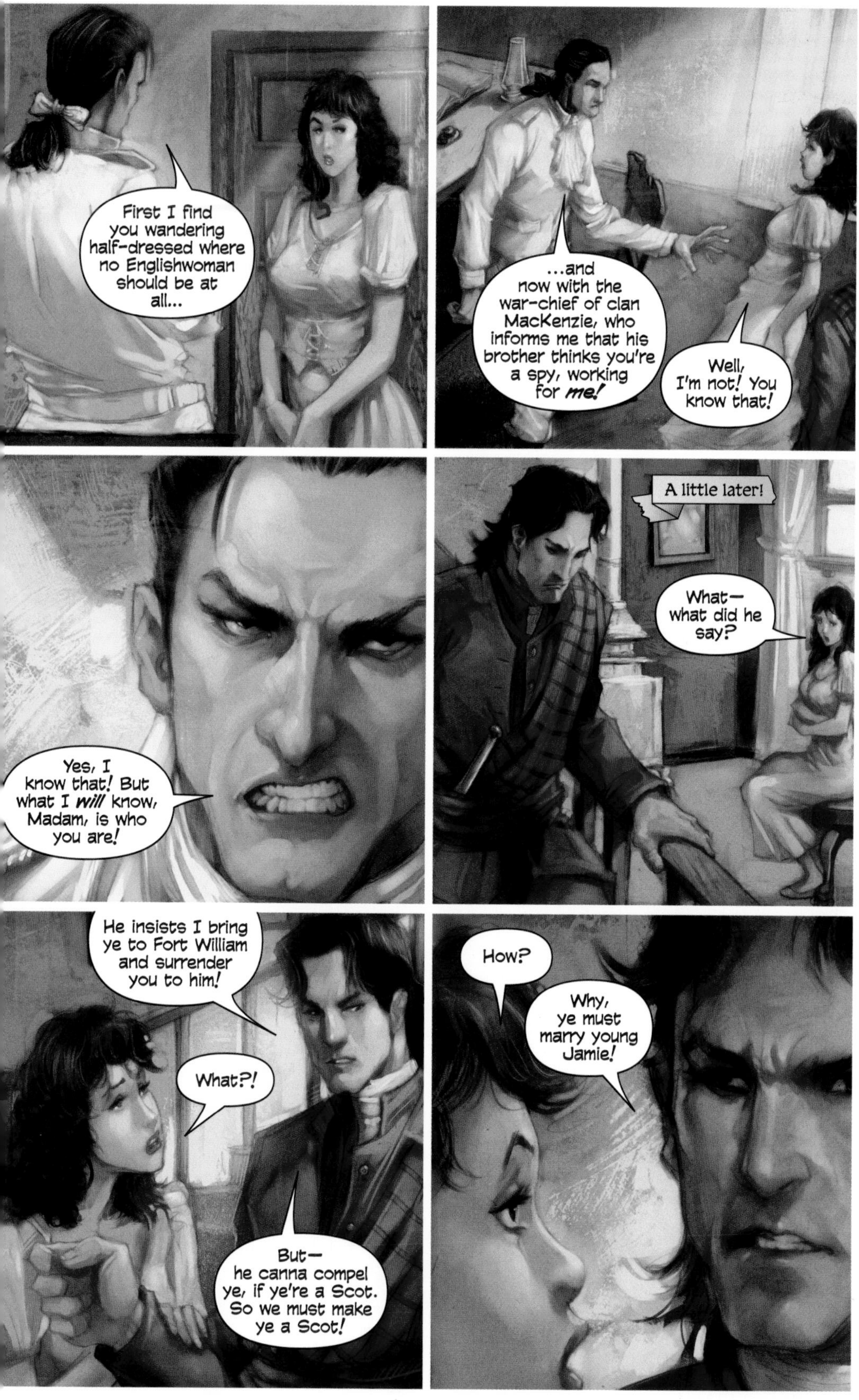

First I find you wandering half-dressed where no Englishwoman should be at all...
...and now with the war-chief of clan MacKenzie, who informs me that his brother thinks you're a spy, working for *me!*
Well, I'm not! You know that!
Yes, I know that! But what I *will* know, Madam, is who you are!
A little later!
What—what did he say?
He insists I bring ye to Fort William and surrender you to him!
What?!
But—he canna compel ye, if ye're a Scot. So we must make ye a Scot!
How?
Why, ye must marry young Jamie!

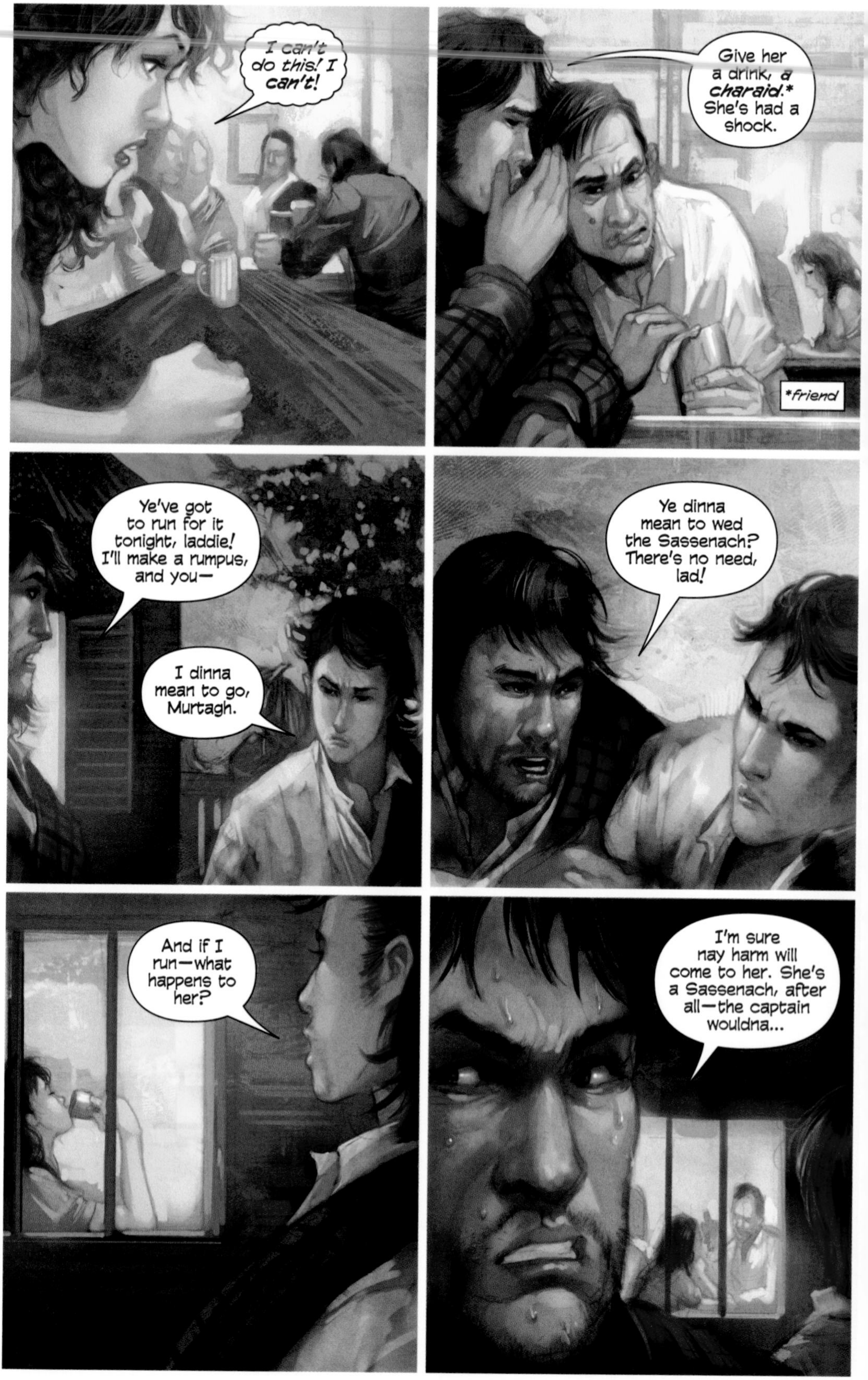
I can't do this! I can't!
Give her a drink, a charaid.* She's had a shock.
*friend
Ye've got to run for it tonight, laddie! I'll make a rumpus, and you—
I dinna mean to go, Murtagh.
Ye dinna mean to wed the Sassenach? There's no need, lad!
And if I run—what happens to her?
I'm sure nay harm will come to her. She's a Sassenach, after all—the captain wouldna...

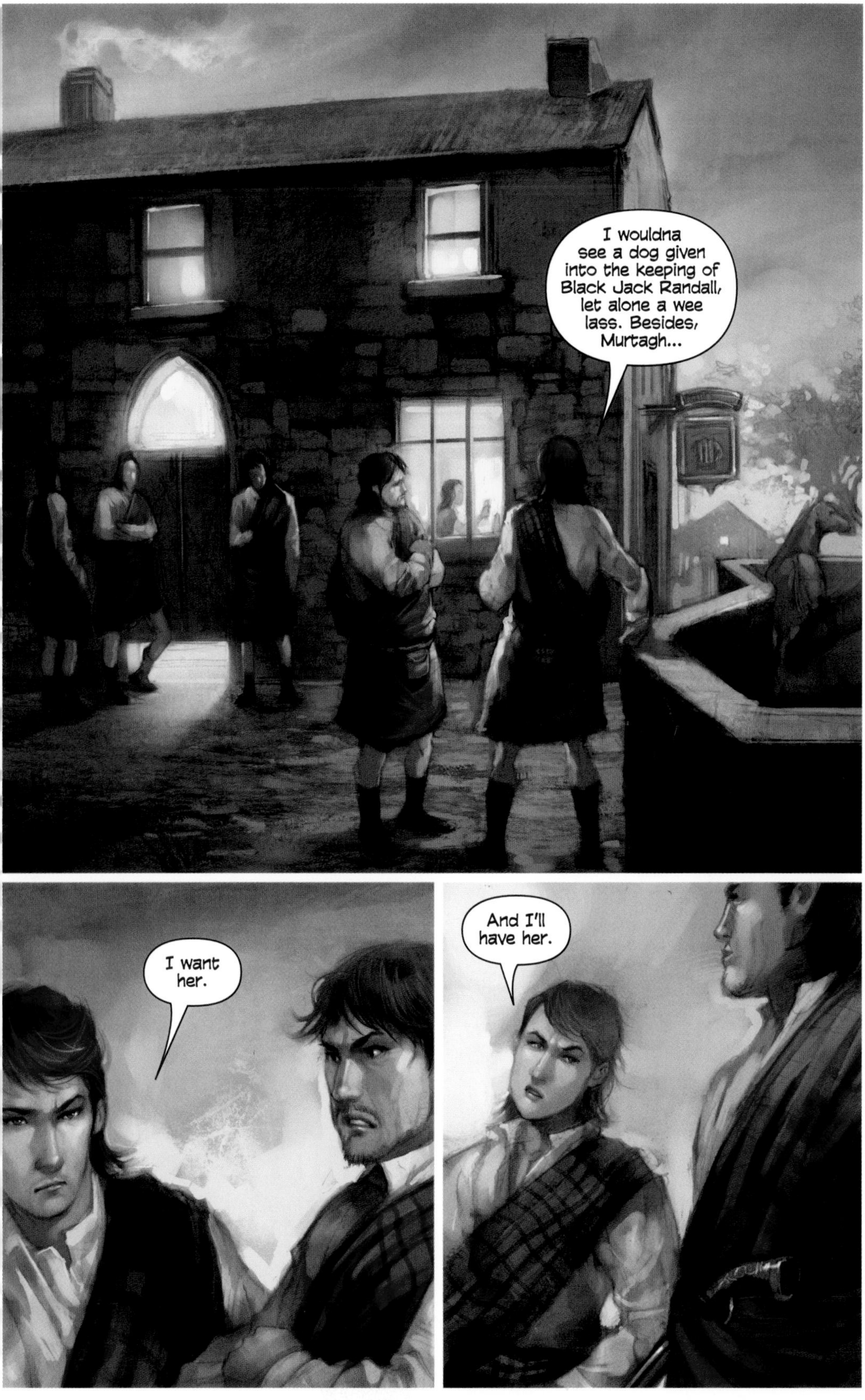
I wouldna see a dog given into the keeping of Black Jack Randall, let alone a wee lass. Besides, Murtagh...
I want her.
And I'll have her.

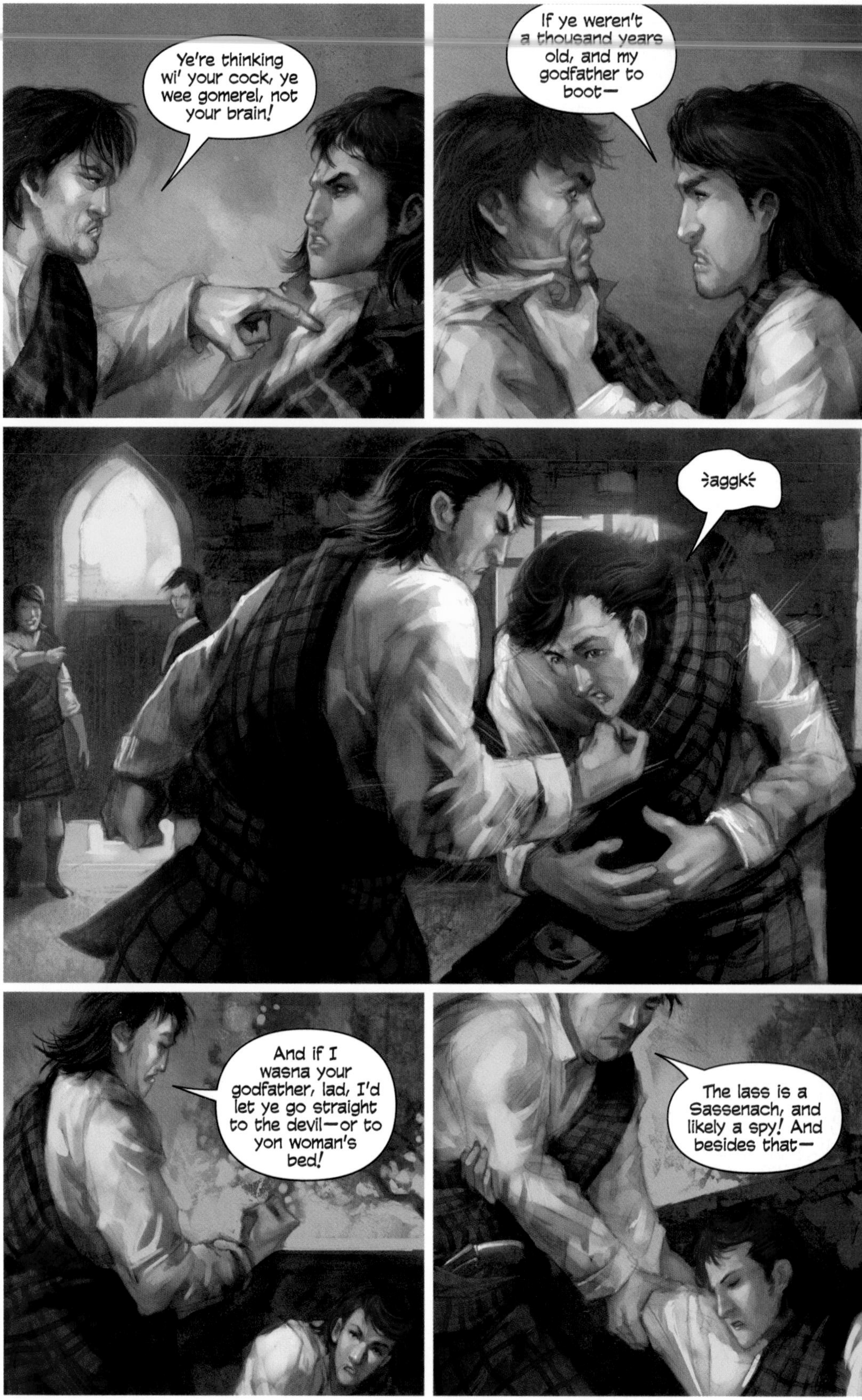
Ye're thinking wi' your cock, ye wee gomerel, not your brain!
If ye weren't a thousand years old, and my godfather to boot—
>aggk<
And if I wasna your godfather, lad, I'd let ye go straight to the devil—or to yon woman's bed!
The lass is a Sassenach, and likely a spy! And besides that—

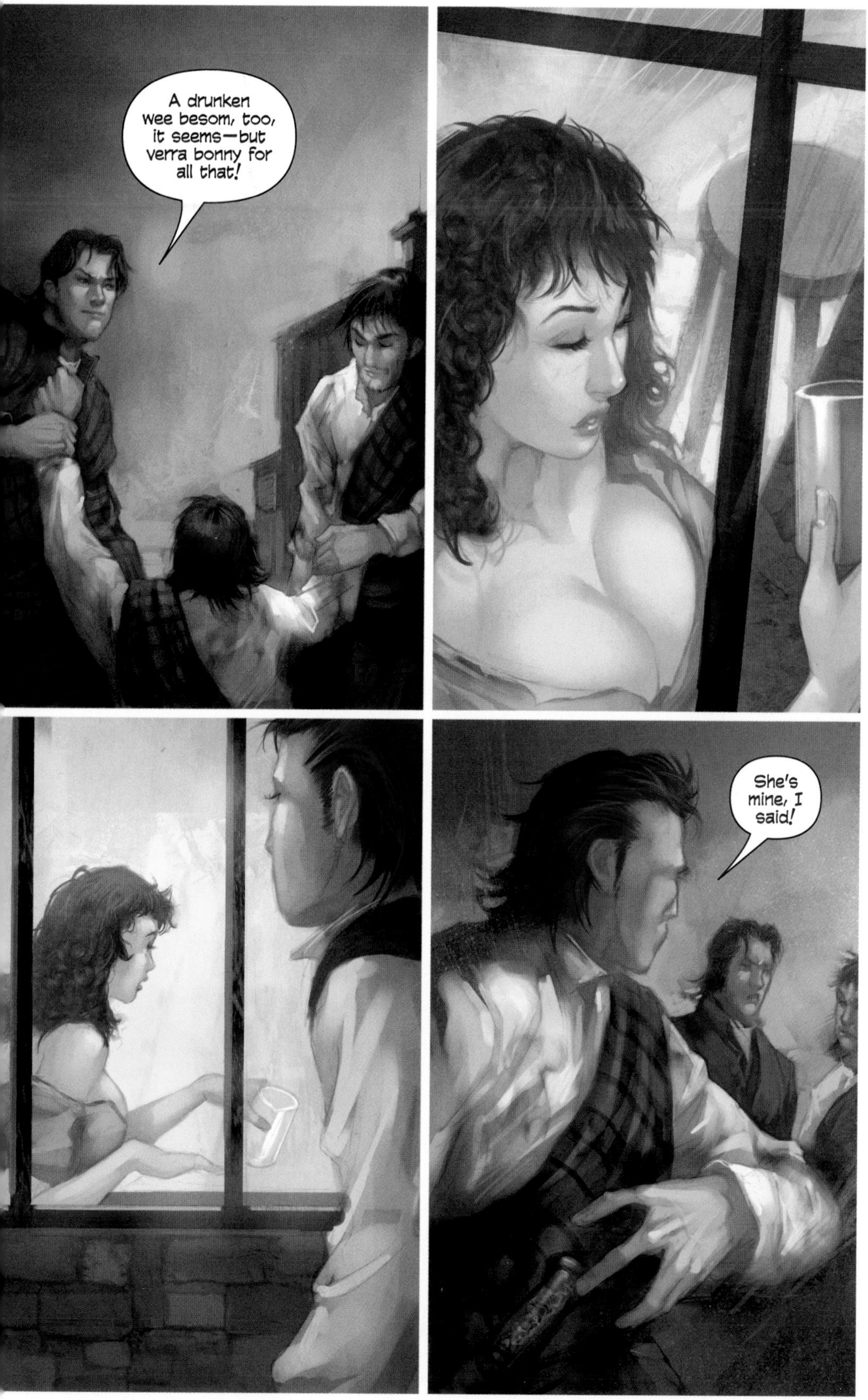
A drunken wee besom, too, it seems—but verra bonny for all that!
She's mine, I said!

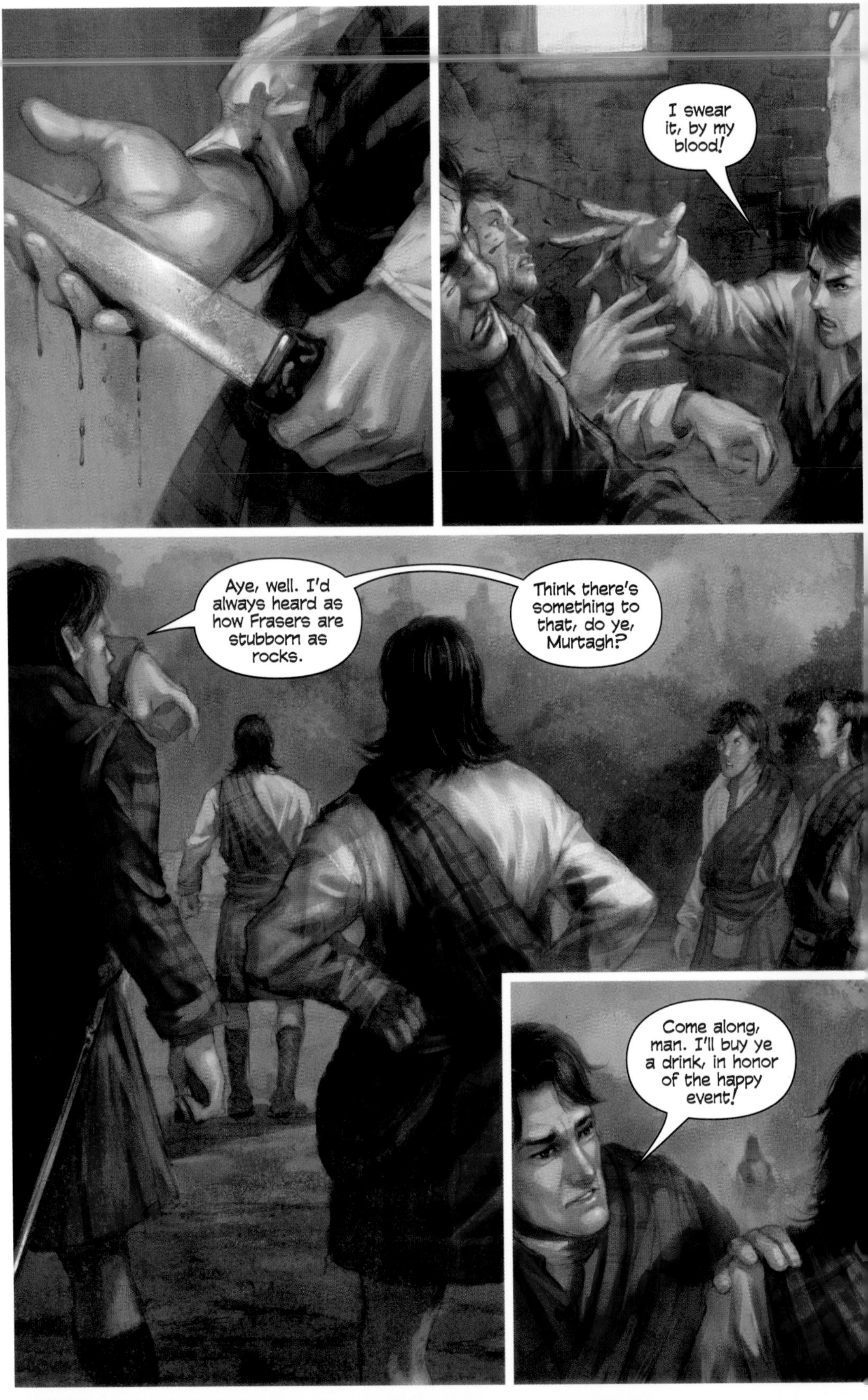
I swear it, by my blood!
Aye, well. I'd always heard as how Frasers are stubborn as rocks.
Think there's something to that, do ye, Murtagh?
Come along, man. I'll buy ye a drink, in honor of the happy event!

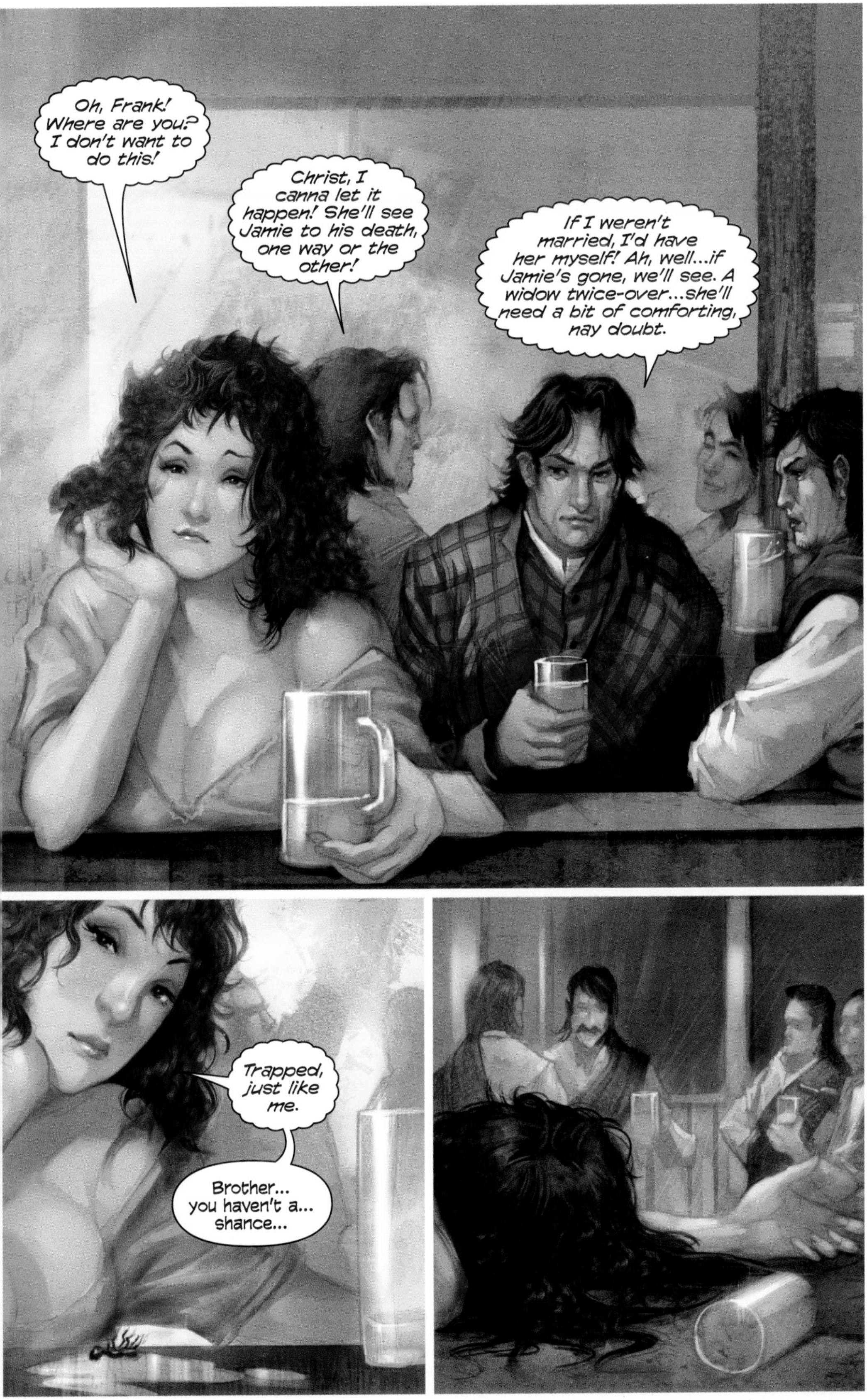
Oh, Frank! Where are you? I don't want to do this!
Christ, I canna let it happen! She'll see Jamie to his death, one way or the other!
If I weren't married, I'd have her myself! Ah, well...if Jamie's gone, we'll see. A widow twice-over...she'll need a bit of comforting, nay doubt.
Trapped, just like me.
Brother... you haven't a... shance...

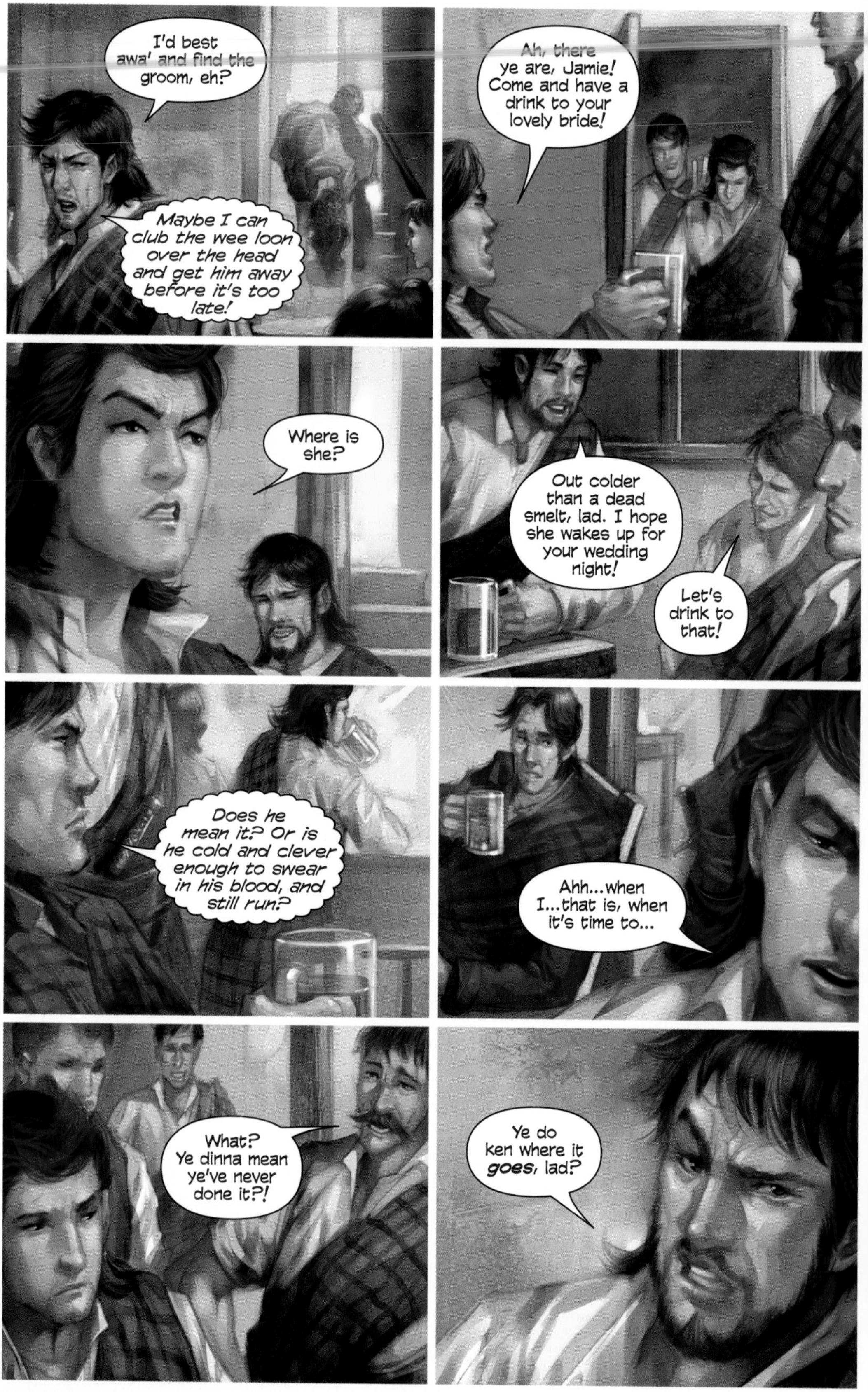
I'd best awa' and find the groom, eh?
Maybe I can club the wee loon over the head and get him away before it's too late!
Ah, there ye are, Jamie! Come and have a drink to your lovely bride!
Where is she?
Out colder than a dead smelt, lad. I hope she wakes up for your wedding night!
Let's drink to that!
Does he mean it? Or is he cold and clever enough to swear in his blood, and still run?
Ahh...when I...that is, when it's time to...
What? Ye dinna mean ye've never done it?!
Ye do ken where it goes, lad?

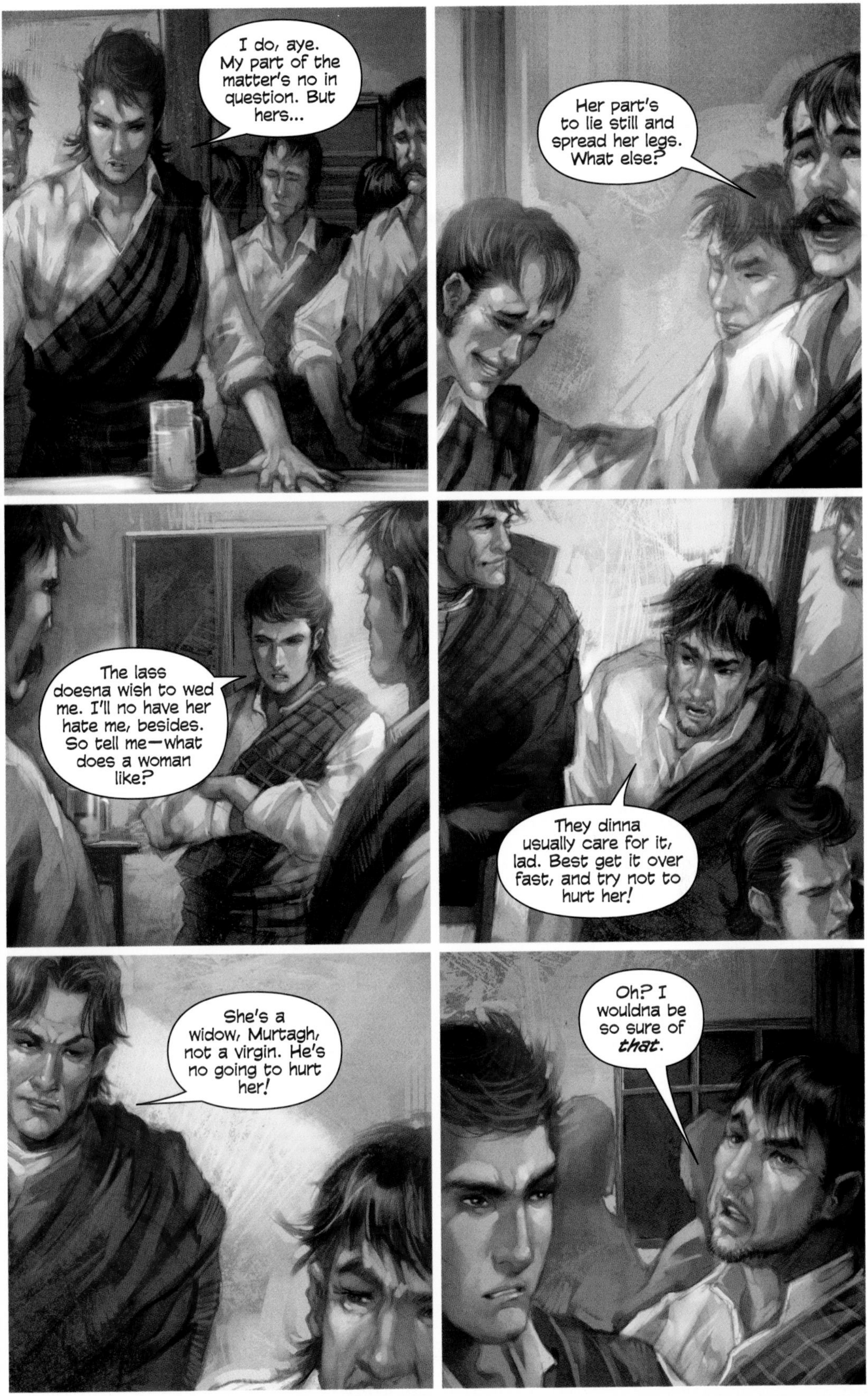
I do, aye. My part of the matter's no in question. But hers...
Her part's to lie still and spread her legs. What else?
The lass doesna wish to wed me. I'll no have her hate me, besides. So tell me—what does a woman like?
They dinna usually care for it, lad. Best get it over fast, and try not to hurt her!
She's a widow, Murtagh, not a virgin. He's no going to hurt her!
Oh? I wouldna be so sure of *that*.

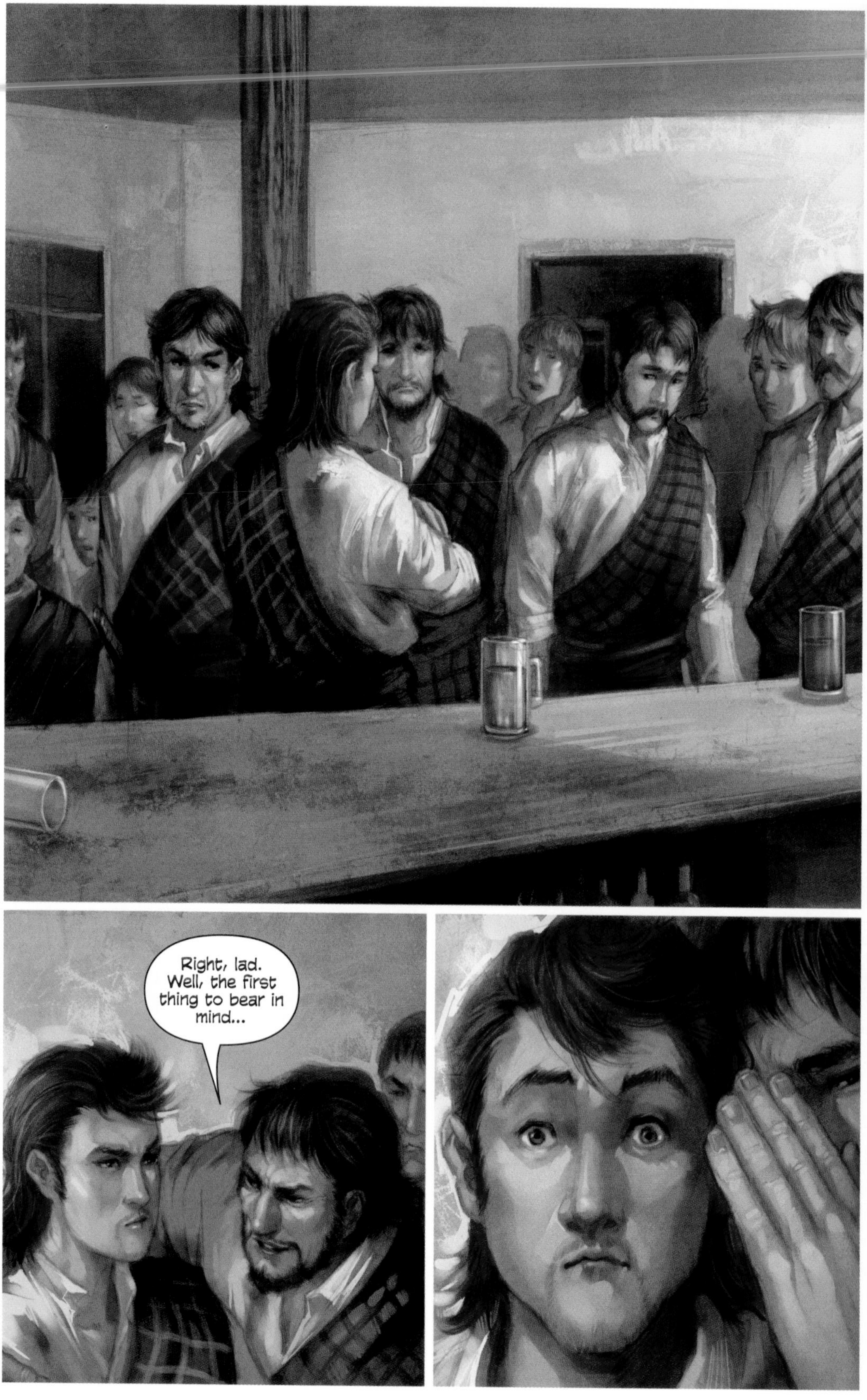
Right, lad. Well, the first thing to bear in mind...

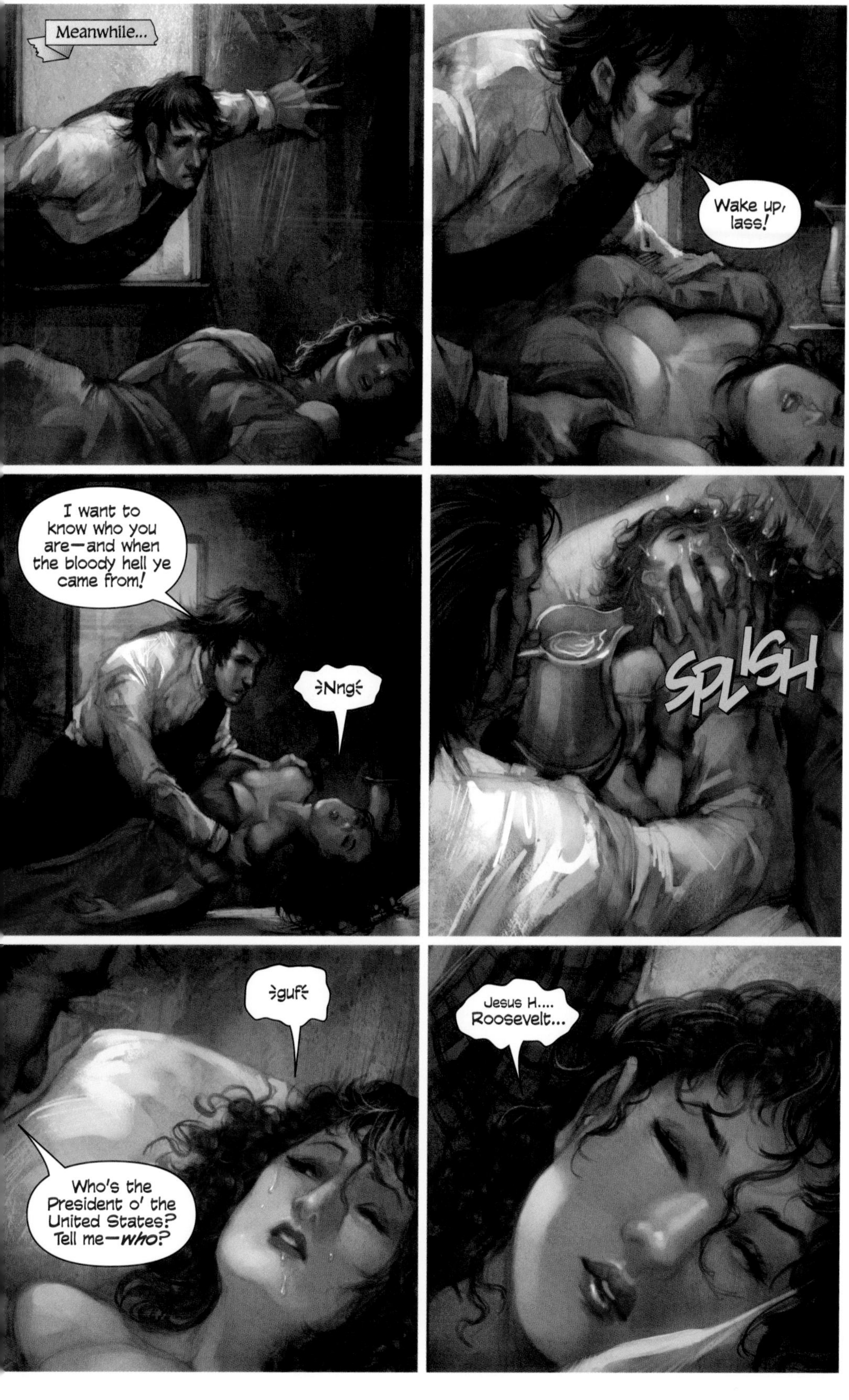
Meanwhile...
Wake up, lass!
I want to know who you are—and when the bloody hell ye came from!
Nng
SPLISH
guf
Who's the President o' the United States? Tell me—*who*?
Jesus H.... Roosevelt...

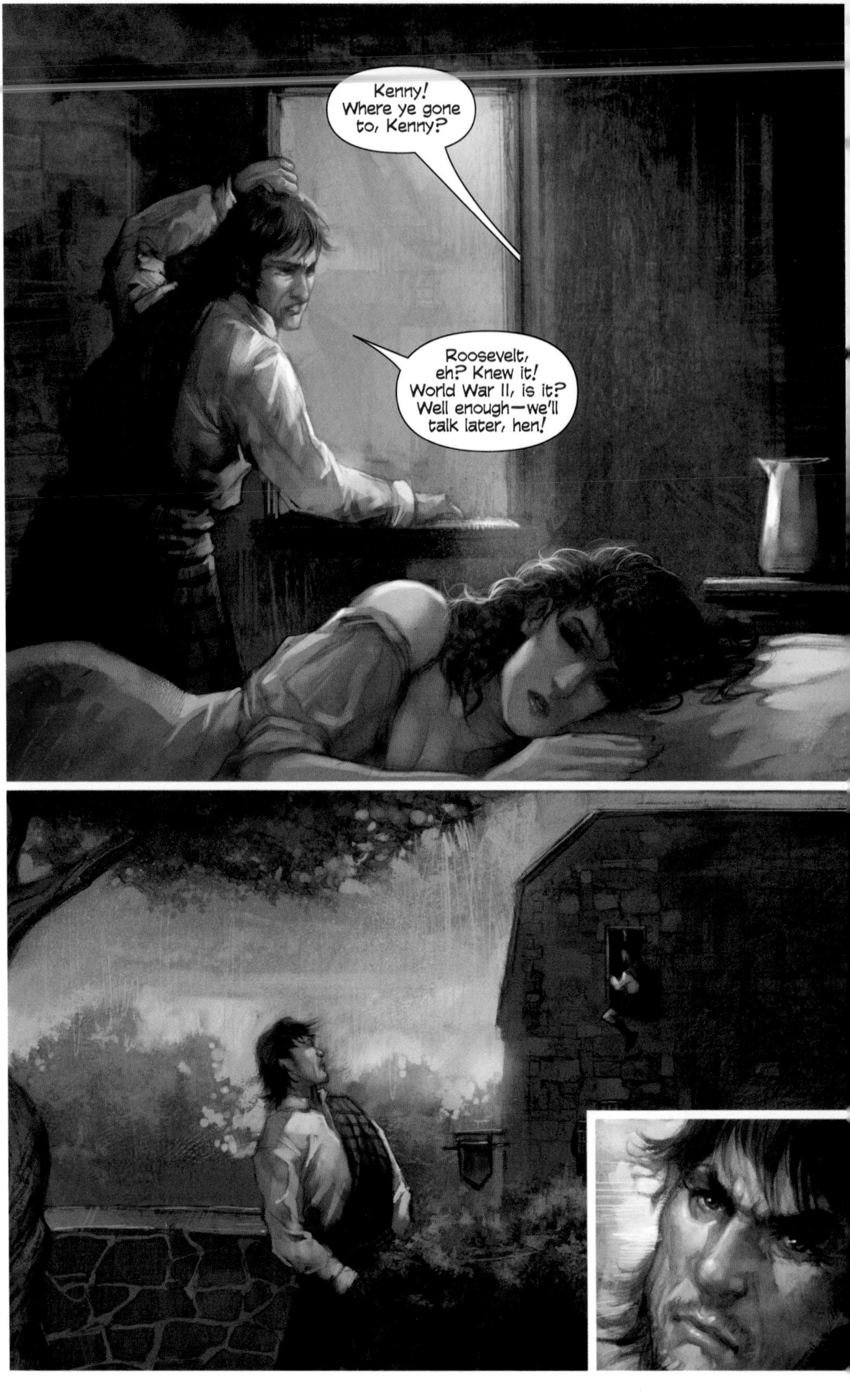
Kenny! Where ye gone to, Kenny?
Roosevelt, eh? Knew it! World War II, is it? Well enough—we'll talk later, hen!

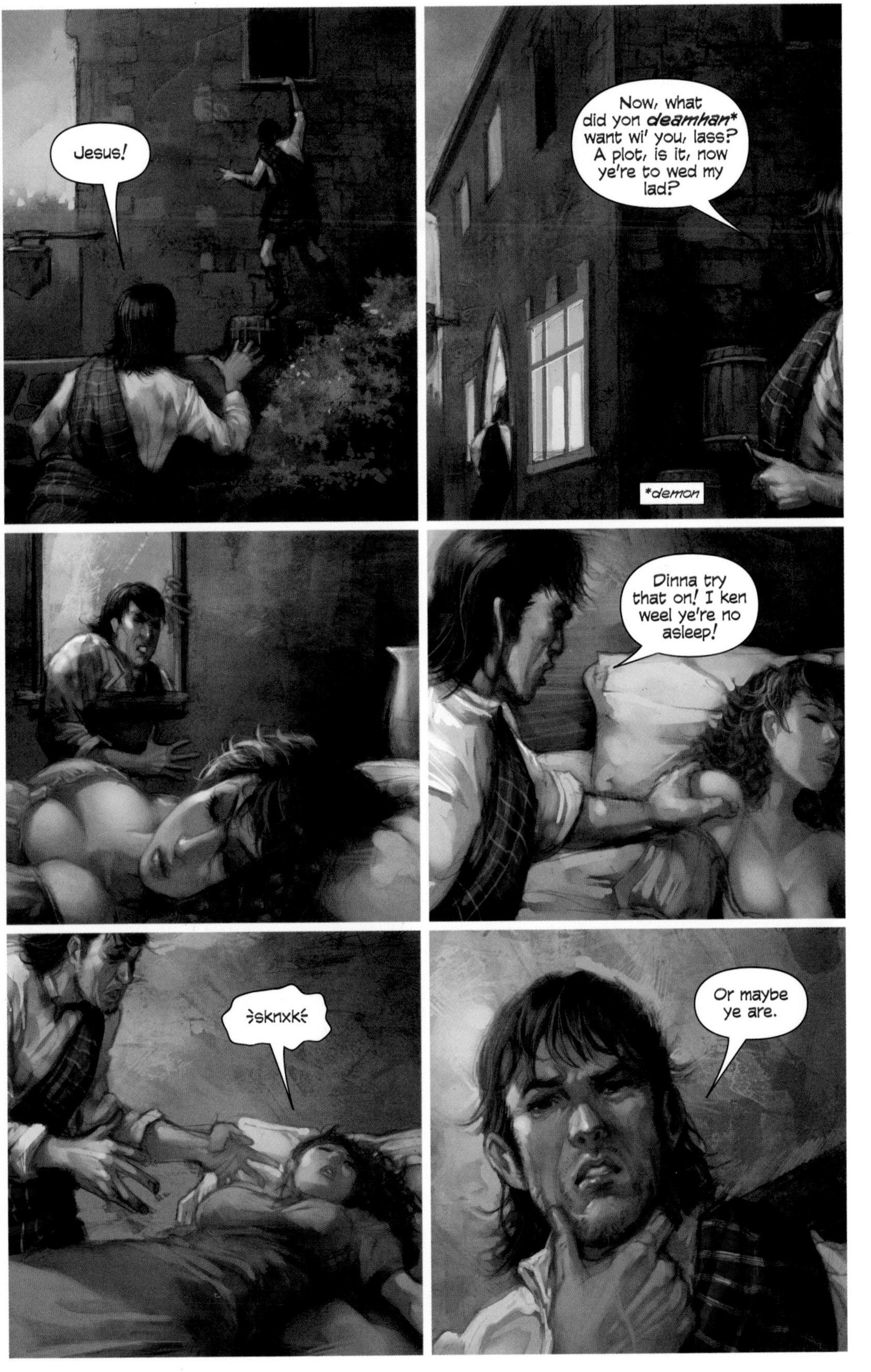
Jesus!
Now, what did yon *deamhan** want wi' you, lass? A plot, is it, now ye're to wed my lad?
*demon
Dinna try that on! I ken weel ye're no asleep!
sknxk
Or maybe ye are.

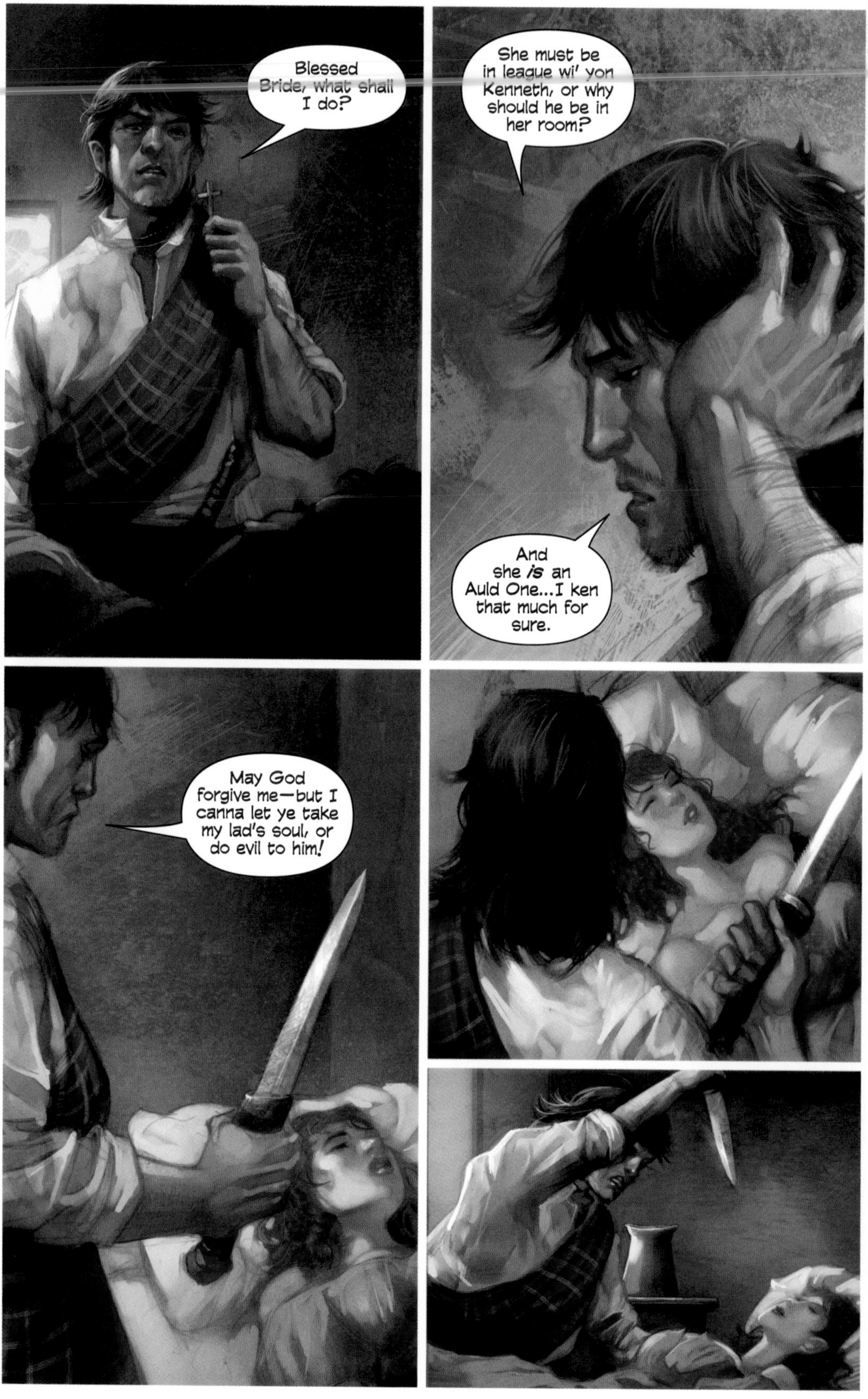
Blessed Bride, what shall I do?
She must be in league wi' yon Kenneth, or why should he be in her room?
And she *is* an Auld One...I ken that much for sure.
May God forgive me—but I canna let ye take my lad's soul, or do evil to him!

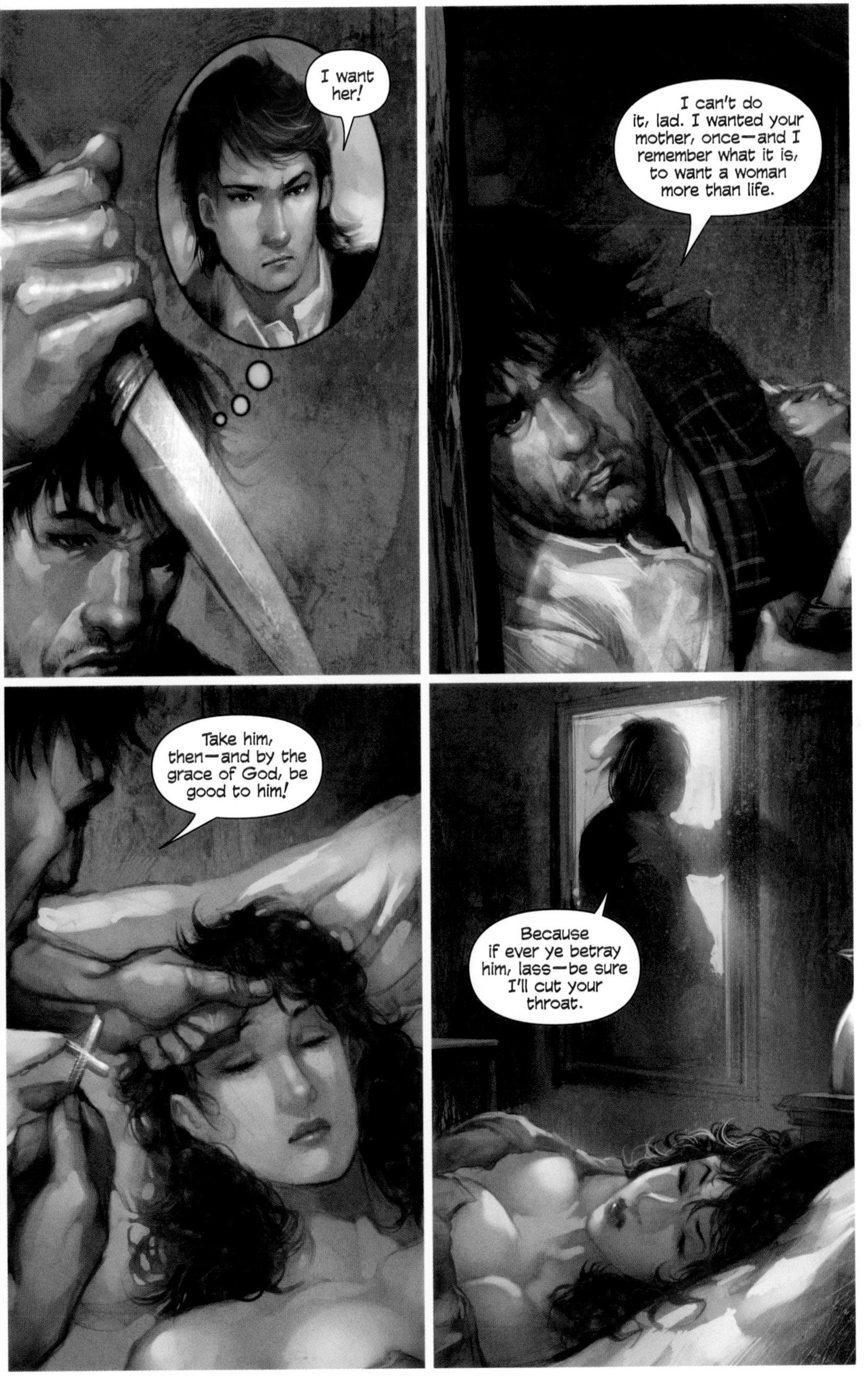
I want her!
I can't do it, lad. I wanted your mother, once—and I remember what it is, to want a woman more than life.
Take him, then—and by the grace of God, be good to him!
Because if ever ye betray him, lass—be sure I'll cut your throat.

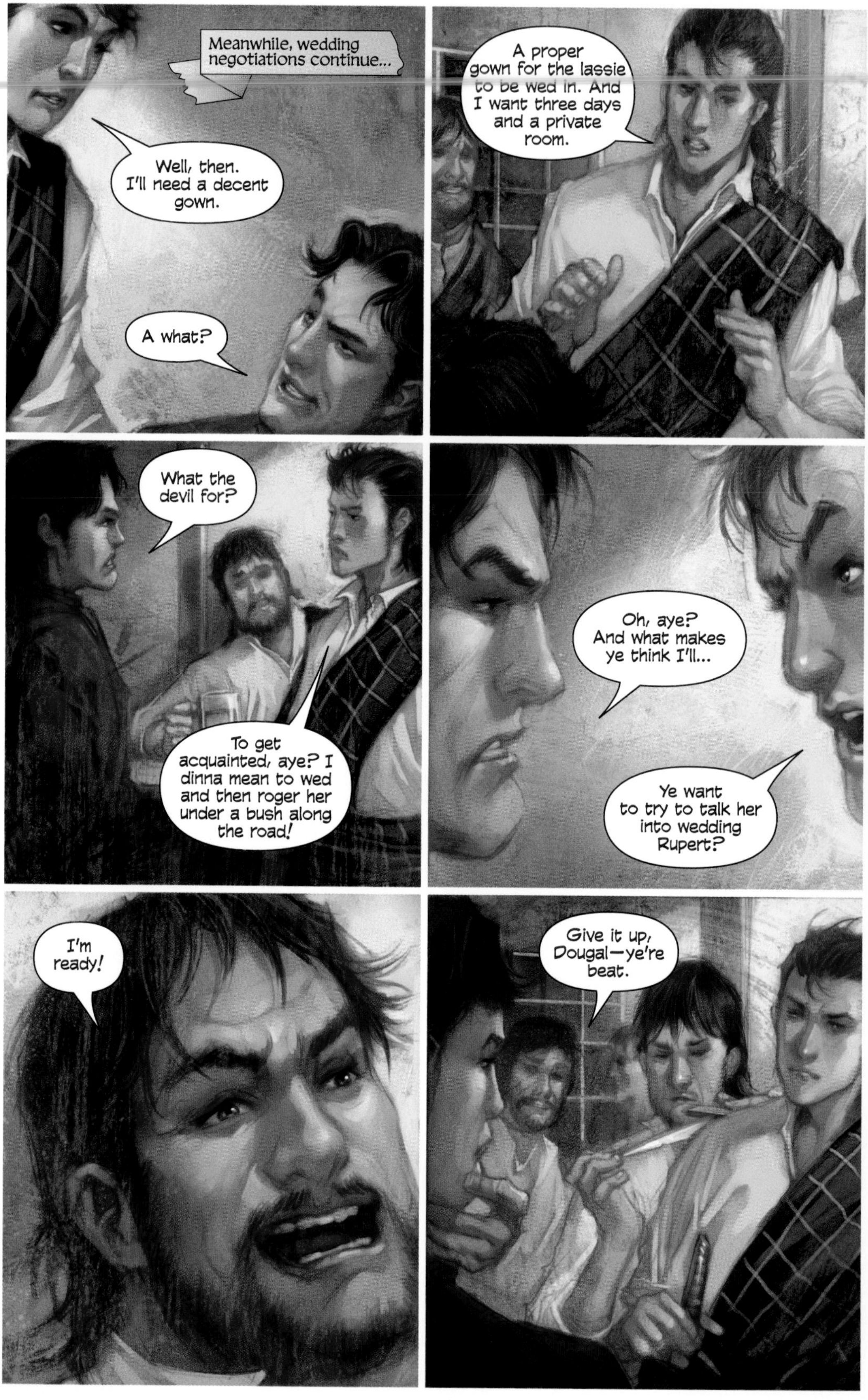
Meanwhile, wedding negotiations continue...
Well, then. I'll need a decent gown.
A what?
A proper gown for the lassie to be wed in. And I want three days and a private room.
What the devil for?
To get acquainted, aye? I dinna mean to wed and then roger her under a bush along the road!
Oh, aye? And what makes ye think I'll...
Ye want to try to talk her into wedding Rupert?
I'm ready!
Give it up, Dougal—ye're beat.

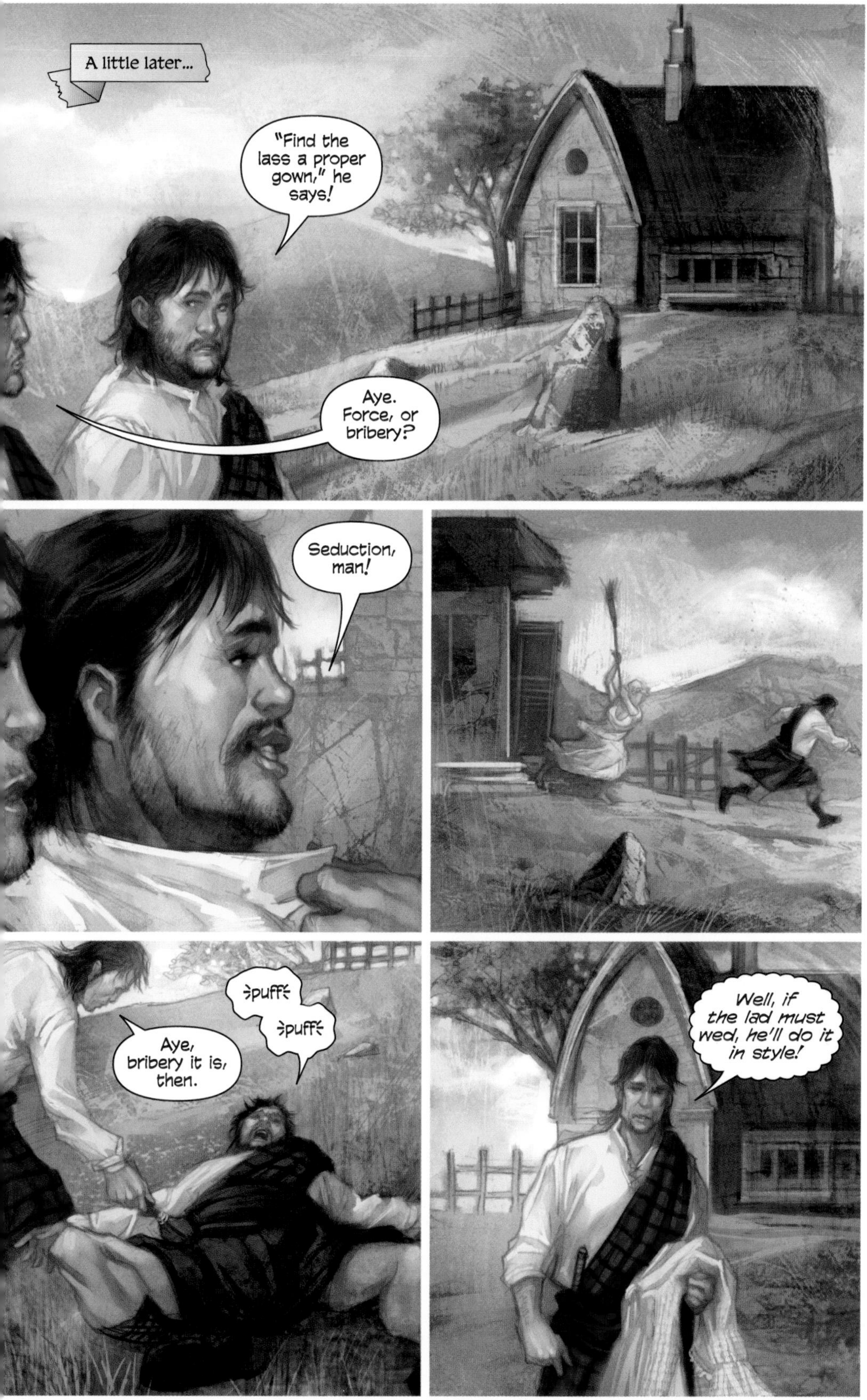
A little later...
"Find the lass a proper gown," he says!
Aye. Force, or bribery?
Seduction, man!
Aye, bribery it is, then.
puff
puff
Well, if the lad must wed, he'll do it in style!

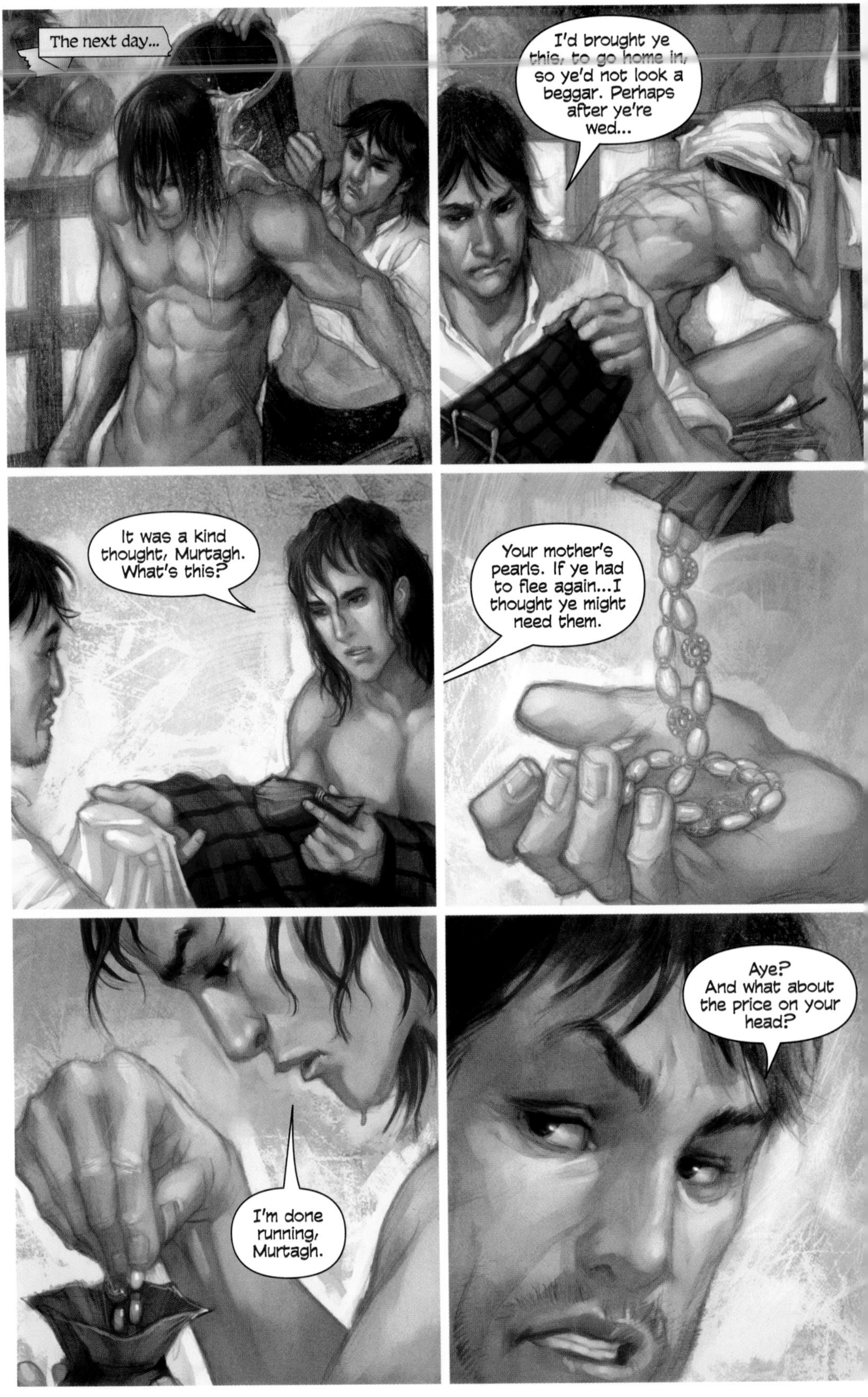
The next day...
I'd brought ye this, to go home in, so ye'd not look a beggar. Perhaps after ye're wed...
It was a kind thought, Murtagh. What's this?
Your mother's pearls. If ye had to flee again...I thought ye might need them.
I'm done running, Murtagh.
Aye? And what about the price on your head?

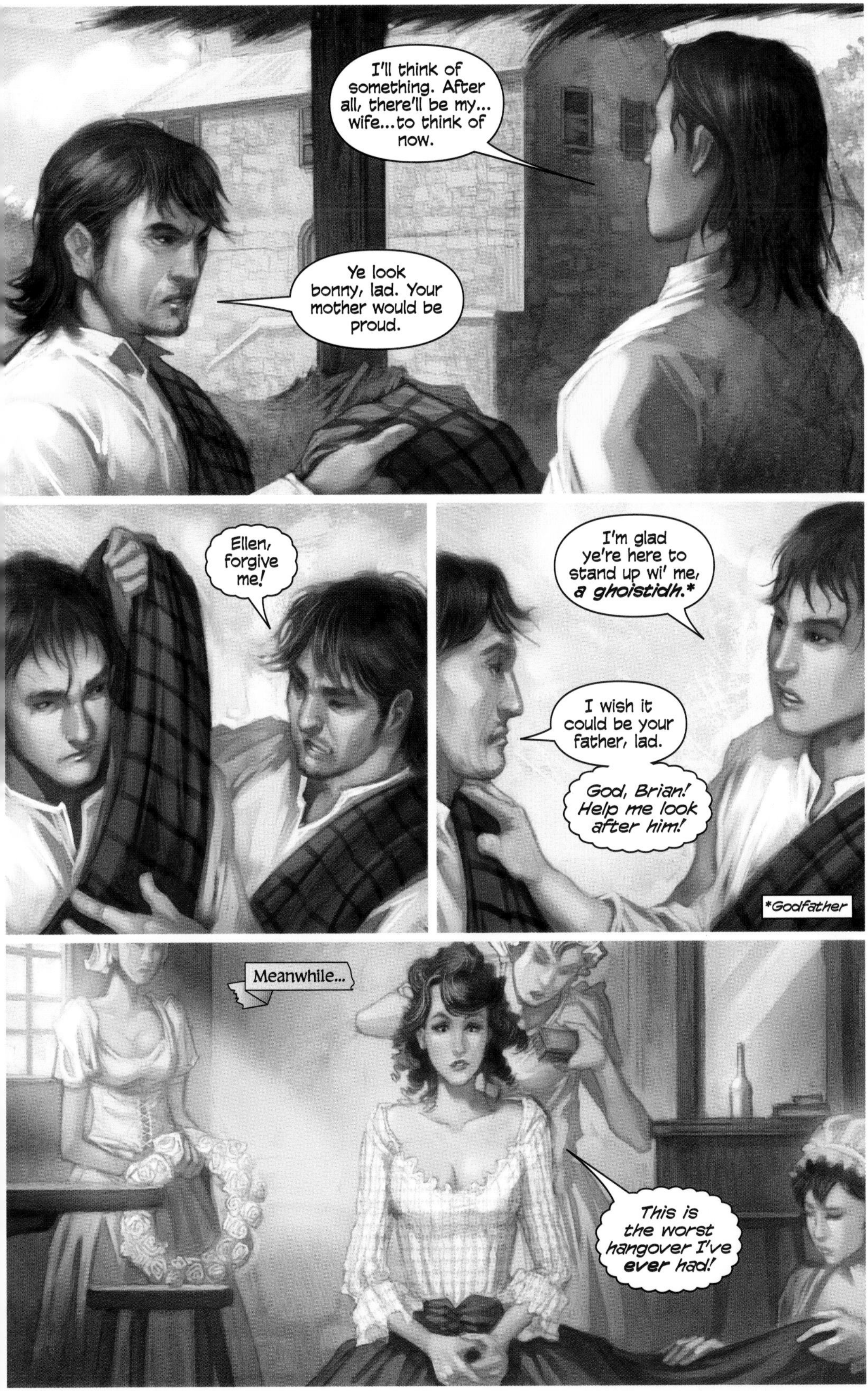
I'll think of something. After all, there'll be my... wife...to think of now.
Ye look bonny, lad. Your mother would be proud.
Ellen, forgive me!
I'm glad ye're here to stand up wi' me, a ghoistidh.*
I wish it could be your father, lad.
God, Brian! Help me look after him!
*Godfather
Meanwhile...
This is the worst hangover I've ever had!

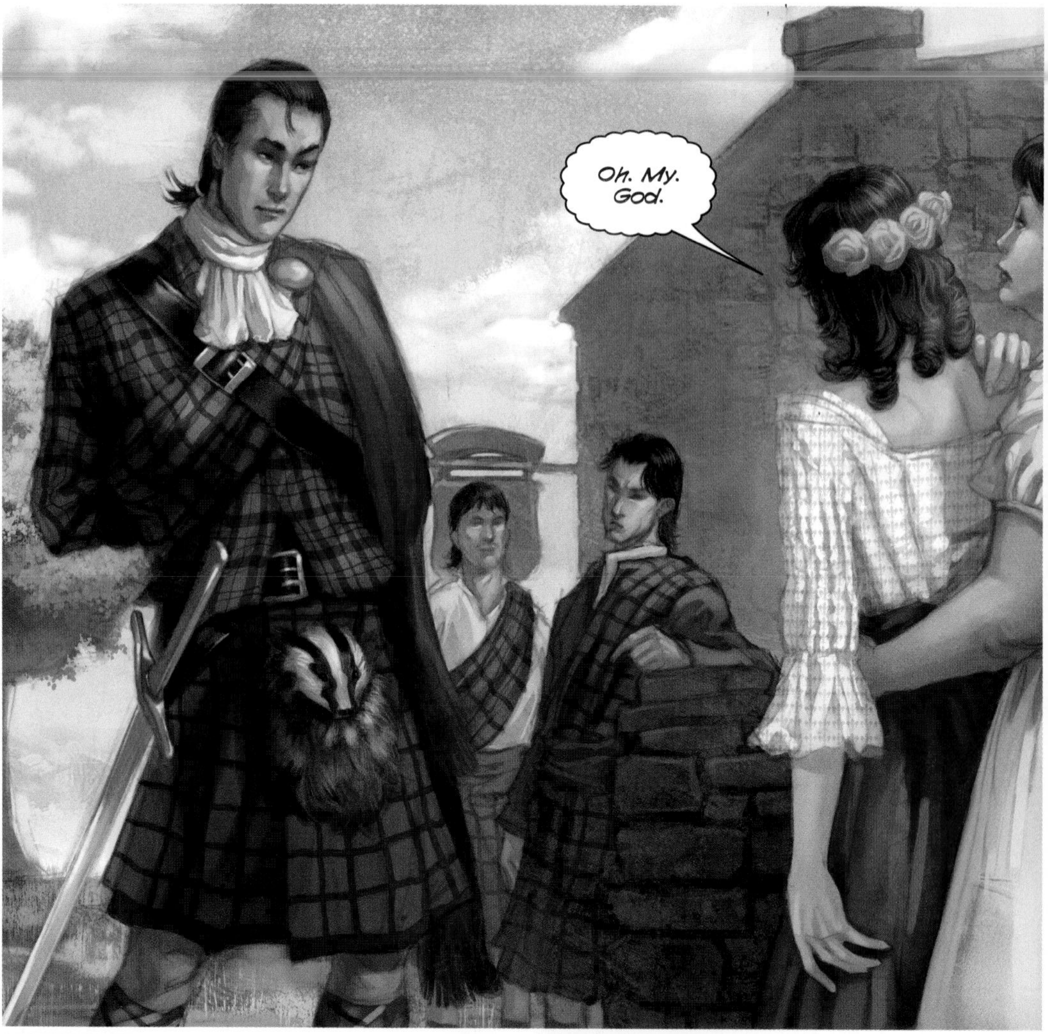
Oh. My. God.

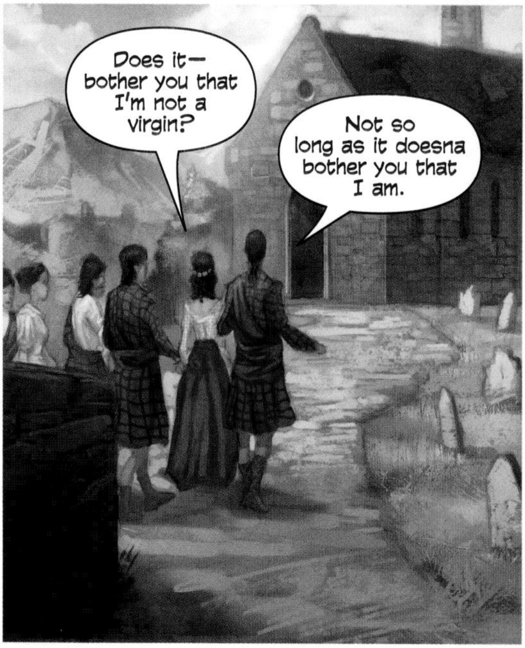
Does it—bother you that I'm not a virgin?
Not so long as it doesna bother you that I am.

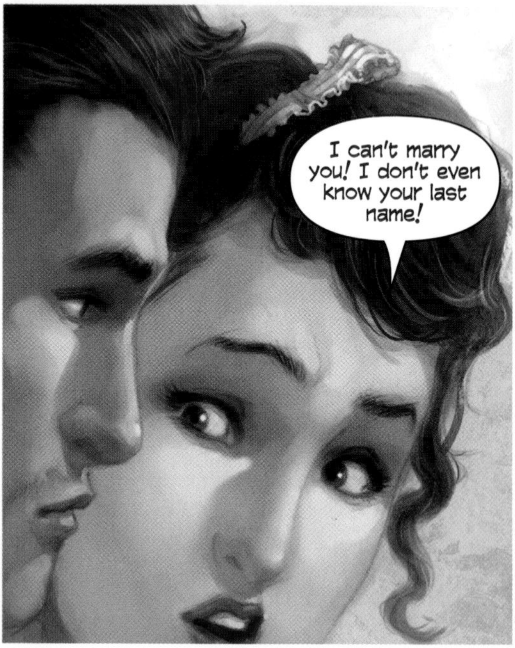
I can't marry you! I don't even know your last name!

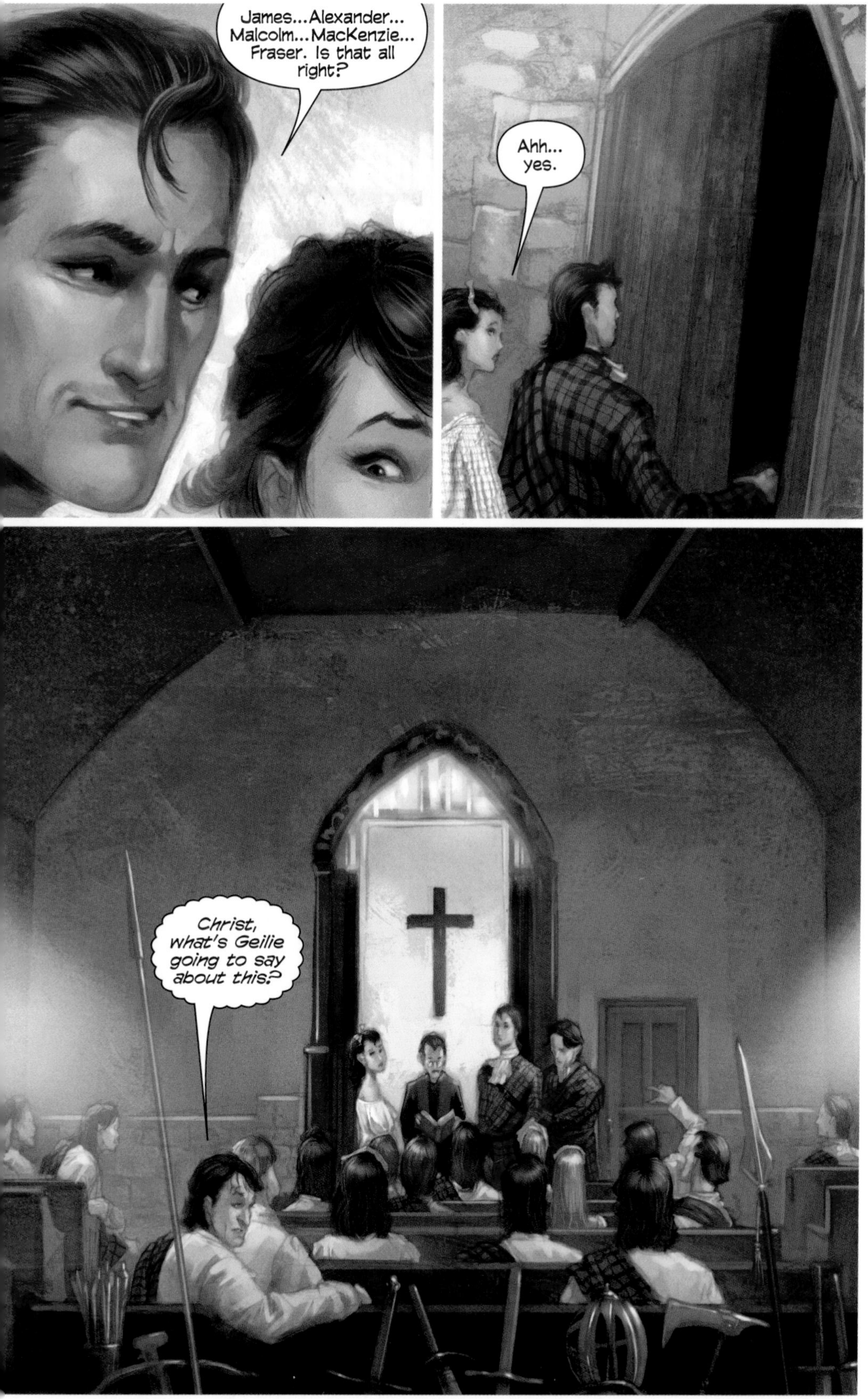
James...Alexander... Malcolm...MacKenzie... Fraser. Is that all right?
Ahh... yes.
Christ, what's Geilie going to say about this?

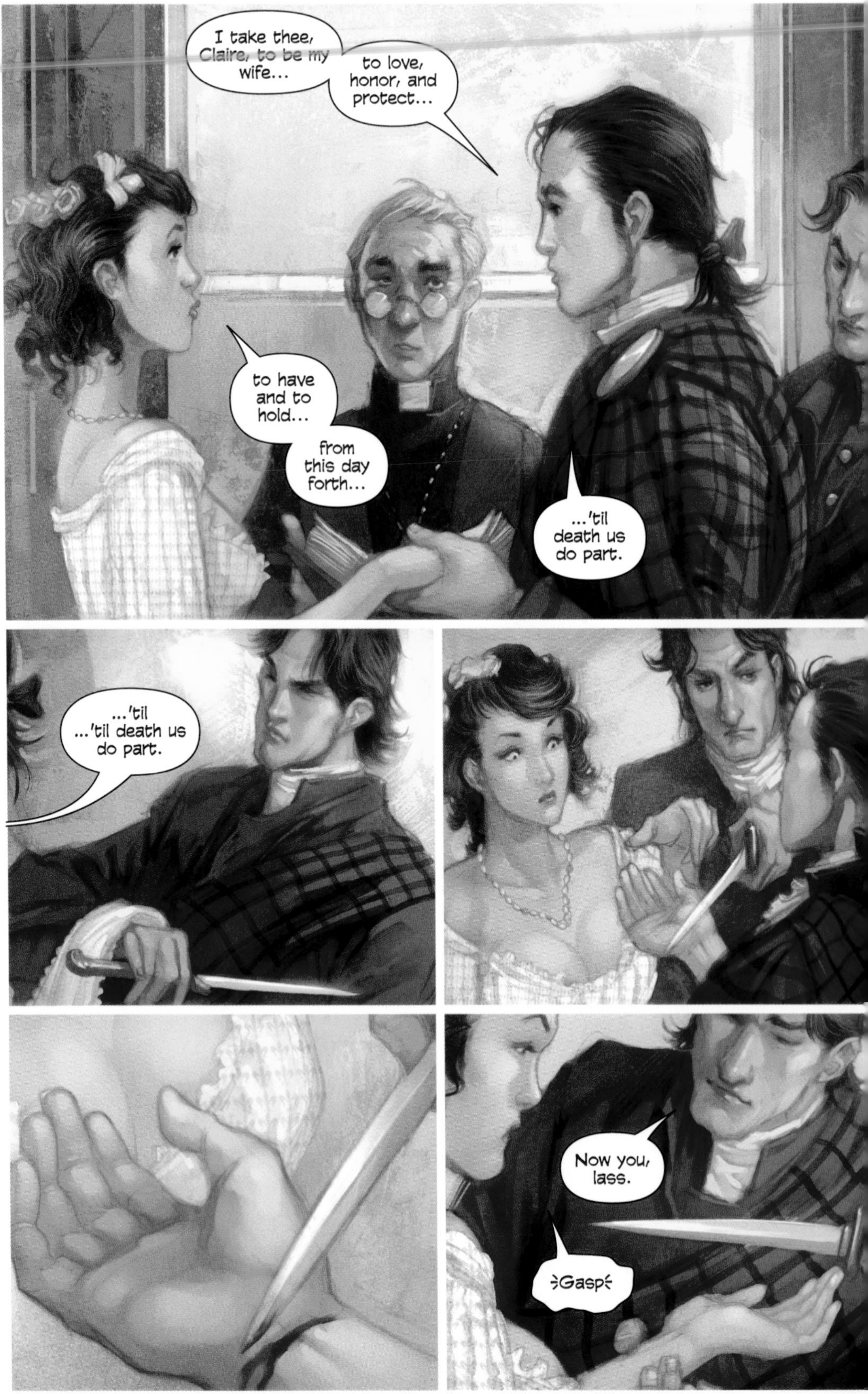
I take thee, Claire, to be my wife...
to love, honor, and protect...
to have and to hold...
from this day forth...
...'til death us do part.
...'til ...'til death us do part.
Now you, lass.
≶Gasp≶

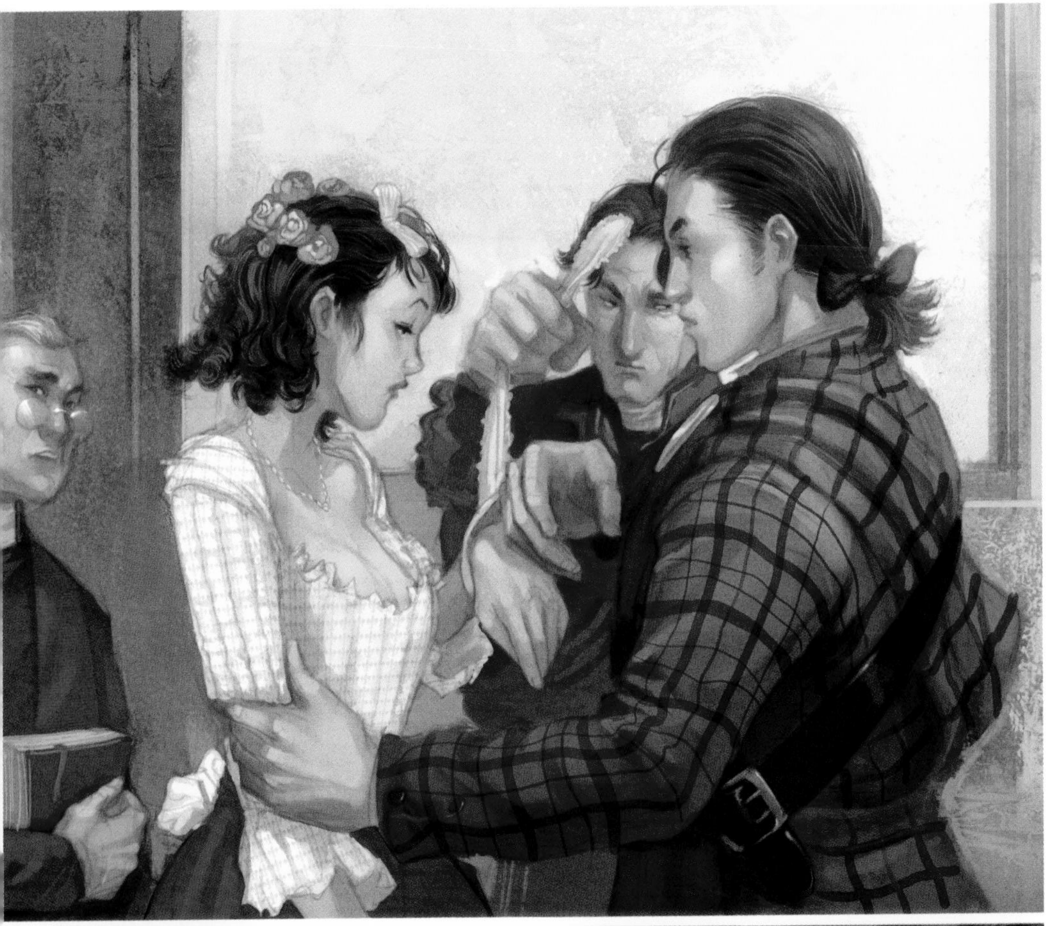

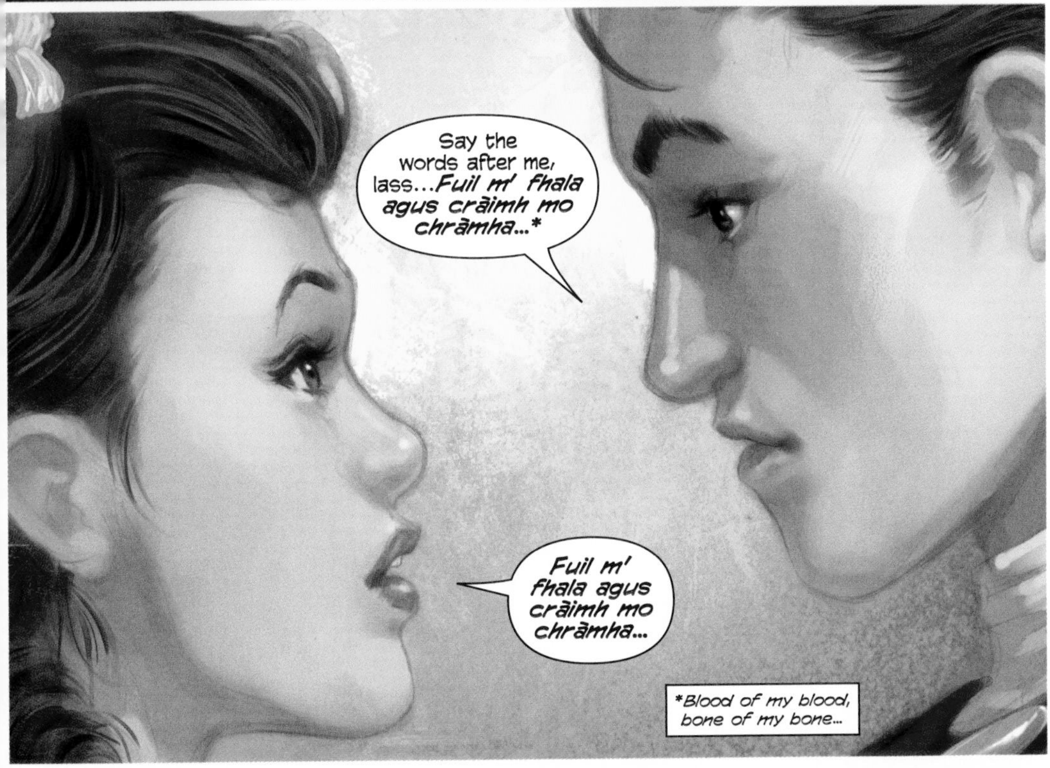
Say the words after me, lass...*Fuil m' fhala agus crāimh mo chrāmha...**
*Fuil m' fhala agus crāimh mo chrāmha...*
*Blood of my blood, bone of my bone...

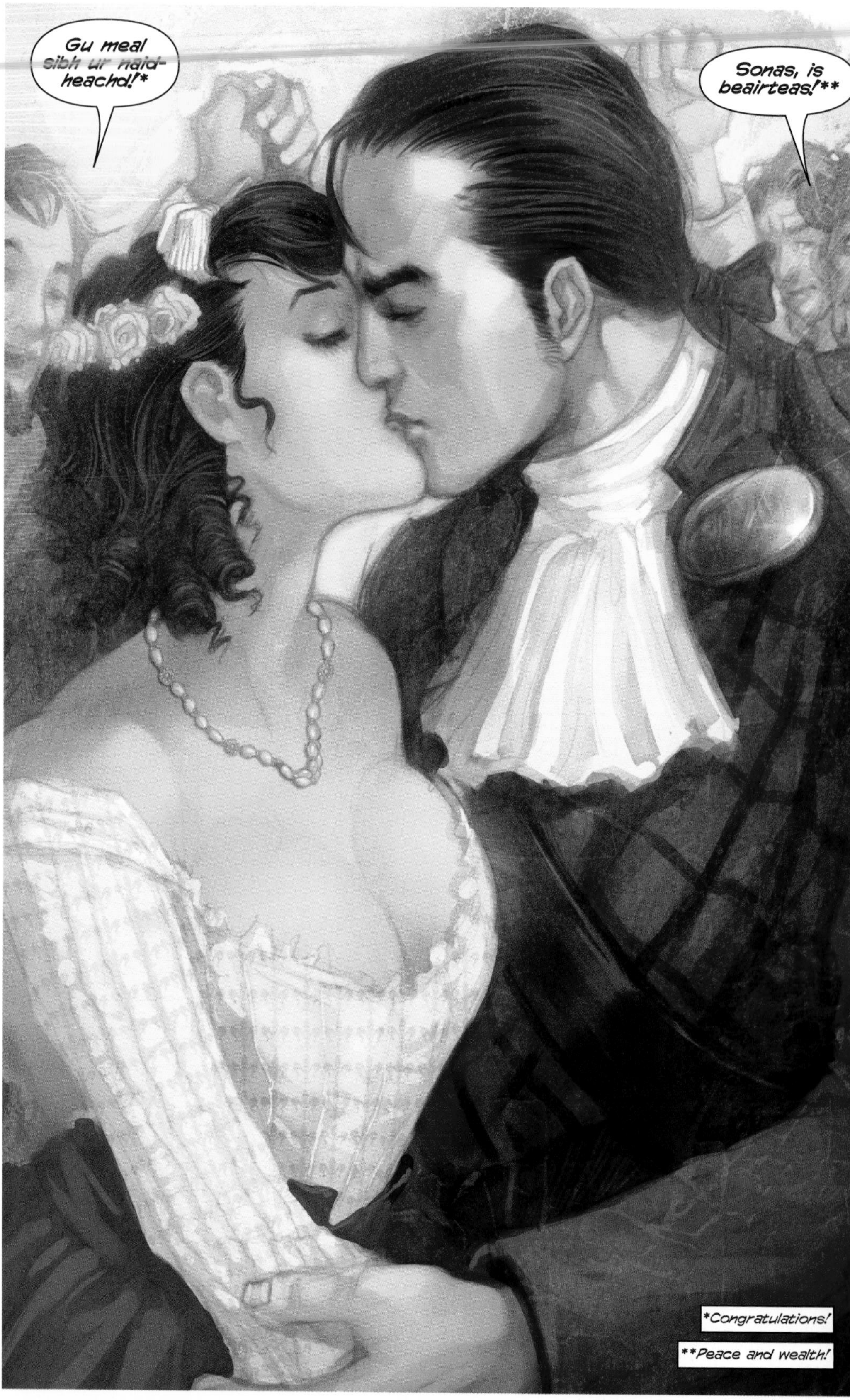

Gu meal sibh ur naid-heachd!*
Sonas, is beairteas!**
*Congratulations!
**Peace and wealth!

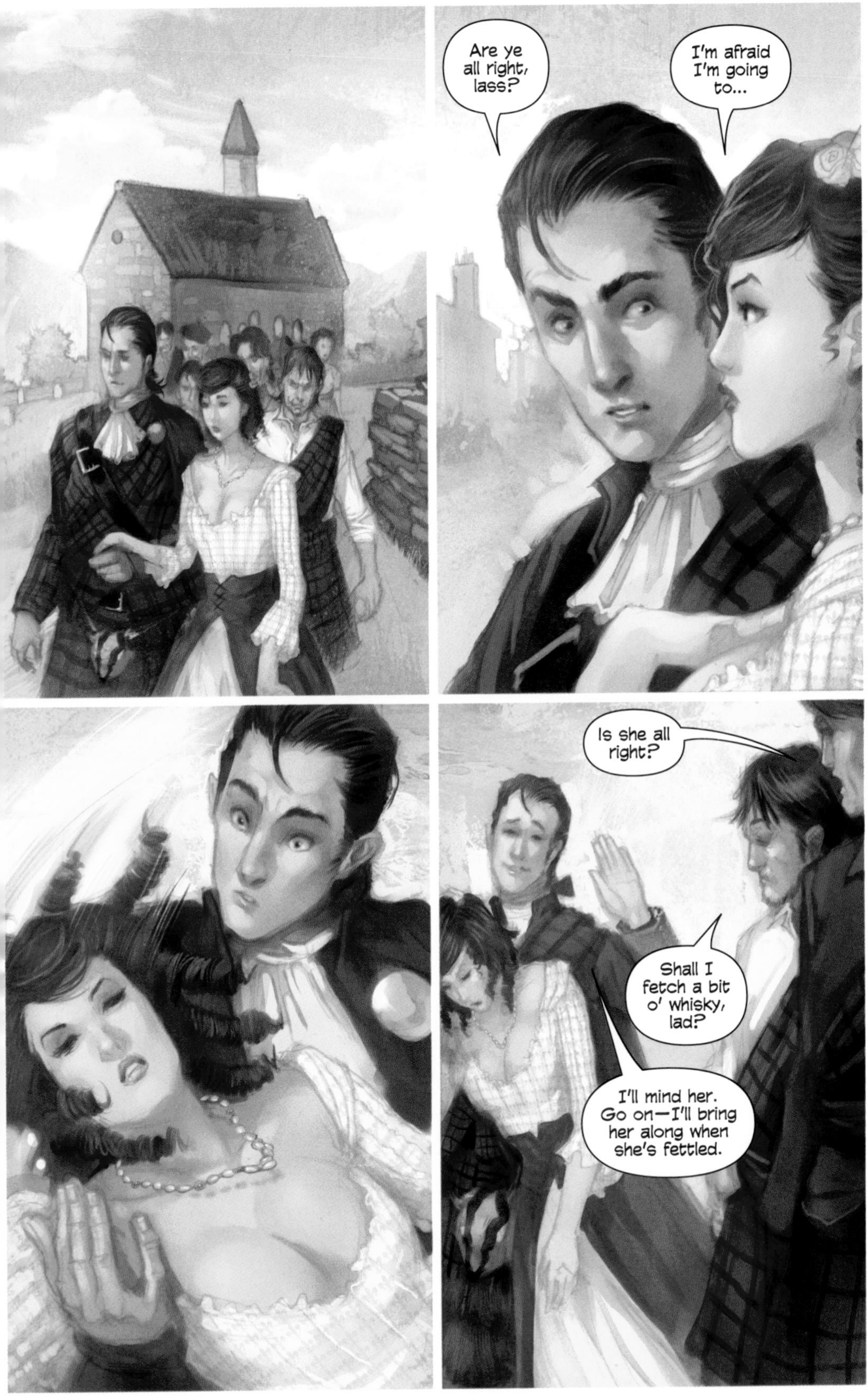
Are ye all right, lass?
I'm afraid I'm going to...
Is she all right?
Shall I fetch a bit o' whisky, lad?
I'll mind her. Go on—I'll bring her along when she's fettled.

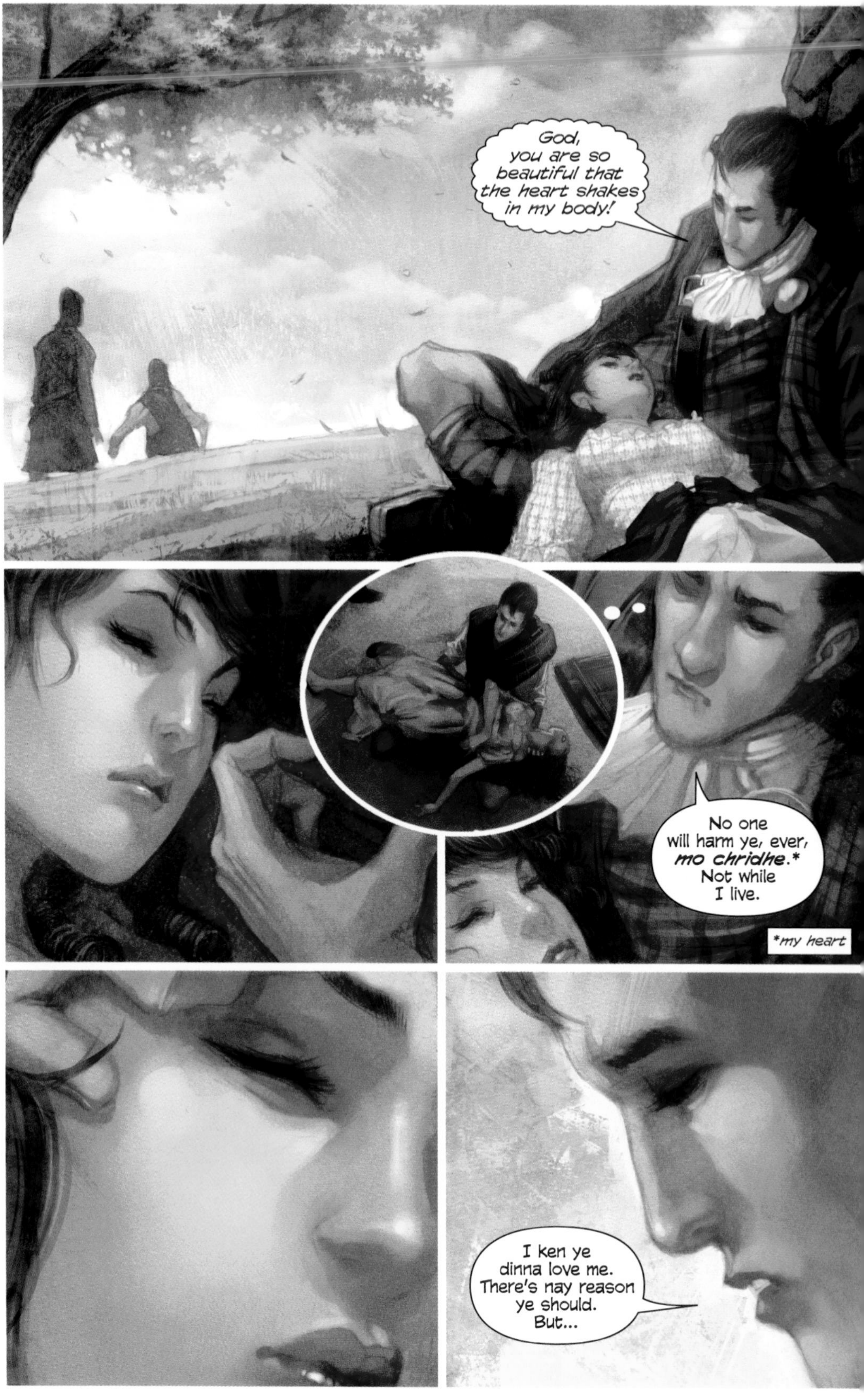
God, you are so beautiful that the heart shakes in my body!
...
No one will harm ye, ever, *mo chridhe*.* Not while I live.
*my heart
I ken ye dinna love me. There's nay reason ye should. But...

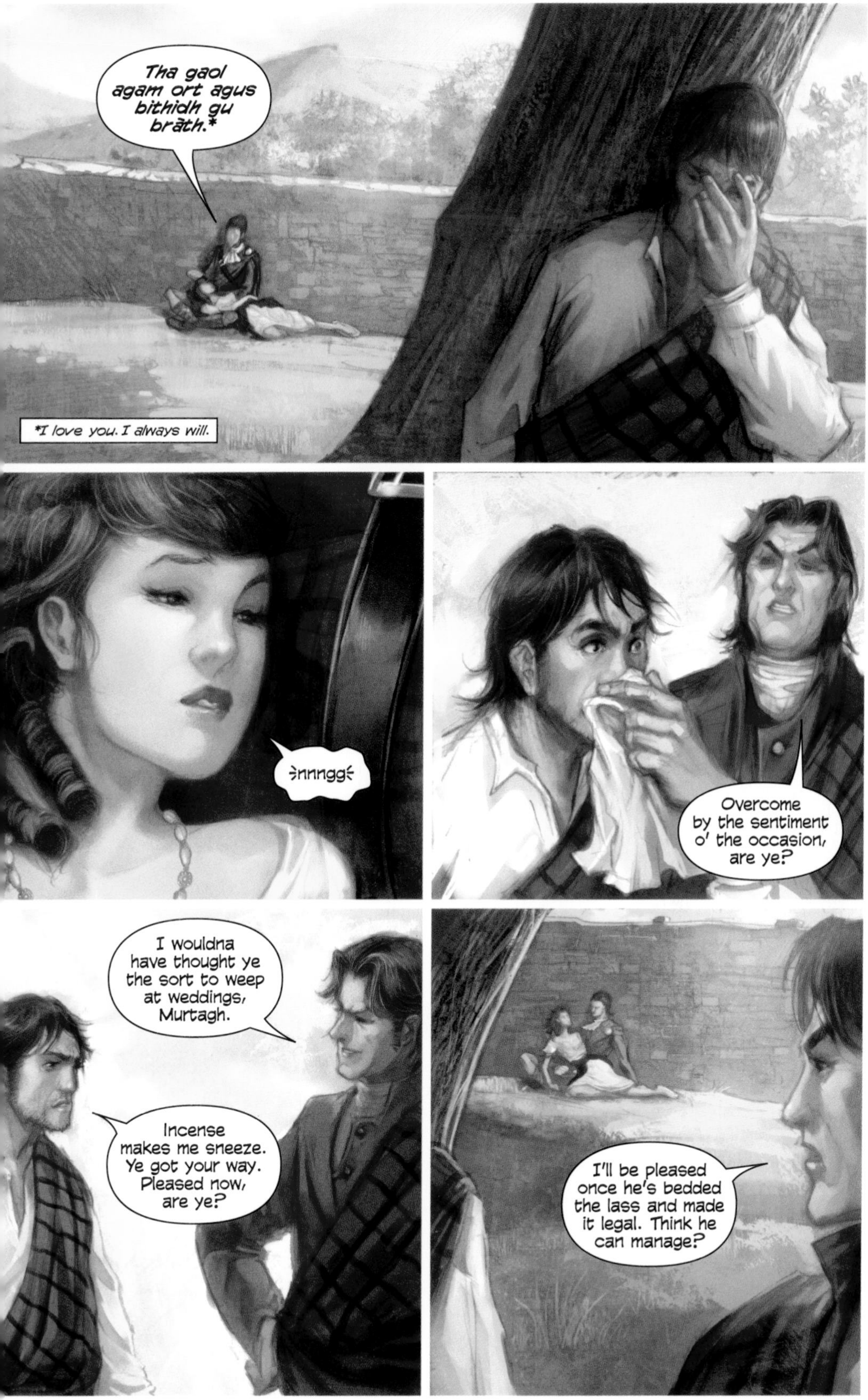
Tha gaol agam ort agus bithidh gu brāth.*
*I love you. I always will.
nnngg
Overcome by the sentiment o' the occasion, are ye?
I wouldna have thought ye the sort to weep at weddings, Murtagh.
Incense makes me sneeze. Ye got your way. Pleased now, are ye?
I'll be pleased once he's bedded the lass and made it legal. Think he can manage?

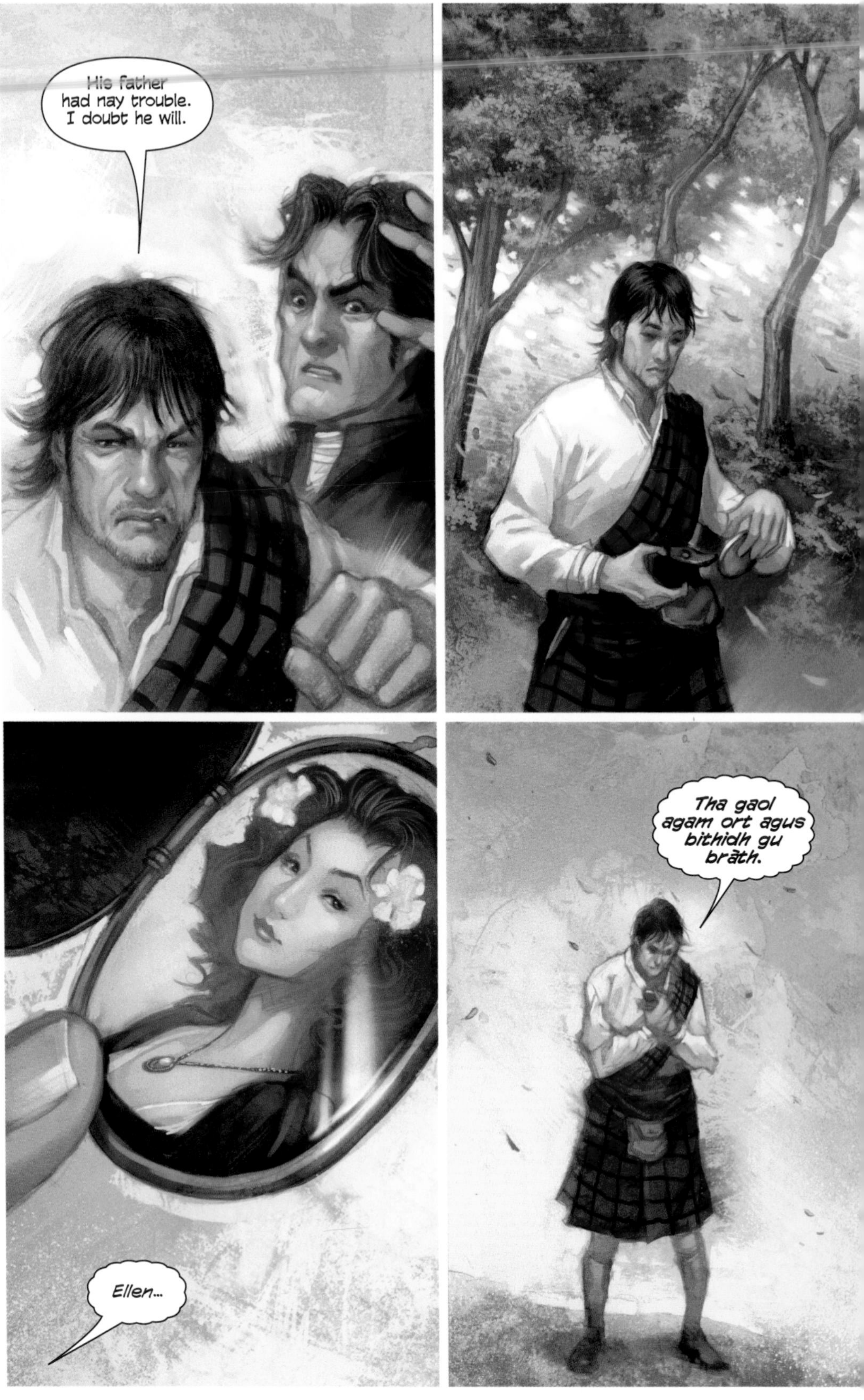
His father had nay trouble. I doubt he will.
Ellen...
Tha gaol agam ort agus bithidh gu bràth.

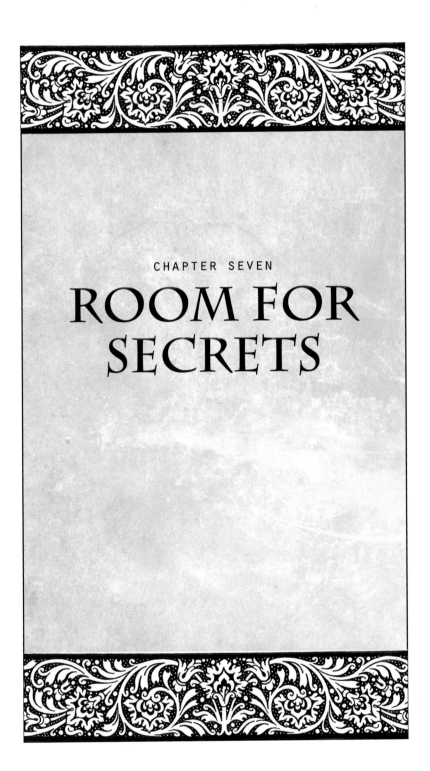

CHAPTER SEVEN

# ROOM FOR SECRETS

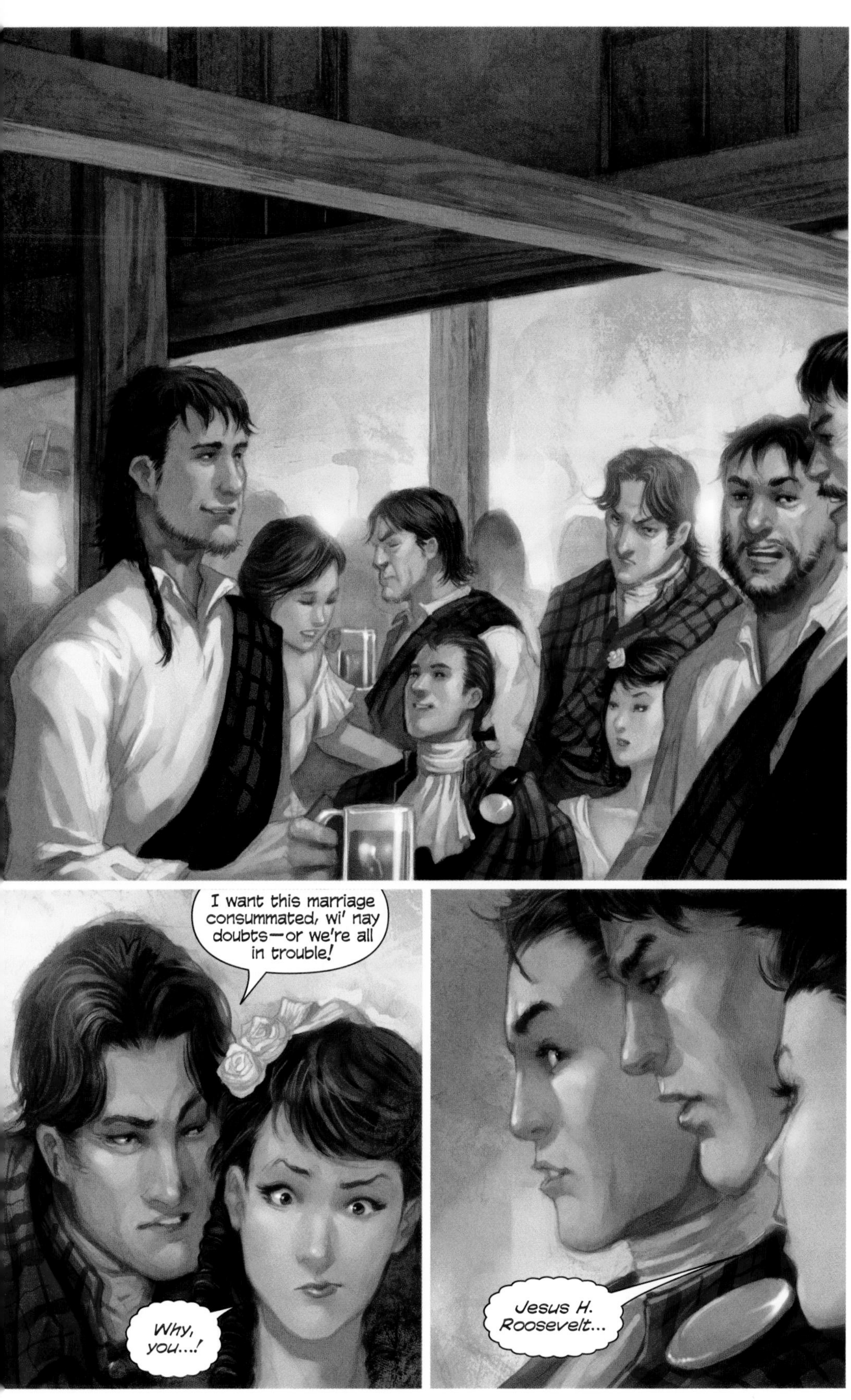
I want this marriage consummated, wi' nay doubts—or we're all in trouble!
Why, you....!
Jesus H. Roosevelt...

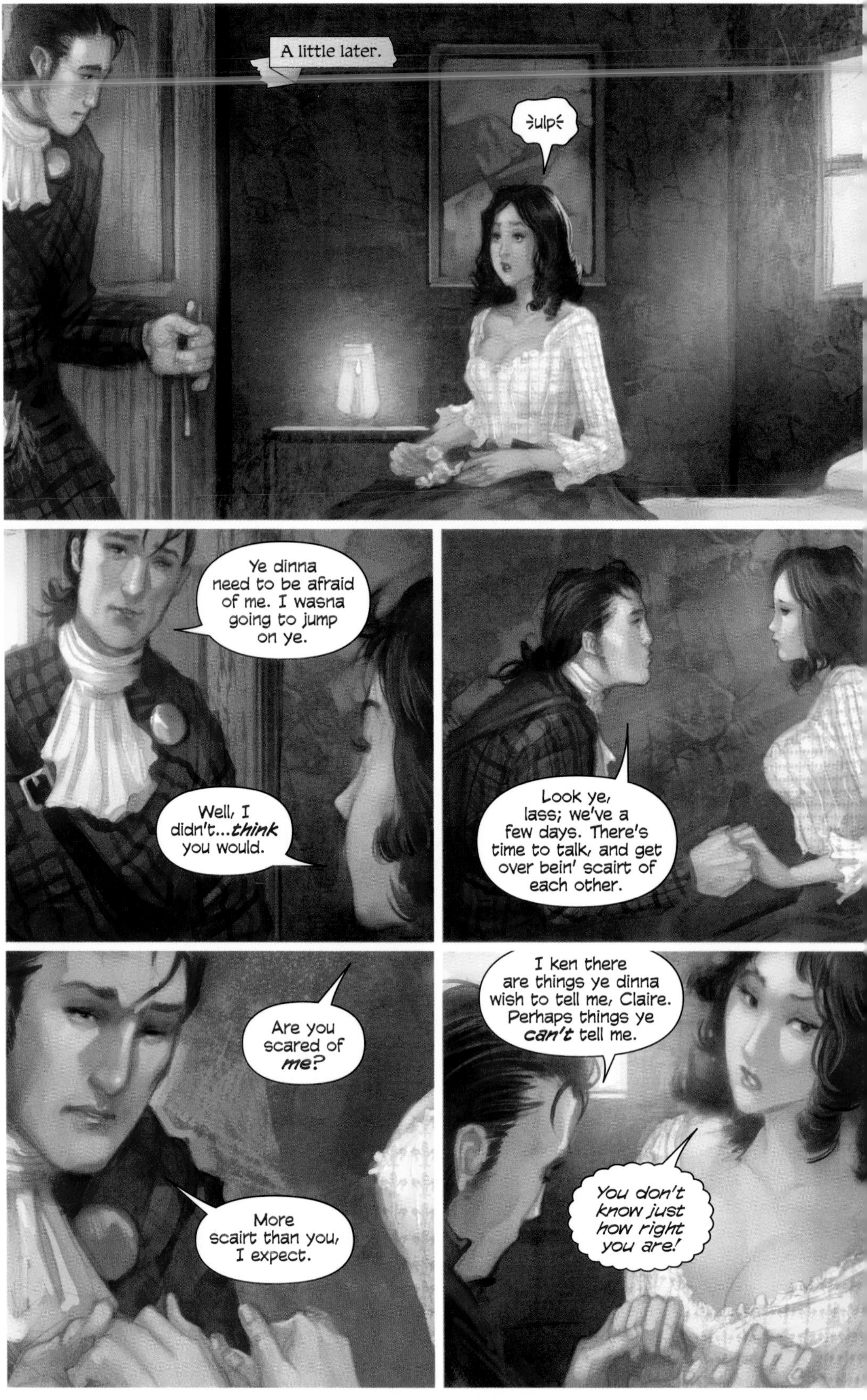
A little later.
ulp
Ye dinna need to be afraid of me. I wasna going to jump on ye.
Well, I didn't...*think* you would.
Look ye, lass; we've a few days. There's time to talk, and get over bein' scairt of each other.
Are you scared of *me*?
More scairt than you, I expect.
I ken there are things ye dinna wish to tell me, Claire. Perhaps things ye *can't* tell me.
*You don't know just how right you are!*

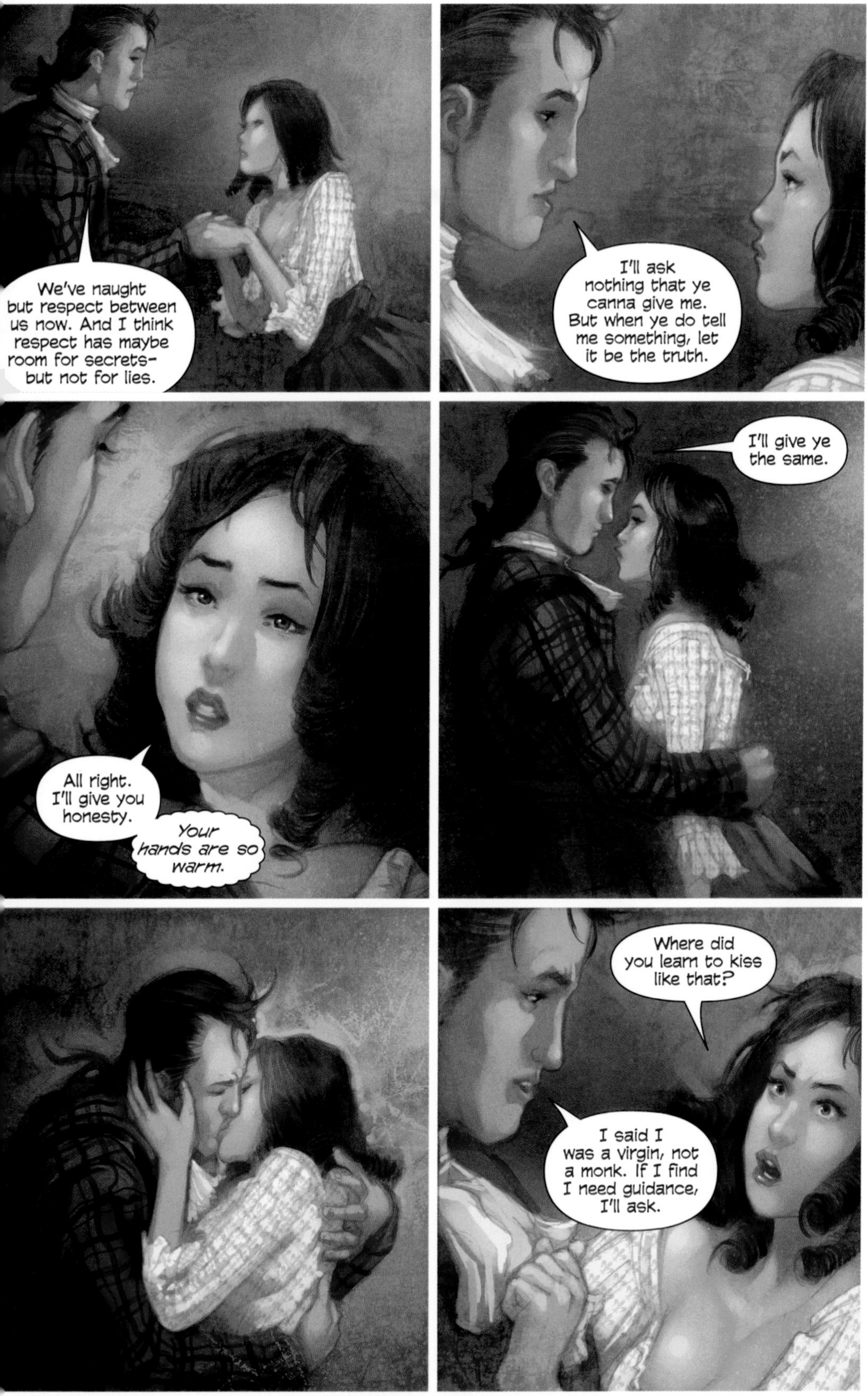
We've naught but respect between us now. And I think respect has maybe room for secrets-but not for lies.
I'll ask nothing that ye canna give me. But when ye do tell me something, let it be the truth.
All right. I'll give you honesty.
Your hands are so warm.
I'll give ye the same.
Where did you learn to kiss like that?
I said I was a virgin, not a monk. If I find I need guidance, I'll ask.

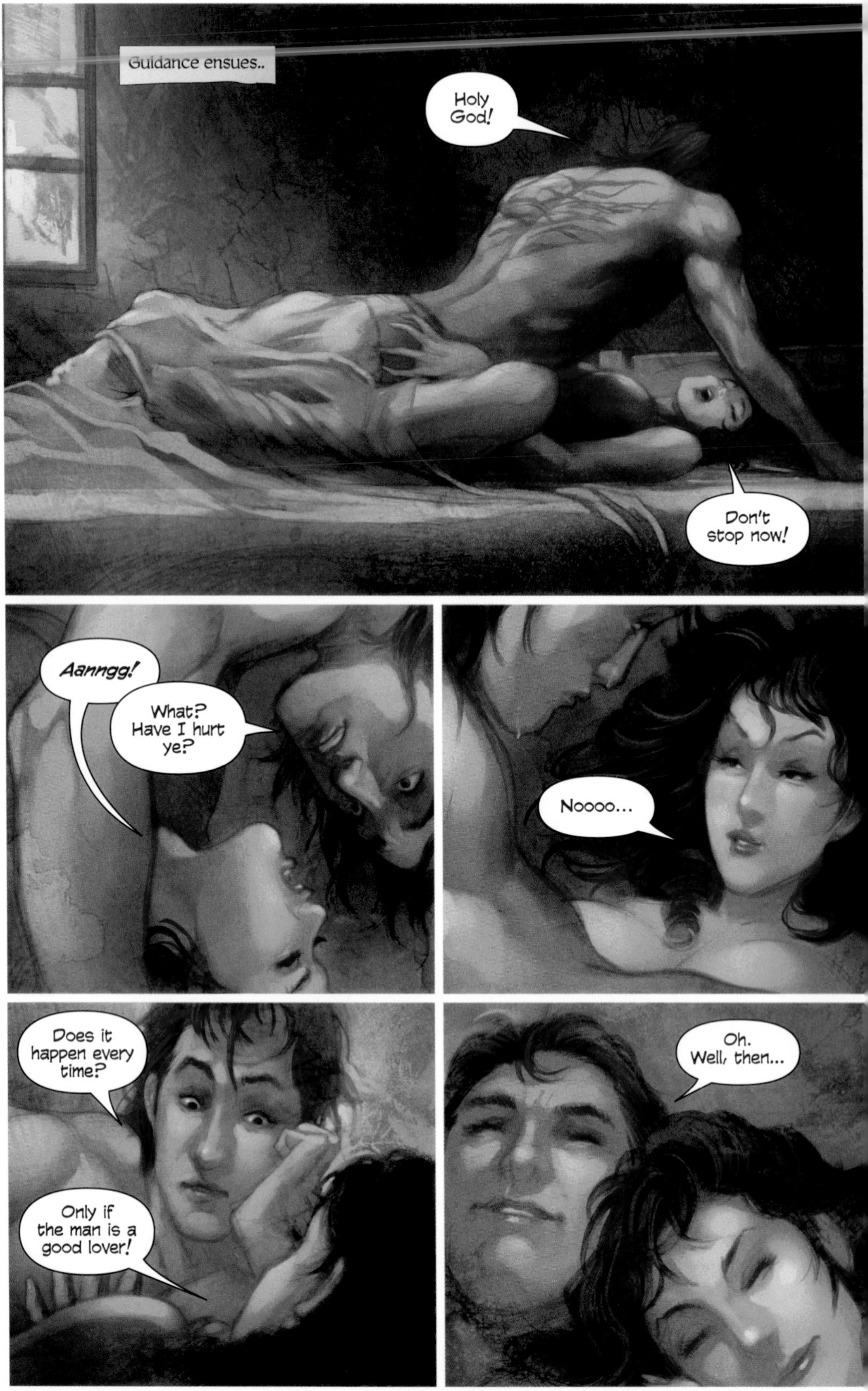
Guidance ensues..
Holy God!
Don't stop now!
Aanngg!
What? Have I hurt ye?
Noooo...
Does it happen every time?
Only if the man is a good lover!
Oh. Well, then...

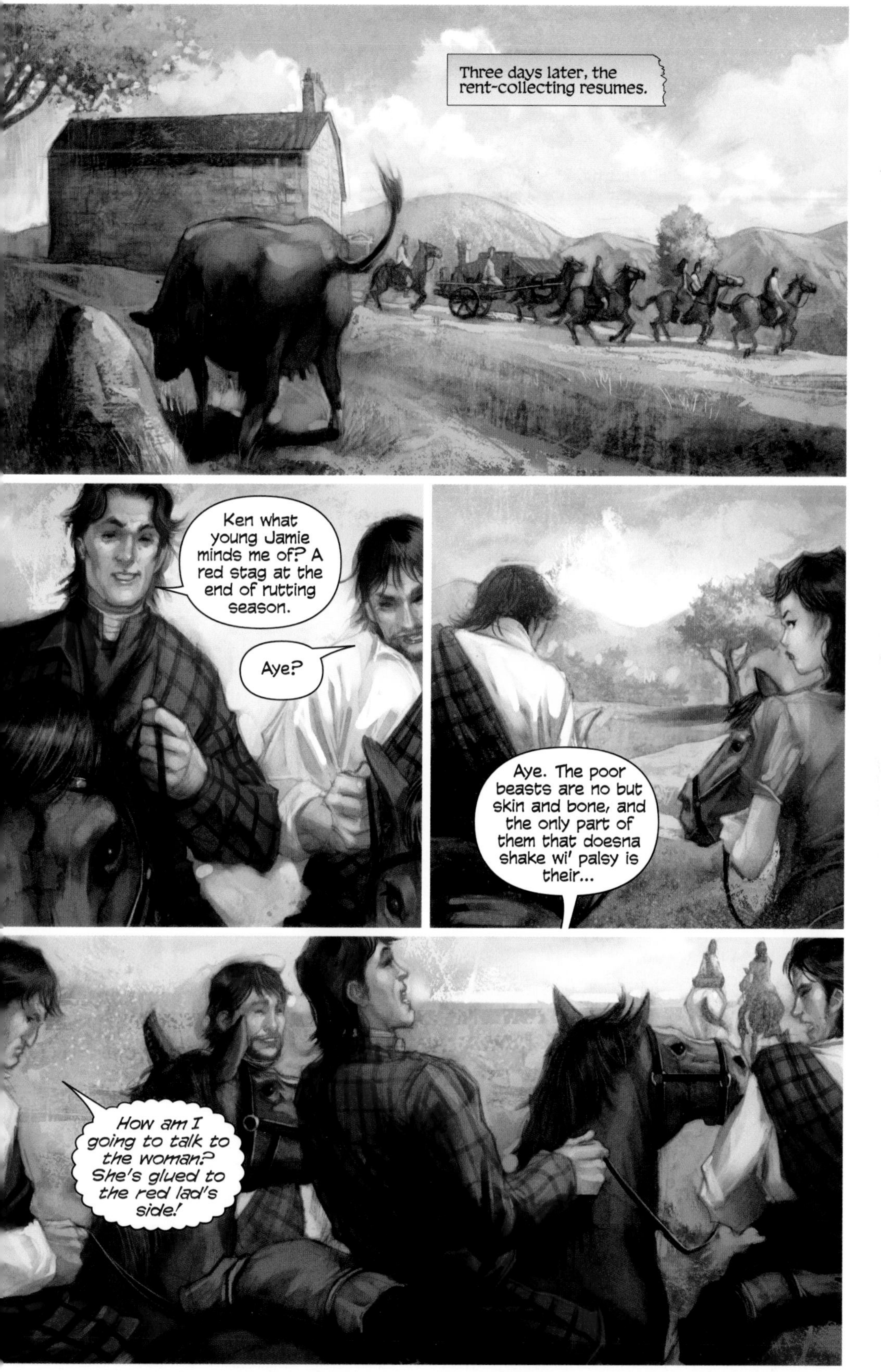
Three days later, the rent-collecting resumes.
Ken what young Jamie minds me of? A red stag at the end of rutting season.
Aye?
Aye. The poor beasts are no but skin and bone, and the only part of them that doesna shake wi' palsy is their...
How am I going to talk to the woman? She's glued to the red lad's side!

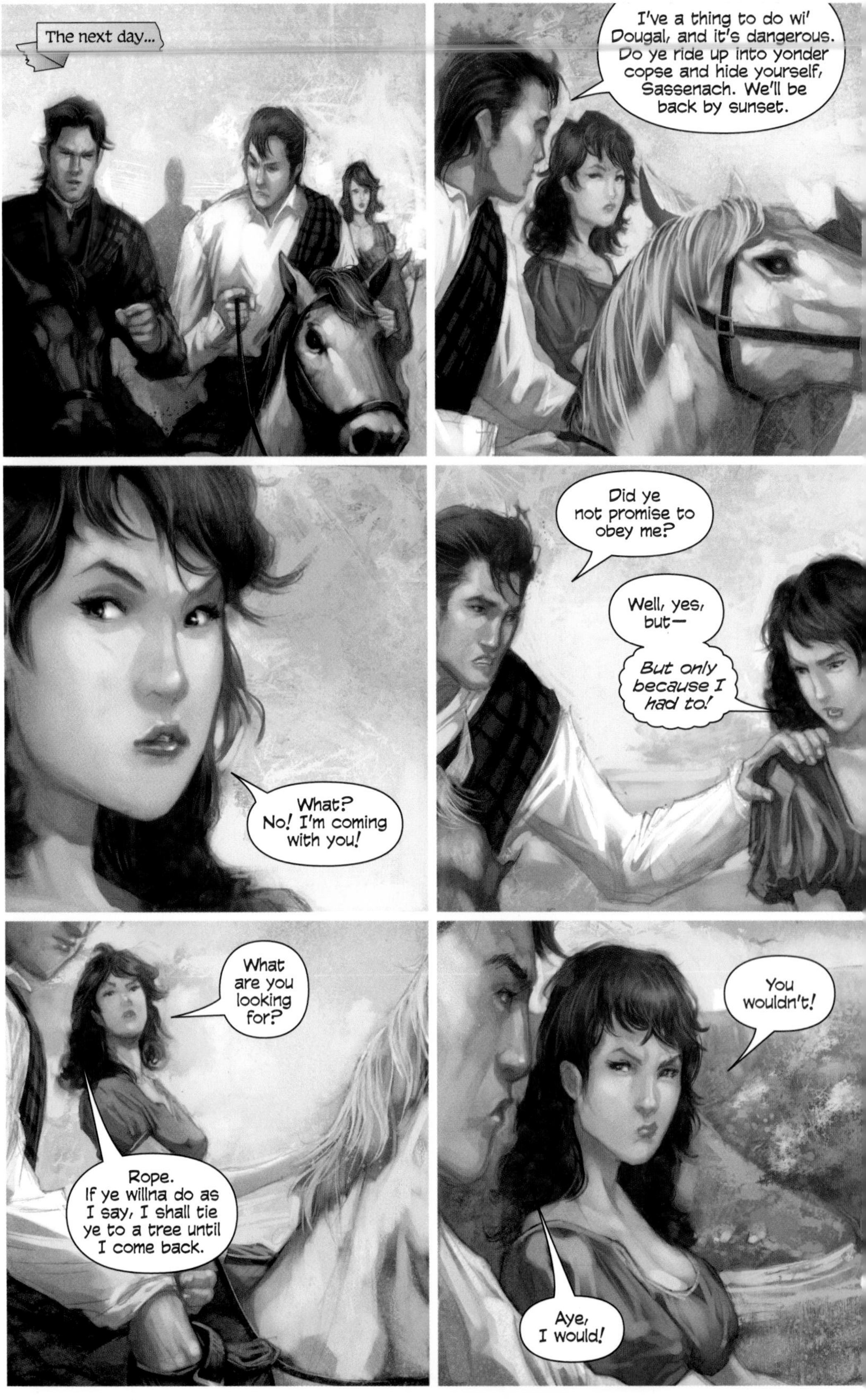
The next day...
I've a thing to do wi' Dougal, and it's dangerous. Do ye ride up into yonder copse and hide yourself, Sassenach. We'll be back by sunset.
What? No! I'm coming with you!
Did ye not promise to obey me?
Well, yes, but—
*But only because I had to!*
What are you looking for?
Rope. If ye willna do as I say, I shall tie ye to a tree until I come back.
You wouldn't!
Aye, I would!

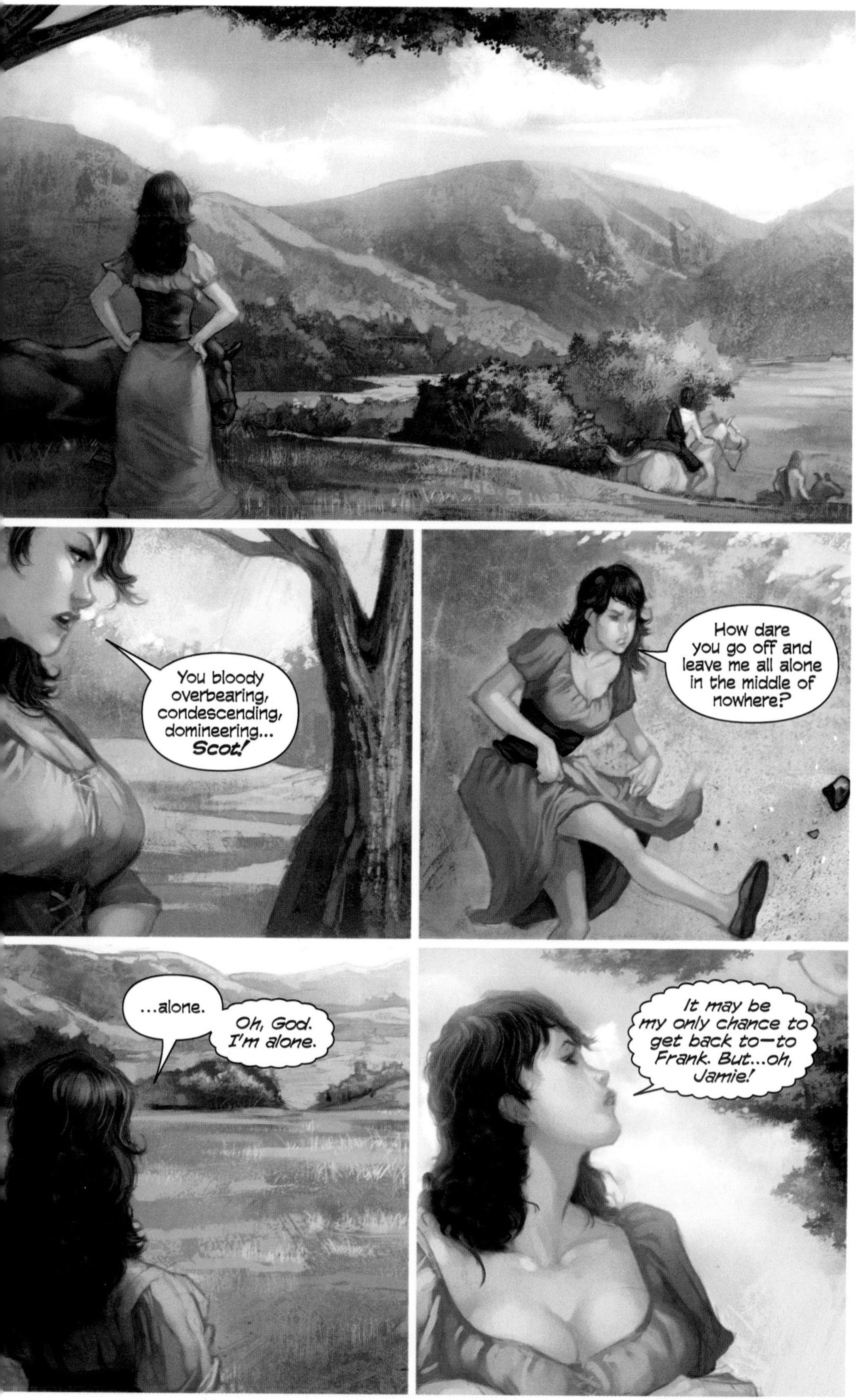

You bloody overbearing, condescending, domineering... *Scot!*
How dare you go off and leave me all alone in the middle of nowhere?
...alone.
*Oh, God. I'm alone.*
*It may be my only chance to get back to—to Frank. But...oh, Jamie!*

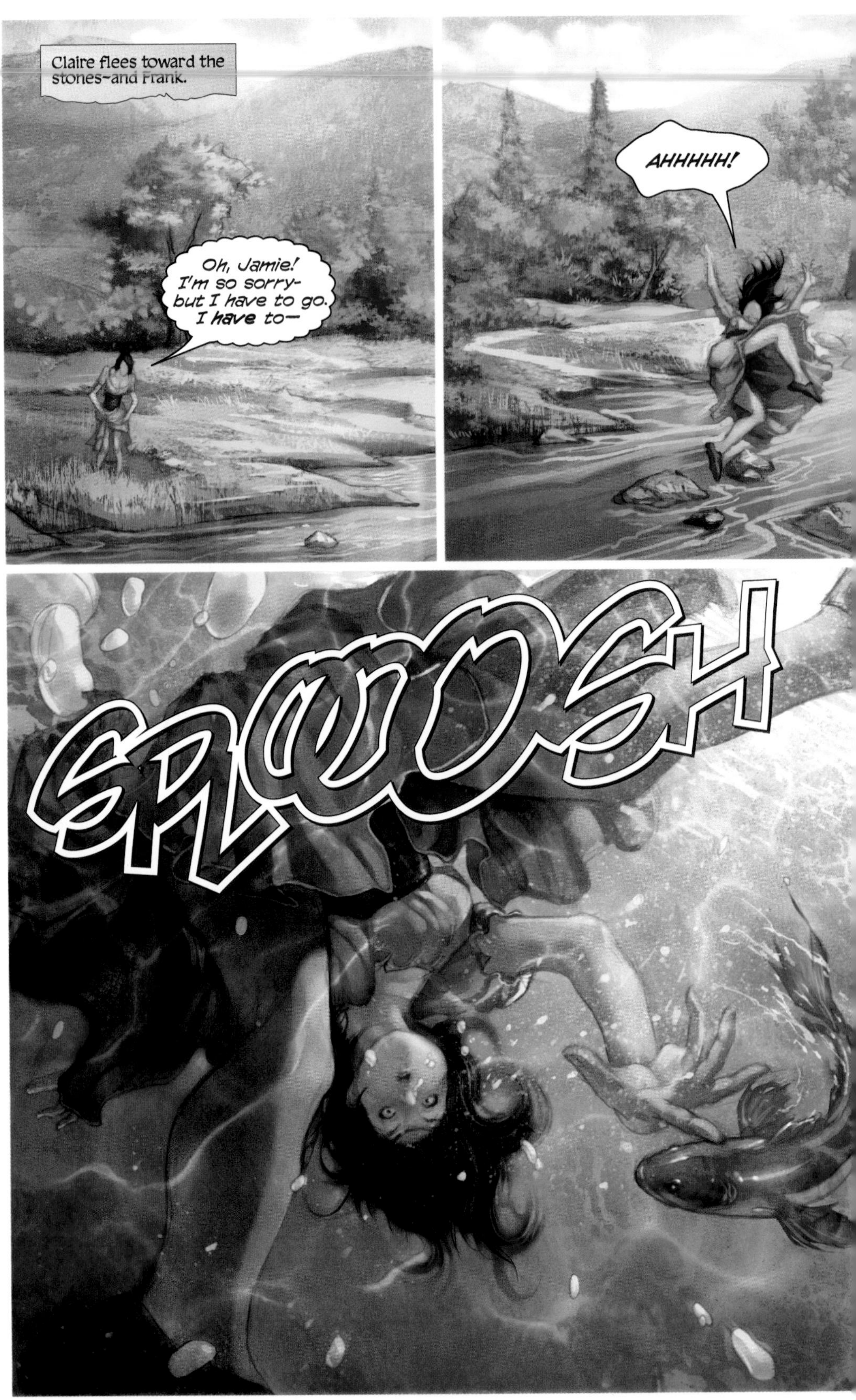
Claire flees toward the stones–and Frank.
Oh, Jamie! I'm so sorry– but I have to go. I have to—
AHHHHH!
SPLOOSH

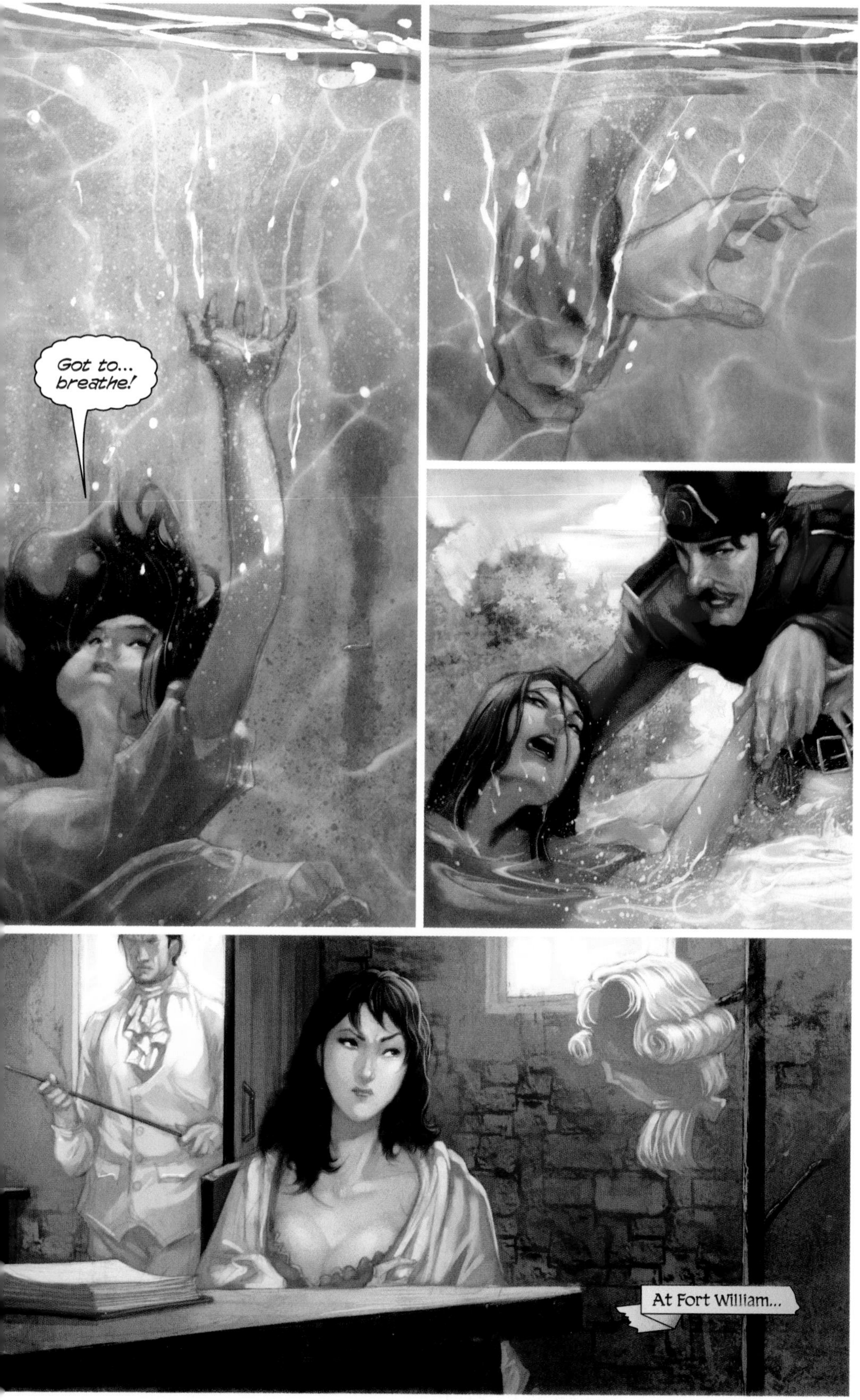
Got to... breathe!
At Fort William...

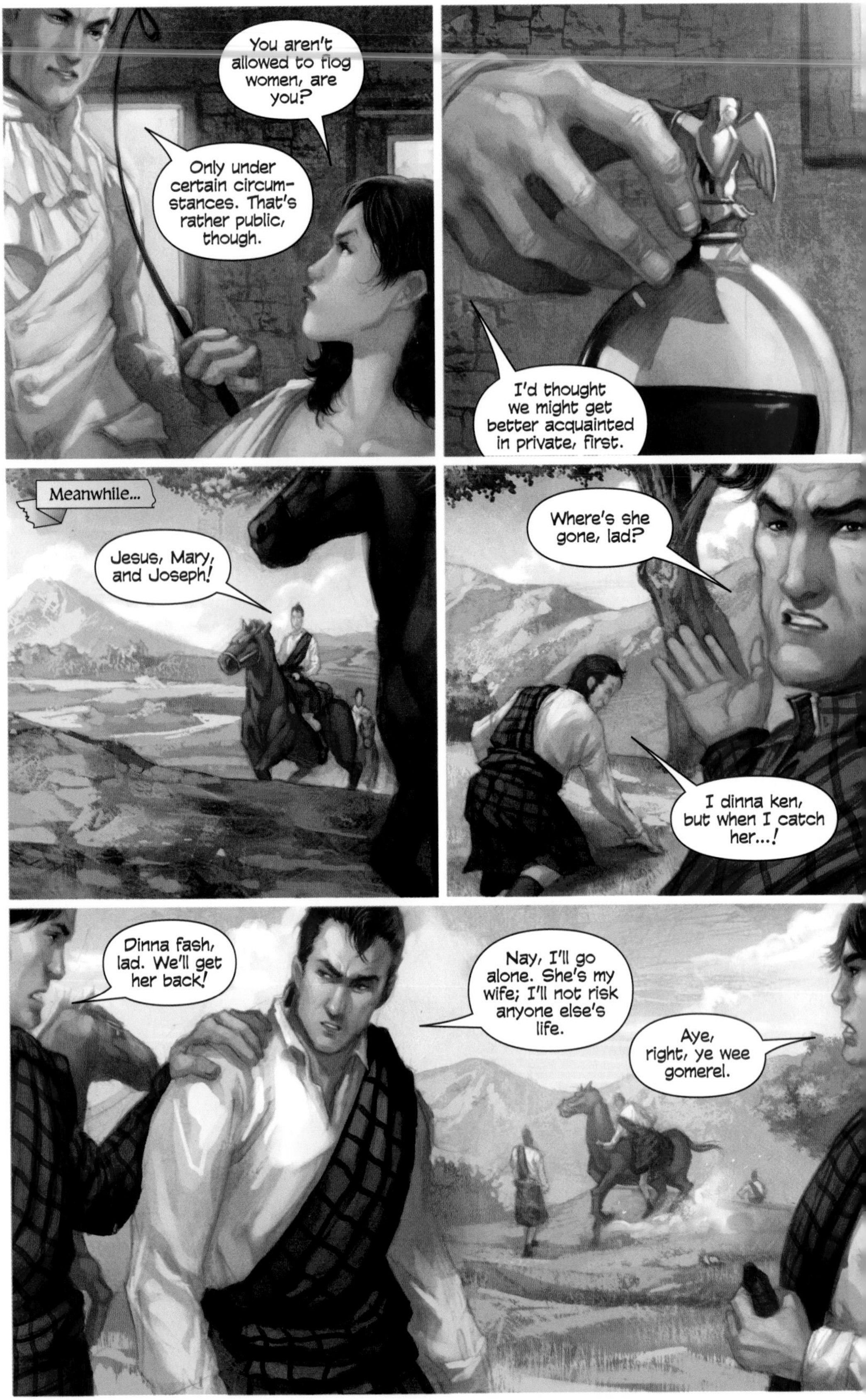
You aren't allowed to flog women, are you?
Only under certain circum-stances. That's rather public, though.
I'd thought we might get better acquainted in private, first.
Meanwhile...
Jesus, Mary, and Joseph!
Where's she gone, lad?
I dinna ken, but when I catch her...!
Dinna fash, lad. We'll get her back!
Nay, I'll go alone. She's my wife; I'll not risk anyone else's life.
Aye, right, ye wee gomerel.

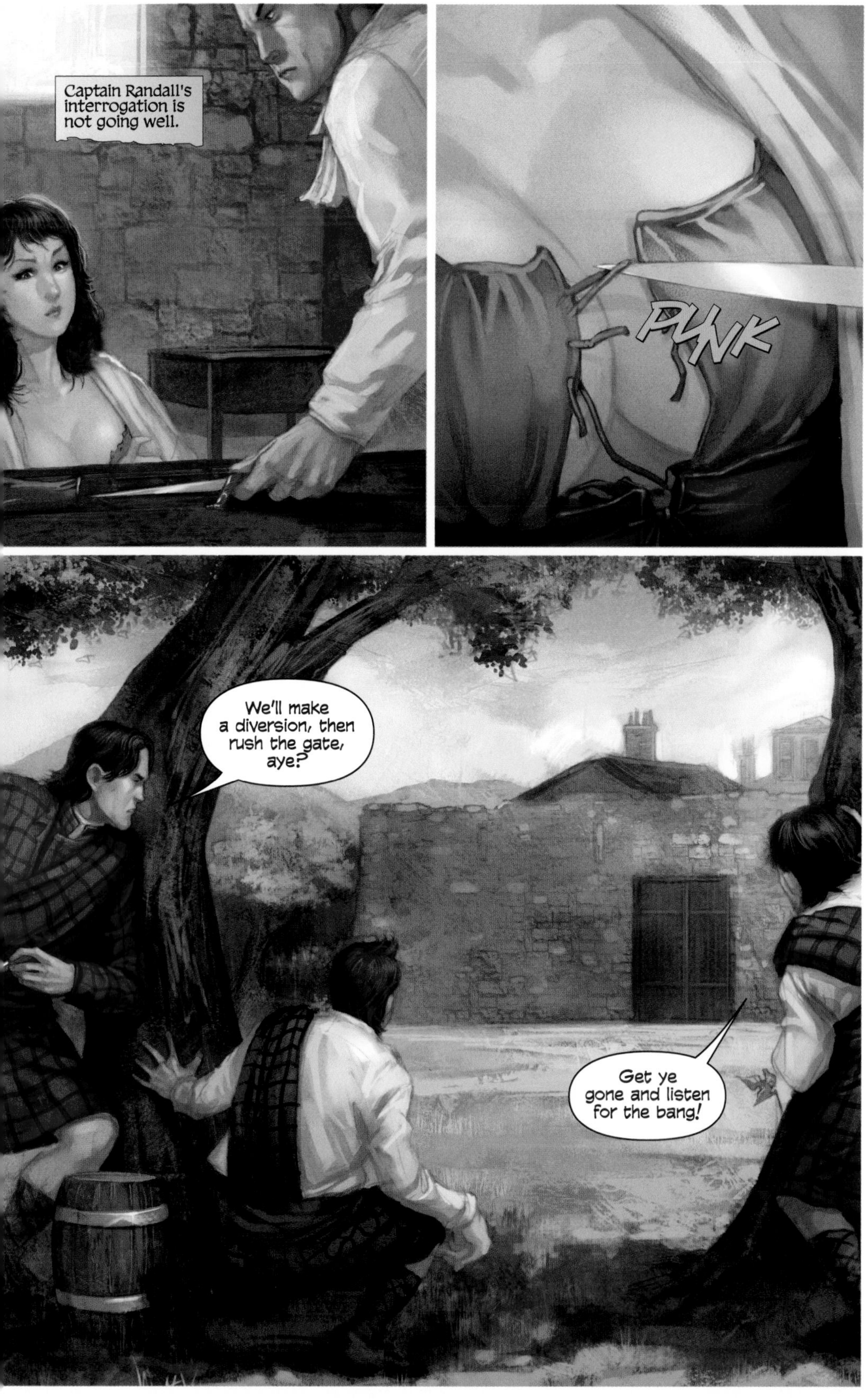
Captain Randall's interrogation is not going well.
PUNK
We'll make a diversion, then rush the gate, aye?
Get ye gone and listen for the bang!

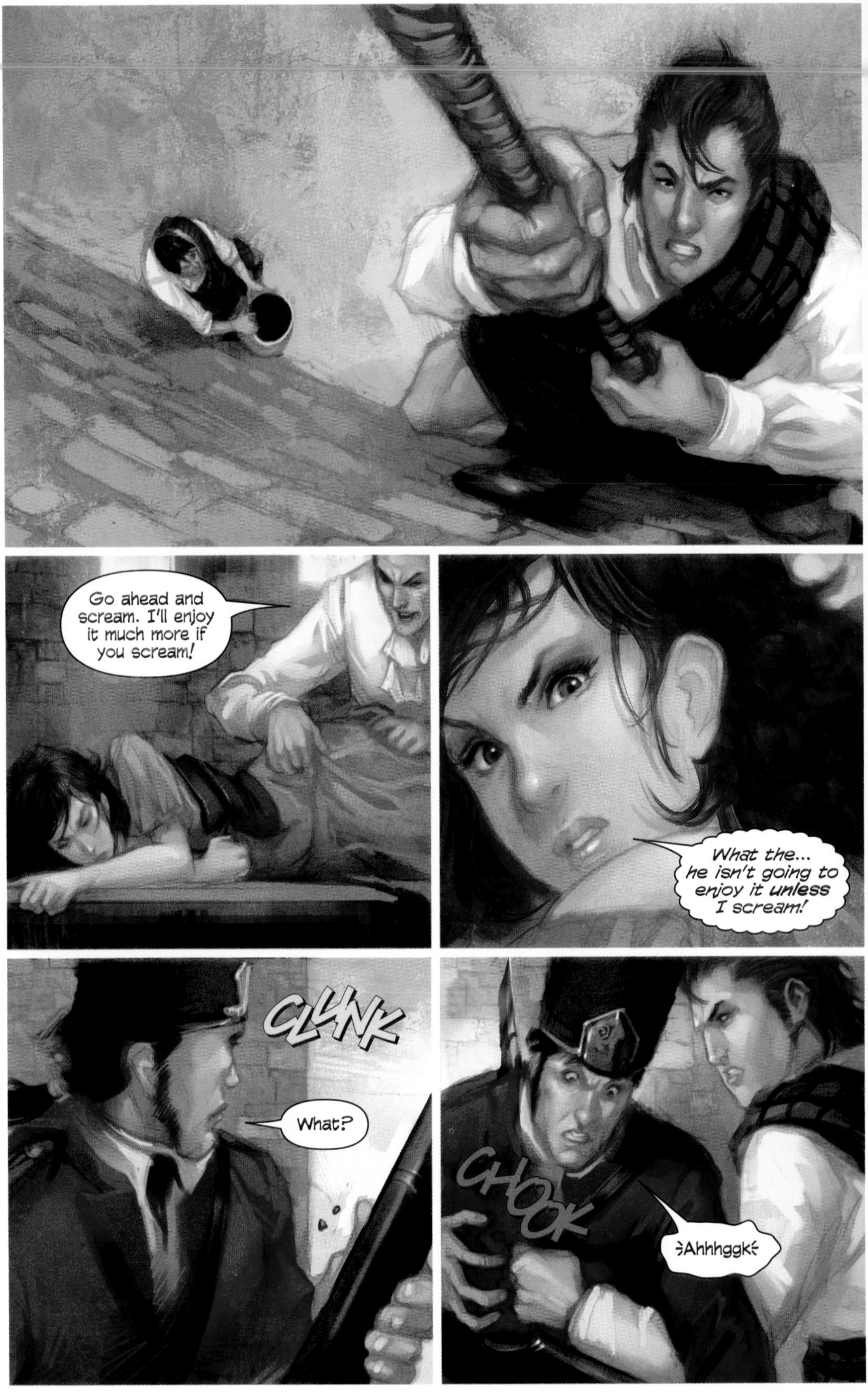
Go ahead and scream. I'll enjoy it much more if you scream!
What the... he isn't going to enjoy it unless I scream!
CLUNK
What?
CHOOK
Ahhhggk

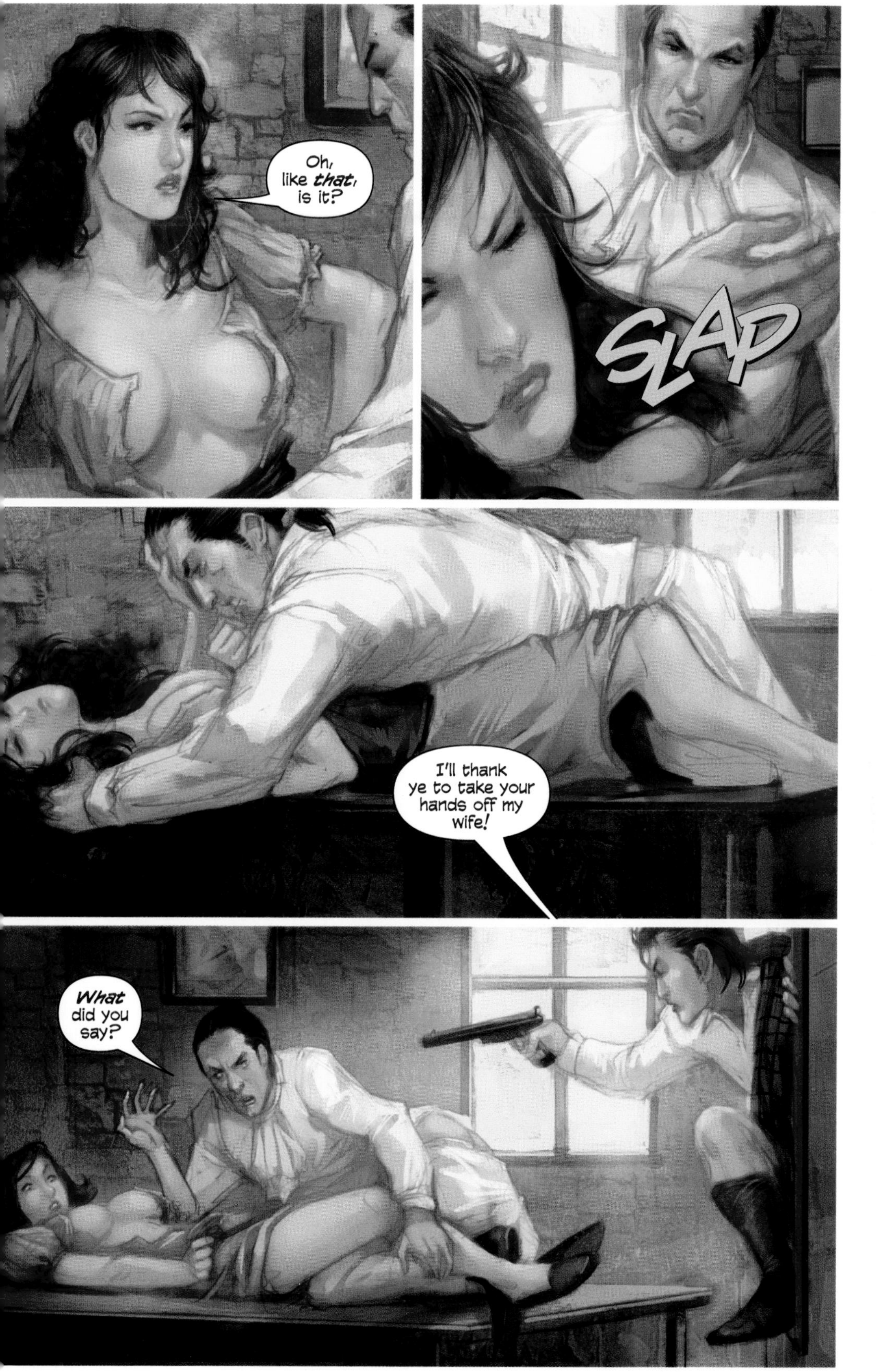
Oh, like *that*, is it?
SLAP
I'll thank ye to take your hands off my wife!
*What* did you say?

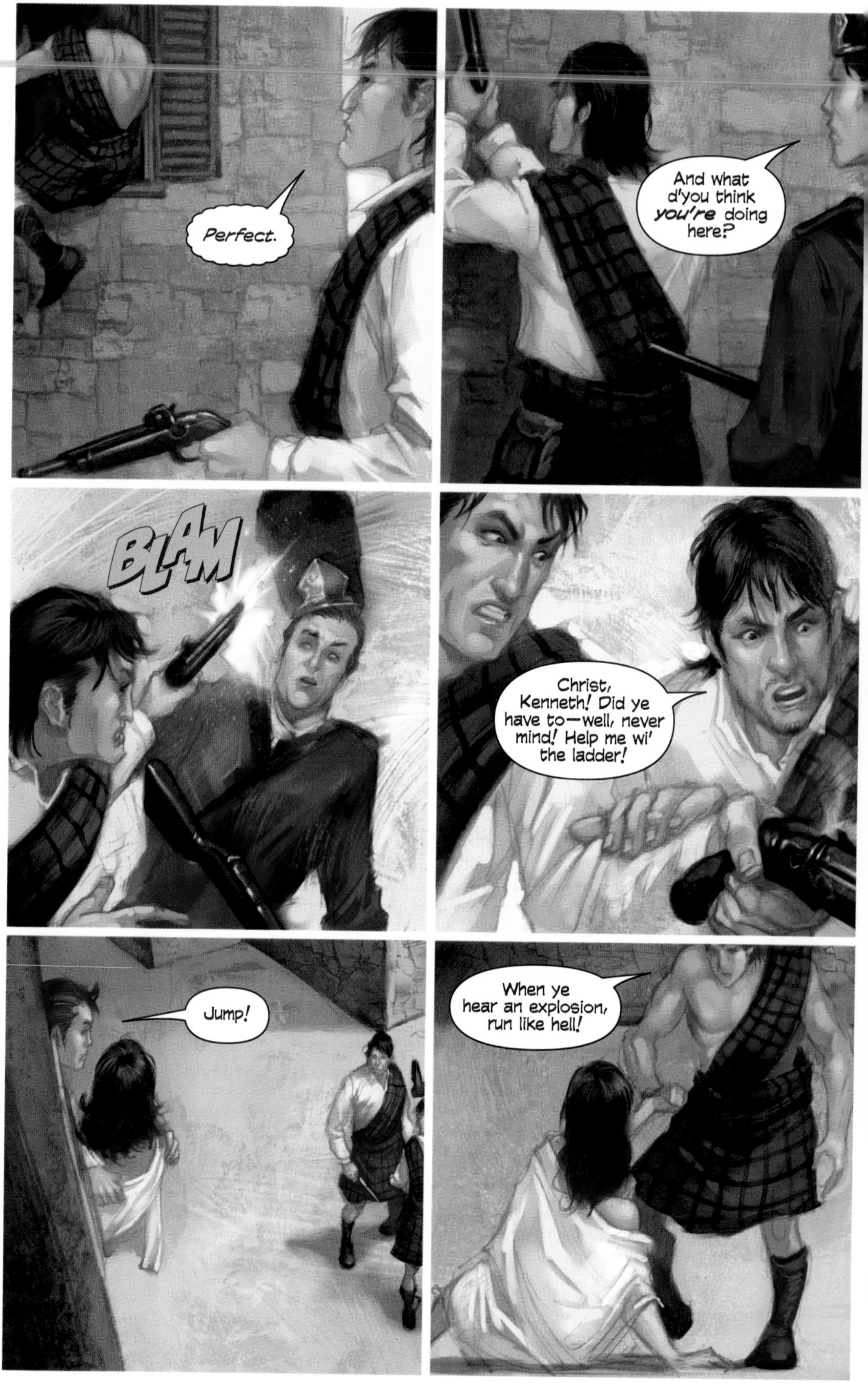
Perfect.
And what d'you think *you're* doing here?
BLAM
Christ, Kenneth! Did ye have to—well, never mind! Help me wi' the ladder!
Jump!
When ye hear an explosion, run like hell!

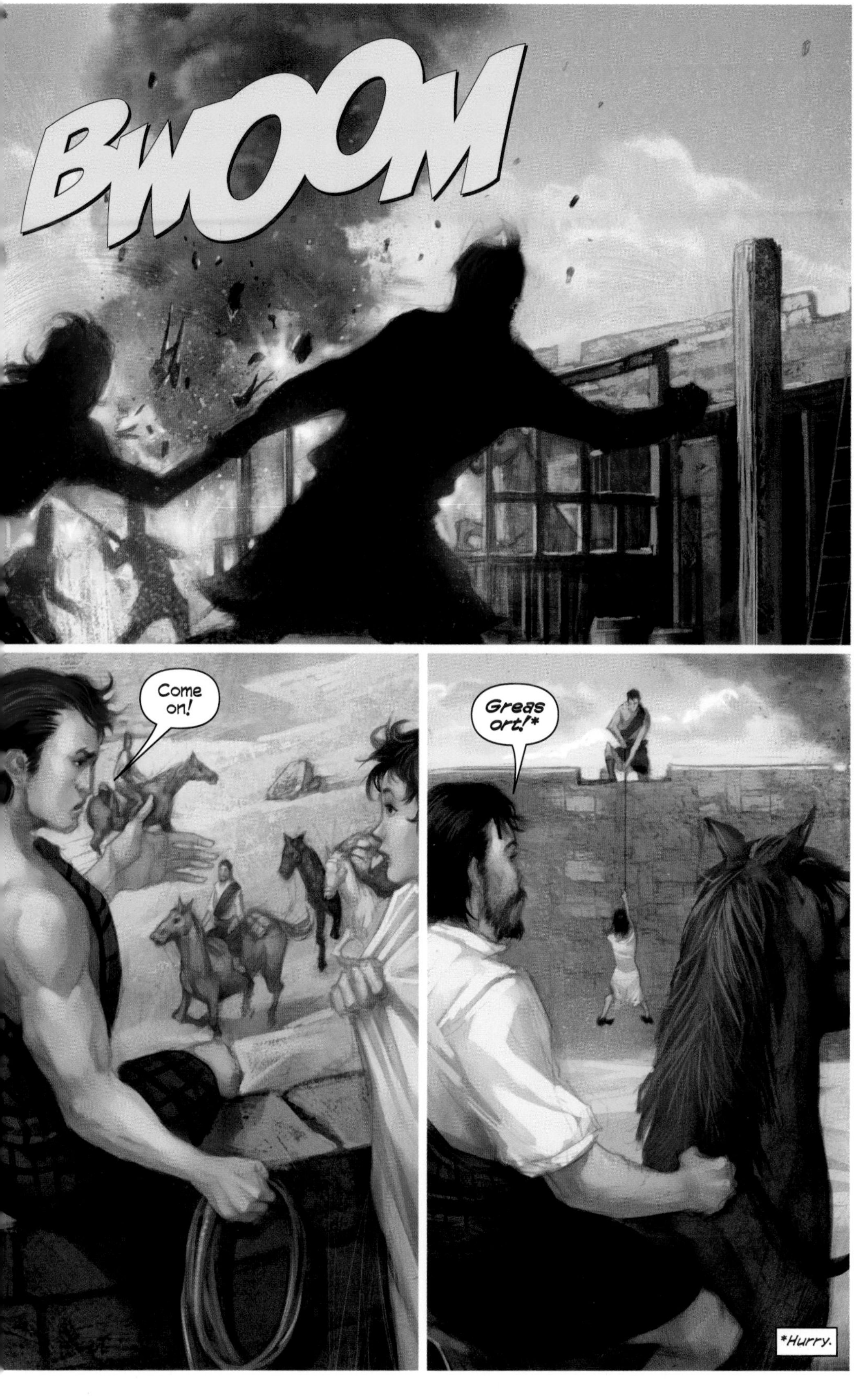
BWOOM
Come on!
Greas ort!*
*Hurry.

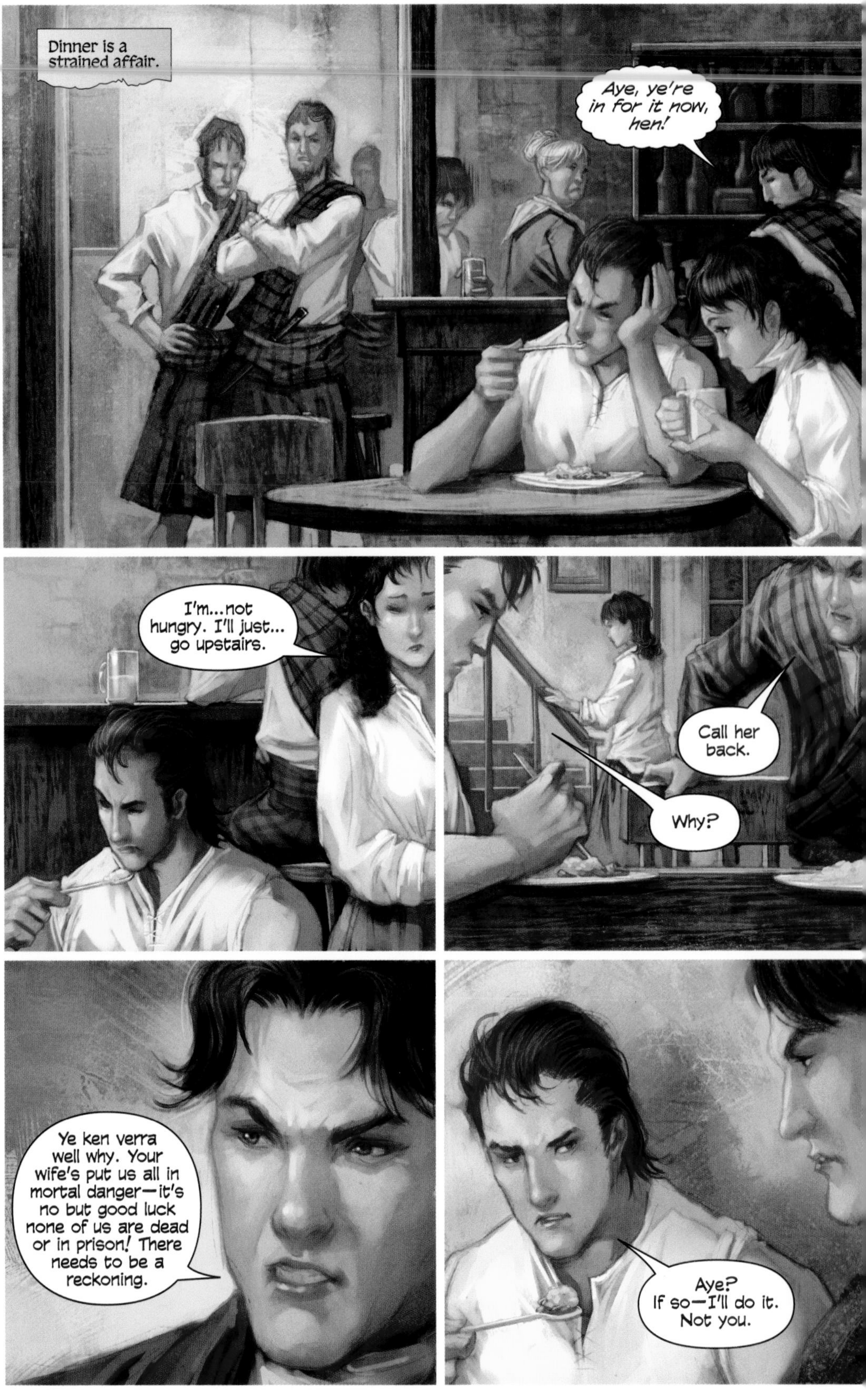
Dinner is a strained affair.
Aye, ye're in for it now, hen!
I'm...not hungry. I'll just... go upstairs.
Call her back.
Why?
Ye ken verra well why. Your wife's put us all in mortal danger—it's no but good luck none of us are dead or in prison! There needs to be a reckoning.
Aye? If so—I'll do it. Not you.

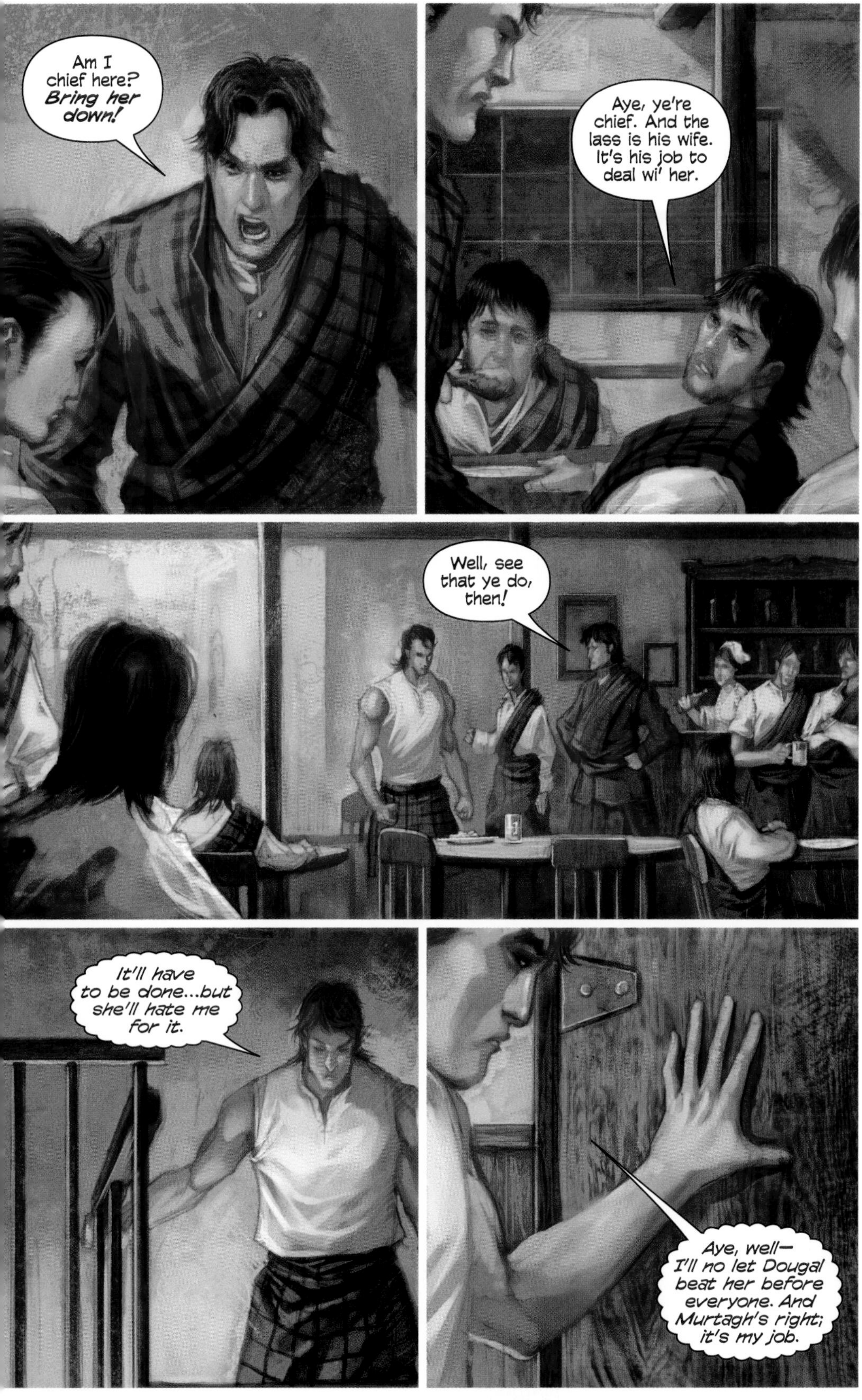
Am I chief here? *Bring her down!*
Aye, ye're chief. And the lass is his wife. It's his job to deal wi' her.
Well, see that ye do, then!
*It'll have to be done...but she'll hate me for it.*
*Aye, well— I'll no let Dougal beat her before everyone. And Murtagh's right; it's my job.*

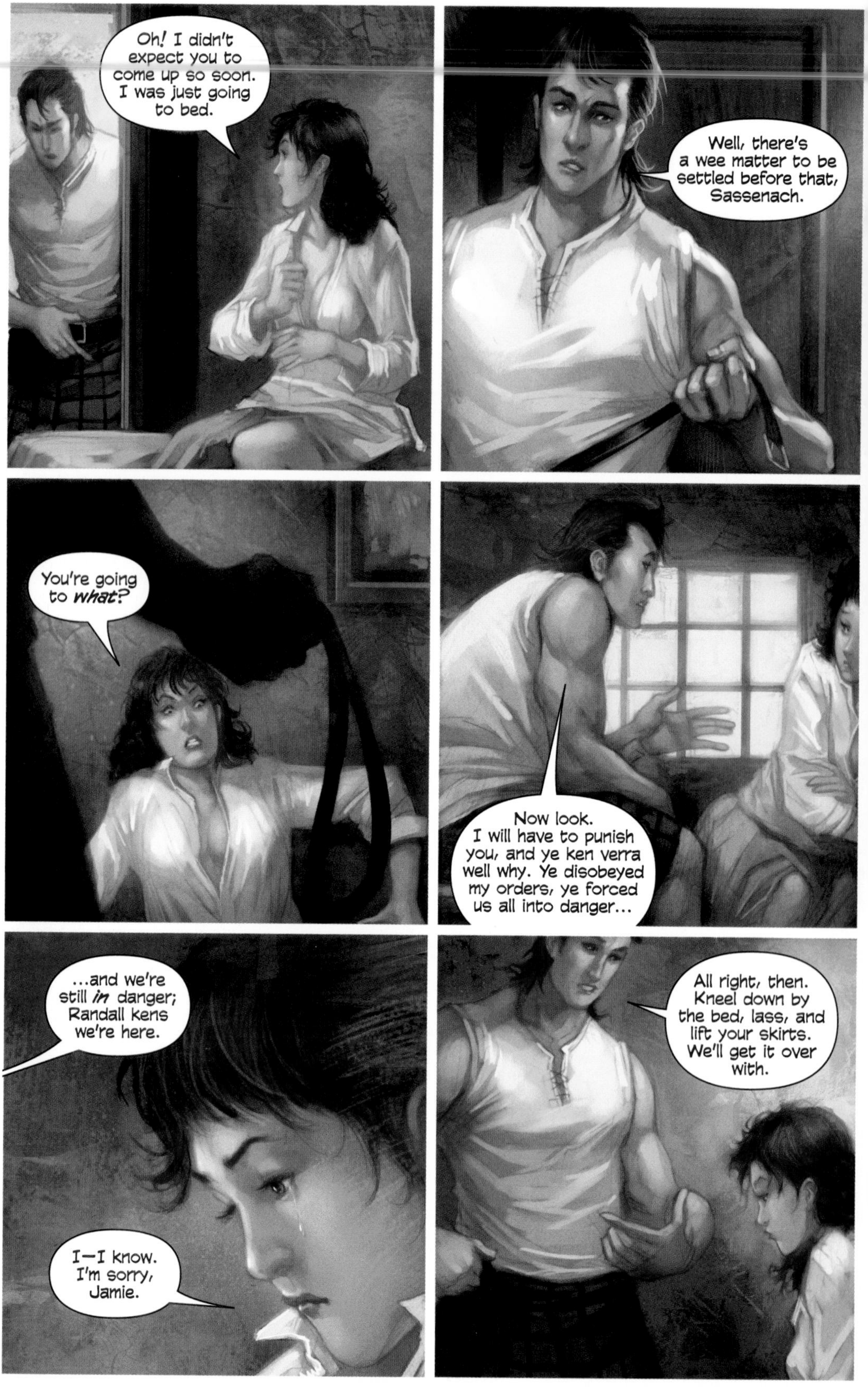
Oh! I didn't expect you to come up so soon. I was just going to bed.
Well, there's a wee matter to be settled before that, Sassenach.
You're going to *what*?
Now look. I will have to punish you, and ye ken verra well why. Ye disobeyed my orders, ye forced us all into danger...
...and we're still *in* danger; Randall kens we're here.
I—I know. I'm sorry, Jamie.
All right, then. Kneel down by the bed, lass, and lift your skirts. We'll get it over with.

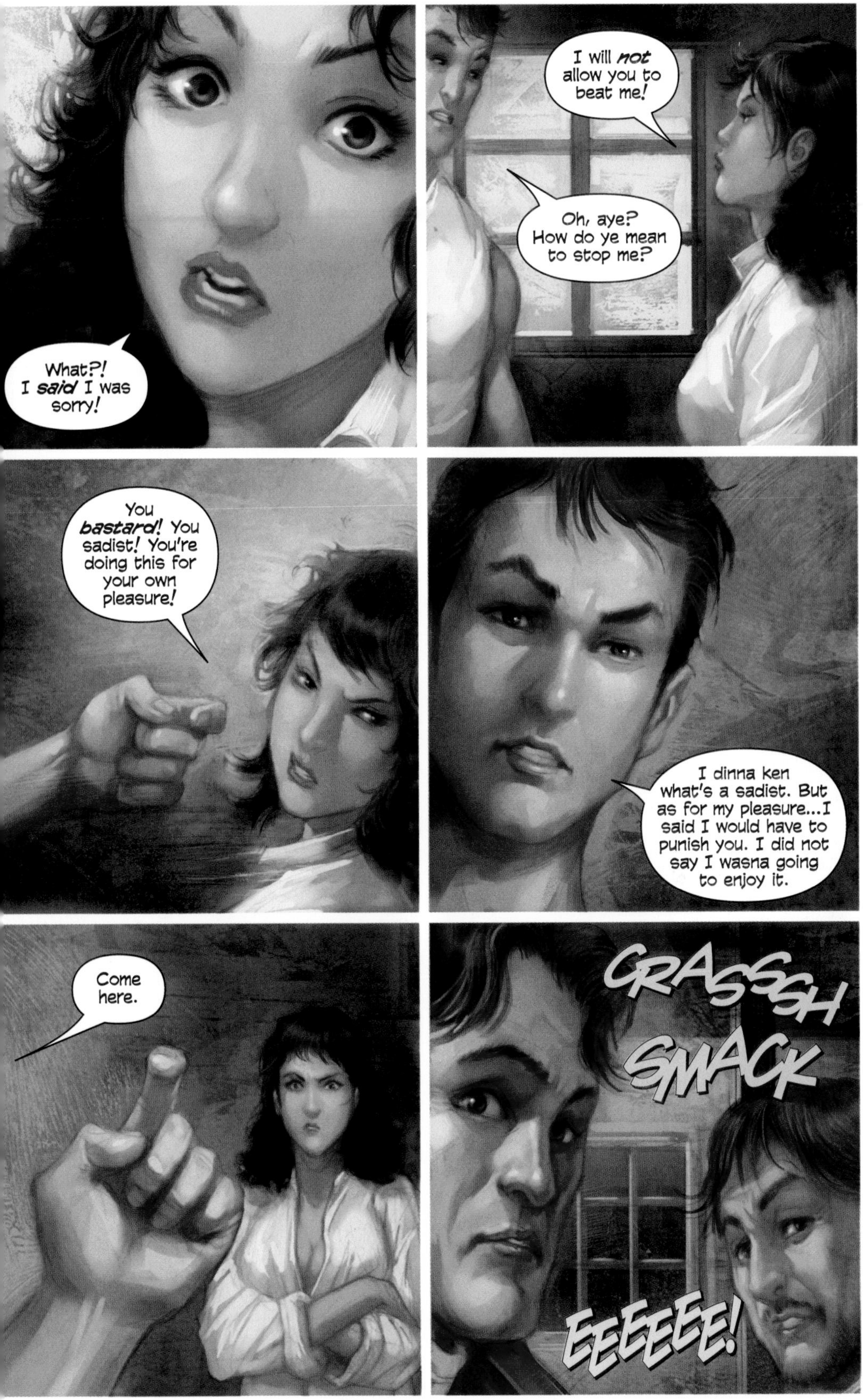
What?! I *said* I was sorry!
I will *not* allow you to beat me!
Oh, aye? How do ye mean to stop me?
You *bastard!* You sadist! You're doing this for your own pleasure!
I dinna ken what's a sadist. But as for my pleasure...I said I would have to punish you. I did not say I wasna going to enjoy it.
Come here.
CRASSSH
SMACK
EEEEEE!

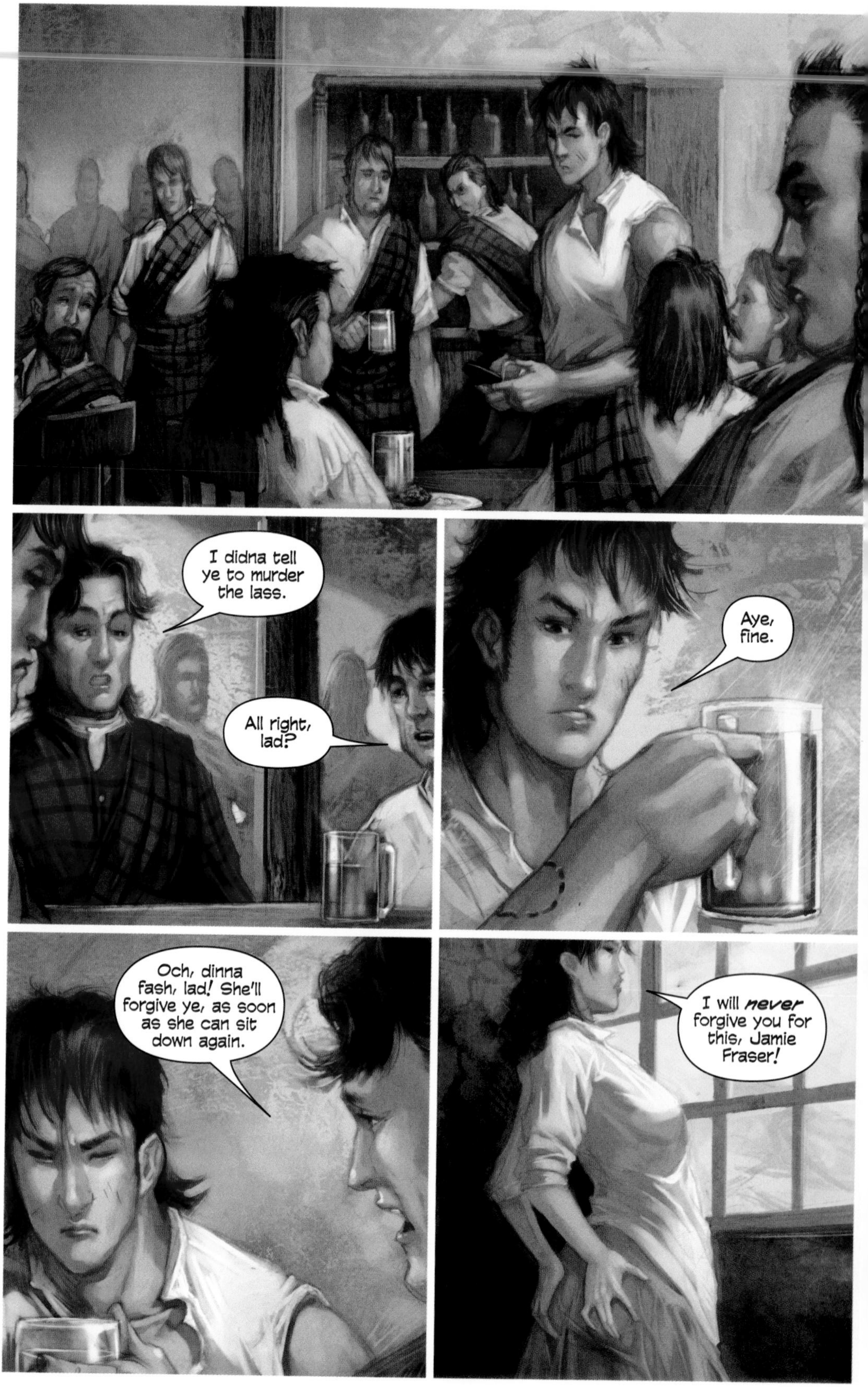
I didna tell ye to murder the lass.
All right, lad?
Aye, fine.
Och, dinna fash, lad! She'll forgive ye, as soon as she can sit down again.
I will *never* forgive you for this, Jamie Fraser!

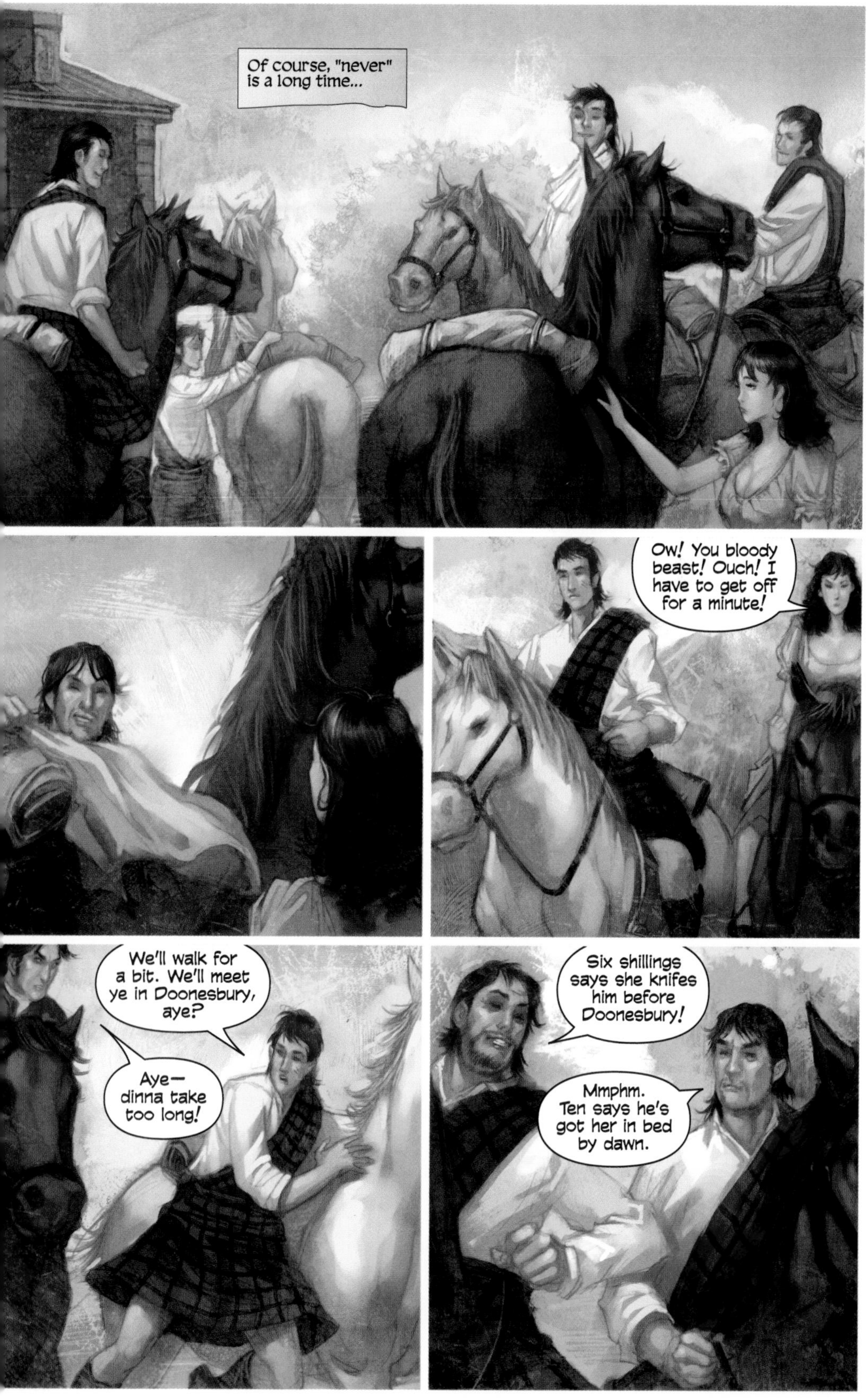
Of course, "never" is a long time...
Ow! You bloody beast! Ouch! I have to get off for a minute!
We'll walk for a bit. We'll meet ye in Doonesbury, aye?
Aye—dinna take too long!
Six shillings says she knifes him before Doonesbury!
Mmphm. Ten says he's got her in bed by dawn.

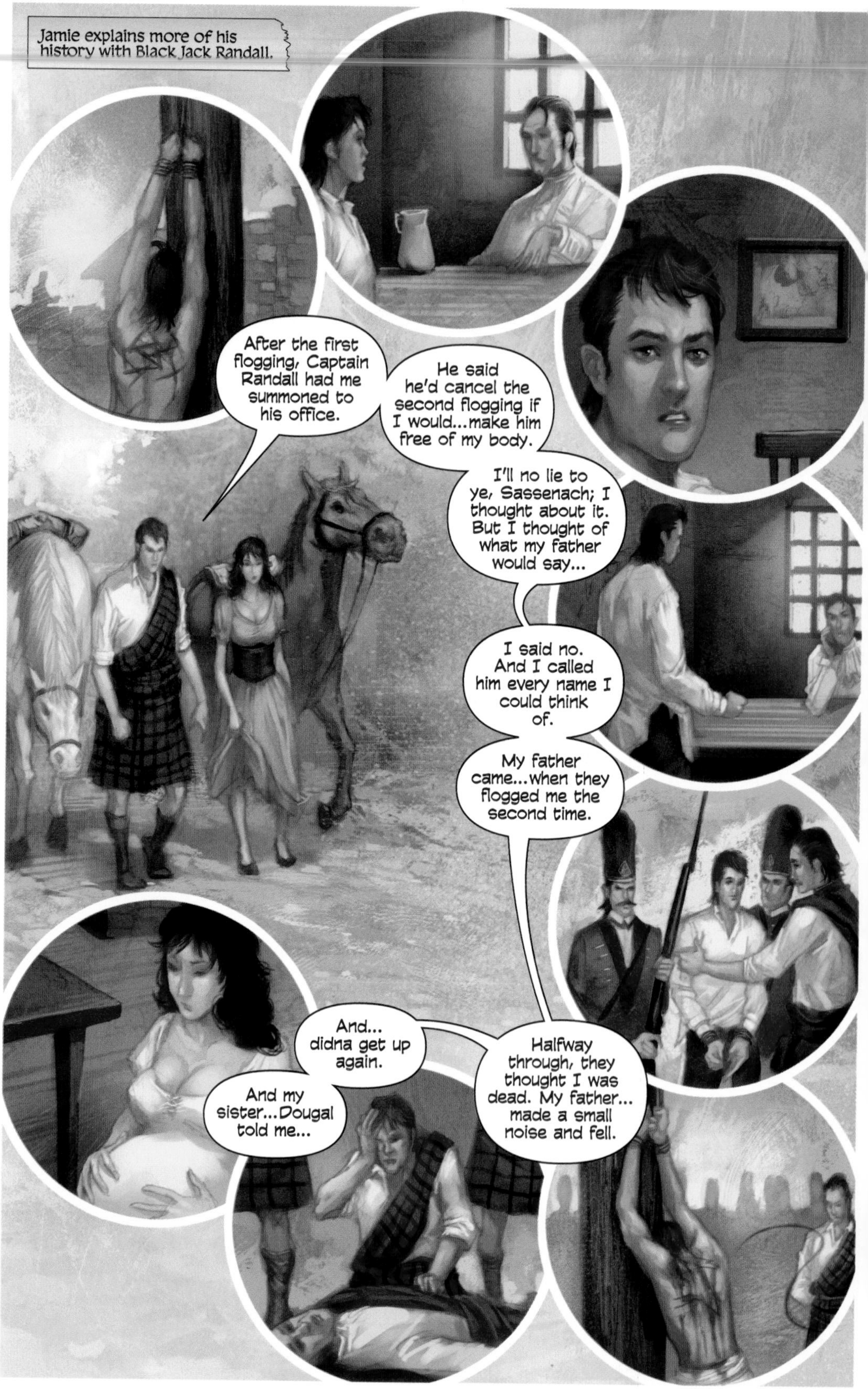
Jamie explains more of his history with Black Jack Randall.
After the first flogging, Captain Randall had me summoned to his office.
He said he'd cancel the second flogging if I would...make him free of my body.
I'll no lie to ye, Sassenach; I thought about it. But I thought of what my father would say...
I said no. And I called him every name I could think of.
My father came...when they flogged me the second time.
Halfway through, they thought I was dead. My father... made a small noise and fell.
And... didna get up again.
And my sister...Dougal told me...

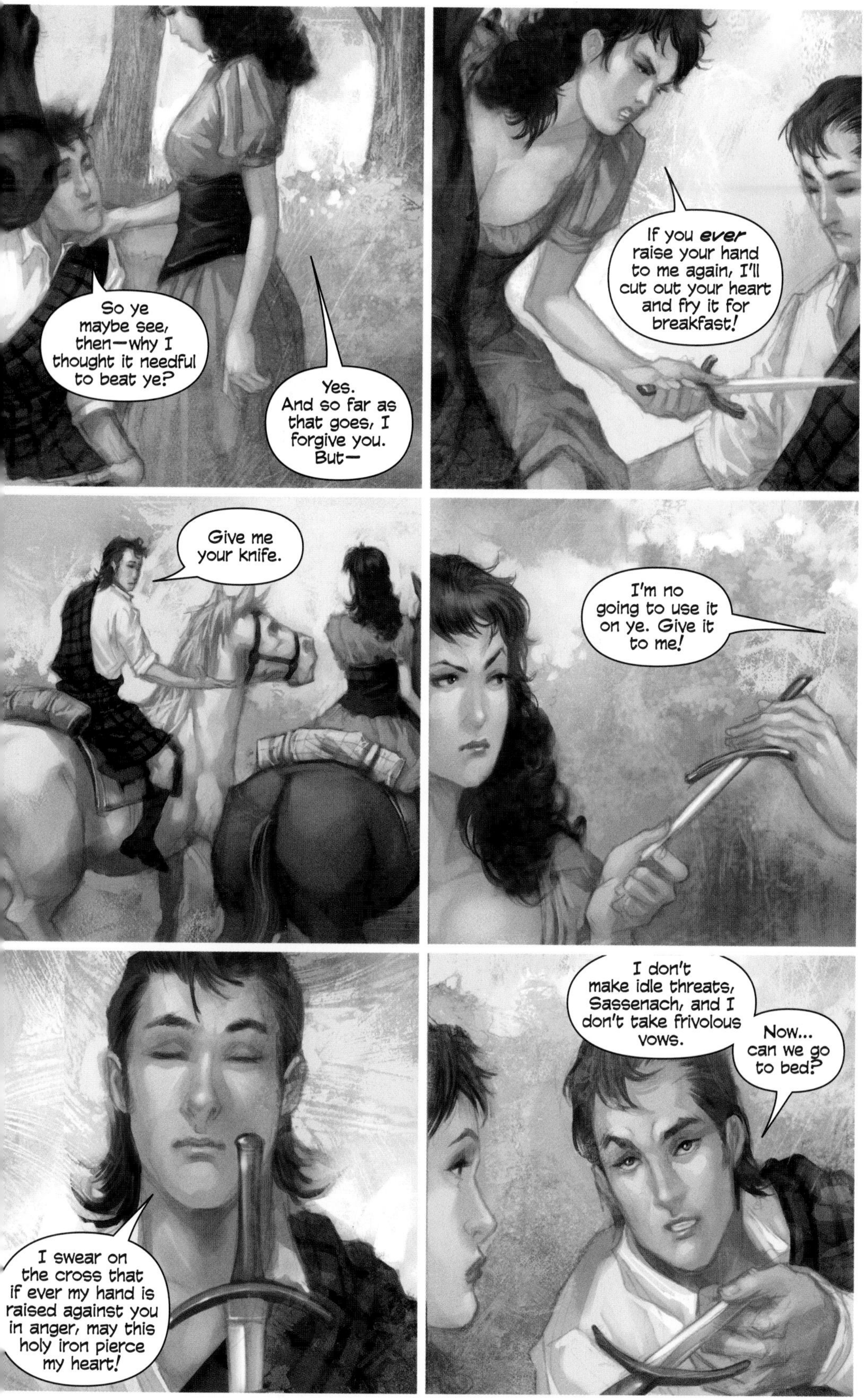
So ye maybe see, then—why I thought it needful to beat ye?
Yes. And so far as that goes, I forgive you. But—
If you *ever* raise your hand to me again, I'll cut out your heart and fry it for breakfast!
Give me your knife.
I'm no going to use it on ye. Give it to me!
I swear on the cross that if ever my hand is raised against you in anger, may this holy iron pierce my heart!
I don't make idle threats, Sassenach, and I don't take frivolous vows.
Now... can we go to bed?

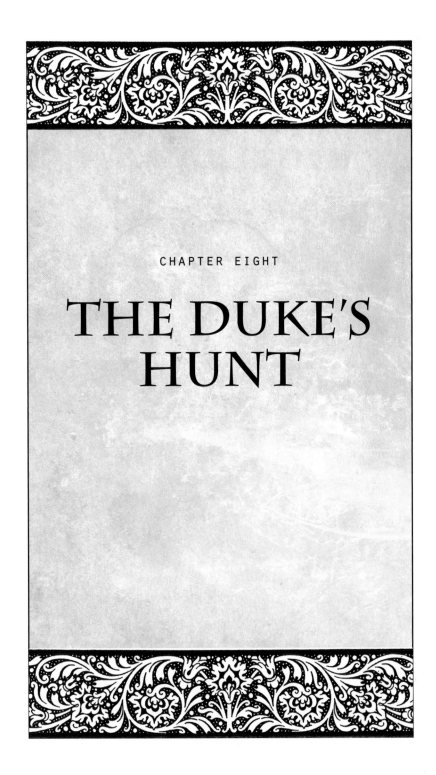

CHAPTER EIGHT

# THE DUKE'S HUNT

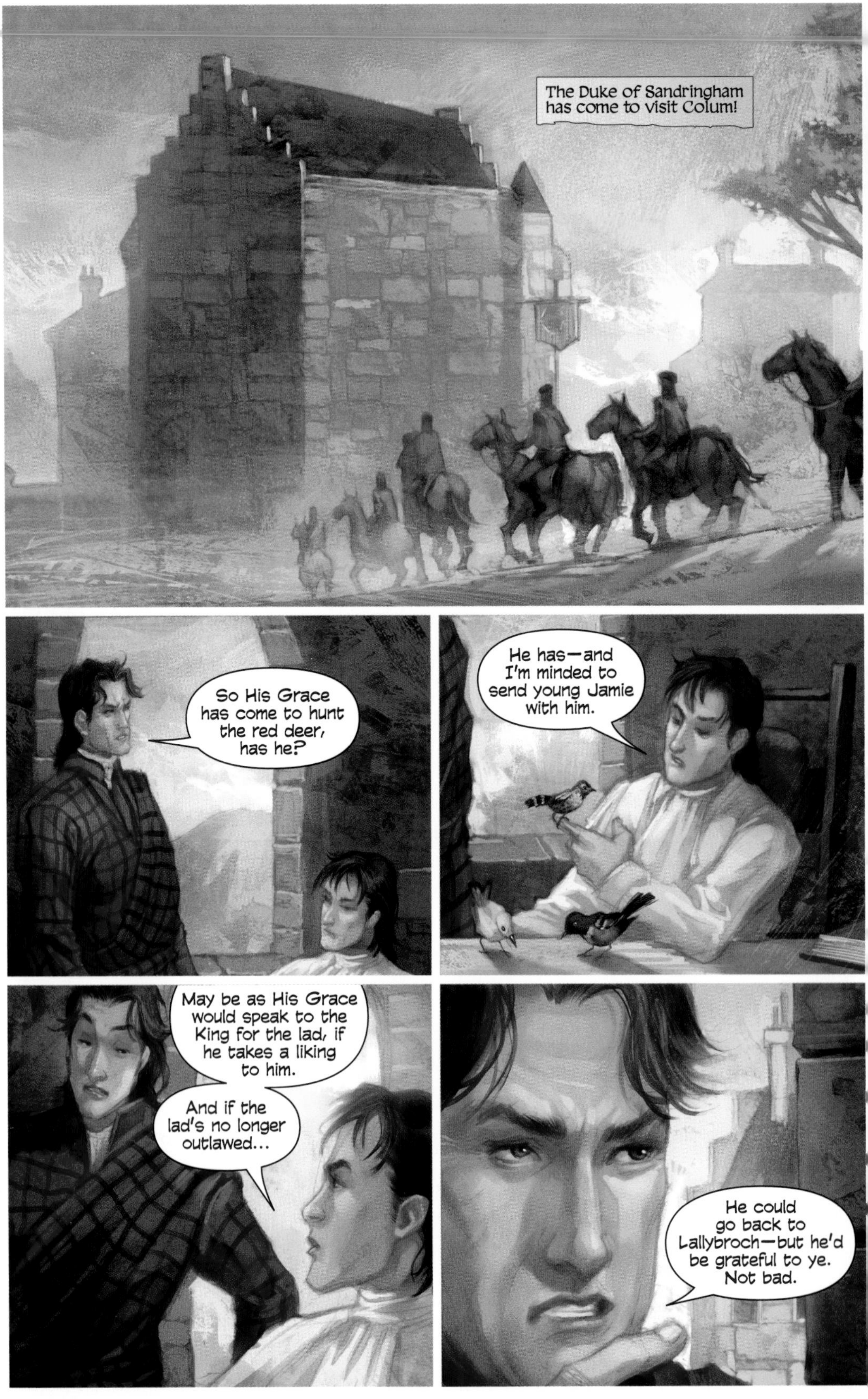

The Duke of Sandringham has come to visit Colum!
So His Grace has come to hunt the red deer, has he?
He has—and I'm minded to send young Jamie with him.
May be as His Grace would speak to the King for the lad, if he takes a liking to him.
And if the lad's no longer outlawed...
He could go back to Lallybroch—but he'd be grateful to ye. Not bad.

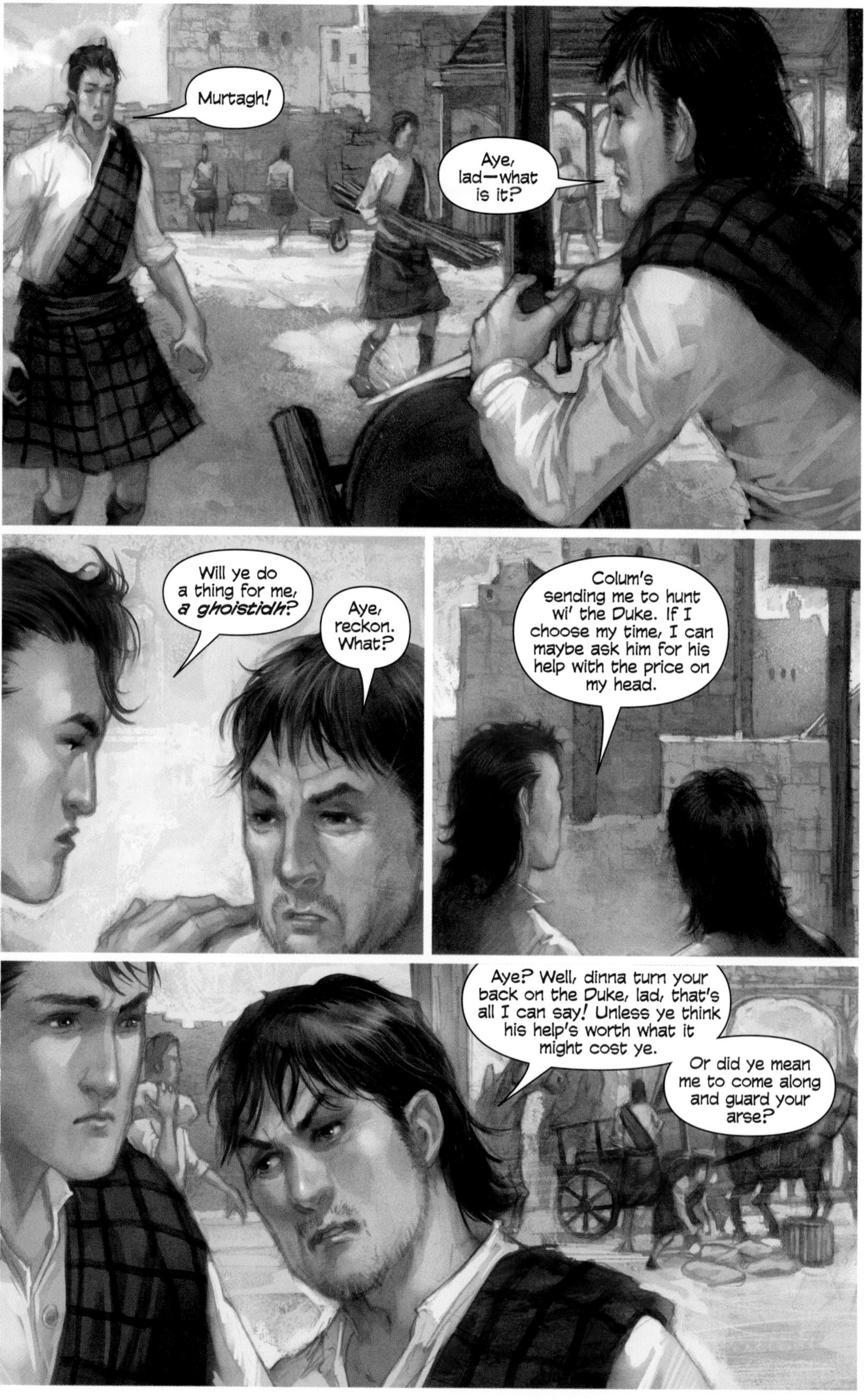
Murtagh!
Aye, lad—what is it?
Will ye do a thing for me, *a ghoistidh*?
Aye, reckon. What?
Colum's sending me to hunt wi' the Duke. If I choose my time, I can maybe ask him for his help with the price on my head.
Aye? Well, dinna turn your back on the Duke, lad, that's all I can say! Unless ye think his help's worth what it might cost ye.
Or did ye mean me to come along and guard your arse?

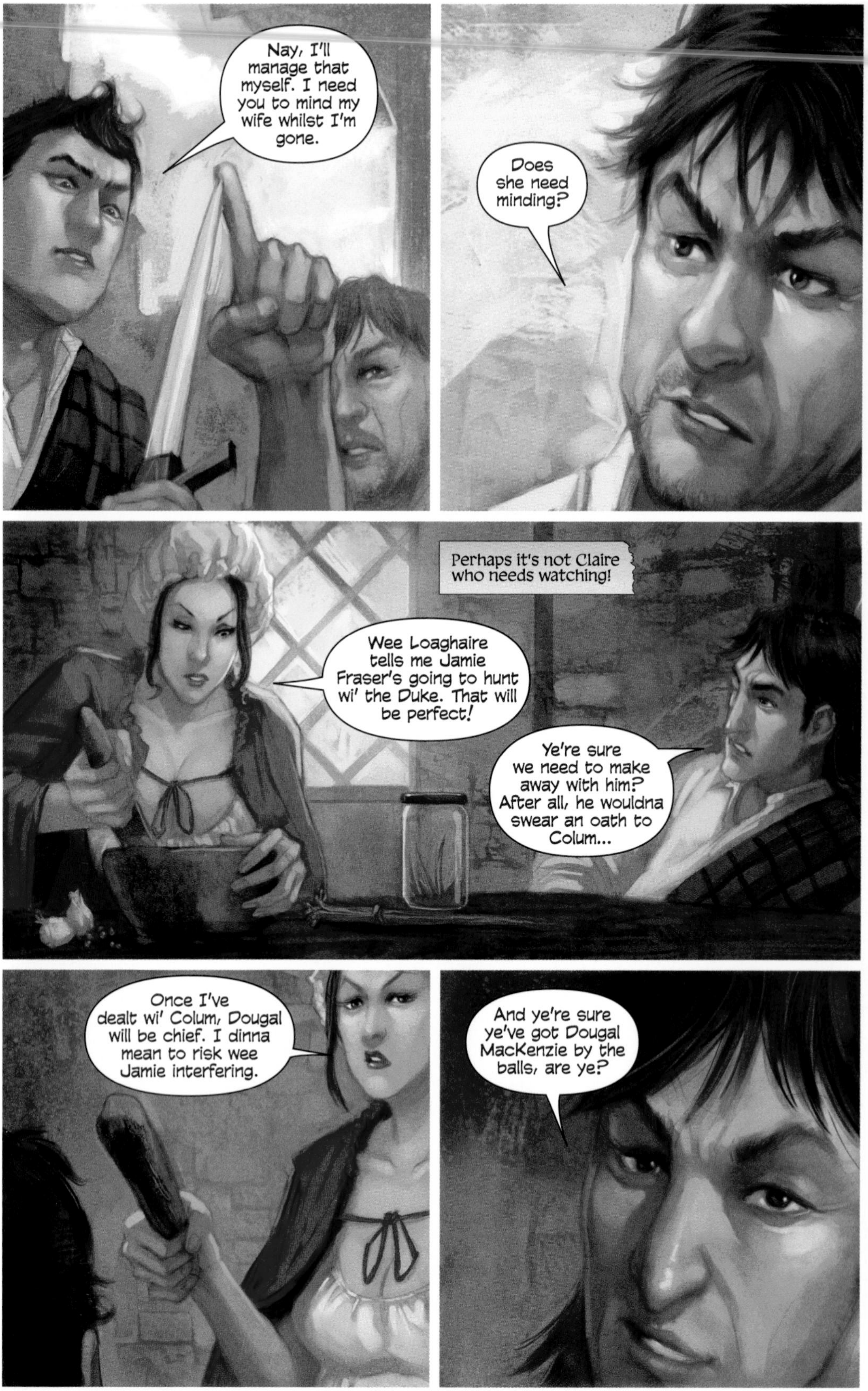
Nay, I'll manage that myself. I need you to mind my wife whilst I'm gone.
Does she need minding?
Perhaps it's not Claire who needs watching!
Wee Loaghaire tells me Jamie Fraser's going to hunt wi' the Duke. That will be perfect!
Ye're sure we need to make away with him? After all, he wouldna swear an oath to Colum...
Once I've dealt wi' Colum, Dougal will be chief. I dinna mean to risk wee Jamie interfering.
And ye're sure ye've got Dougal MacKenzie by the balls, are ye?

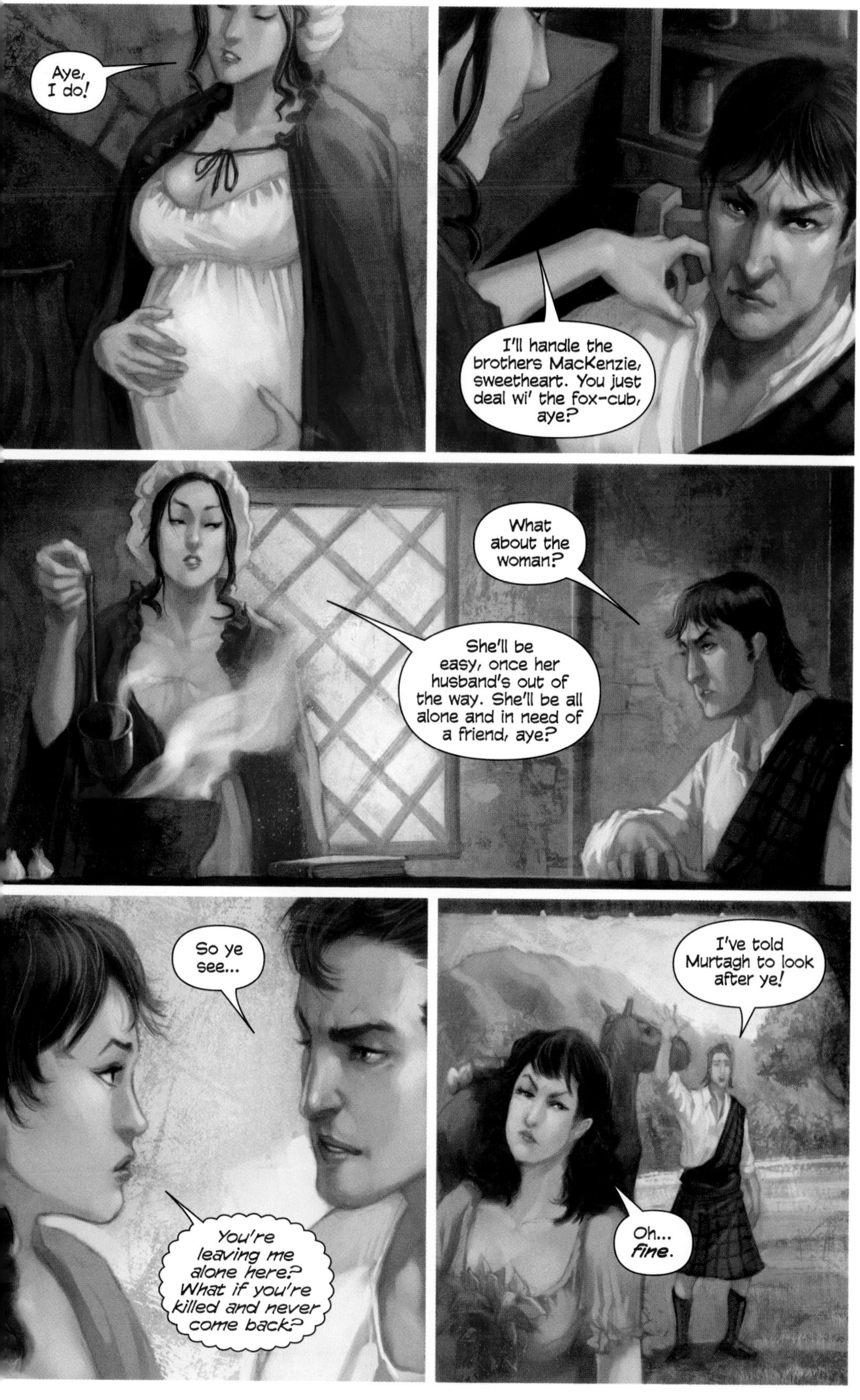
Aye, I do!
I'll handle the brothers MacKenzie, sweetheart. You just deal wi' the fox-cub, aye?
What about the woman?
She'll be easy, once her husband's out of the way. She'll be all alone and in need of a friend, aye?
So ye see...
*You're leaving me alone here? What if you're killed and never come back?*
I've told Murtagh to look after ye!
Oh... *fine*.

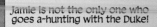
Jamie is not the only one who goes a-hunting with the Duke!

I'll find a gang of broken men, near the saint's pool in the Great Glen, Geilie says. How the devil does she ken these things?

Toward sunset that day...

I suppose she **would** know; she's a bloody witch, after all...

*Gasp!*

Stand and deliver!

Oh, I will! I've a proposition for ye, gentle-men!

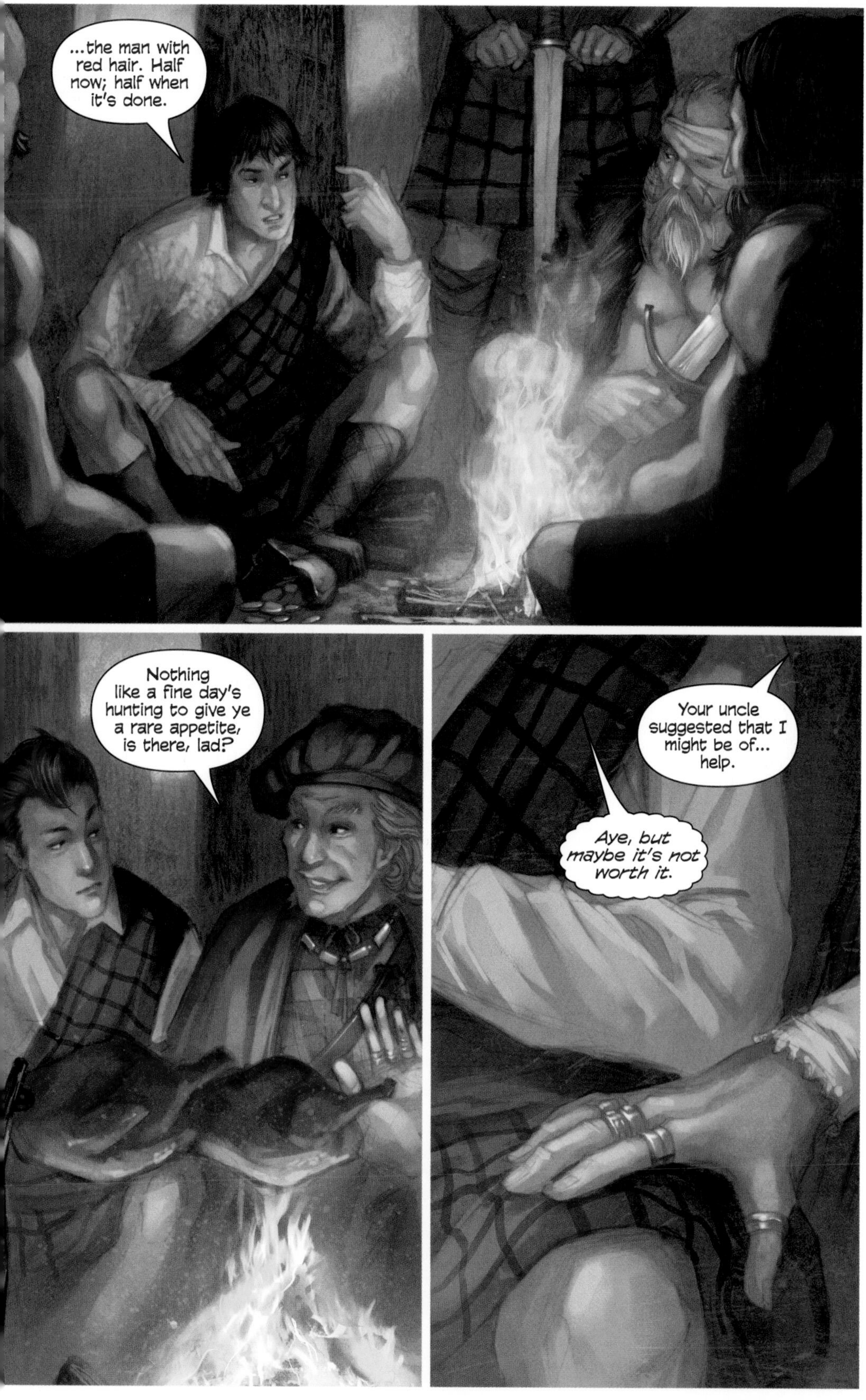
...the man with red hair. Half now; half when it's done.
Nothing like a fine day's hunting to give ye a rare appetite, is there, lad?
Your uncle suggested that I might be of... help.
*Aye, but maybe it's not worth it.*

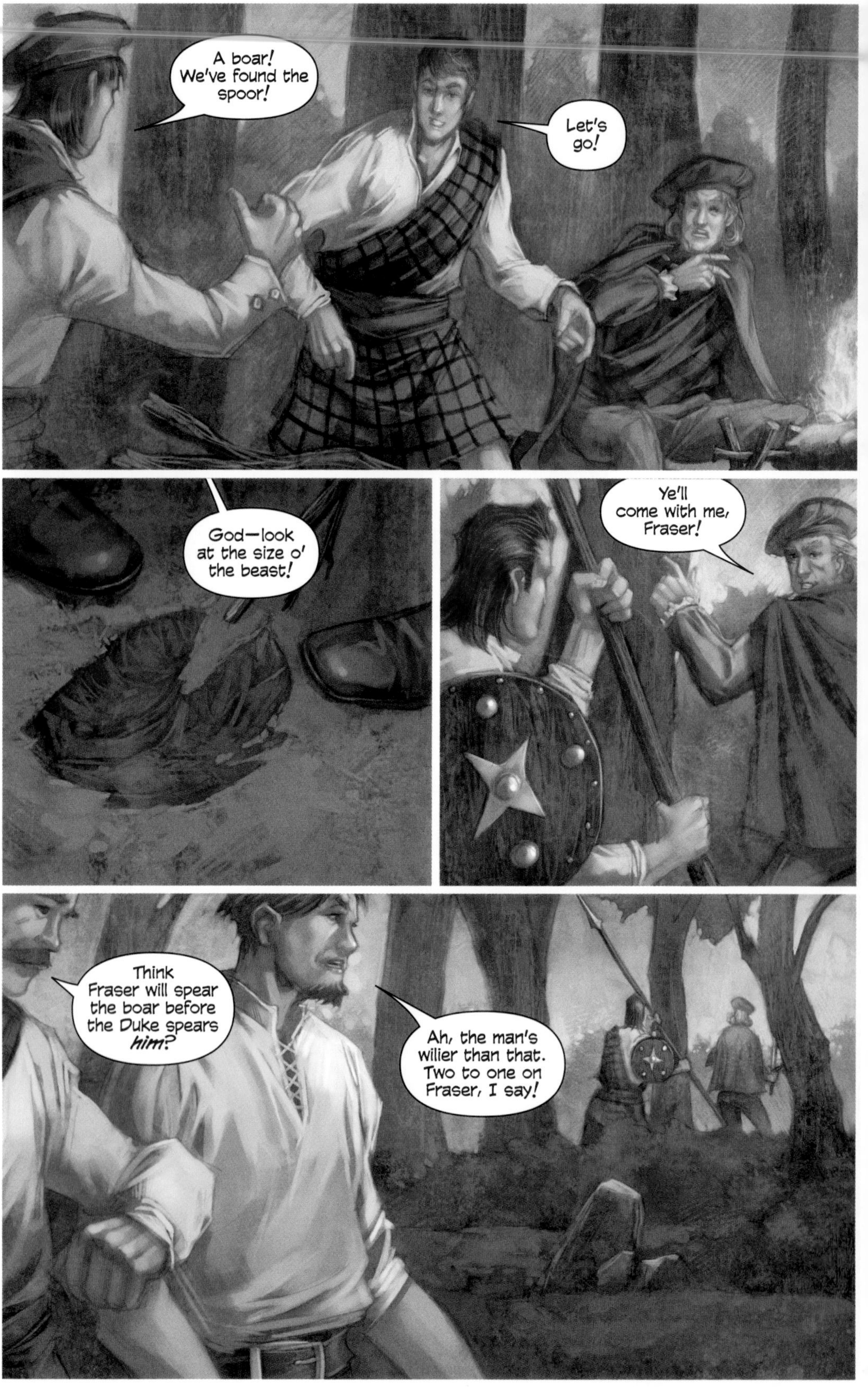
A boar! We've found the spoor!
Let's go!
God—look at the size o' the beast!
Ye'll come with me, Fraser!
Think Fraser will spear the boar before the Duke spears *him*?
Ah, the man's wilier than that. Two to one on Fraser, I say!

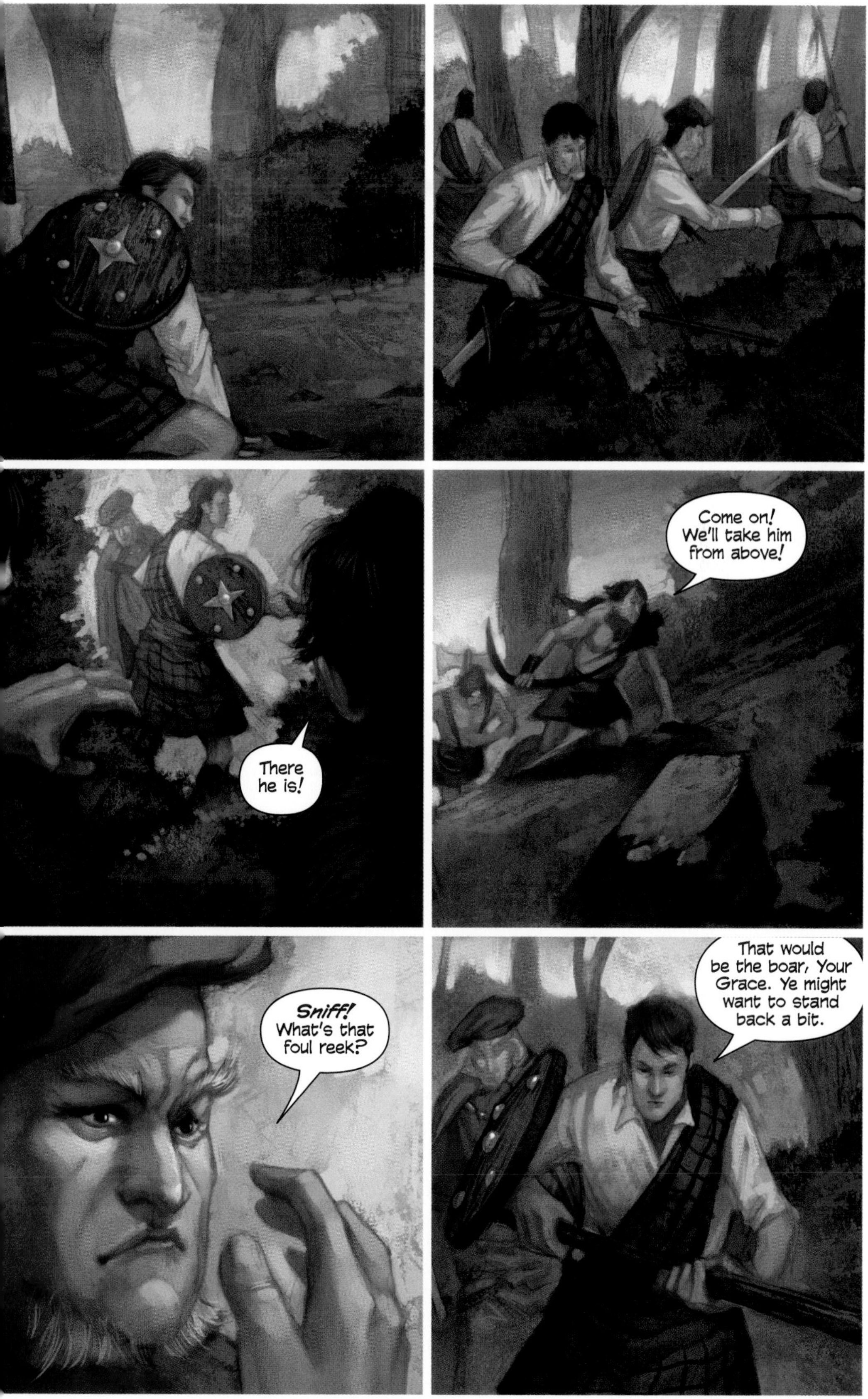
There he is!
Come on! We'll take him from above!
Sniff! What's that foul reek?
That would be the boar, Your Grace. Ye might want to stand back a bit.

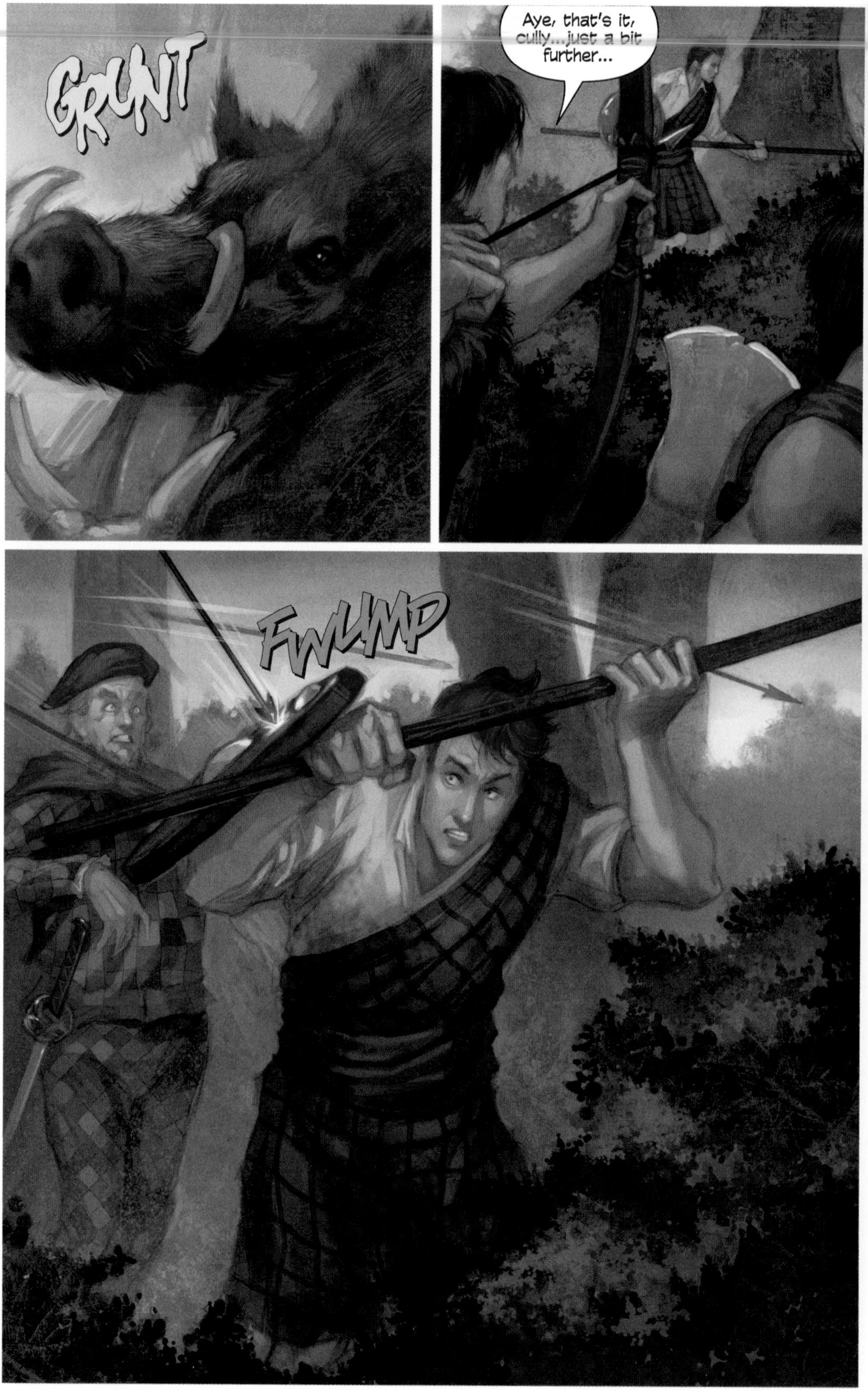
GRUNT
Aye, that's it, cully...just a bit further...
FWUMP

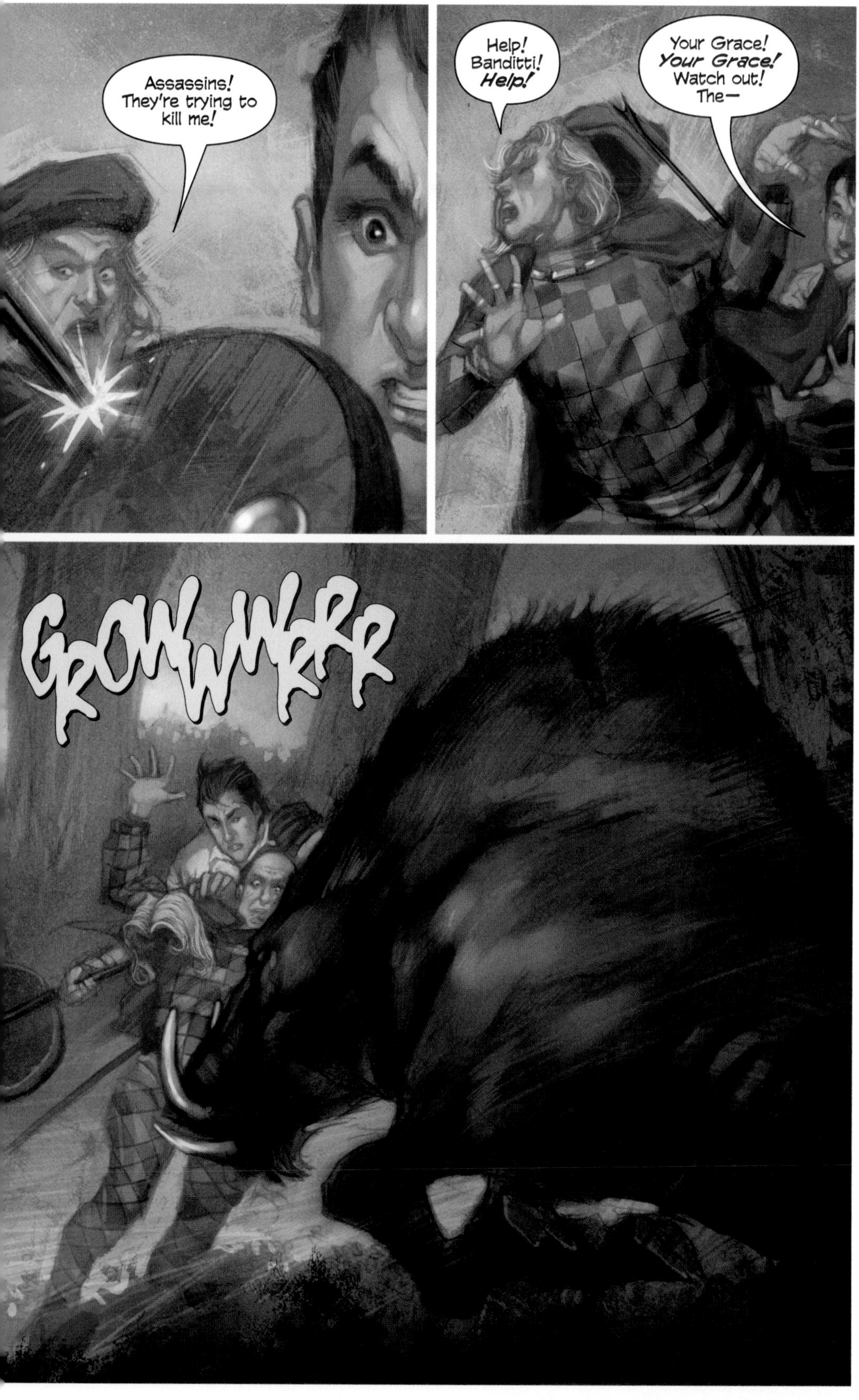
Assassins! They're trying to kill me!
Help! Banditti! *Help!*
Your Grace! *Your Grace!* Watch out! The—
GROWWRR

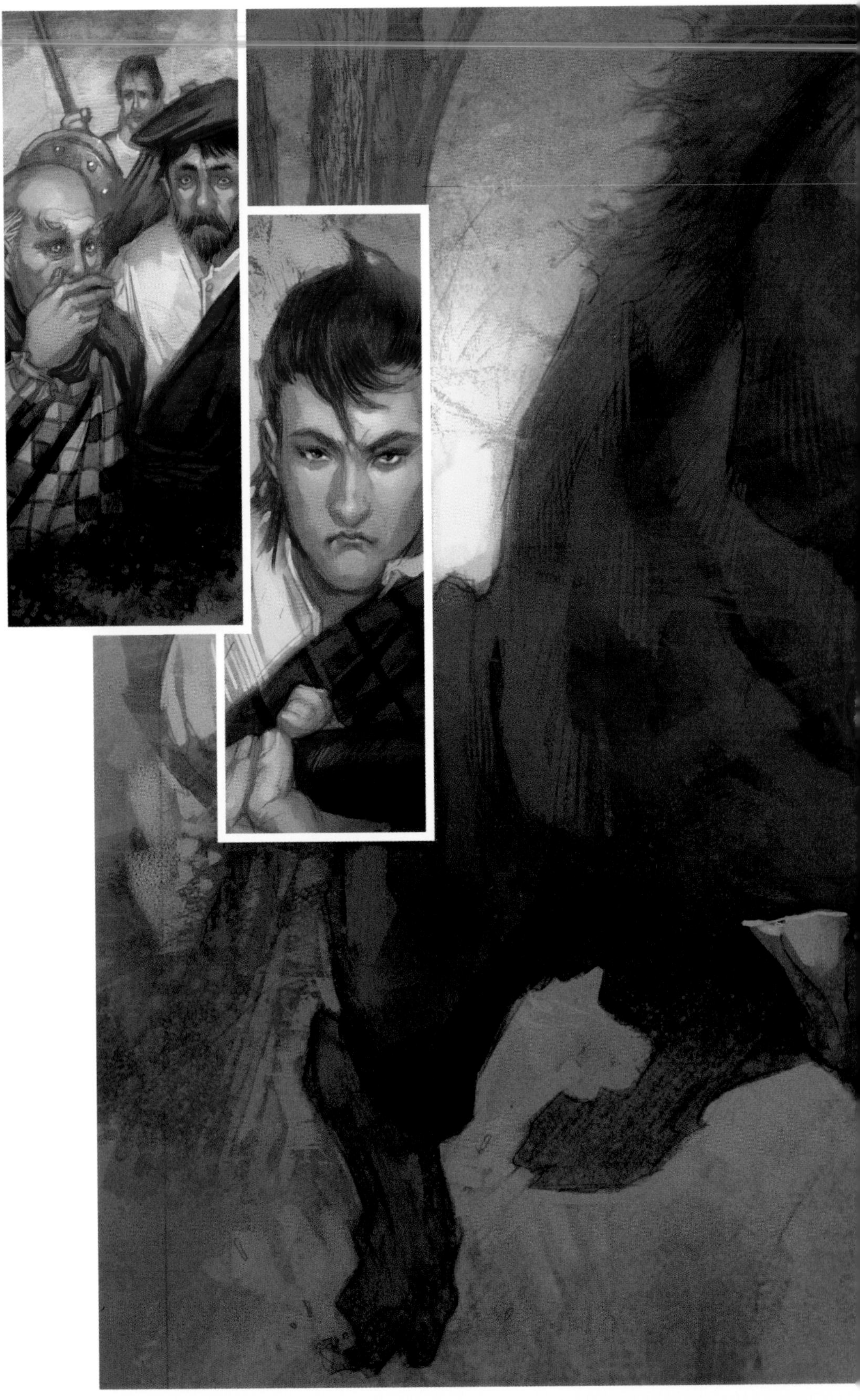

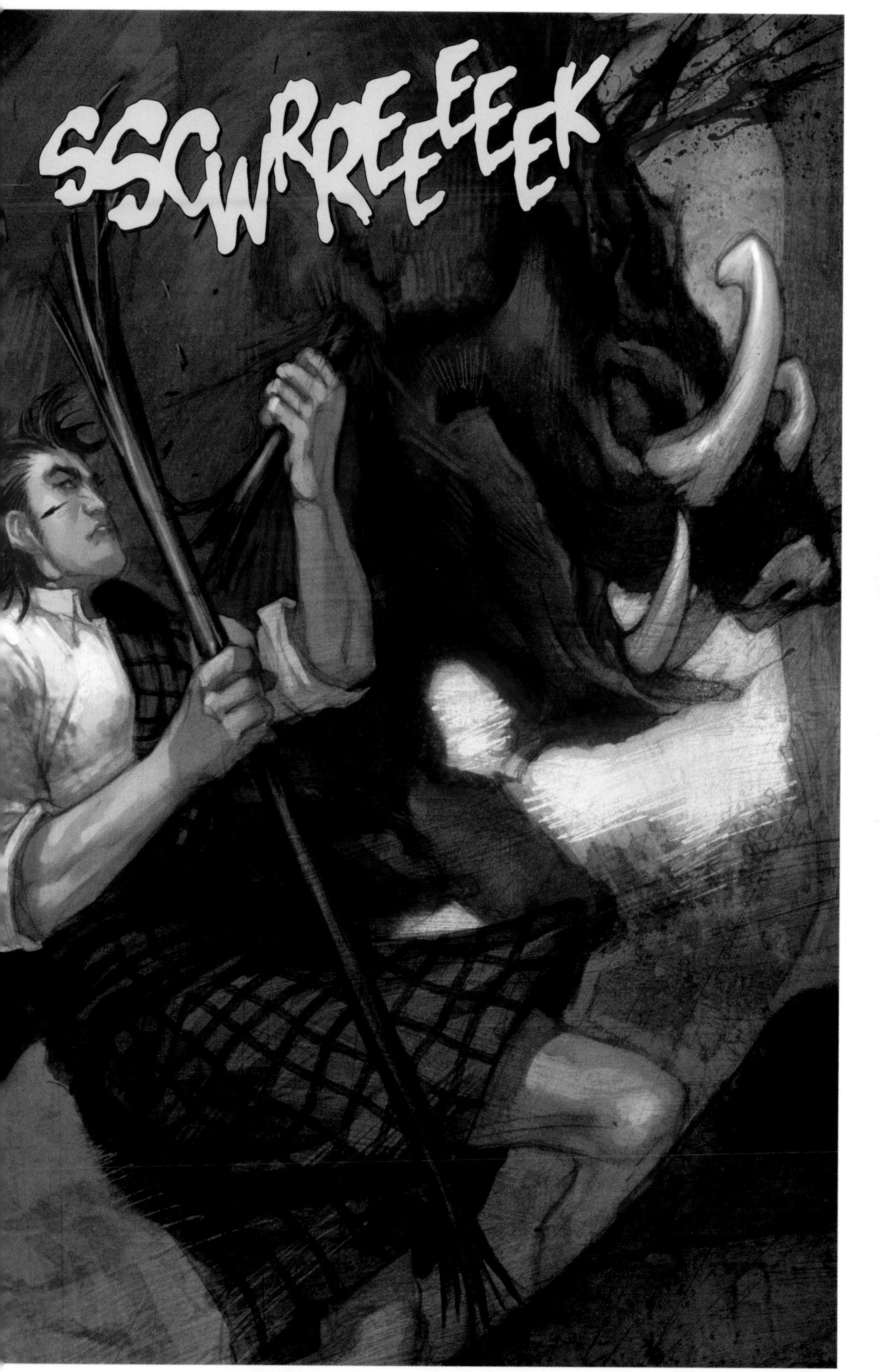
SSCWRREEEEEK

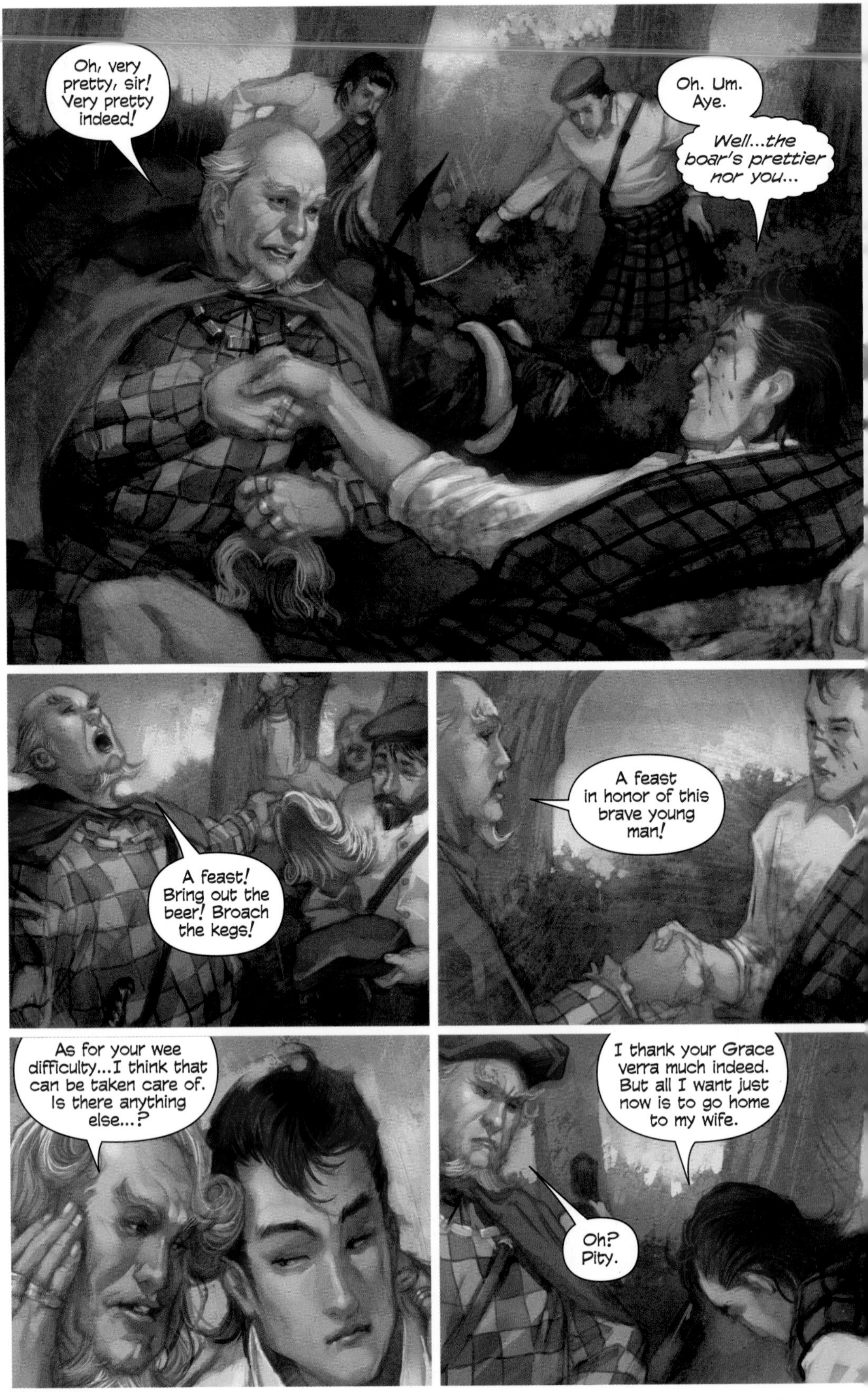
Oh, very pretty, sir! Very pretty indeed!
Oh. Um. Aye.
Well...the boar's prettier nor you...
A feast! Bring out the beer! Broach the kegs!
A feast in honor of this brave young man!
As for your wee difficulty...I think that can be taken care of. Is there anything else...?
I thank your Grace verra much indeed. But all I want just now is to go home to my wife.
Oh? Pity.

CHAPTER NINE

# SUFFER
# A WITCH

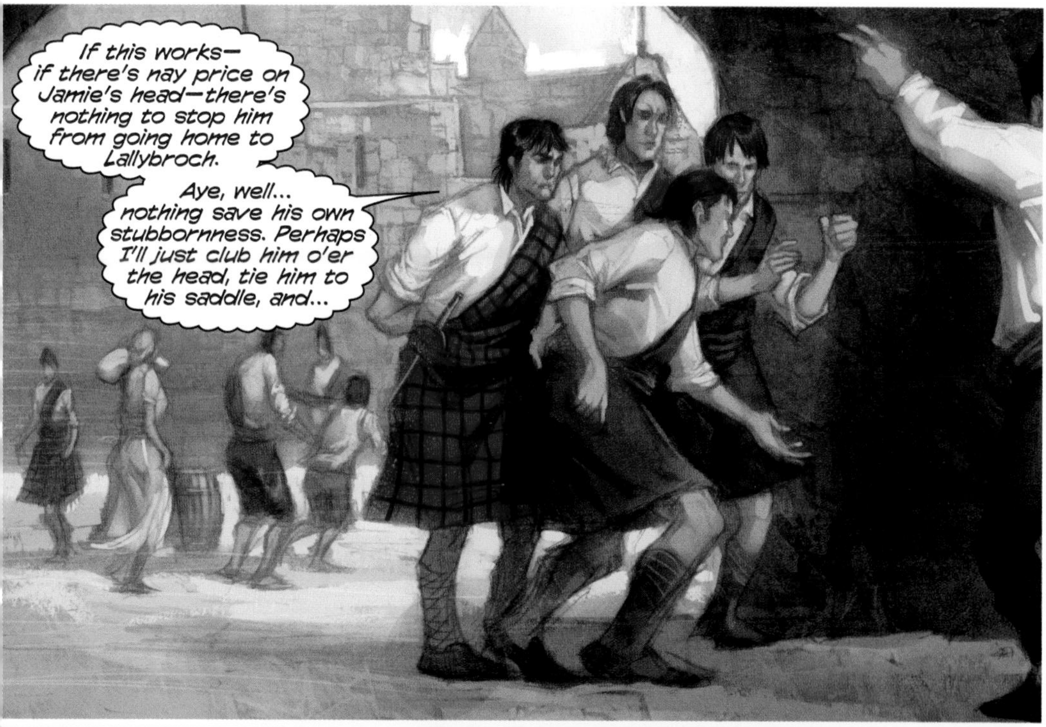
If this works—if there's nay price on Jamie's head—there's nothing to stop him from going home to Lallybroch.
Aye, well... nothing save his own stubbornness. Perhaps I'll just club him o'er the head, tie him to his saddle, and...

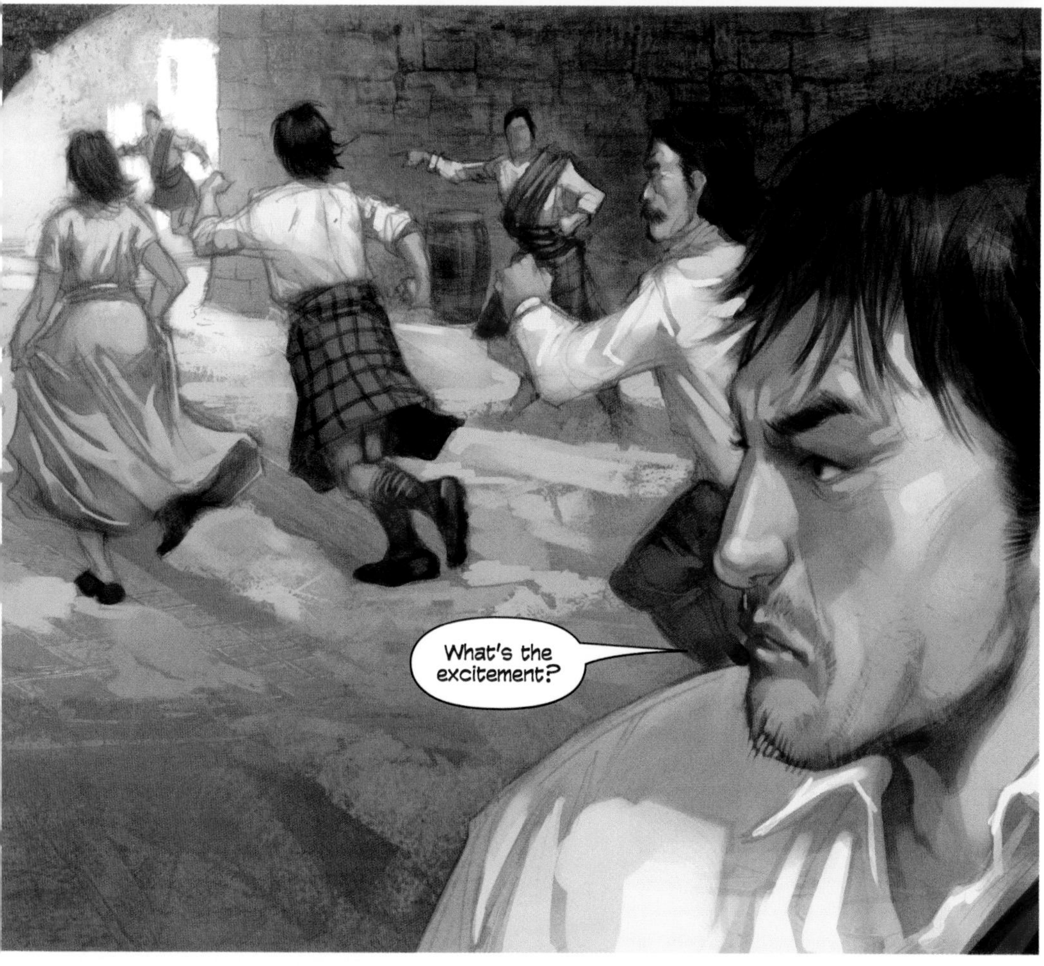
What's the excitement?

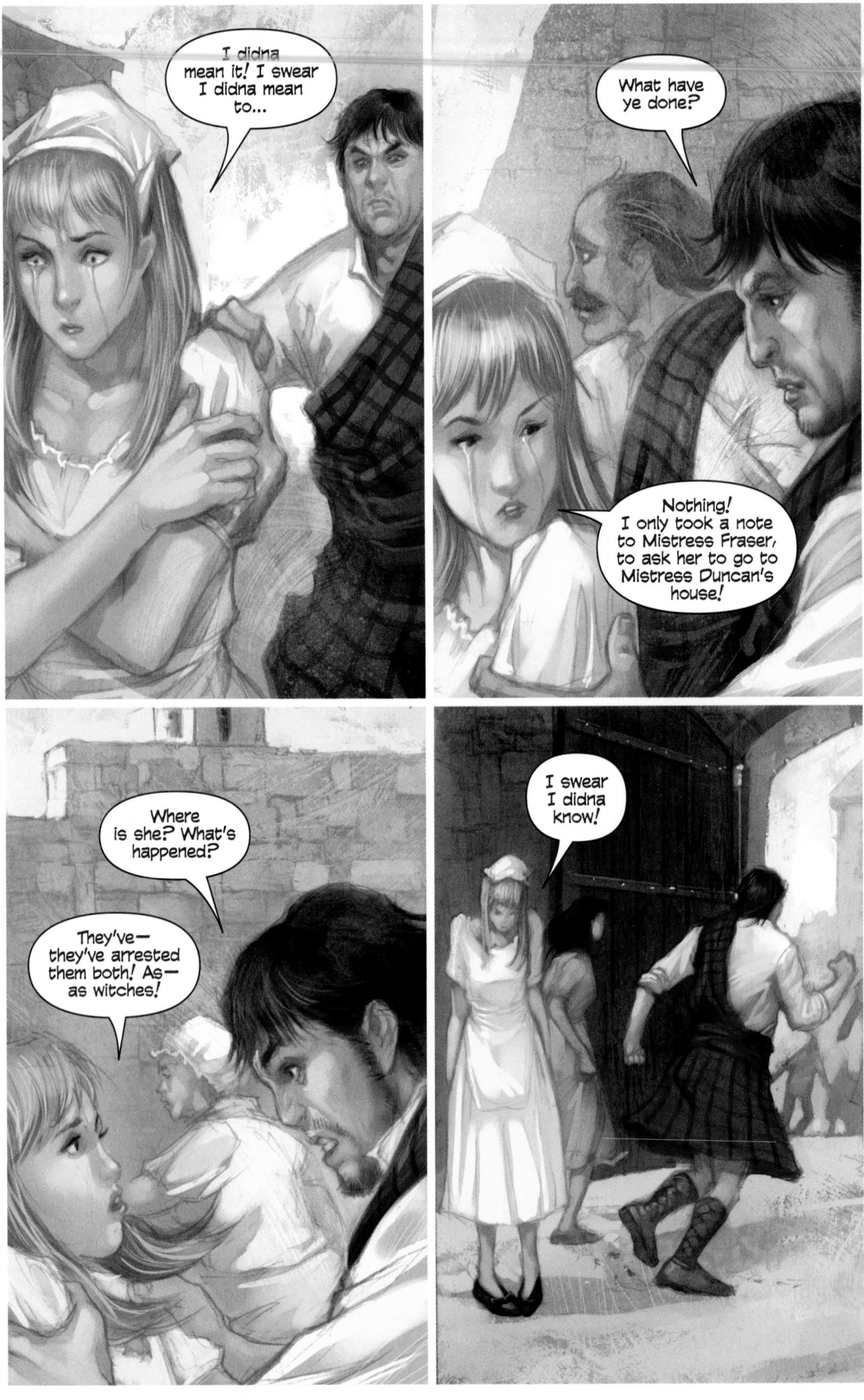
I didna mean it! I swear I didna mean to...
What have ye done?
Nothing! I only took a note to Mistress Fraser, to ask her to go to Mistress Duncan's house!
Where is she? What's happened?
They've— they've arrested them both! As— as witches!
I swear I didna know!

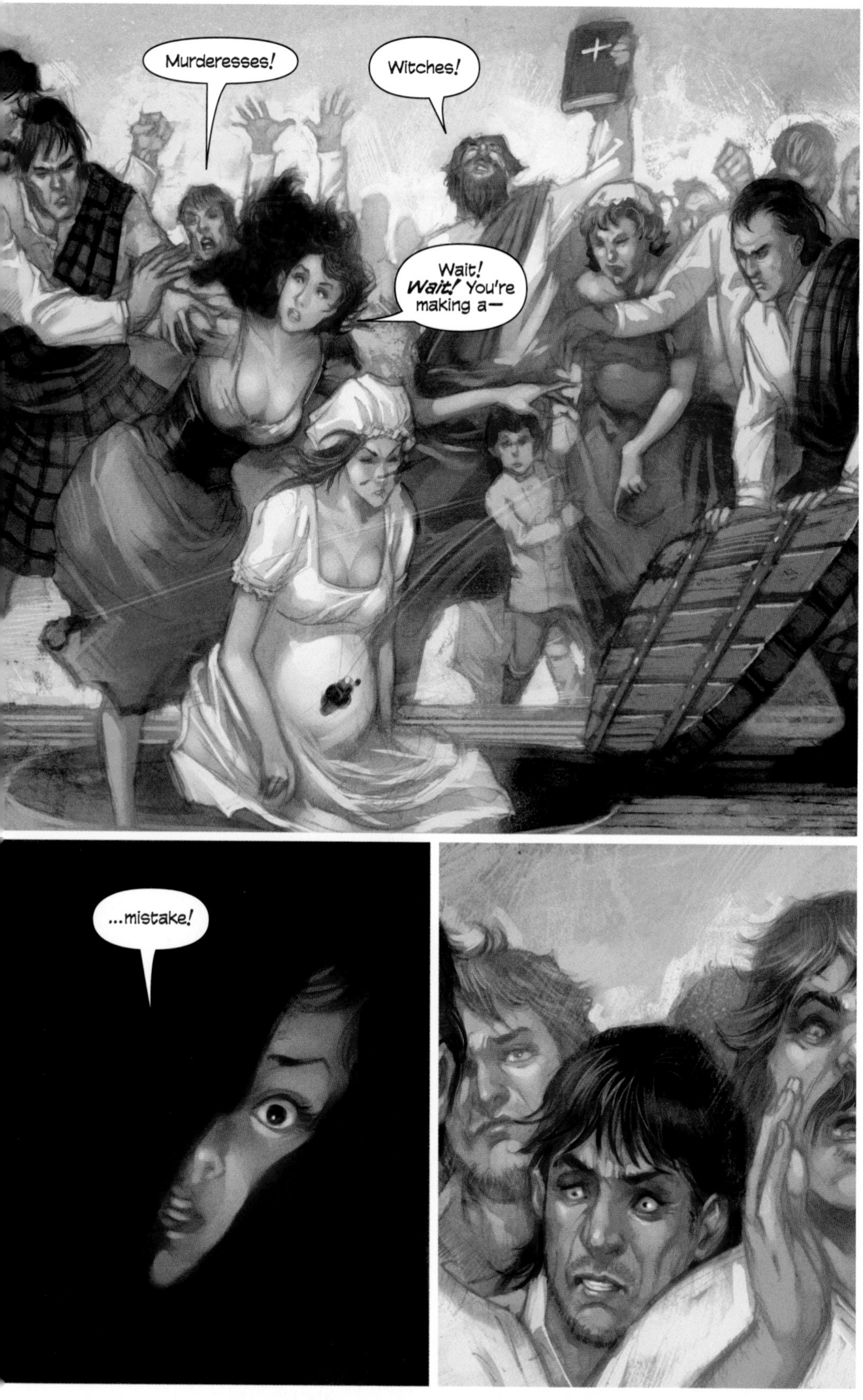
Murderesses!
Witches!
Wait! *Wait!* You're making a—
...mistake!

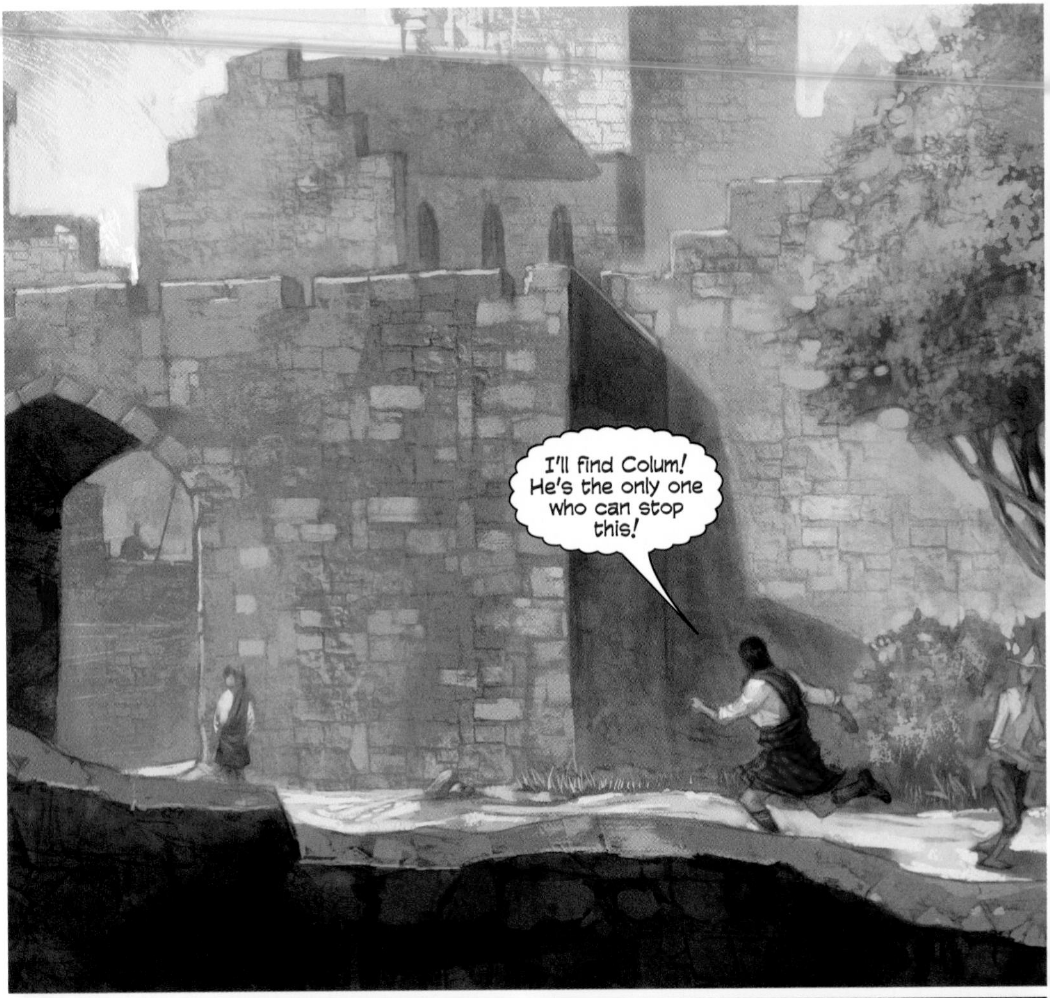
I'll find Colum! He's the only one who can stop this!

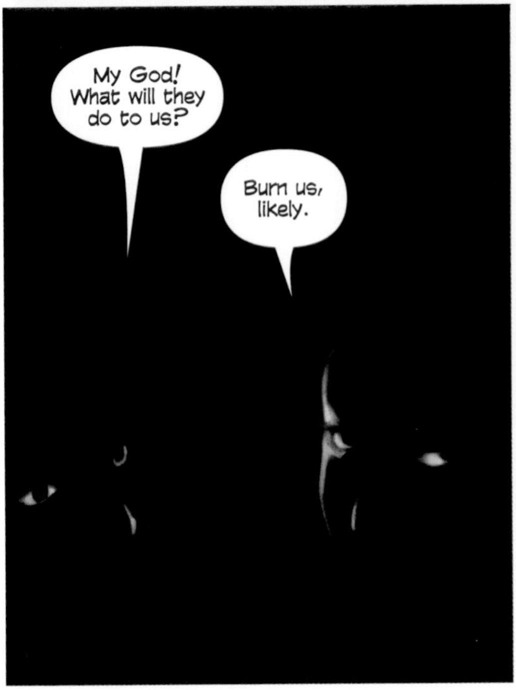
My God! What will they do to us?
Burn us, likely.

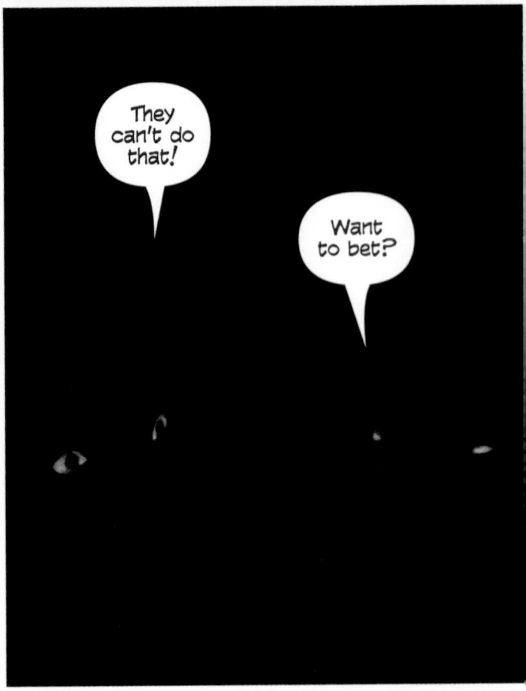
They can't do that!
Want to bet?

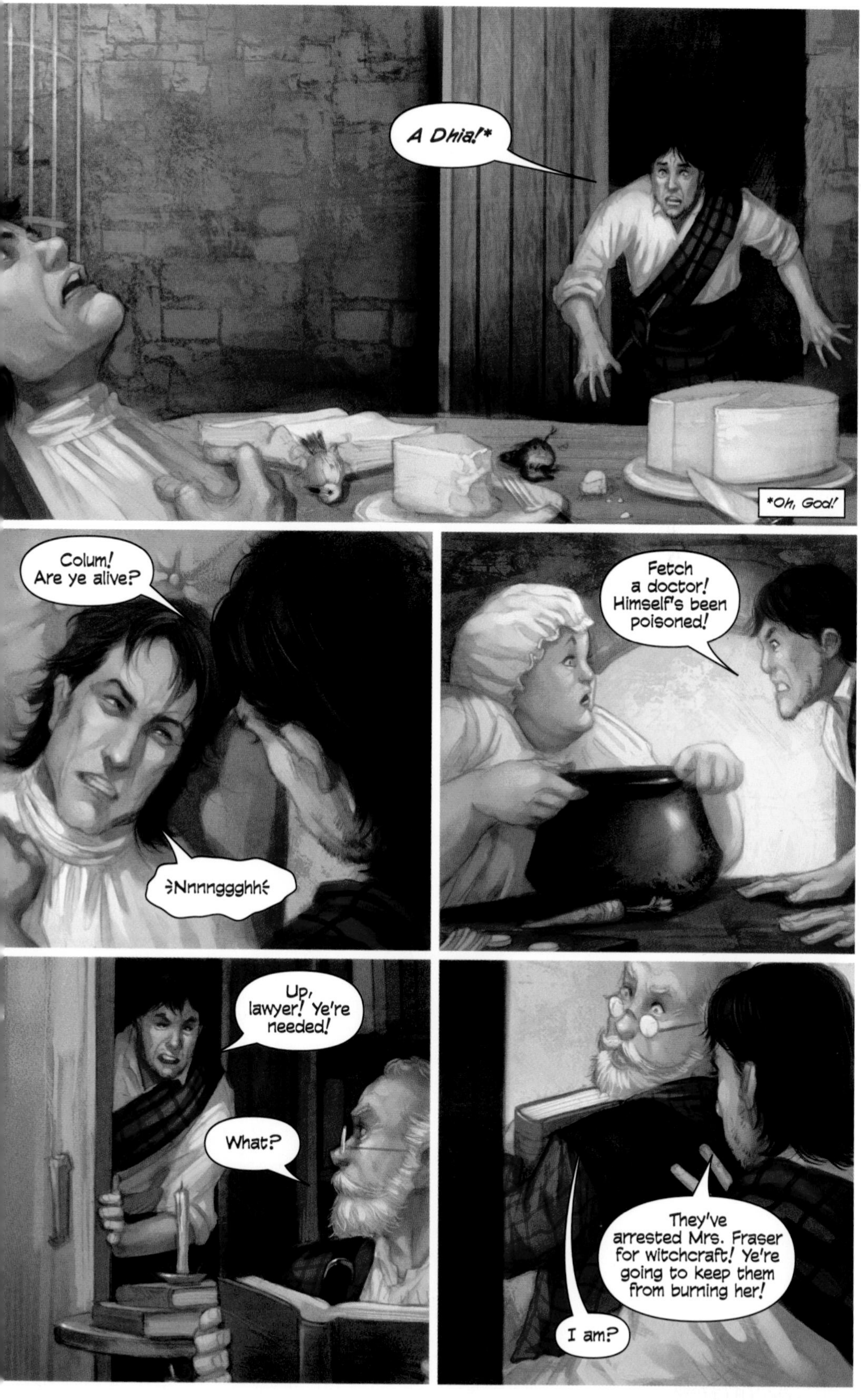
A Dhia!*
*Oh, God!
Colum! Are ye alive?
Nnnnggghh
Fetch a doctor! Himself's been poisoned!
Up, lawyer! Ye're needed!
What?
They've arrested Mrs. Fraser for witchcraft! Ye're going to keep them from burning her!
I am?

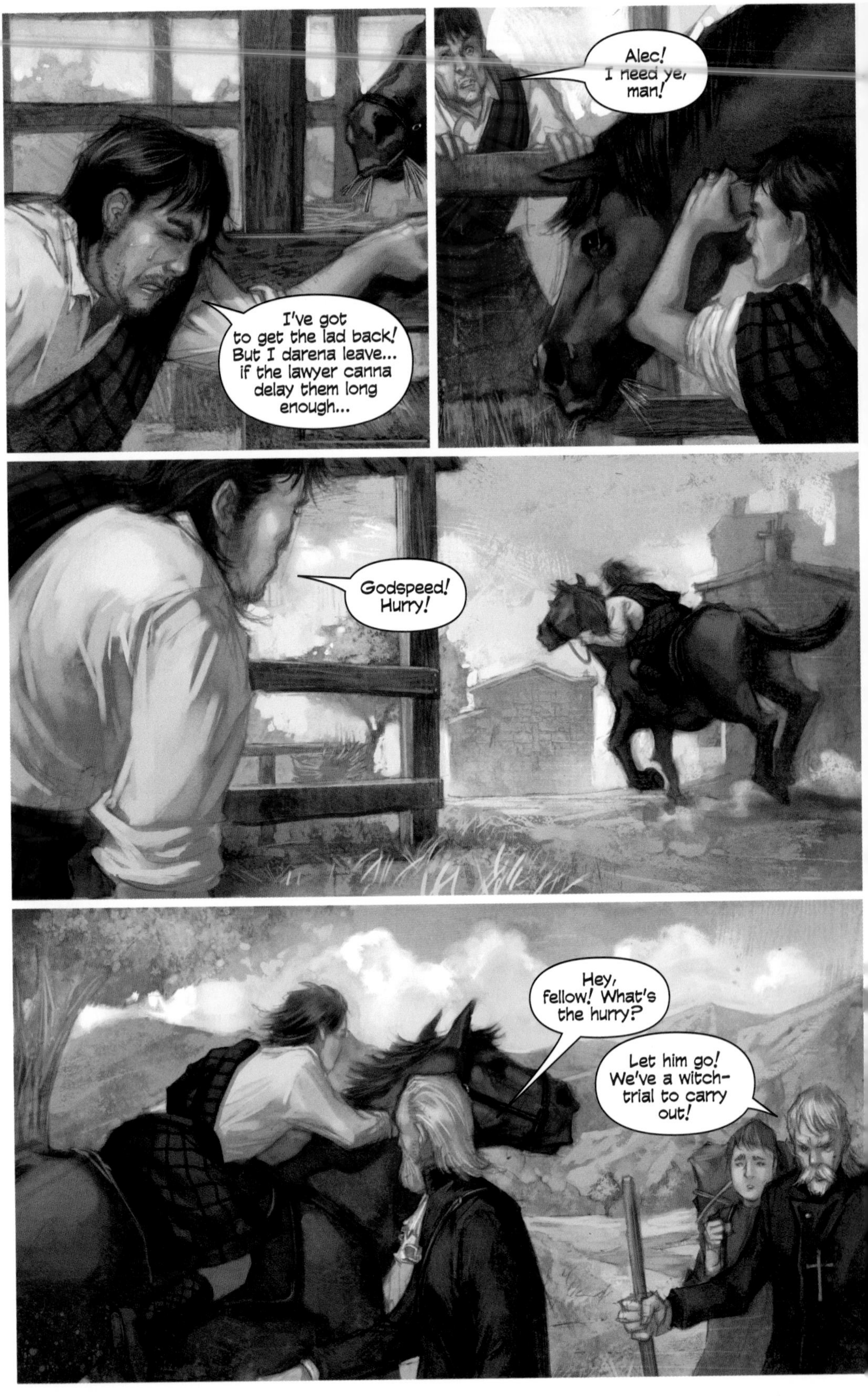
I've got to get the lad back! But I darena leave... if the lawyer canna delay them long enough...
Alec! I need ye, man!
Godspeed! Hurry!
Hey, fellow! What's the hurry?
Let him go! We've a witch-trial to carry out!

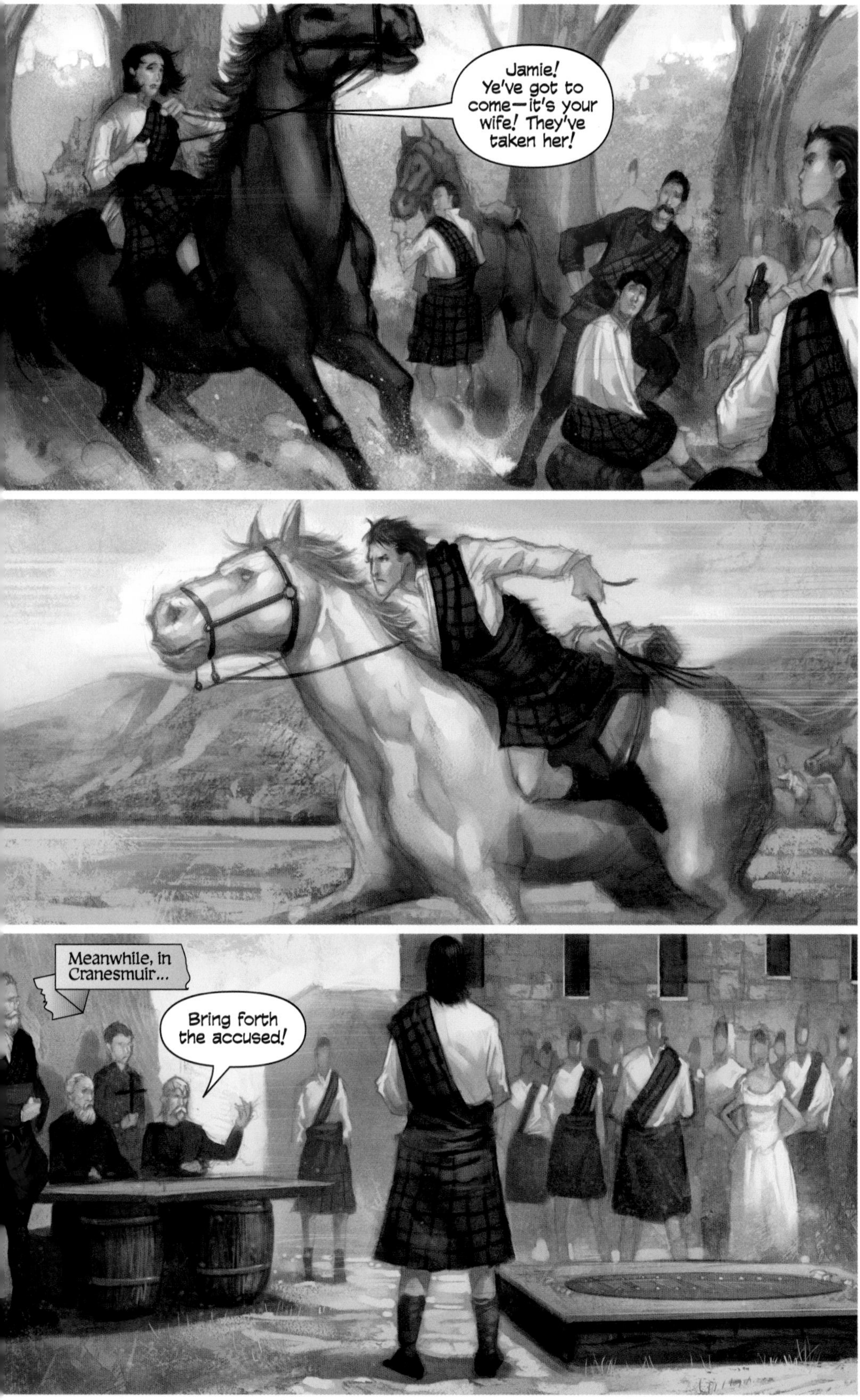

Jamie! Ye've got to come—it's your wife! They've taken her!
Meanwhile, in Cranesmuir...
Bring forth the accused!

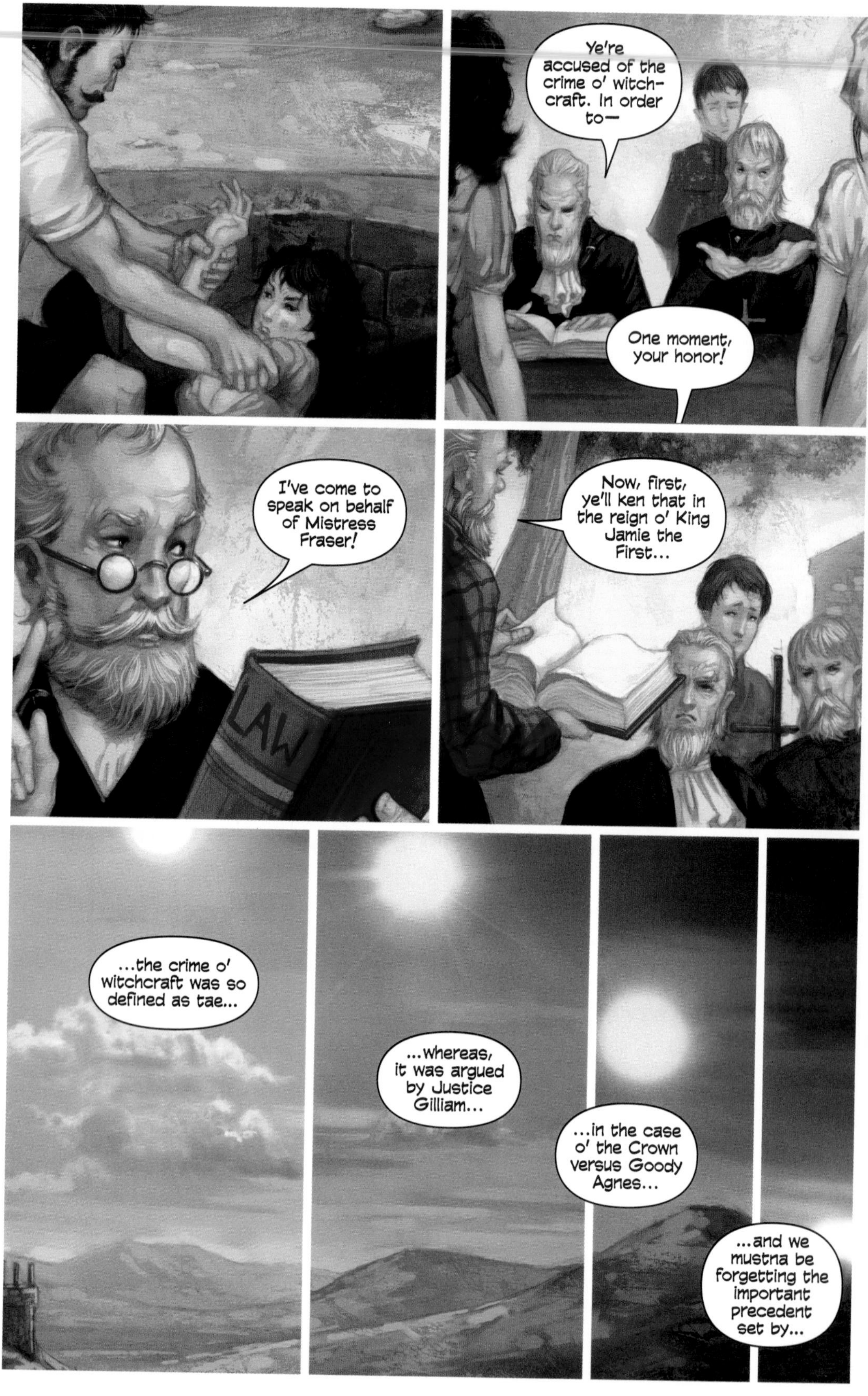
Ye're accused of the crime o' witch-craft. In order to—
One moment, your honor!
I've come to speak on behalf of Mistress Fraser!
Now, first, ye'll ken that in the reign o' King Jamie the First...
...the crime o' witchcraft was so defined as tae...
...whereas, it was argued by Justice Gilliam...
...in the case o' the Crown versus Goody Agnes...
...and we mustna be forgetting the important precedent set by...

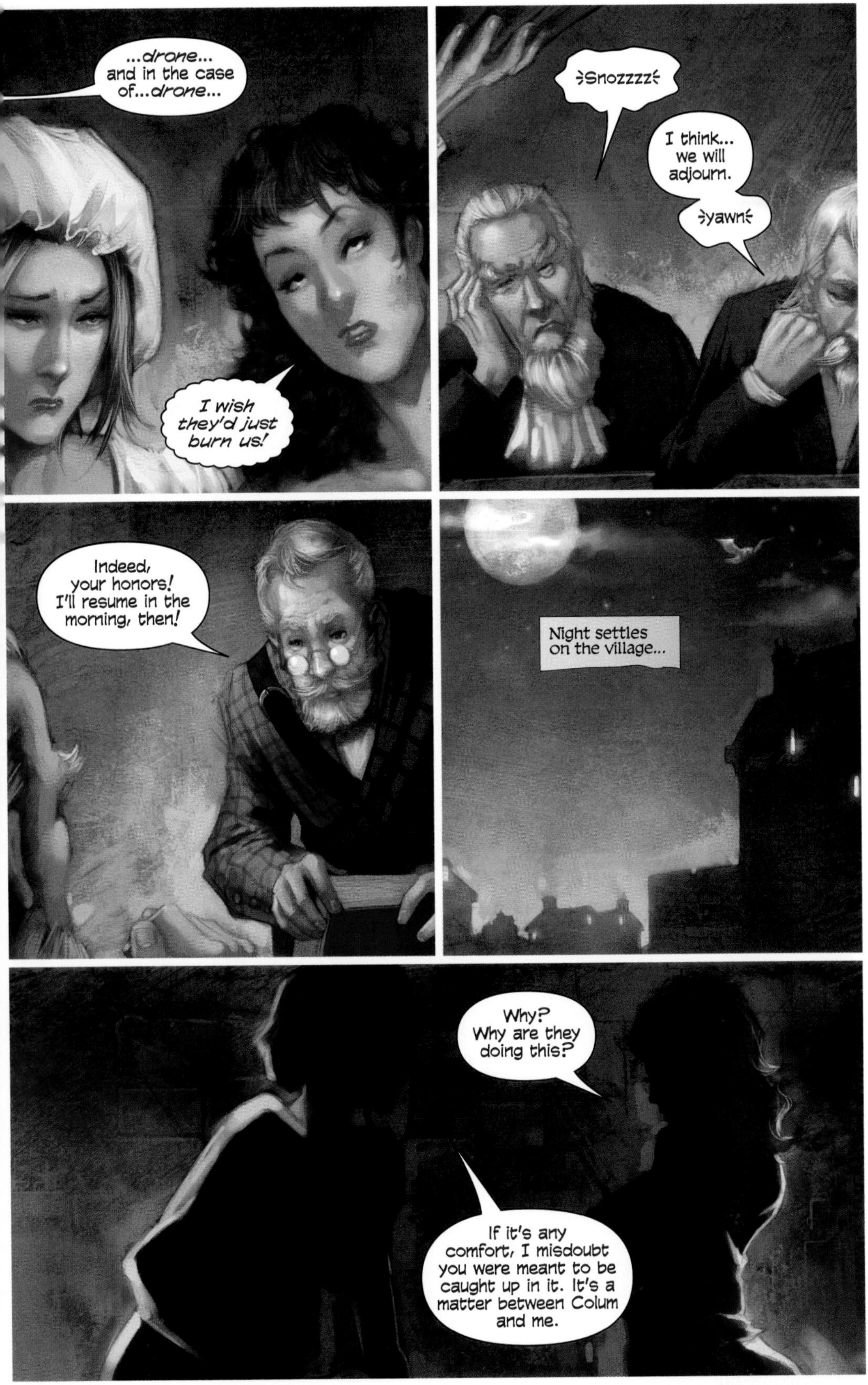
...drone... and in the case of...drone...
I wish they'd just burn us!
Snozzzz
I think... we will adjourn.
yawn
Indeed, your honors! I'll resume in the morning, then!
Night settles on the village...
Why? Why are they doing this?
If it's any comfort, I misdoubt you were meant to be caught up in it. It's a matter between Colum and me.

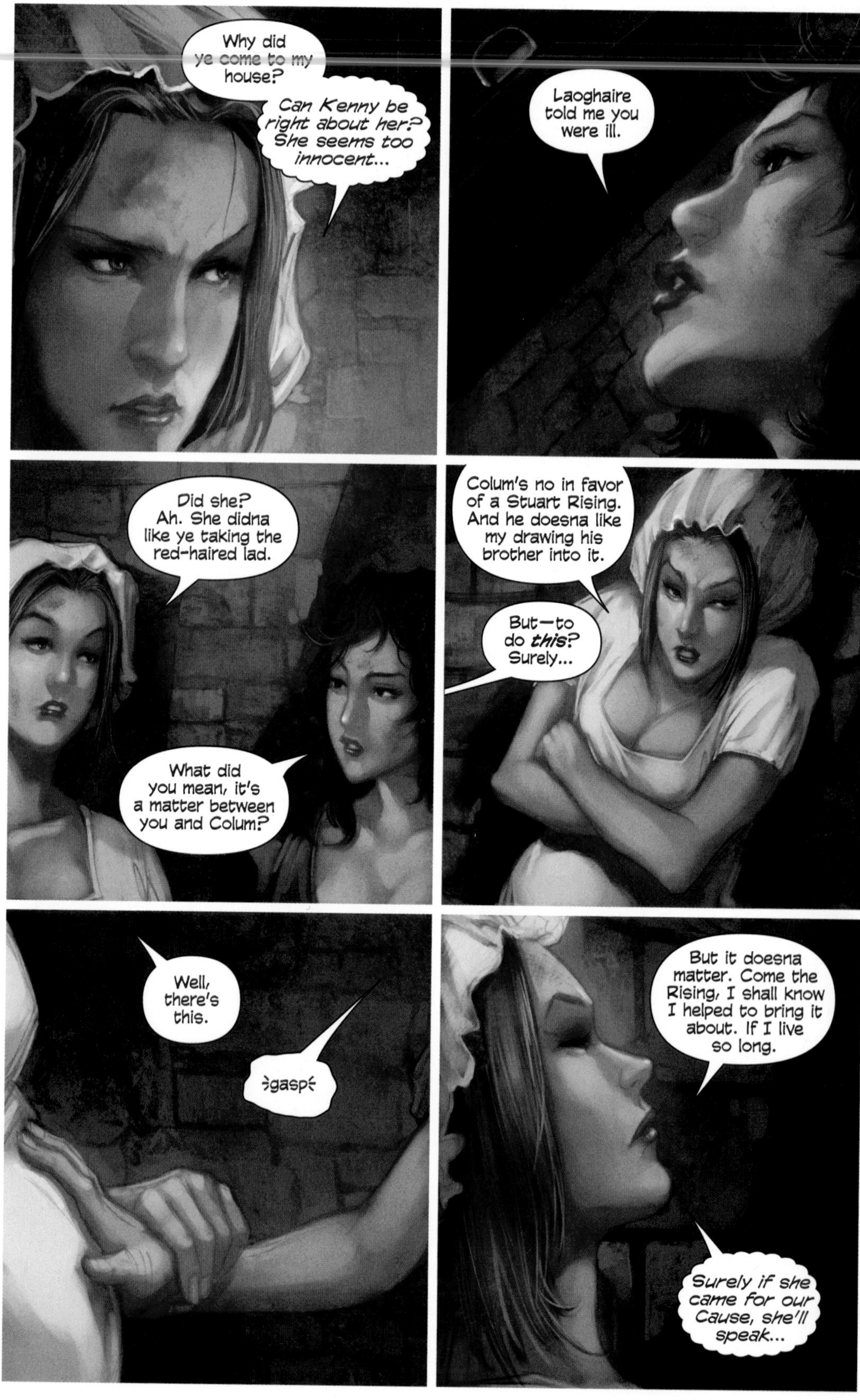
Why did ye come to my house?
*Can Kenny be right about her? She seems too innocent...*
Laoghaire told me you were ill.
Did she? Ah. She didna like ye taking the red-haired lad.
What did you mean, it's a matter between you and Colum?
Colum's no in favor of a Stuart Rising. And he doesna like my drawing his brother into it.
But—to do ***this***? Surely...
Well, there's this.
gasp
But it doesna matter. Come the Rising, I shall know I helped to bring it about. If I live so long.
*Surely if she came for our Cause, she'll speak...*

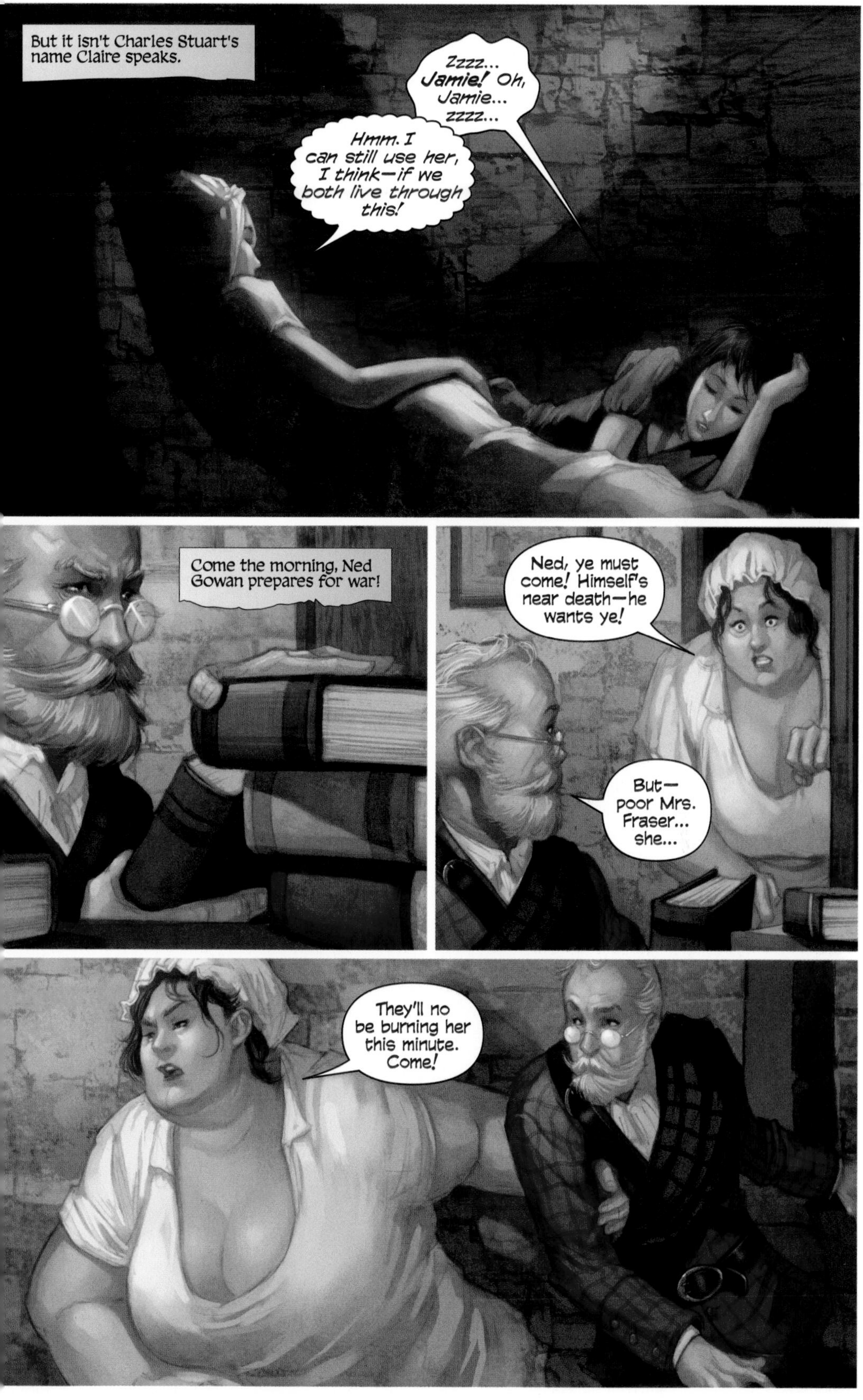
But it isn't Charles Stuart's name Claire speaks.
Zzzz... Jamie! Oh, Jamie... zzzz...
Hmm. I can still use her, I think—if we both live through this!
Come the morning, Ned Gowan prepares for war!
Ned, ye must come! Himself's near death—he wants ye!
But—poor Mrs. Fraser... she...
They'll no be burning her this minute. Come!

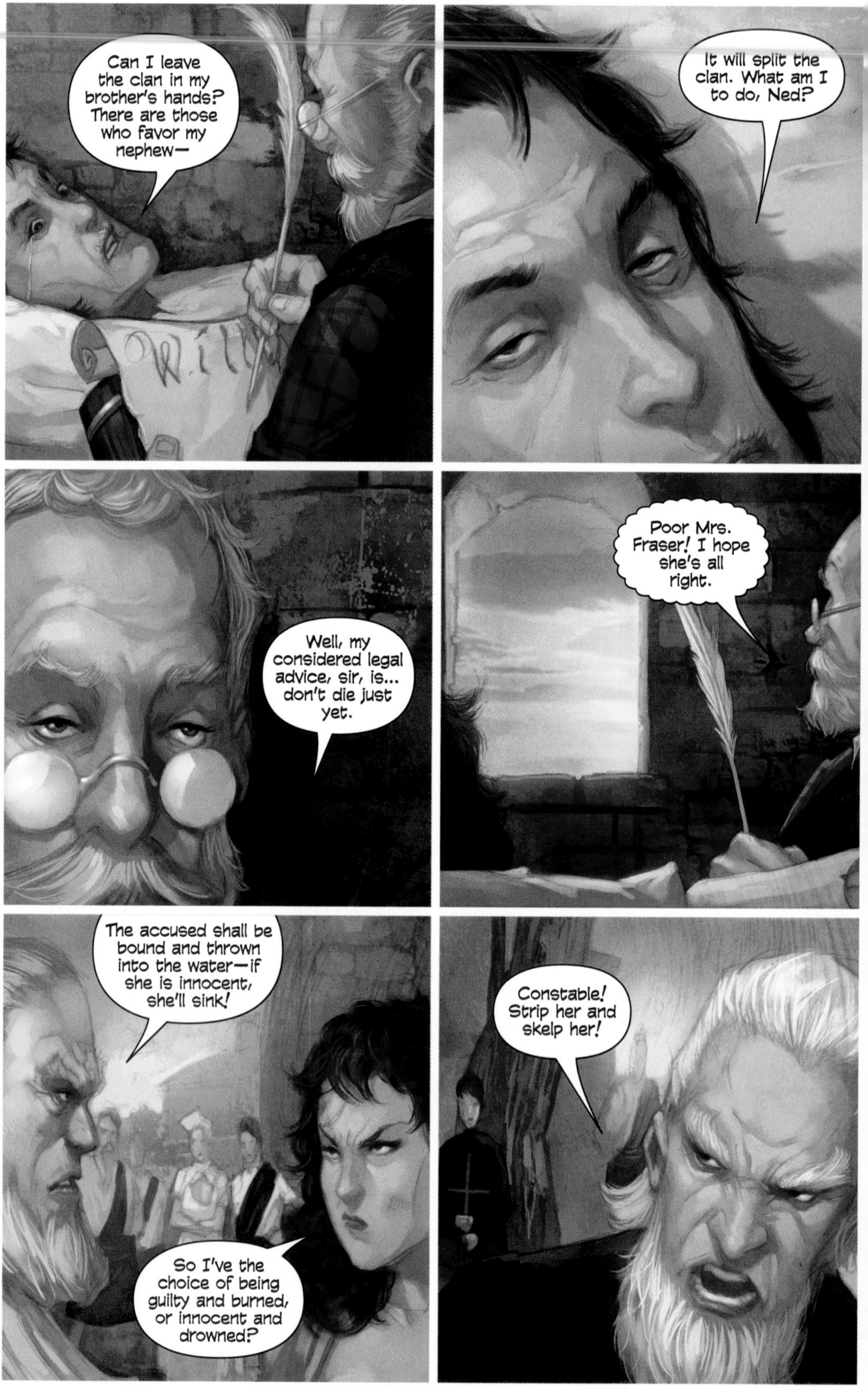
Can I leave the clan in my brother's hands? There are those who favor my nephew—
It will split the clan. What am I to do, Ned?
Well, my considered legal advice, sir, is... don't die just yet.
Poor Mrs. Fraser! I hope she's all right.
The accused shall be bound and thrown into the water—if she is innocent, she'll sink!
So I've the choice of being guilty and burned, or innocent and drowned?
Constable! Strip her and skelp her!

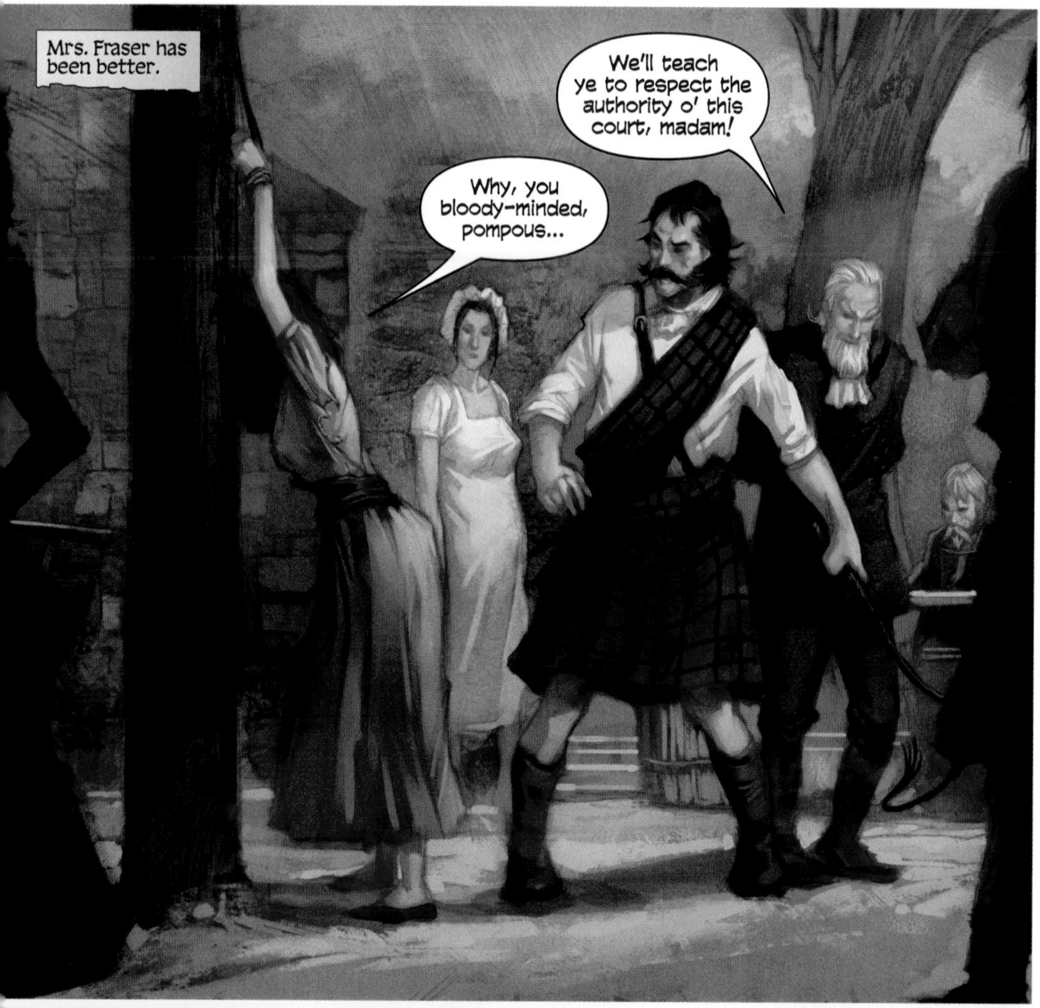

Mrs. Fraser has been better.
We'll teach ye to respect the authority o' this court, madam!
Why, you bloody-minded, pompous...


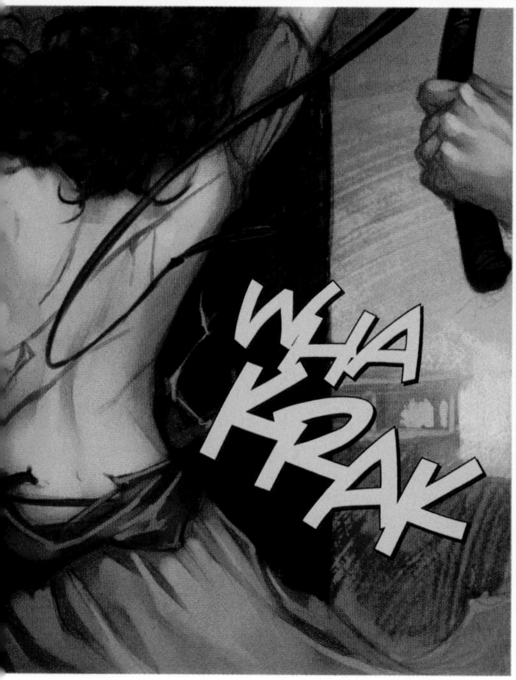

WHA KRAK


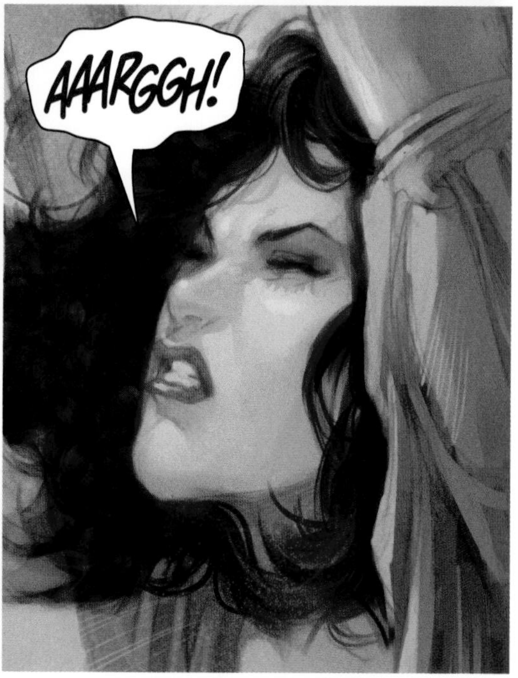

AAARGGH!

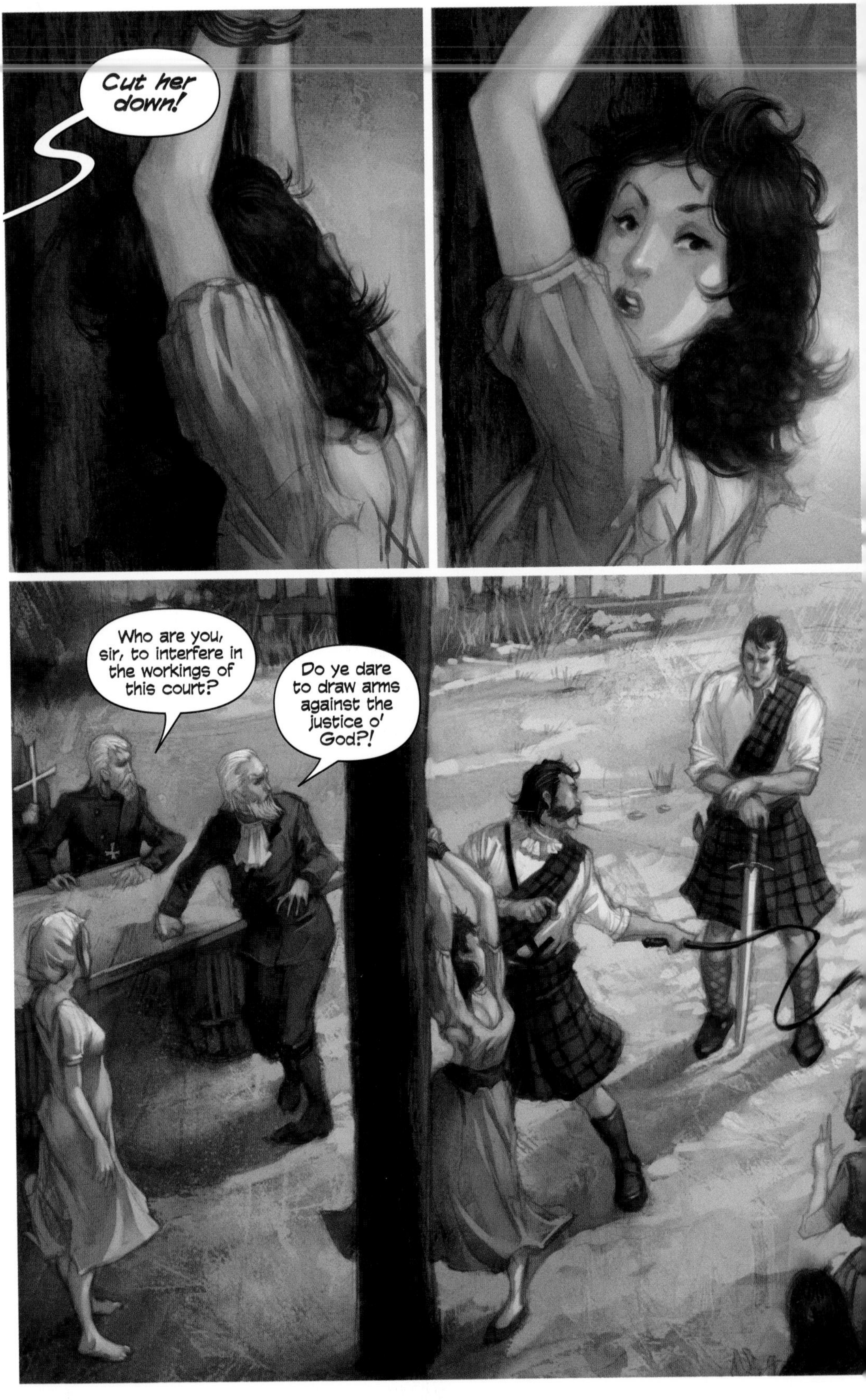
Cut her down!
Who are you, sir, to interfere in the workings of this court?
Do ye dare to draw arms against the justice o' God?!

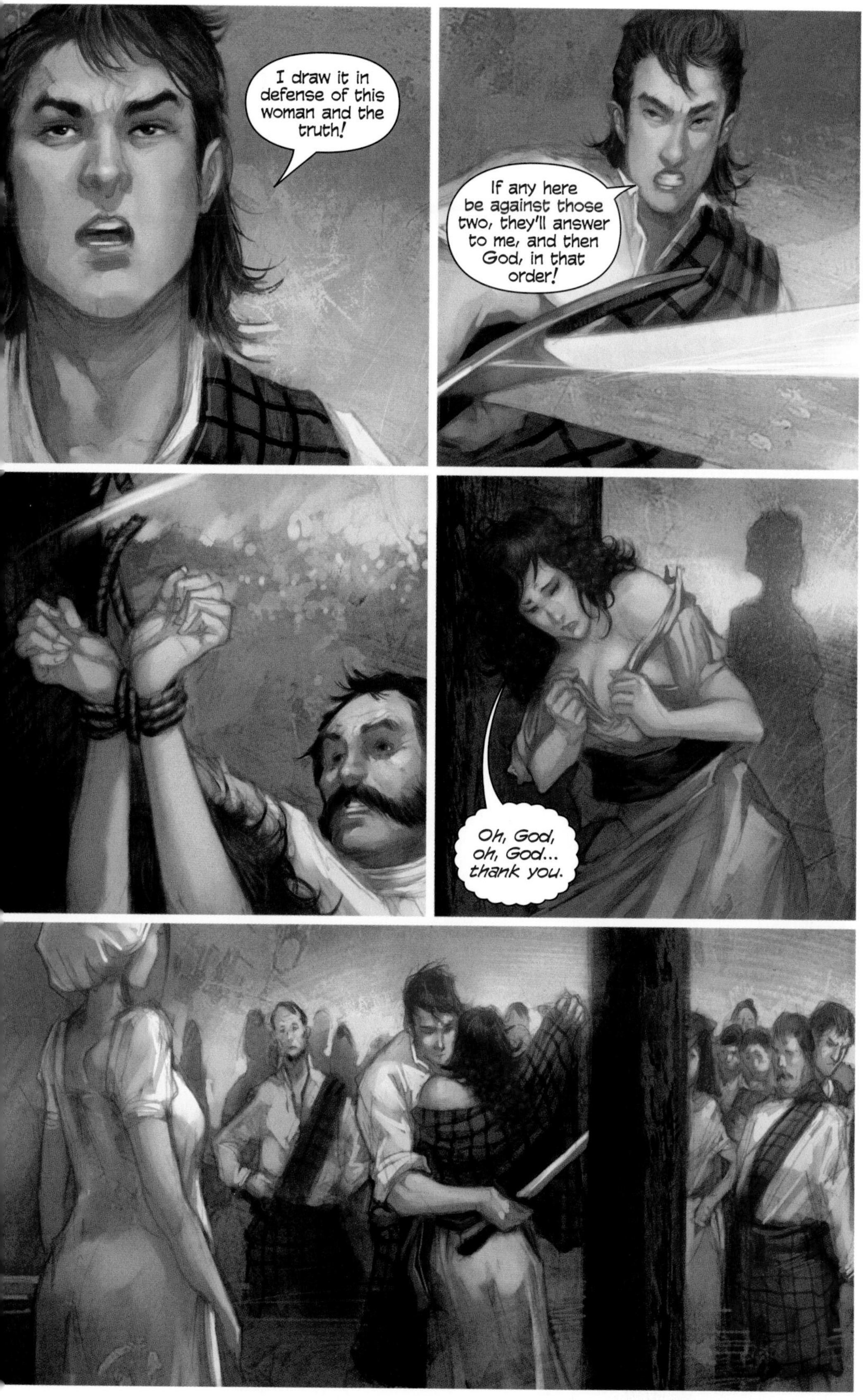
I draw it in defense of this woman and the truth!
If any here be against those two, they'll answer to me, and then God, in that order!
Oh, God, oh, God... thank you.

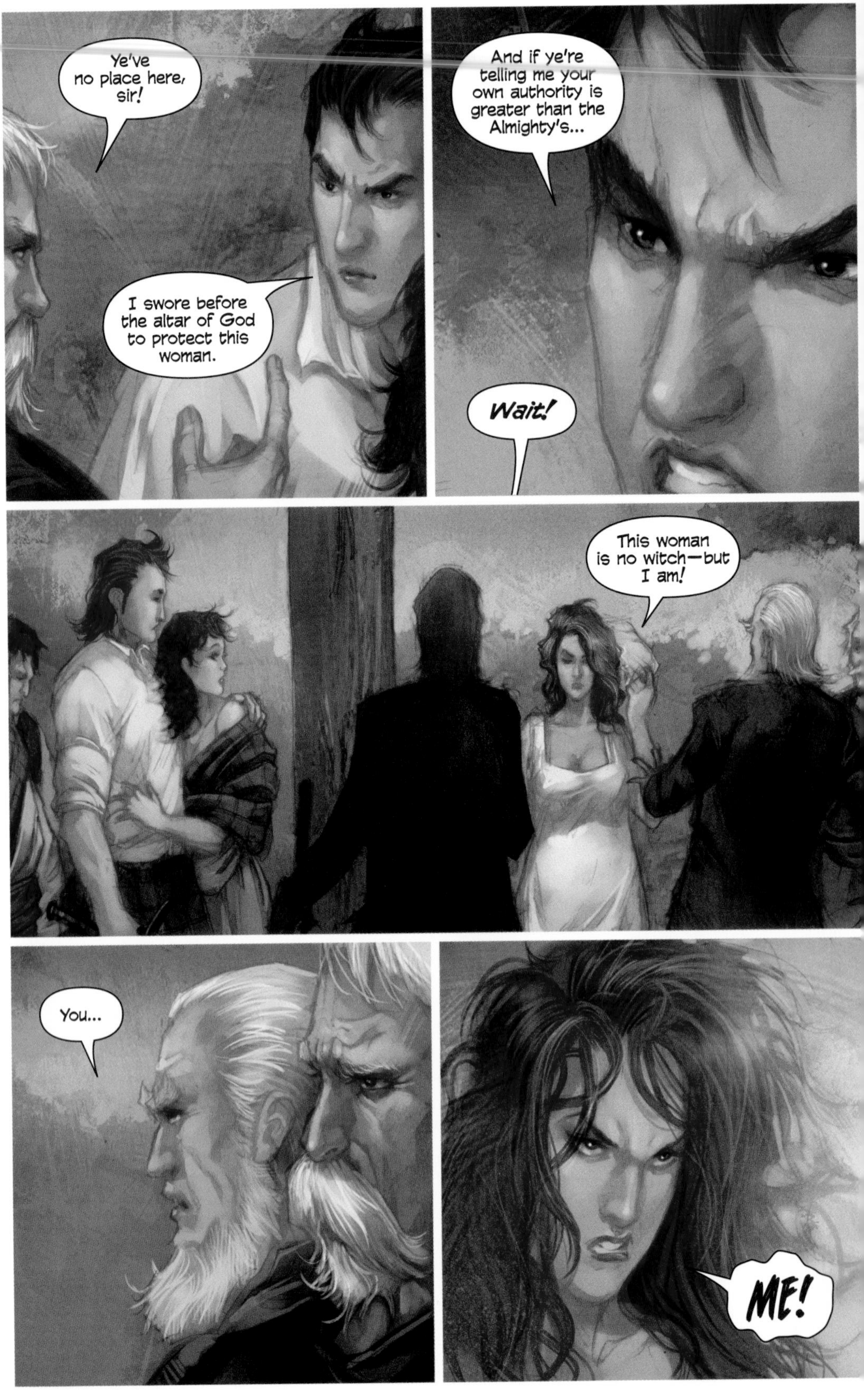
Ye've no place here, sir!
I swore before the altar of God to protect this woman.
And if ye're telling me your own authority is greater than the Almighty's...
Wait!
This woman is no witch—but I am!
You...
ME!

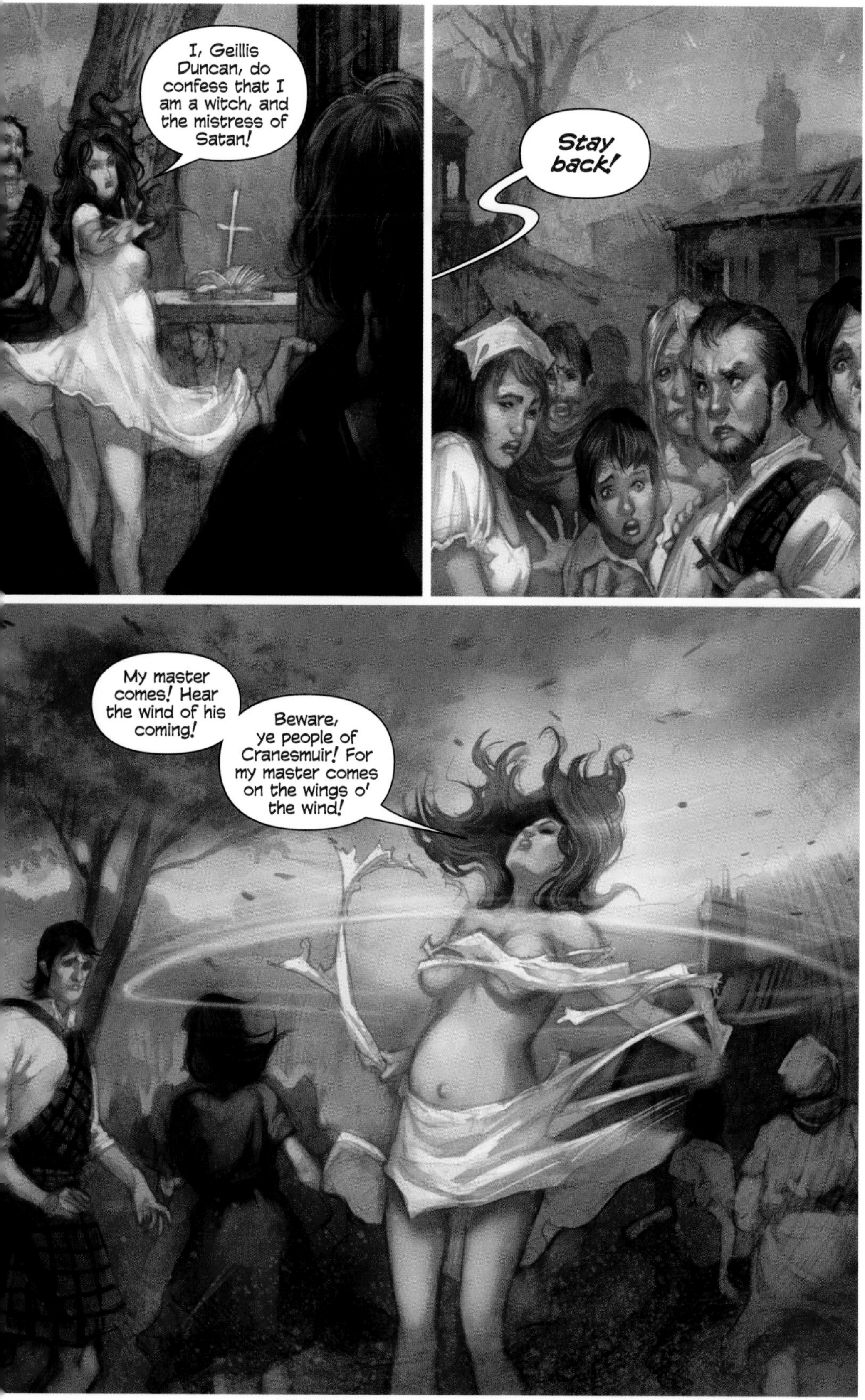
I, Geillis Duncan, do confess that I am a witch, and the mistress of Satan!
Stay back!
My master comes! Hear the wind of his coming!
Beware, ye people of Cranesmuir! For my master comes on the wings o' the wind!

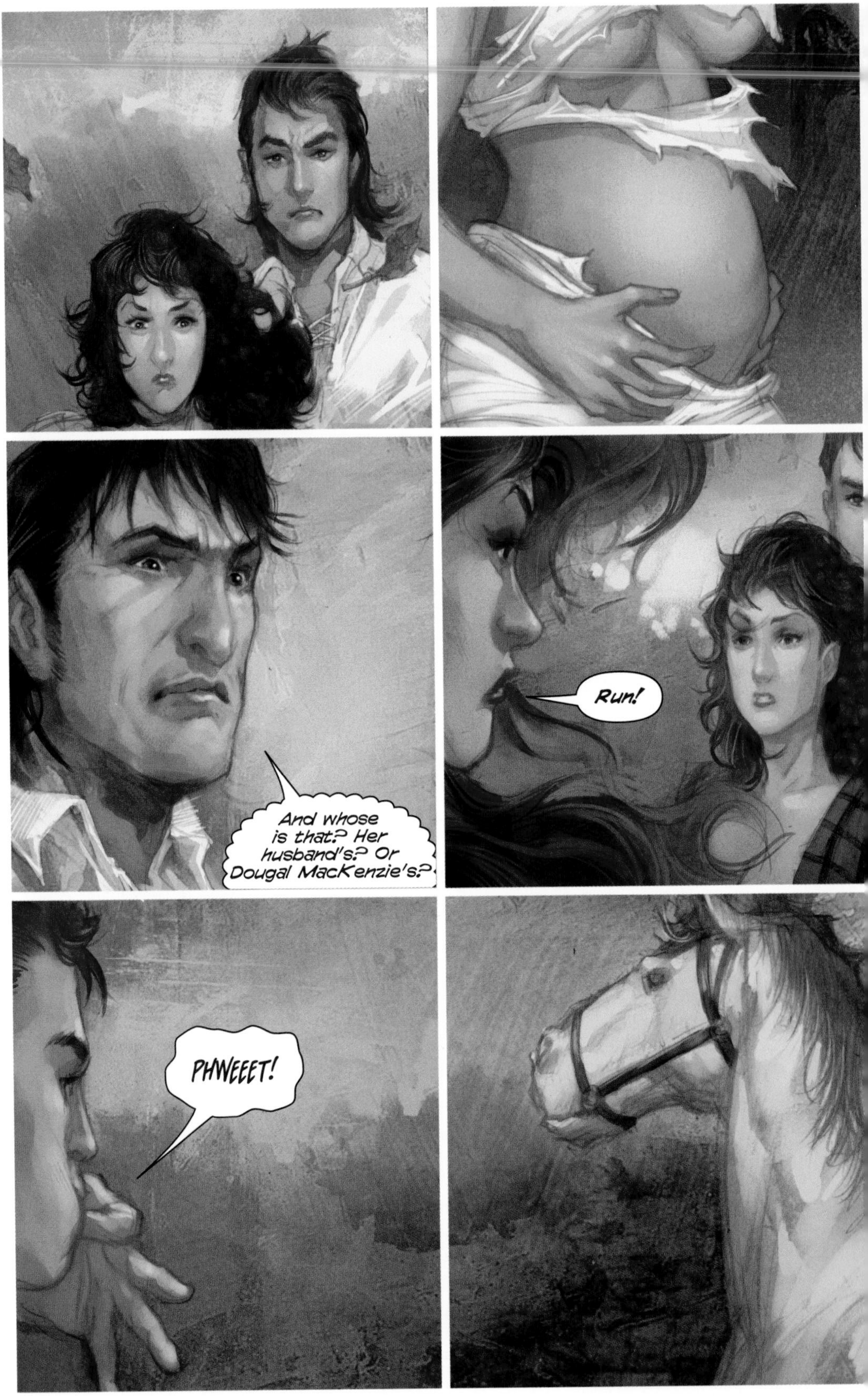
And whose is that? Her husband's? Or Dougal MacKenzie's?
Run!
PHWEEET!

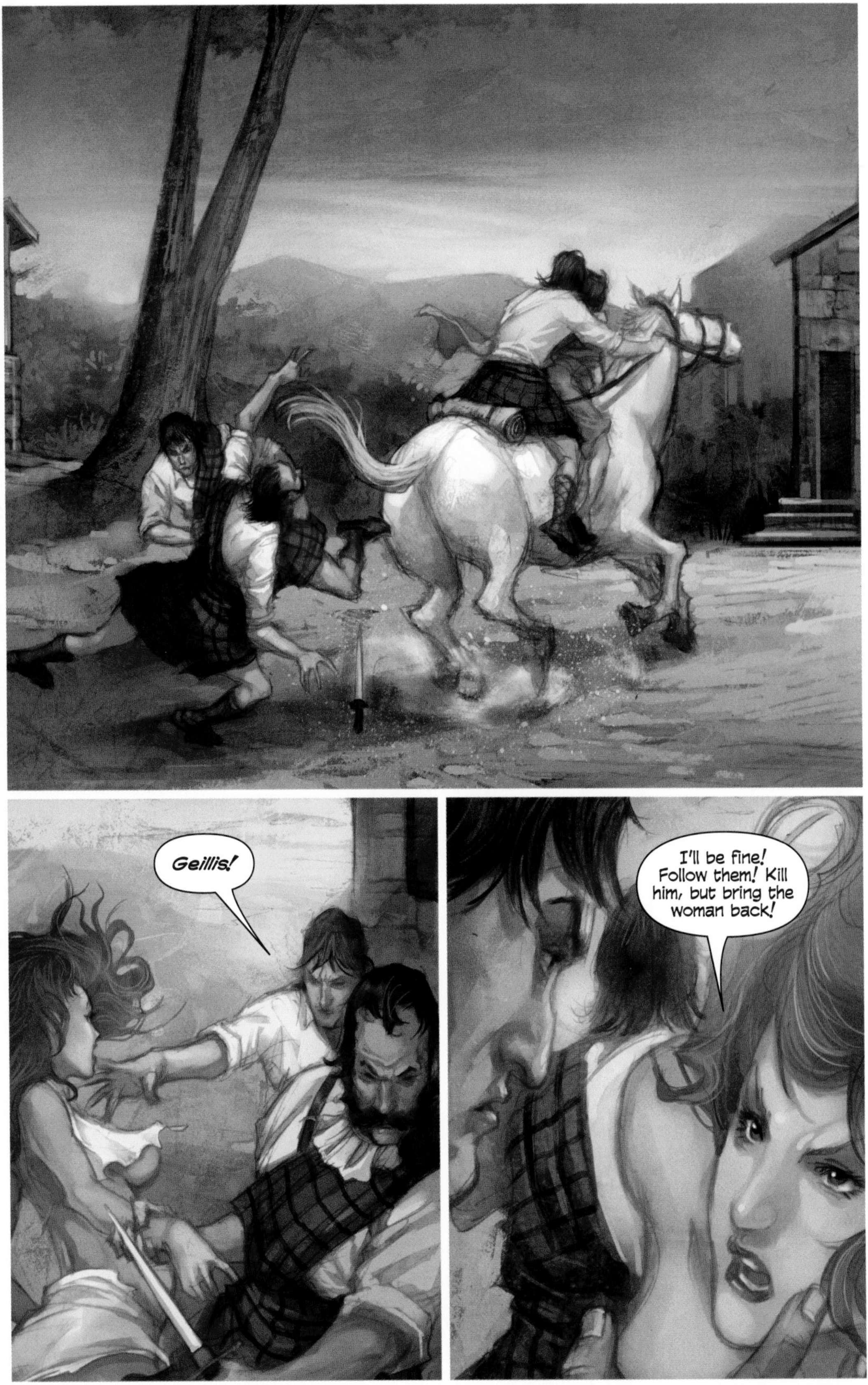
Geillis!
I'll be fine! Follow them! Kill him, but bring the woman back!

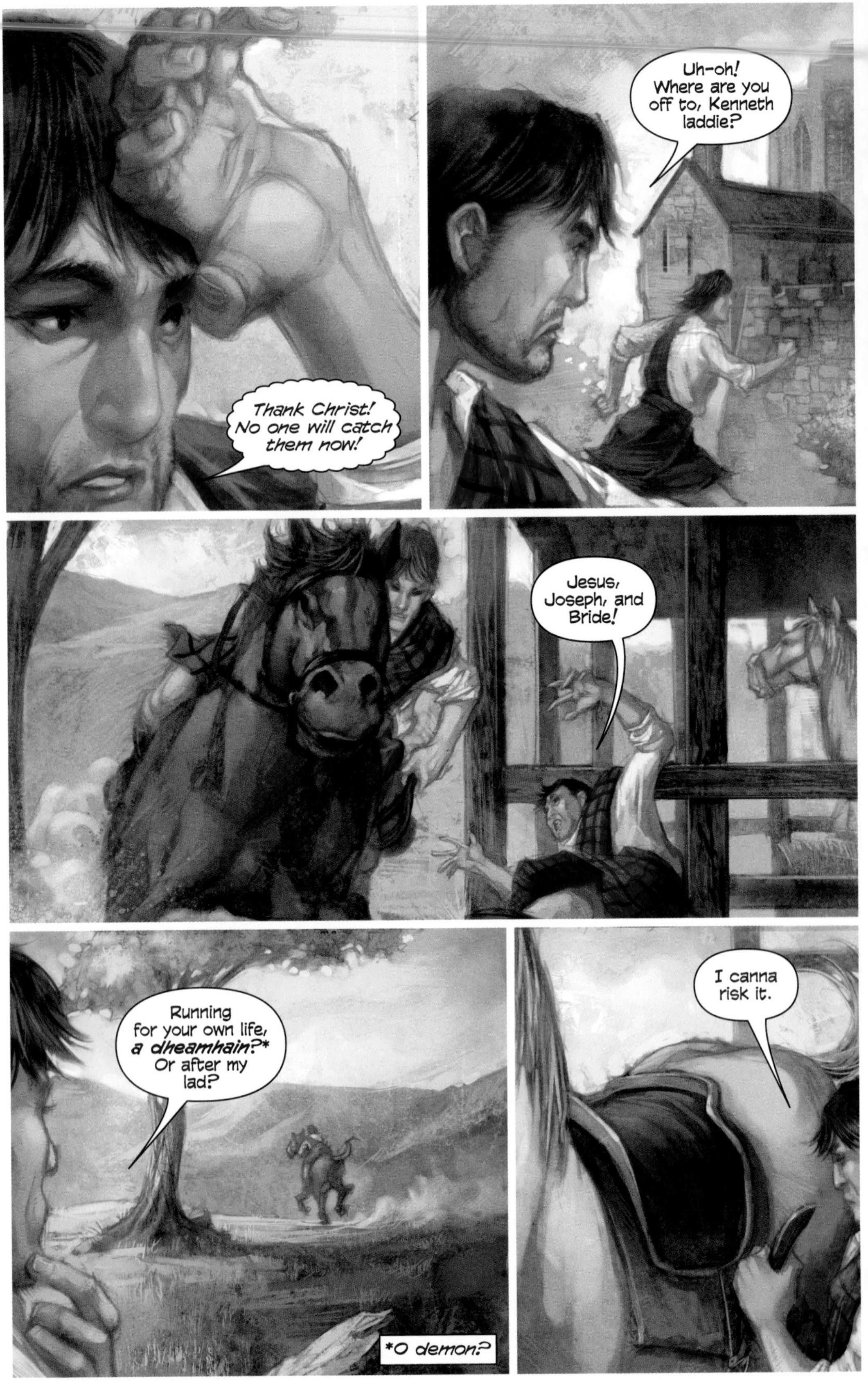
Thank Christ! No one will catch them now!
Uh-oh! Where are you off to, Kenneth laddie?
Jesus, Joseph, and Bride!
Running for your own life, ***a dheamhain?**** Or after my lad?
*O demon?
I canna risk it.

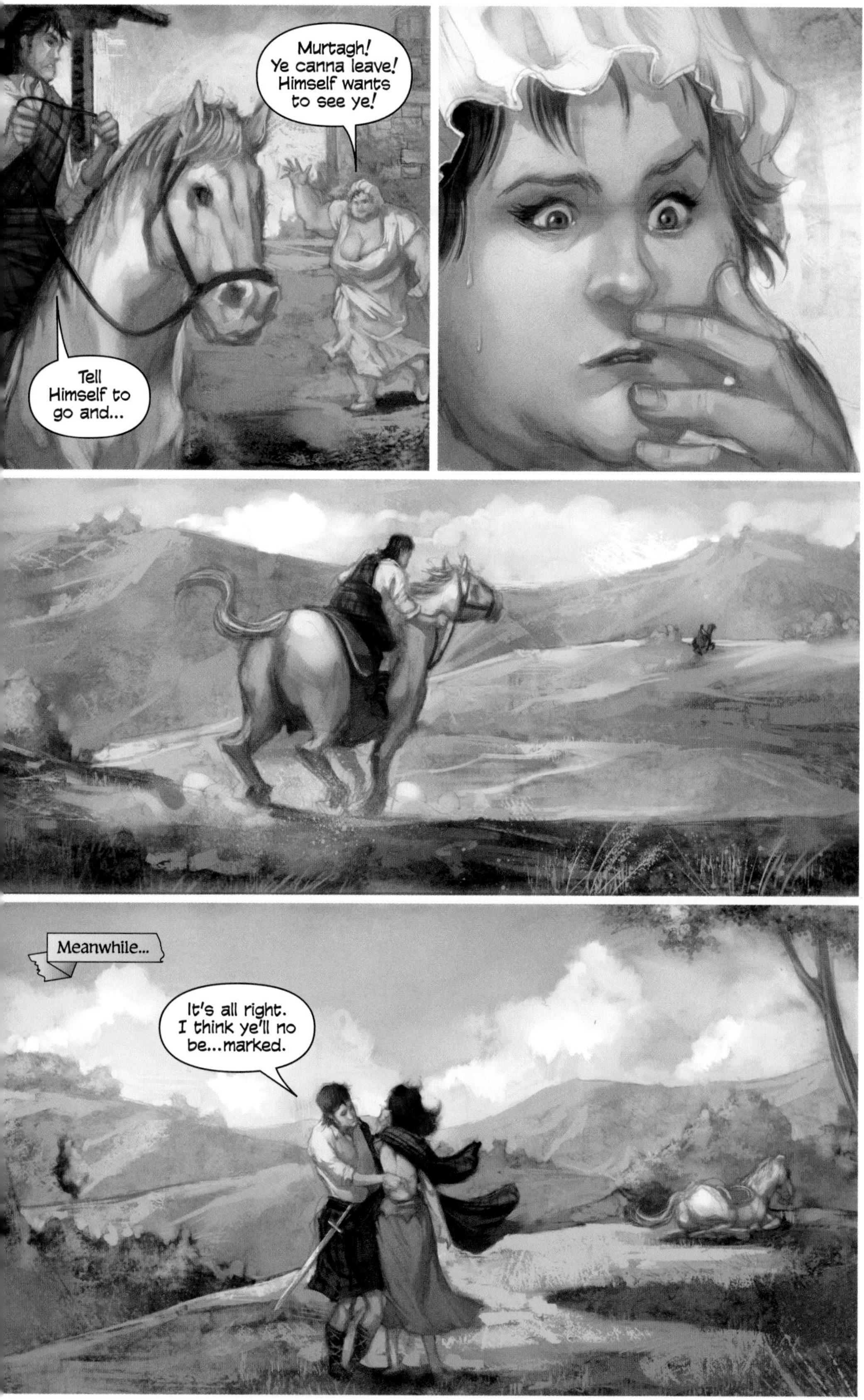
Murtagh! Ye canna leave! Himself wants to see ye!
Tell Himself to go and...
Meanwhile...
It's all right. I think ye'll no be...marked.

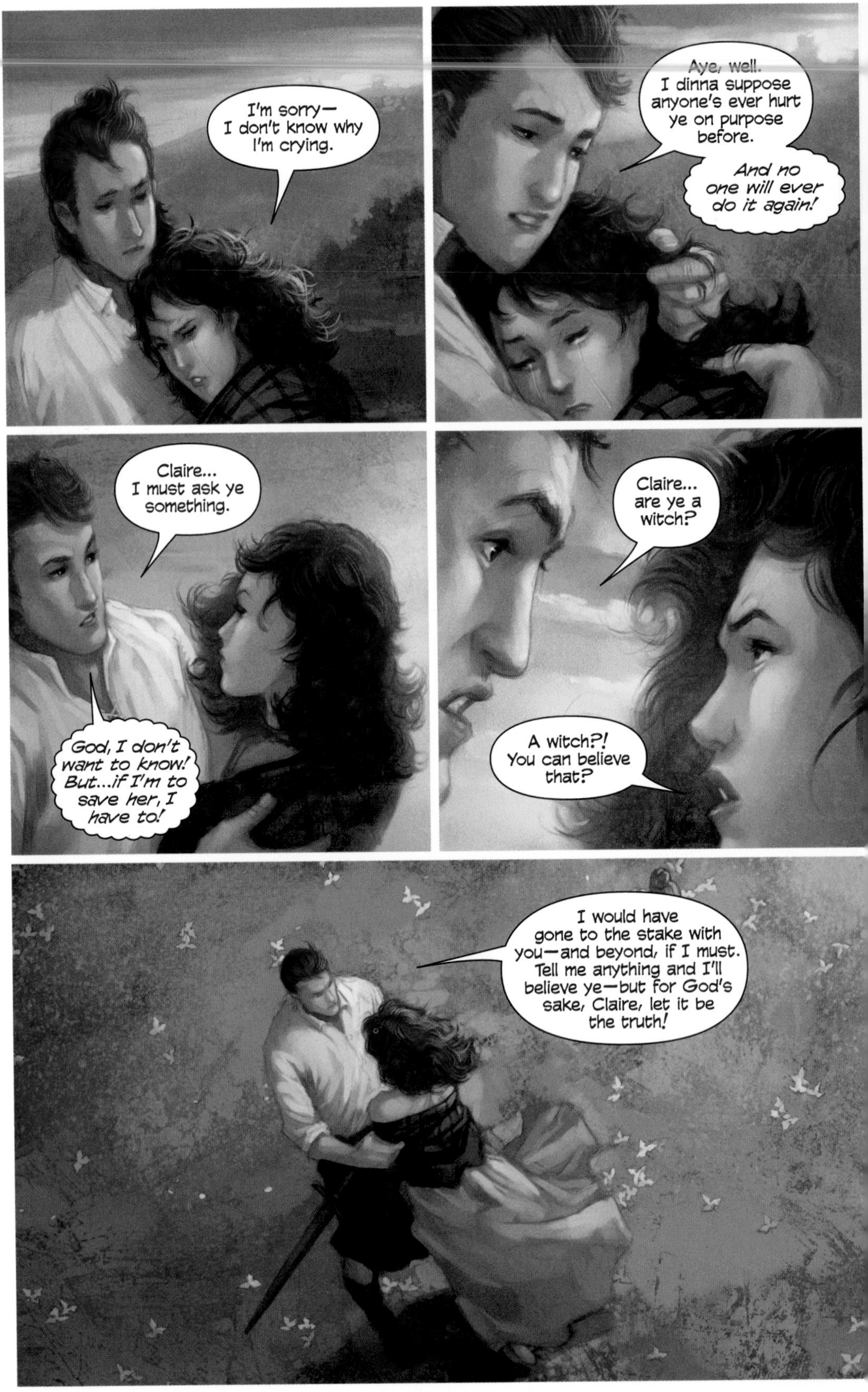
I'm sorry—
I don't know why
I'm crying.
Aye, well.
I dinna suppose
anyone's ever hurt
ye on purpose
before.
*And no one will ever do it again!*
Claire...
I must ask ye
something.
*God, I don't want to know! But...if I'm to save her, I have to!*
Claire...
are ye a
witch?
A witch?!
You can believe
that?
I would have
gone to the stake with
you—and beyond, if I must.
Tell me anything and I'll
believe ye—but for God's
sake, Claire, let it be
the truth!

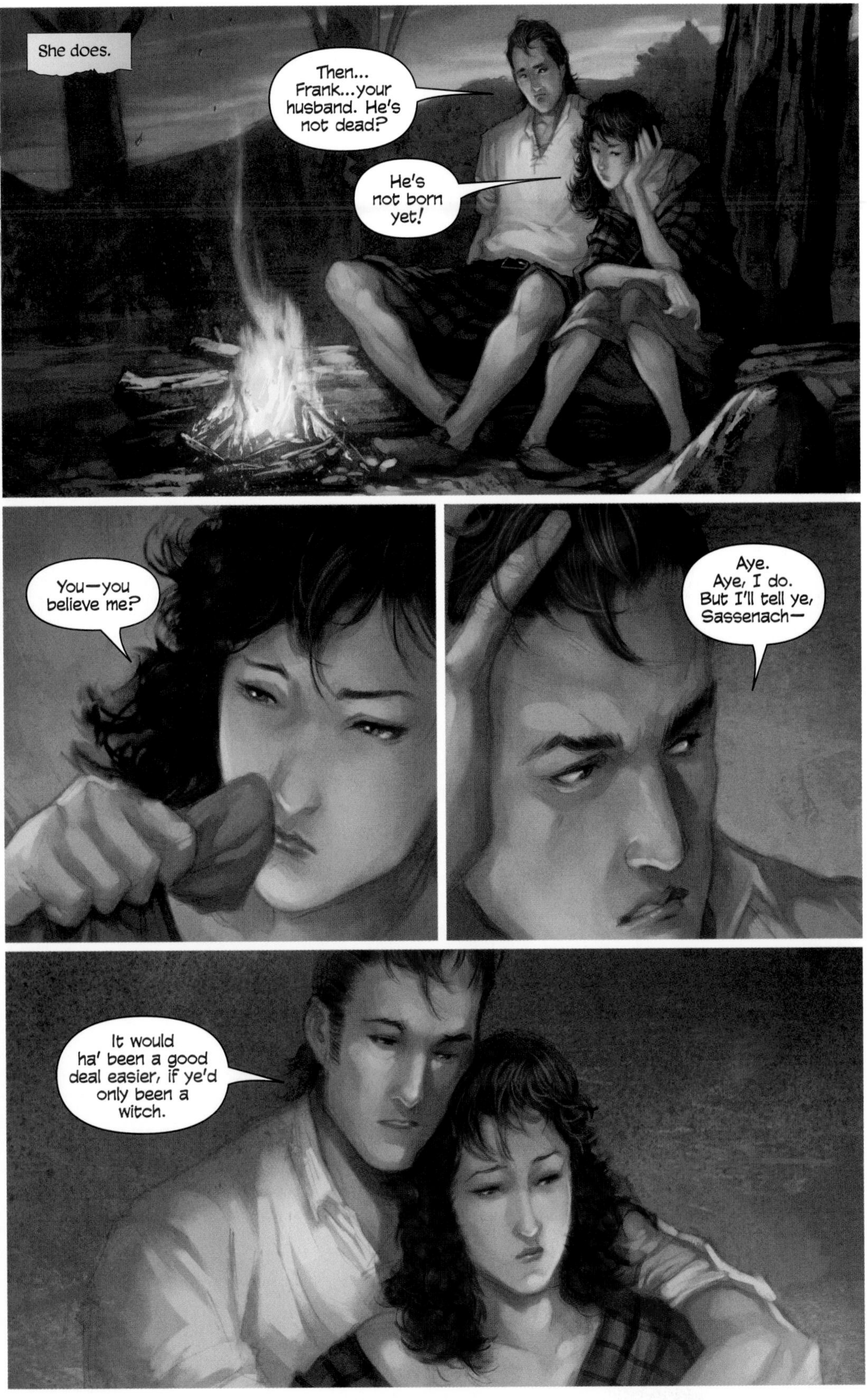
She does.
Then... Frank...your husband. He's not dead?
He's not born yet!
You—you believe me?
Aye. Aye, I do. But I'll tell ye, Sassenach—
It would ha' been a good deal easier, if ye'd only been a witch.

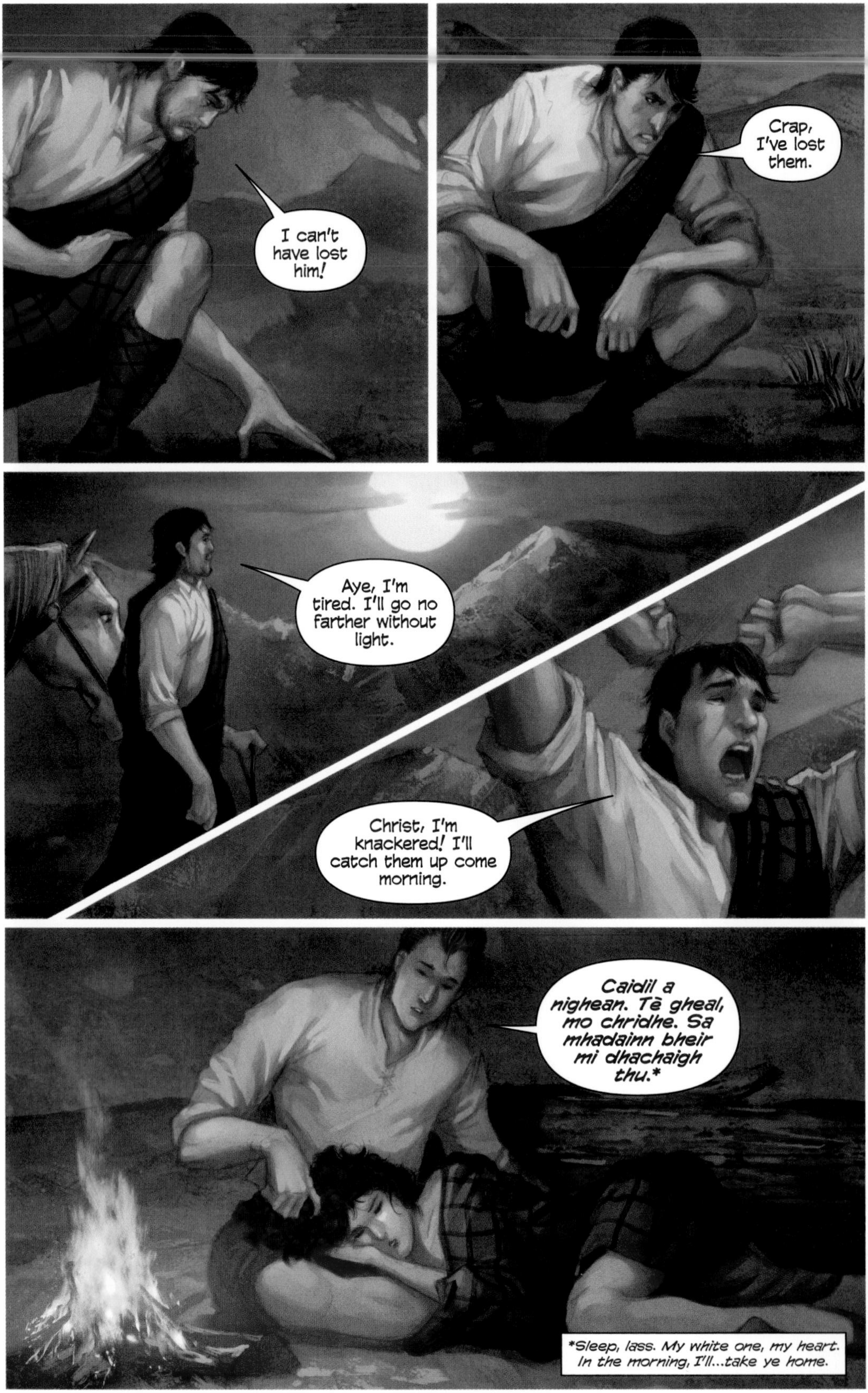
I can't have lost him!
Crap, I've lost them.
Aye, I'm tired. I'll go no farther without light.
Christ, I'm knackered! I'll catch them up come morning.
*Caidil a nighean. Tè gheal, mo chridhe. Sa mhadainn bheir mi dhachaigh thu.**
*Sleep, lass. My white one, my heart. In the morning, I'll...take ye home.*

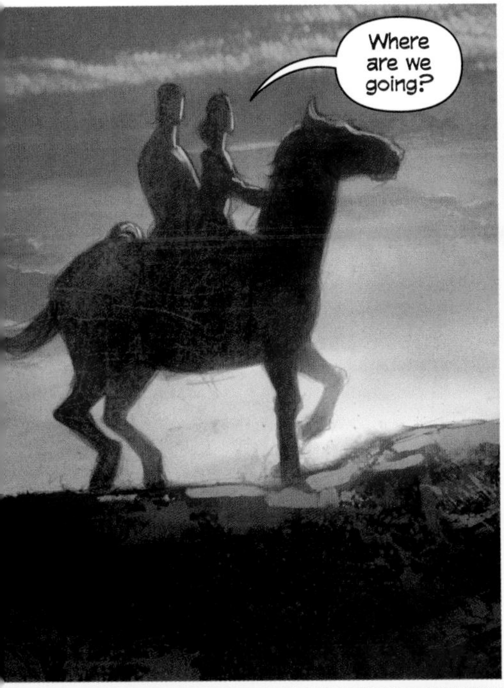
Where are we going?

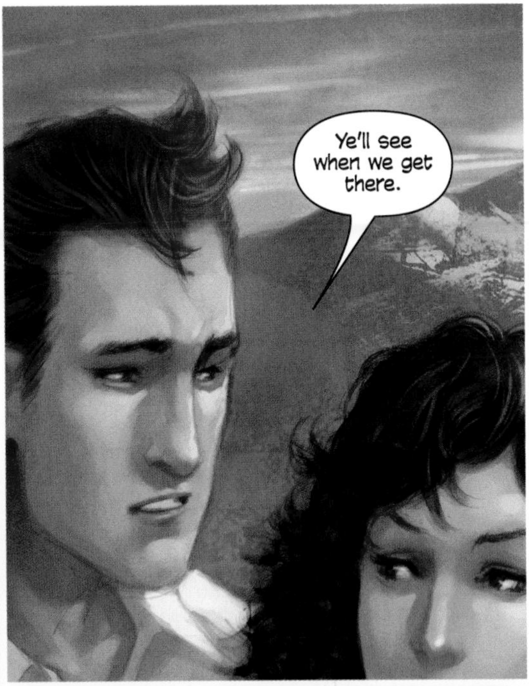
Ye'll see when we get there.

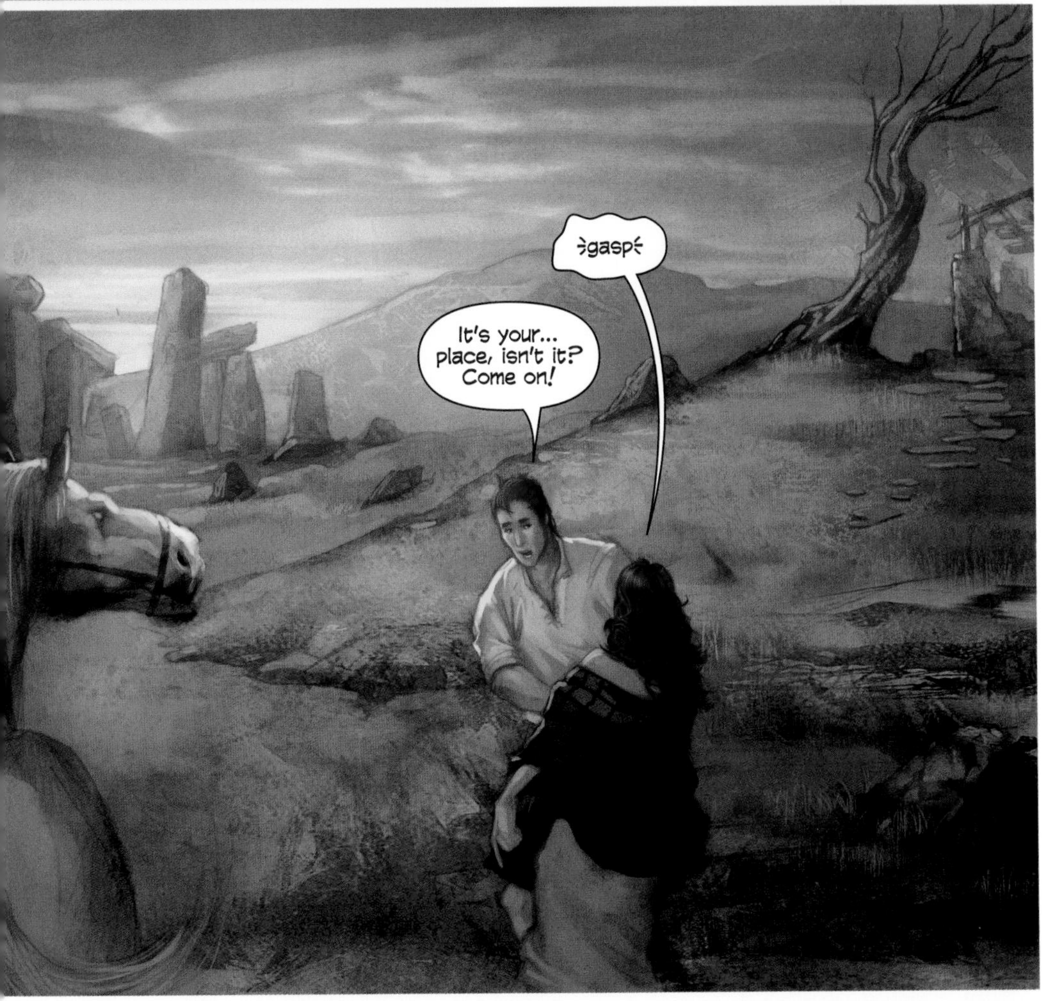
It's your... place, isn't it? Come on!
gasp

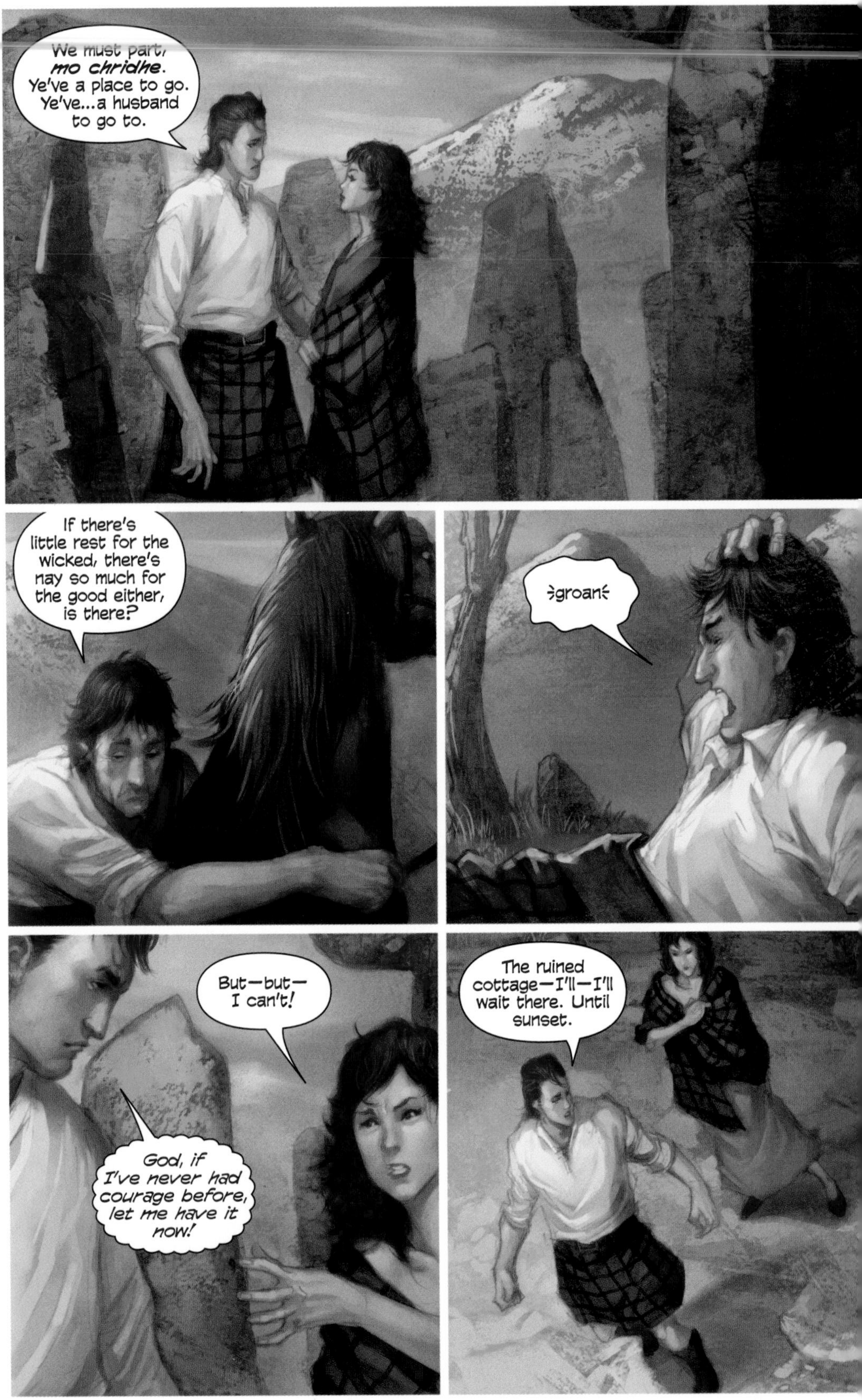
We must part, *mo chridhe*. Ye've a place to go. Ye've...a husband to go to.
If there's little rest for the wicked, there's nay so much for the good either, is there?
groan
But—but— I can't!
*God, if I've never had courage before, let me have it now!*
The ruined cottage—I'll—I'll wait there. Until sunset.

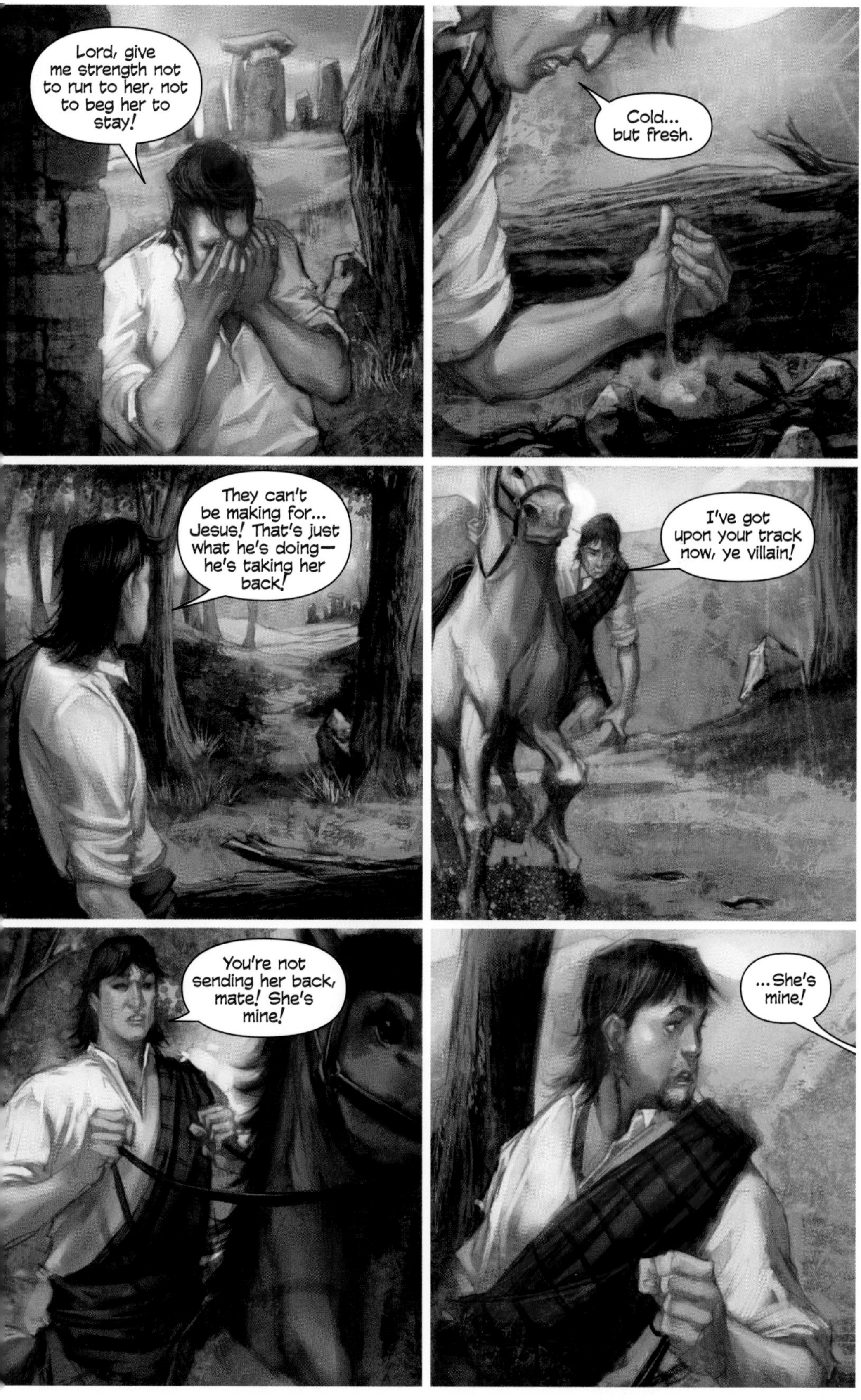
Lord, give me strength not to run to her, not to beg her to stay!
Cold... but fresh.
They can't be making for... Jesus! That's just what he's doing— he's taking her back!
I've got upon your track now, ye villain!
You're not sending her back, mate! She's mine!
...She's mine!

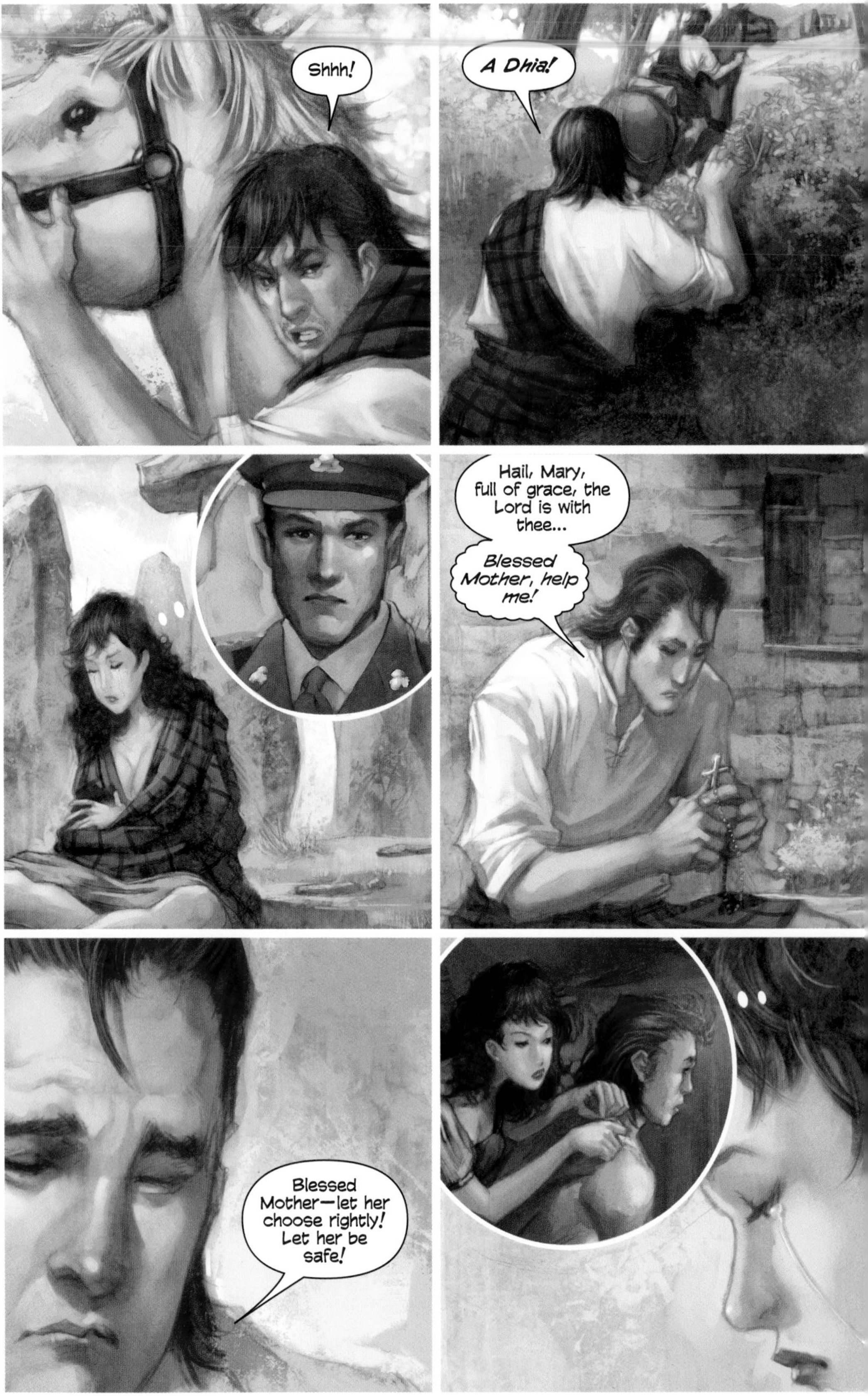
Shhh!
A Dhia!
Hail, Mary, full of grace, the Lord is with thee...
Blessed Mother, help me!
Blessed Mother—let her choose rightly! Let her be safe!

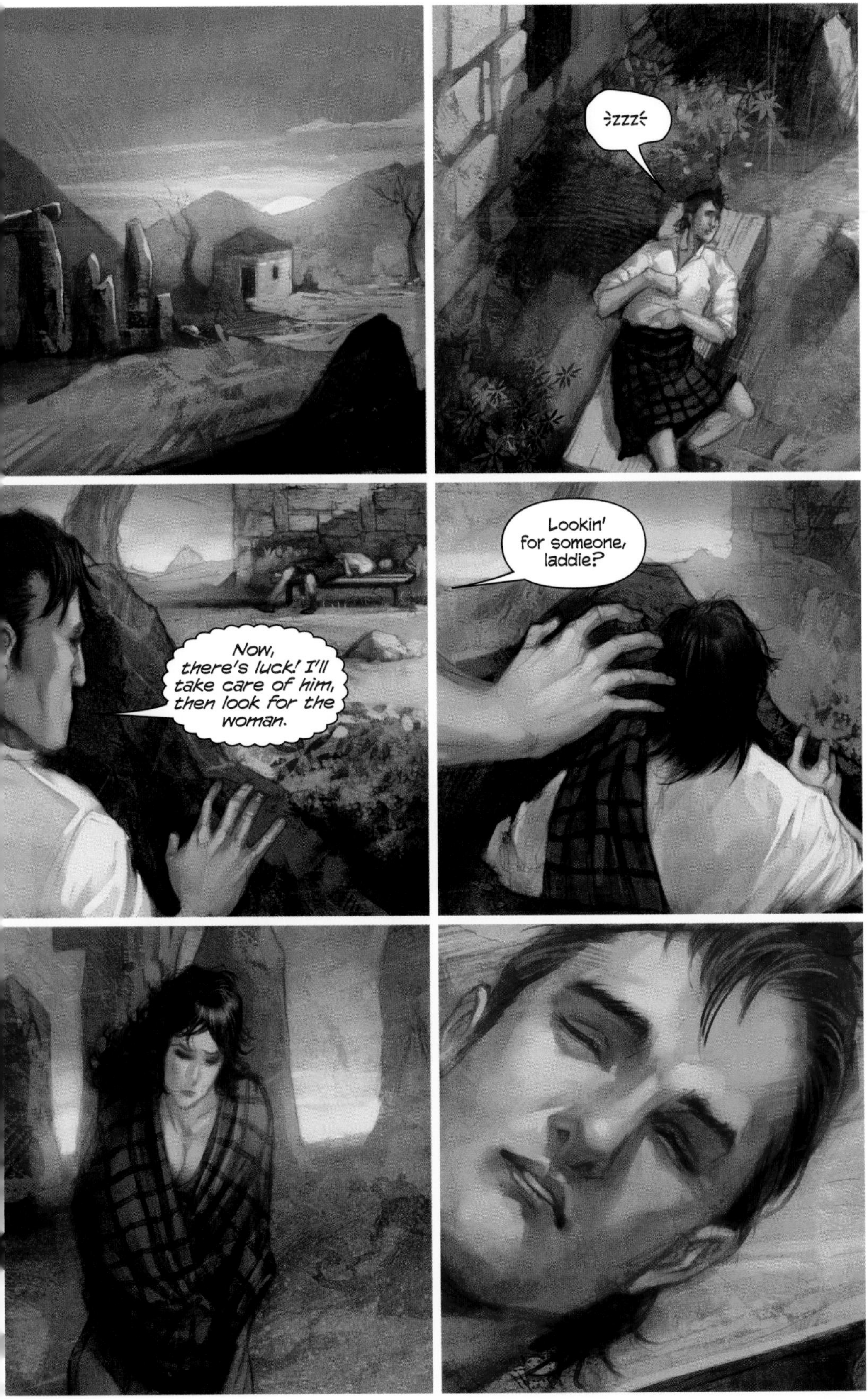
ZZZ
Now, there's luck! I'll take care of him, then look for the woman.
Lookin' for someone, laddie?

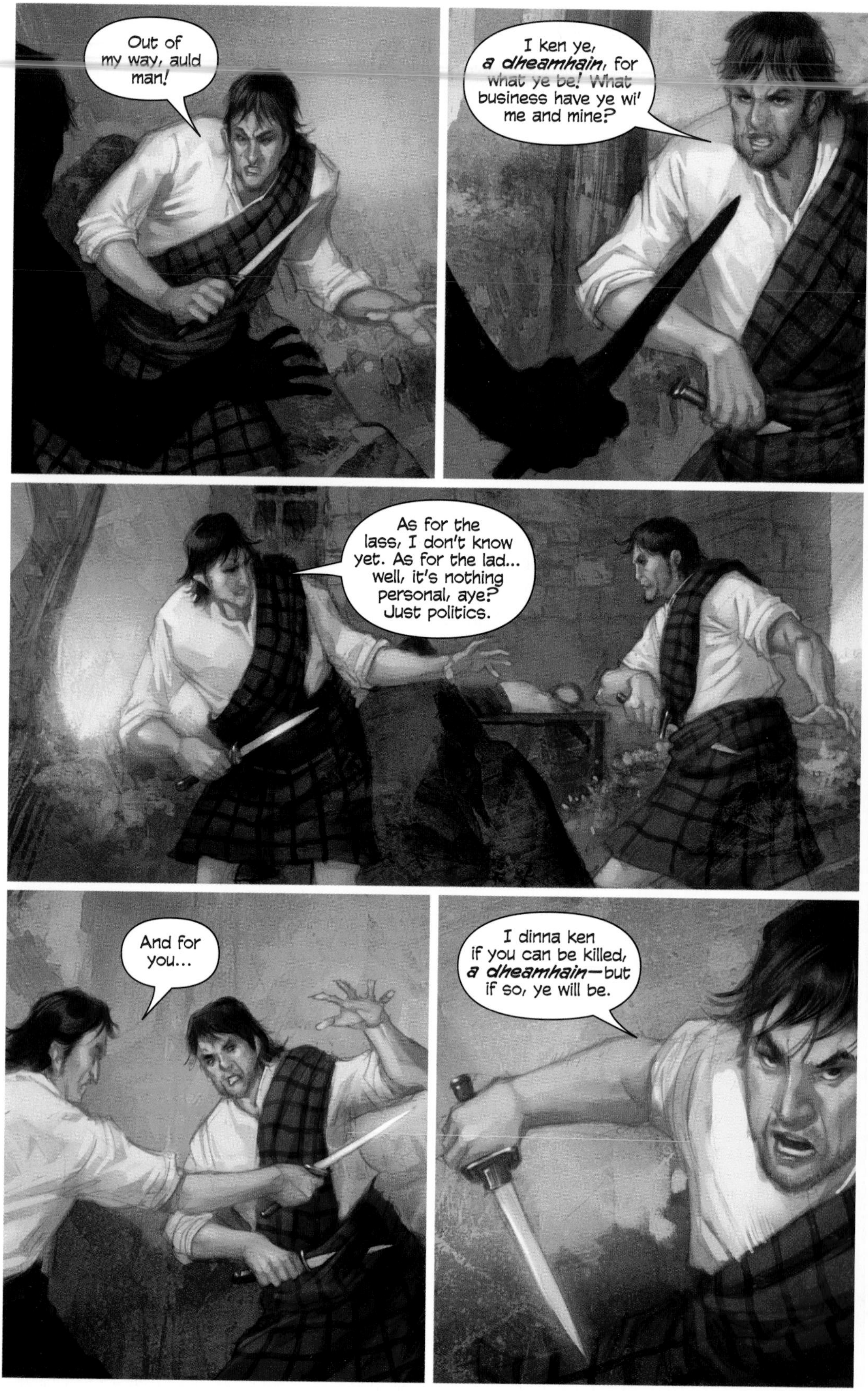
Out of my way, auld man!
I ken ye, a dheamhain, for what ye be! What business have ye wi' me and mine?
As for the lass, I don't know yet. As for the lad... well, it's nothing personal, aye? Just politics.
And for you...
I dinna ken if you can be killed, a dheamhain—but if so, ye will be.

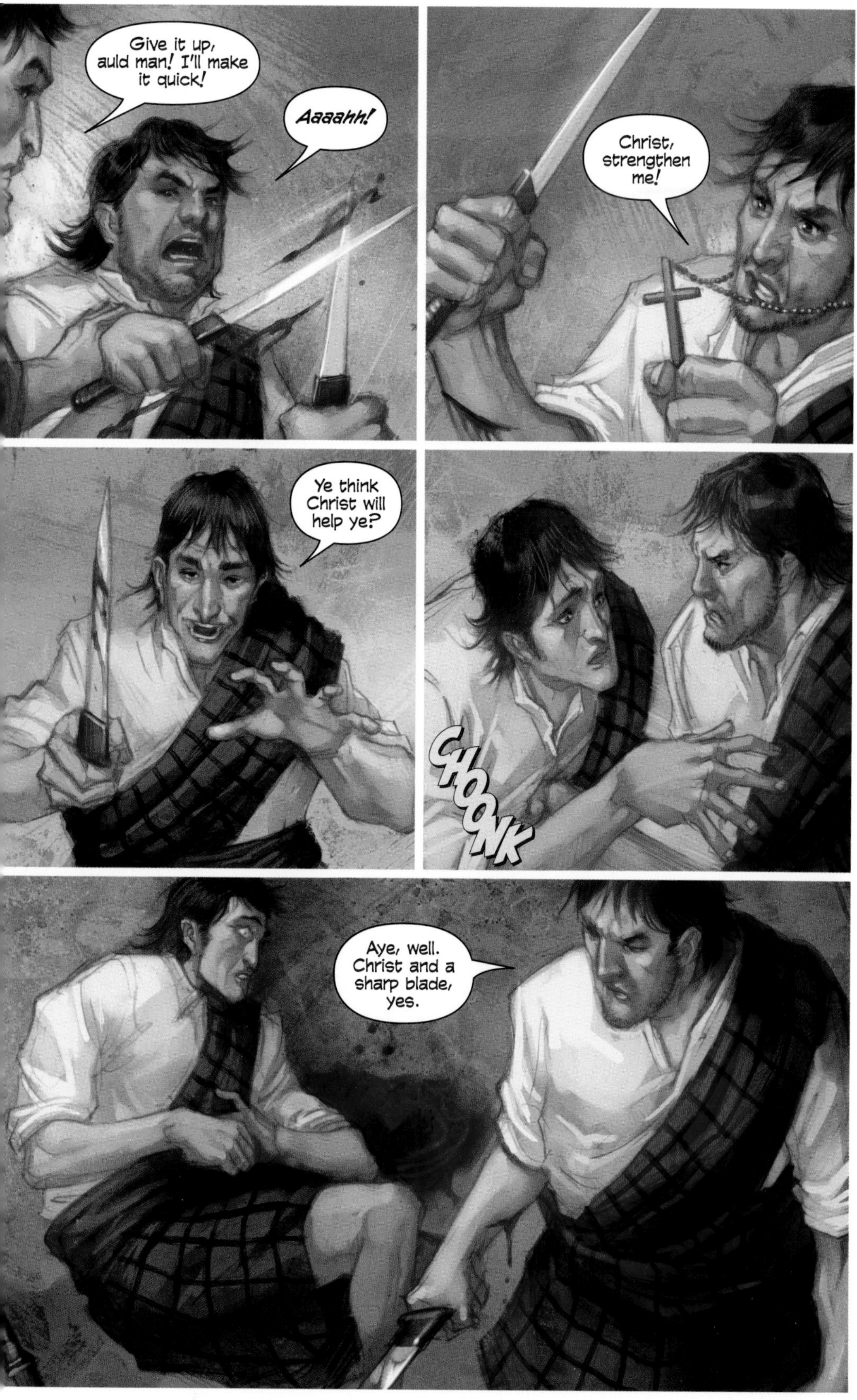
Give it up, auld man! I'll make it quick!
Aaaahh!
Christ, strengthen me!
Ye think Christ will help ye?
CHOONK
Aye, well. Christ and a sharp blade, yes.

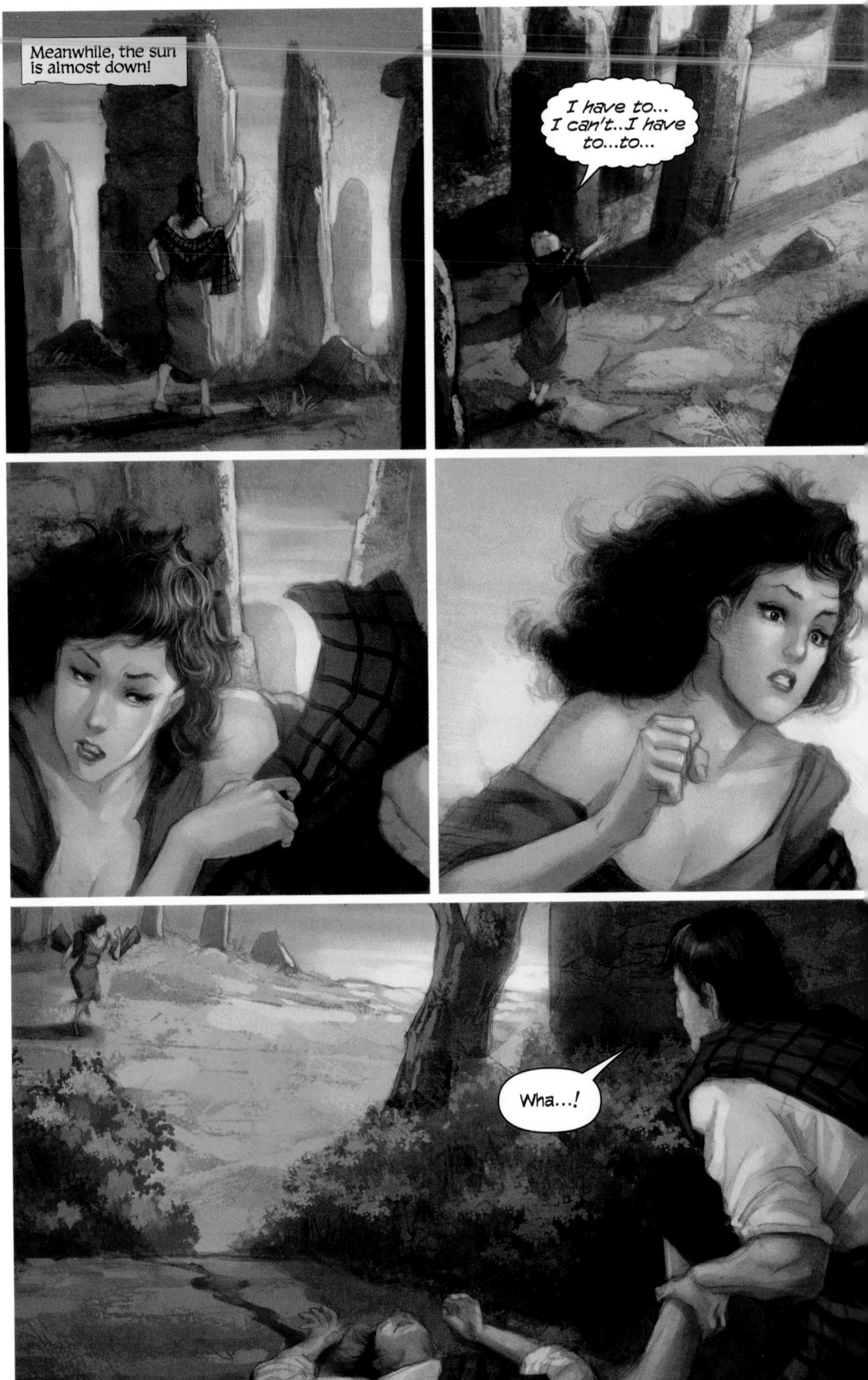
Meanwhile, the sun is almost down!
I have to... I can't...I have to...to...
Wha...!

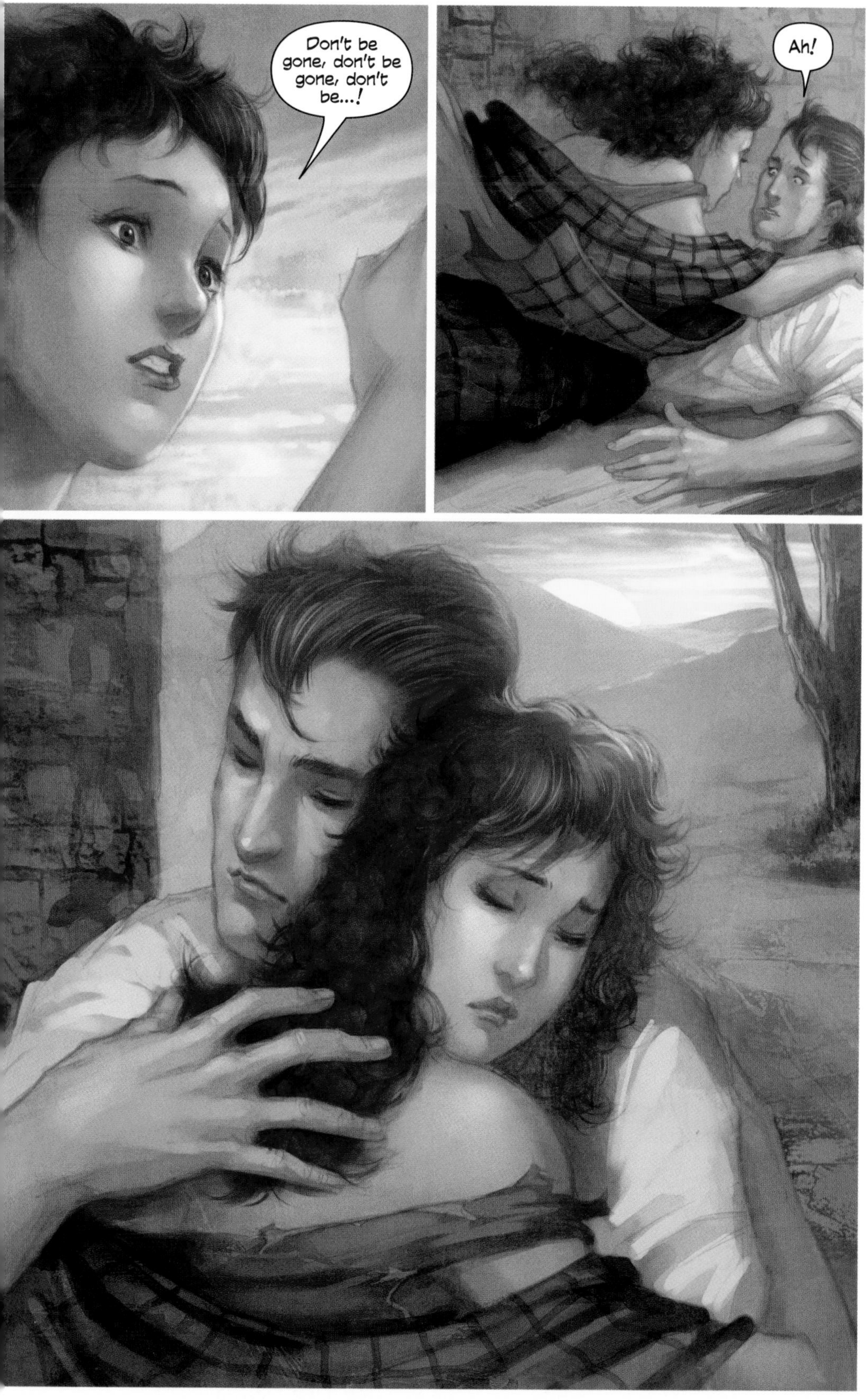
Don't be gone, don't be gone, don't be...!
Ah!

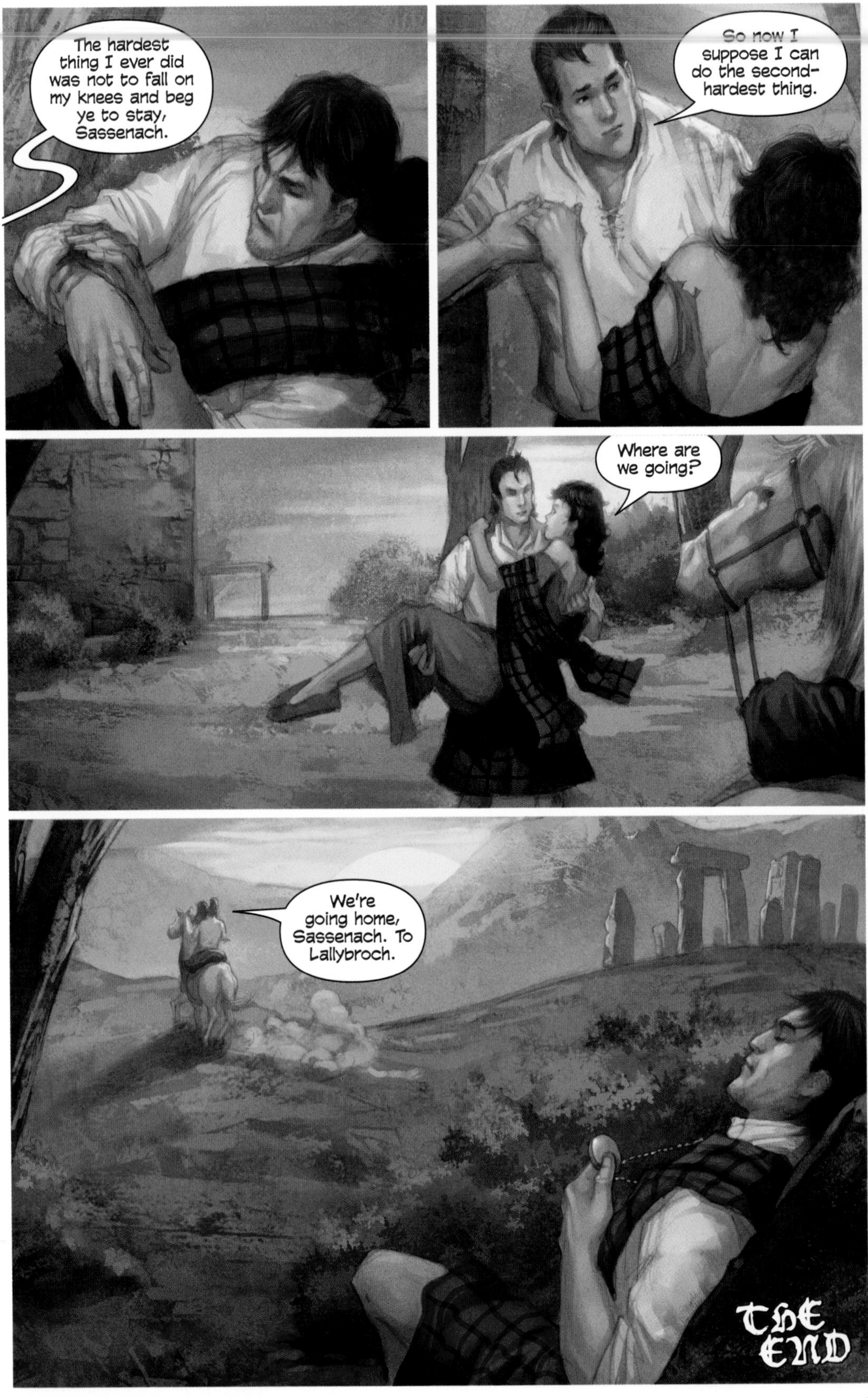
The hardest thing I ever did was not to fall on my knees and beg ye to stay, Sassenach.
So now I suppose I can do the second-hardest thing.
Where are we going?
We're going home, Sassenach. To Lallybroch.
THE END

# THE MAKING OF THE EXILE

A graphic novel is very much a collaborative work between author and artist, and the most important decision in the early creation of this project was selecting the art style that would best tell the story of *The Exile*. Diana Gabaldon deliberated over a number of art samples by possible artists. One was Hoang Nguyen, a California artist who was born in Vietnam and came to this country when he was nine years old. Nguyen's website, liquidbrush.com, overflowed with beautifully rendered female faces, many showing an influence from the popular Japanese manga style in which eyes are enlarged and faces delicate and elfin. But his talent was obvious—and when asked to supply additional samples, he provided a work in progress: a graphic novel set during World War I that showed his capabilities with male characters, action, and historical settings, all of which would be integral to bringing *The Exile*'s script to the sequential art form.

## CHARACTER DEVELOPMENT

Before he would be named the official artist, however, Hoang had to prove that he could bring to life the characters who have dwelled for so long in the author's imagination: Jamie Fraser and Claire Randall. His next task was to work up sample character designs based on Diana's descriptions.

### Jamie Fraser

*Diana's description:*

"A head taller than anyone else (he's 6'4", in a time when the average man stood 5'8"), wide-shouldered and muscular, but lean—built like a basketball player, not a football player or a superhero. A long, straight nose, faintly slanted dark-blue eyes, broad cheekbones, high brow, solid jaw with a wide mouth, usually turned up at one corner—thick, dark red hair (worn short but shaggy in opening, later in the story long enough to tie back), 'the color of a red deer's pelt.' He has a cowlick that lifts the hair off his brow (it's not standing on end; it just isn't hanging in his face). Young—he's 22—but well grown into himself, with a sense of strength and confidence. A smart-ass who knows he can back it up—but able to be gentle and thoughtful in private."

Diana gave this response to one early sketch.

*Notes in re Jamie—your second study of him has great presence and power, and isn't that far off. Of course, getting him just right is particularly tricky, because (as you saw in the first book) since it's written from Claire's viewpoint, she describes him minutely and repeatedly—which means all the readers (who've read all the books, often multiple times), have very detailed and fixed notions of him.*

BEFORE

*I did (out of curiosity) show the sketch to a group of fans who were hosting a private party for me at a recent conference, just to see how their impressions matched with my own. They all went, "Ooh!" but then said (basically), "He's too pretty." Mostly a function of the mouth, I think, though (trying to get as specific as possible in terms of features here) this drawing has too much chin and not quite enough nose. Also a little too thick and burly through the neck; he is a warrior, but we also need an impression of youth and some vulnerability. The most general comment that wasn't based on features was that they wished they could see him smiling. He is, as you'll have noticed, possessed of a marked sense of humor, and it generally shows on his face.*

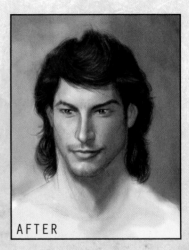

AFTER

The Internet abounds with fan-created artistic renderings of the *Outlander* characters, and as it happened, two of Diana's readers supplied pieces that turned out to be extremely helpful in finalizing Jamie's appearance. One was this piece, described by Diana:

> *The attached drawing was sent to me by a German fan. It's a very young Jamie, aged about 13 or 14, and by good fortune, it actually does look very much like him. This is definitely his nose and heavy eyebrows, and the facial bones and proportions are pretty close, too. He doesn't have a cleft in his chin, though.*

ART BY CHRISTINA SPIELBAUER,
HTTP://79CHRISTINAS.DEVIANTART.COM

The second photo reference was created by a fan who touched up a photograph of model Gabriel Aubrey to give him red hair and the background of a Scottish loch. We don't have Aubrey's permission to use the resulting piece in our book, but at press date it could be found at this URL:

HTTP://SMG.PHOTOBUCKET.COM/ALBUMS/V514/AAG567/
ROLE%20PLAYING/?ACTION=VIEW&CURRENT=JAMIE12.JPG

Another...useful, shall we say...photo of Mr. Aubrey appeared on theinsider .com in their "Shirtless Celebrity of the Day" section. Says Diana:

> *That sort of long, lean body in the "shirtless" pose is what Jamie looks like, though he's a good bit more "cut" than Mr. Aubrey, owing to an active life. <cough>*
> *Now, if we can just find a good shot of Mr. Aubrey's naked behind...*

That final comment was part of a lengthy discussion among author, artist, and editor regarding just how Jamie should look in the nude scene on page 11. Suffice it to say that the version which appears in this book is the result of extensive research.

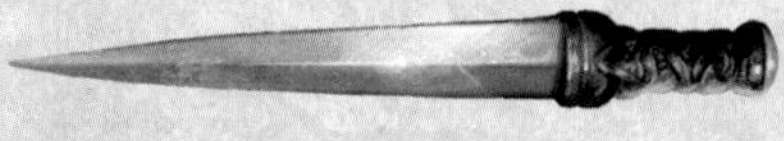

**Claire Beauchamp Randall**

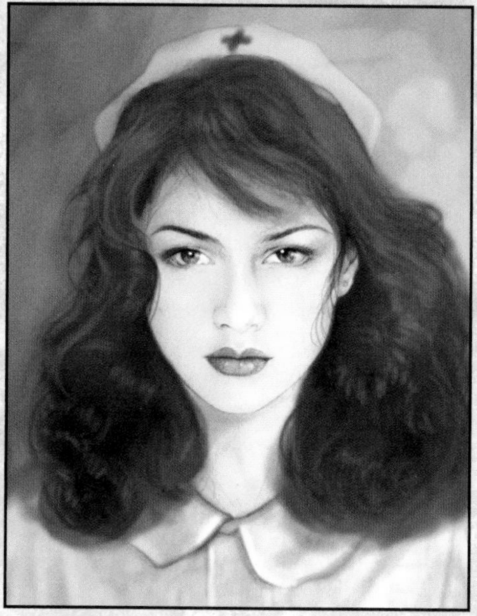

*Diana's description:*

"Tall for a woman—5'6", versus an average of 5'1"—with wildly curly light-brown hair. (About shoulder-length to begin, longer later in the story. Her hair has a personality of its own.) Dark brows and lashes, arresting whisky-colored eyes. Noticeably pale, translucent skin and a strong sexual presence (well-developed breasts and round bottom, though generally slender build). Oval face, well-defined cheekbones, and a lush but determined-looking mouth. Nose not remarkable. Definitely not a teenager; she's 27 here, and should look intelligent and competent—she's been a combat nurse during World War II. Major-league sense of humor, but not willing to be messed with."

Hoang's vision of Claire emerged quickly. Diana asked him to make her hair curlier, but she ended up essentially unchanged from this early sketch. Her figure came in for discussion at various points as the graphic novel proceeded. The original version of the scene in which Claire stumbles across Jamie in the stable during her aborted attempt to escape Castle Leoch presented her as quite voluptuous. As Diana wrote to Hoang:

*I second Betsy's motion regarding Claire's breasts on page 96 (panel 3). What my daughters refer to as "the boobage" might be getting a trifle out of hand on some of the later pages in this sequence, too; I think it's great for Claire to be buxom, but she's about twice as big in the bosom here as she was back on pages 34 and 35. Her figure in the early pages, right after she comes through the stones, is very good, I think.*

## CLOTHING AND ACCESSORIES

Scotland in the eighteenth century required visual research on dozens of topics, and Diana supplied numerous reference books for Hoang's use. She filled frequent emails with further information. Here is one of particular interest.

*The Scottish clans did wear kilts (and women's shawls, called arisaids) made in checkered-weave patterns called tartans, and it was known in the eighteenth century for families to have a specific pattern (or sett). But there was no such thing as a traditional clan sett. You would see groups of related men wearing similar colors and patterns, just because they were all getting their cloth from the same local weaver, and the weaver was using the dye-plants that grew nearby, and a limited number of variations on his (weavers were mostly men) usual pattern. But there was no custom of a clan all wearing a particular clan tartan. There's* not a lot of pictorial evidence from the Highlands, because only the very wealthy had their portraits painted—but there is one well-known painting of the two sons of the Duke of Argyll, wearing tartan. One boy is wearing a kilt, waistcoat, and jacket; his brother's wearing trews (tight-fitting trousers), a waistcoat, and jacket—and between them, they're wearing six different setts, even though all of them are done in the same colors.

Then along came the Rising under Bonnie Prince Charlie, and when the Scots were defeated at Culloden, the British government passed the Diskilting Act, which prohibited Highlanders from wearing tartan, owning weapons, or playing the bagpipes (which were considered a weapon of war). So no tartans at all were worn in the Highlands (at least officially) from 1746 to 1786, when the Act was repealed.

OK, along comes Queen Victoria and her husband—and Sir Walter Scott—and among the three of them, they romanticized the Highlands and made it fashionable to go to Scotland (which previously was considered a howling wilderness). And the Prince Consort took to wearing a kilt when he was in Scotland. Whereupon the Lowland woolen merchants (the Lowlands of Scotland are culturally distinct from the Highlands, being more or less English-speaking and not Gaelic) recognized a Good Thing, and swung into gear, producing "traditional" clan tartans. All of what most people think are traditional setts were in fact invented by these nineteenth-century woolen manufacturers.

The thing is, these merchants did such a good job of promotion (and people are so generally ignorant of history) that now everyone assumes that these tartans are in fact traditional, and that the Frasers, for instance, have always worn a scarlet, green, and black dress tartan and a blue and brown hunting tartan, while the MacKenzies wore dark green and white, etc. Whereas in fact, a lot of MacKenzies may have worn some variation of green and white—but not necessarily, and not all of them.

*The problem, of course, is that "everybody knows" that clansmen are supposed to wear distinctive tartans. It wasn't possible to stop the story (in* Outlander*) dead and explain all this about tartans (Claire wouldn't have known it, in any case) so I had to sort of walk the line between what I knew to be historically accurate, and this very popular misconception.*

*And that's probably way more than you wanted to know about tartans.*

## THE MATTER OF THE QUAICH

Having never seen a quaich, Hoang drew it the first time at almost the diameter of a dinner plate. Diana sent the attached photos and note.

*Attached are some photos of two quaichs I have—I've never seen one bigger than the larger one of these (and drinking one of these full of undiluted whisky would knock a normal person on their ass, believe me—assuming they could do it without strangling). I have very small hands, and you can see how the quaich fits me—I should really have made my husband hold it and taken the picture myself, but didn't think of that.*

# THE MATTER OF THE WEDDING-NIGHT SCENE

There was no drawing of the veil of night over Jamie and Claire's wedding bed. Hoang's original version of the scene on page 142 was quite revealing—so much so that this editor printed out the page in full color and carried it around to various departments of Random House to ask others whether it was too graphic, even for a "graphic novel." And although that version of the art brightened the day of many a hardworking publicist, editor, and marketing manager, it was decided to go with a slightly less revealing version. Diana acquiesced:

> *I like the original very much myself, though I think moving Claire's arm to obscure her nipple wouldn't ruin it. If we do need to tone it down, though, I'd vote for discreet blanket-draping, rather than tucking the legs out of sight—that doesn't seem realistic.*

Interested readers may access the original version on Diana's website at www.dianagabaldon.com.

# A FINAL WORD FROM DIANA

Those of you who've read the original *Outlander* novel (the record, I believe, is held by the woman who wrote to tell me she'd read it twenty-three times. I'm very flattered, of course, but I sort of hope she actually has a life, too....) may notice small variations of detail from the text. This was deliberate, and done either to accommodate the original dialogue in a constrained space, or for visually artistic reasons. For example, while in the original novel Claire arrives in 1743 wearing a dress sprigged with peonies, she's wearing a plain blue 1940s housedress here. The style of the dress is exactly what she would have been wearing, but using a solid color instead of a print makes the composition of the panels more striking. (For the same reason, tartan colors occasionally vary from their original description.)

A collaborative project ideally gives both artists scope for their individual talents, and it was a thrill to me when I could put a direction in the script like, "I need a half-page scene here where Angus Mhor beats the s— out of Jamie, but details not important. Go for it!" and see what Hoang's imagination and talent came up with. The results were always more than gratifying.

Do keep in mind, though, that what you're seeing here is really not a literal transcription of what's inside my head when I see these characters. They can't be, for one thing—collaboration has its limits, and those usually stop well short of telepathy—and for another, this is a graphic novel; characters are approximations appropriate to the form. Naturally, every reader brings his or her own background, expectations, and personal preferences to the visualization of fictional characters. All you have to do to realize this is to glance at some of the *Outlander* fan art available on the Web, which ranges from the sublime to the...er...well. <cough>

Just bear in mind that if you could see inside my head, almost all of you would exclaim, "That's not what I thought Jamie looked like!"

Anyway, I hope you've enjoyed this book, and its unique angle on the *Outlander* story. For those of you who haven't read the original novel... *The Exile* covers approximately the first third of *Outlander*. So if you want to find out what happens next, see the following page for a complete list of the books in the Outlander series.

*Le meas agus,**

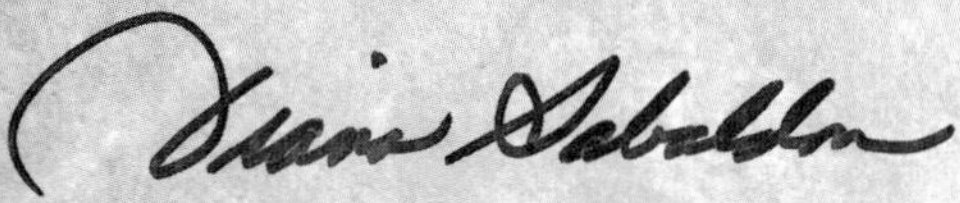

**With respect and best wishes*

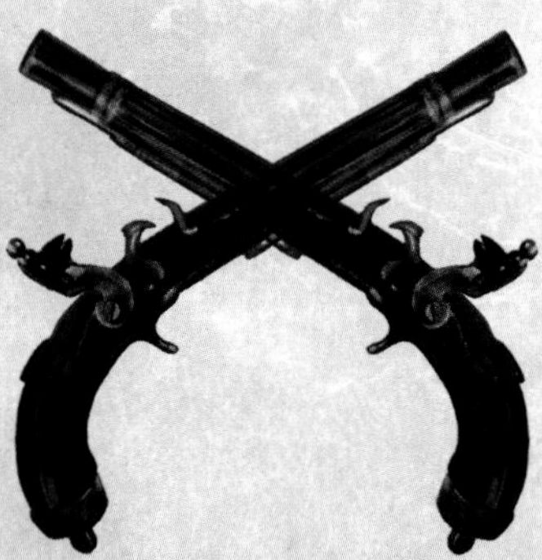

*Also by Diana Gabaldon*

## THE OUTLANDER SERIES

DIANA
GABALDON
OUTLANDER
A NOVEL

DIANA
GABALDON
DRAGONFLY
IN AMBER
A NOVEL

DIANA
GABALDON
VOYAGER
A NOVEL

DIANA
GABALDON
DRUMS OF
AUTUMN
A NOVEL

DIANA
GABALDON
THE FIERY
CROSS

DIANA
GABALDON
A BREATH OF
SNOW AND ASHES

DIANA
GABALDON
AN ECHO
IN THE BONE

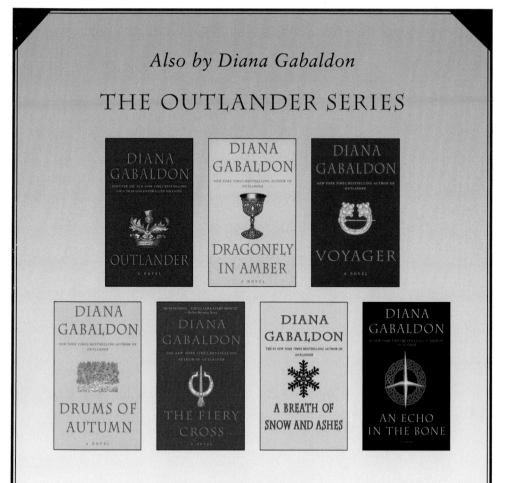

## THE COMPANION VOLUME

DIANA
GABALDON
THE OUTLANDISH
COMPANION
In Which Much Is Revealed
Regarding Claire and Jamie
Fraser, their Lives and Times, Antecedents,
Adventures, Companions, and Progeny,
with Learned Commentary (and Many
Footnotes) by their Humble Creator

THE RANDOM HOUSE PUBLISHING GROUP
www.DianaGabaldon.com